THE LEGACY OF
Rousseau

D1547435

THE LEGACY OF
Rousseau

EDITED BY
CLIFFORD ORWIN AND NATHAN TARCOV

THE UNIVERSITY OF CHICAGO PRESS
Chicago & London

CLIFFORD ORWIN is professor of political science at the University of Toronto. He is the author of *The Humanity of Thucydides*. NATHAN TARCOV is professor of political science and in the Committee on Social Thought and the College at the University of Chicago. He is the author of *Locke's Education for Liberty* and the translator, with Harvey C. Mansfield, of Machiavelli's *Discourses on Livy*.

THE UNIVERSITY OF CHICAGO PRESS, CHICAGO 60637
THE UNIVERSITY OF CHICAGO PRESS, LTD., LONDON

© 1997 by The University of Chicago
All rights reserved. Published 1997
Printed in the United States of America

06   05   04   03   02   01   00   99   98   97   1   2   3   4   5

ISBN: 0-226-63855-3 (cloth)
ISBN: 0-226-63856-1 (paper)

Library of Congress Cataloging-in-Publication Data

The legacy of Rousseau / edited by Clifford Orwin and Nathan Tarcov.
    p.   cm.
Includes bibliographical references and index.
ISBN 0-226-63855-3 (alk. paper). — ISBN 0-226-63856-1 (pbk. : alk. paper)
1. Rousseau, Jean Jacques, 1712–1778—Contributions in political science.
2. Rousseau, Jean Jacques, 1712–1778—Contributions in political culture. I. Orwin,
Clifford, 1947– . II. Tarcov, Nathan, 1948– .
JC179.R9L44   1997
320.1—dc20   96-8908
                                                                                CIP

♾ The paper used in this publication meets the minimum requirements of the American National Standard for Information Sciences—Permanence of Paper for Printed Library Materials, ANSI Z39.48-1984.

To the memory of Allan Bloom
Translator, interpreter, and critic of the work of Rousseau

❧Contents❧

✤Acknowledgments✤

This book was first conceived and the original invitations to most of the contributors were issued by Allan Bloom and Nathan Tarcov in the months before Bloom's death in October 1992. They intended to invite Judith N. Shklar, who died suddenly shortly before Bloom. After Bloom's death, Clifford Orwin agreed to replace him as coeditor. The original contributors first presented their chapters in a lecture series and conference in 1992–93 sponsored by the University of Chicago's John M. Olin Center for Inquiry into the Theory and Practice of Democracy, whose activities are made possible by funding from the John M. Olin foundation. Those chapters benefited in their revision from the comments made on those occasions by the conference chairs and discussants, Walter Berns, Carey McWilliams, James H. Nichols, Abram Shulsky, and Richard Zinman, as well as by the many other participants. The staff of the Olin Center, Stephen B. Gregory, its administrative coordinator, and Anne Gamboa, then its administrative assistant, assisted in countless ways at every stage. Michael Freeman prepared the index.

The dedication expresses the manifold debts that the editors, contributors, and all those interested in the legacy of Rousseau owe to Allan Bloom. All the contributors were friends of his and at one time or another were his colleagues, students, or fellow students, and they freely acknowledge his abiding influence on their reflections about the thought of Jean-Jacques Rousseau and its sway over the world we live in.

*

Bloom's work, of course, was not limited to the question of Rousseau; readers can consult a volume that does justice to the range of his writing and teaching, *Political Philosophy and the Human Soul: Essays in Memory of Allan Bloom*, edited by Michael Palmer and Thomas L. Pangle (Lanham, Md.: Rowman and Littlefield, 1995). We thank the estate of Allan Bloom and the American Enterprise Institute for Public Policy Research, Washington, D.C., for permission to reprint the chapter by Bloom, which appeared originally as "Rousseau—the Turning Point," in *Confronting the Constitution: The Challenge to Locke, Montesquieu, Jefferson, and the Federalists from Utilitarianism, Historicism, Marxism, Freudianism, Pragmatism, Existentialism* . . . , edited by Allan Bloom with the assistance of Steven J. Kautz (Washington, D.C.: AEI Press, 1990).

Introduction

CLIFFORD ORWIN AND NATHAN TARCOV

We asked prospective contributors to this book to address the question of what in Rousseau's thought on a certain issue continues, for better or worse, to shape (or to challenge) current perceptions of that issue. We were attracted to Rousseau's profundity and charm and impressed by his often unacknowledged influence on our ways of understanding the world and the different human types that inhabit it. It was Rousseau who originated modern dissatisfaction with modernity, and he is the source of the multiple polarities through which that dissatisfaction still expresses itself today: nature versus society; sincerity versus socialization; repression and sublimation; the self versus the other; community versus the individual; participation versus representation; nationalism versus cosmopolitanism; compassion versus competitiveness; wholeness versus alienation.

The fundamental polarity in Rousseau's thought, which seems to underlie all the others, is that between nature and society. Rousseau followed Hobbes and Locke in rejecting the older claim that society is itself natural because human beings possess speech and reason. But he went much further than they had in purging our conception of the natural of any trace of the social. He was the first to try to conceive of us as beings for whom speech and reason as well as society are artificial, beings constituted not by nature but by culture or history. At the same time he inverted Hobbes's presentation of the state of nature as a negative standard for human life. Instead he portrayed it as a condition of freedom, equality, wholeness, and goodness, contrasting it with the despotism, inequality, alienation, and corruption of modern society. It was Rousseau who taught us to think of ourselves as good and to blame our sufferings and crimes on society.

Caught in the crosshairs of Rousseau's critique of modern (postclassical, post-Christian) society is its typical product, the bourgeois. This book's unity, inspired by the work of Allan Bloom, derives from Rousseau's critique of the bourgeois, the divided human being of modern society, whose division stems ultimately from the tension between natural individuality and artificial sociality. In their criticism of the bourgeois, all subsequent modern dissatisfaction with modernity and all revolutionary projects to transcend it, whether from the Left or the Right, have occupied Rousseauian ground. The bourgeois is the focus of modern dissatisfaction with modernity precisely because that is the distinctively modern type, which has superseded all others. It was the bourgeois who basked in the approbation of the first wave of modern writers, those who promoted a society characterized by commerce, tolerance, the priority of "society" to "government," and a decent devotion to private pleasures and private gains. It is in opposition to the bourgeois that later moderns have turned to such Rousseauian alternatives as the artist, the bohemian, the citizen, and the lover. It is in opposition to bourgeois self-interest that we have tried to cultivate our new virtues of sincerity, compassion, community, and diversity. That in the centuries since Rousseau the bourgeoisie has itself increasingly adopted the trappings, fashions, and jargon of the movement to subvert its authority affords an ambiguous confirmation of the power of his critique of them. Today everyone preaches something incompatible with remaining a bourgeois, while not for all that ceasing to remain one—which would not have surprised Rousseau.

Yet it was not only because Rousseau inspired so many of our contemporary ways of talking, feeling, thinking, and complaining that we turned to him. It is also because current discourse so often impoverishes Rousseau's complex analysis by magnifying some aspects of it while ignoring others, thus transforming his paradoxes into slogans. The Left preserves his love of justice at the expense of his love of greatness, and his critique of conventional inequalities at the expense of his affirmation of natural ones; the Right does the opposite. Some adopt his morality of compassion while ignoring his insistence on rigorous justice, or echo his praise of "participation" or "community" while neglecting his call for austerity, homogeneity, and civil religion. We therefore encouraged our contributors to return from these broken shards of Rousseau's understanding to the intact original. We asked them not only to look back on Rousseau and all he has wrought from the vantage point of the late twentieth century, but also to survey present realities from the heights afforded by his thought.

The past two centuries of turbulence in the realms of both life and thought have yielded no finally persuasive answers to the questions confronting us as human beings. If we are thoughtful, however, they may have sharpened our grasp of these questions. A thesis common to the essays in this volume is that Rousseau stands as a pivotal figure in this process by which the increasing self-awareness of modernity has fostered a growing radicalization but also a growing self-questioning. Januslike, his gaze seems to encompass both his predecessors, such as Machiavelli, Bacon, Hobbes, and Locke—of whose projects his own is at the same time a critique and a fulfillment—and his successors from Kant through Marx and Nietzsche to Freud and Heidegger. Rousseau was a sober skeptic of all solutions to these problems, even his own, and his grasp of the durability and complexity of the problems he articulated exceeded that of his successors in their eagerness to achieve solutions. Yet our contributors do not treat Rousseau's thought as a collection of paradoxes but understand the paradoxes as aspects of a comprehensive view of human problems.

Given the scope and richness of Rousseau's thought, there is scarcely an aspect of life for which it lacks implications—or for which these implications are unequivocal. We have not tried to cover every significant aspect of Rousseau's multifaceted and pervasive legacy. In particular, we have not included an exploration of romantic love and domestic felicity, those alternatives to bourgeois vanity depicted so enchantingly by Rousseau and developed by the great romantic novelists. For that we refer readers to part 1 of Allan Bloom's *Love and Friendship*.

Each of the chapters in this volume, with the exception of the one by Allan Bloom, was written expressly for it and appears in print for the first time. Of the scholars who have contributed to this project, some are specialists in Rousseau or in either his predecessors or his successors, others are best known as analysts of contemporary thought or affairs. This diversity is evident in the resulting essays, and we regard this as one of the strengths of the book. The reader will find some chapters that concentrate primarily on the thought of Rousseau himself or that convey his importance to his successors by articulating his transformation of the outlook of his predecessors, and others that concentrate almost exclusively on later thinkers who, while furthering or responding to Rousseau's project, ended up at a considerable distance from him. Other chapters scrutinize aspects of the current situation from a perspective at the same time informed by Rousseau and critical of him, and still others seek to open a dialogue between Rousseau and contemporary thinkers or schools of thought. What unites the authors is a lively admiration for the genius of Rousseau leavened by an awareness of the questionableness of his teaching.

They oppose the trivialization of Rousseau's thought, whether wrought by uncritical acceptance or uncritical rejection.

The barriers to coming to grips with Rousseau today include that residual Anglo-Saxon smugness that dismissed him from the outset as "unsystematic" and therefore hopelessly unsound. This spirit lives on in some academic departments whose inmates call themselves philosophers but refuse to recognize Rousseau as one. Rousseau not only encouraged us to look at the artist and novelist, understood as a creative genius, as a source of human understanding superior to academic or systematic philosophy; he led us to see philosophers as themselves engaging in a kind of poetry, fiction, or art.

Also insistent today are the voices of that "postmodernism" whose zeal to "deconstruct" old texts is not supported by an equal resolve to understand them. Sometimes postmodernists claim Rousseau as a kindred spirit, and a few of them have written insightfully on him. On the whole, however, self-congratulation for one's up-to-dateness yields patronizing interpretations of old books.

Certainly the postmodernists are correct that modernity itself has become radically questionable to us; indeed, the question is whether they do not at the same time both underestimate its resources and take its authority too much for granted. On the one hand, they are in an awful hurry to bury it, and with it such substantial (if imperfect) achievements as liberal democracy. On the other hand, for all of their questioning of the authority of modernity, they never adequately reopen the issues supposedly settled by its fundamental claim to have adequately disposed of its predecessors, the classical tradition and the prophetic one. As a result they may remain unthinkingly modern, prisoners of the premises that distinguish modernity. In Rousseau theoretical modernity puts its best foot forward; he offers a dazzling demonstration of its power to address the human situation. There is hardly a respect in which he does not appear to have had his finger on the pulse of modernity, or in which his thought and its seismic impact did not serve to quicken that pulse. At the same time there are few thinkers who while remaining true to modernity have so thoroughly grasped its problematic character or have been so capable of confronting it with the classics and the Bible. Our hope is that this book will contribute to renewed appreciation and discussion of a Rousseau who transcends the various hidden assumptions that have emanated from him. Like every whole that is too vast for ready comprehension, the thought of Rousseau may be approached only through its parts, yet the ultimate justification for taking up the parts must be to lead the reader back to the whole.

I

Bourgeois versus Artist

❧ 1 ❦

The Problem of the Bourgeois

WERNER J. DANNHAUSER

I

When one speaks of the bourgeois or the bourgeoisie today, one employs terms made popular as well as inescapable by Karl Marx. Formal definitions are not very helpful at the beginnings of inquiries like this, so none will be attempted here. Instead, one does better to begin with the simple but necessary observation that the bourgeoisie appears as something bad. That is especially true of Marx, but not only of him, as the case of Flaubert suffices to show. Curiously enough, it is not the same with the English term "the middle class," its near equivalent. For example, in the United States almost everyone thinks of himself or herself as belonging to the middle class, but almost no one wants to be accused of being bourgeois.

But what is so bad about being bourgeois? The criticisms one hears are confusing, probably confused, and certainly contradictory, but they are worth examining because they can advance one's understanding of the problem of the bourgeois.

First, to be bourgeois means to be deficient in aesthetic refinement, to live in an ugly house furnished with uncomfortable chairs ornamented by doilies, where one sits while listening to lackluster music. On a somewhat higher level, the charge is that the bourgeoisie replaces the poetic with the prosaic in all aspects of life, thus rendering life a spiritual wasteland.

One can and should, however, occasionally turn from this depressing image to contemplate a glorious galaxy of bourgeois artists: Bach, Mozart, Beethoven, and Schubert; Stendhal, Austen, Heine, Dostoyevsky—the list could be extended indefinitely even without the necessary addition of painters, architects, and others. Stories do abound, of course, of artists who starved in garrets because the bourgeoisie had no use for either their lives or their art, but it is not all that rare to find bourgeois artists who are lionized by the bourgeoisie. In fact, even if these artists prefer to live "on the margins" as bohemians, they may find that the middle class indulges their transgressions of manners and morals.

Is the charge that the bourgeois is philistine, then, valid or invalid? Could it possibly be both? Marxists are known to distinguish between an early, epic era of genuine bourgeois productivity and a decadent late capitalism;[1] this is a genuinely helpful distinction in many cases, but it raises the vexing question whether the bourgeois has a nature or only a history.

Either answer causes the problem of the bourgeois to emerge. It also comes to the fore when one discusses what have come to be known as family values. It can be maintained that to be bourgeois means to dote on one's own family to the extent of neglecting the welfare of one's nation, to practice the love of one's own until it obliterates the love of the good. Yet one can also argue that the bourgeoisie destroys family values, reducing the family to an economic unit; bourgeois man sees his wife as "a mere . . . instrument of production," all the while practicing both official and unofficial prostitution. The quotation—as well as the surrounding thought—comes from two acknowledged experts on the bourgeoisie, Karl Marx and Friedrich Engels in *The Communist Manifesto*.[2]

A final example may be useful. According to Marxists, the bourgeois is a dour churchgoer, shackled by myth and religion. According to Marx's great nineteenth-century antagonist Friedrich Nietzsche, however, to be bourgeois means to realize that "God is dead"[3] and to replace the soul's traditional reverence with a degrading and deadening concern for comfortable self-preservation at the expense of loftier goals.

One needs help in coming to grips with these and many other contradictions, or seeming contradictions, about the bourgeoisie; no real understanding is possible without engaging such paradoxes. One of the most useful guides to nineteenth-century thought, Karl Löwith's *From Hegel to Nietzsche*, points one in the right direction. Löwith maintains: "Rousseau's writings contain the first and clearest statement of the human problem of bourgeois society. It consists in the fact that man in bourgeois society is not a unified whole."[4] If one assumes, as one should, that Löwith is correct, one realizes that the lack of unity he points to almost suffices by itself to explain the divergent characteristics ascribed to bourgeois man: lacking unity, he is a battlefield for contradictory impulses.

II

This chapter will deal only cursorily with the thought of Jean-Jacques Rousseau. Compelling reasons exist for this relative neglect. My own knowledge of Rousseau is thin and entirely derivative, based on the writings of Leo Strauss[5] and Allan Bloom.[6] Moreover, the contributions of a number of eminent authorities on Rousseau can be found in this book, and I have neither the ability nor the desire to compete with them. Finally, the theme of this book is not simply Rousseau but *the legacy* of Rousseau, and I know more about the legacy, especially as it can be seen in the works of Marx and Nietzsche. In dealing with the legacy of Rousseau, however, I will attempt to be mindful of a cautionary remark by Leo Strauss, in *Natural Right and History*, to the effect that though Rousseau's disciples clarified his views, one may wonder whether they preserved the breadth of his views.[7]

The most central passage from Rousseau for our purposes, and identified as a critically important statement by Allan Bloom in his edition of *Emile*, occurs near the beginning of book 1:

> He who in the civil order wants to preserve the primacy of the sentiments of nature does not know what he wants. Always in contradiction with himself, always floating between his inclinations and his duties, he will never be either man or citizen. He will be good neither for himself nor for others. He will be one of these men of our days: a Frenchman, an Englishman, a bourgeois. He will be nothing.[8]

According to Rousseau, the bourgeois is someone or something in between. In the passage above, the bourgeois is both between and beneath man as fashioned by nature and man as molded by the city, as citizen. This "inbetweenness" of bourgeois man is central to one's understanding of the problem of the bourgeois. Even if one thinks of a bourgeois as simply "middle class," which Rousseau does at times, the problem appears. After all, the middle class is the class between the nobility on the one hand and the poor peasants and workers on the other.

After Rousseau, Tocqueville developed this train of thought. This can be seen in his analysis of the advent of democratic egalitarianism. He ascribes to the nobility such characteristics as wealth, strength, and a leisure amid far-reaching luxuries, refinements of tastes, pleasures of the mind, and the attractions of the arts. On the other end of the scale, among the lower classes, one finds work, coarseness, and ignorance, but also lively passions, generous feelings, deep beliefs, and untamed virtues. The bourgeois—though that is not

Tocqueville's term in *Democracy in America*—exists between and beneath these two ends of the scale,[9] lacking both the rich vigor of the lower orders and the spiritual refinements of the higher ones.

One may note that this "in-betweenness and beneathness" is attributed, perhaps with some justice, to the bourgeoisie to this very day. To be bourgeois in the twentieth century is to be attacked by communists for being pro-fascist and by fascists for being fellow travelers, by the very poor for being haughty and by the very rich for being coarse, by feminists for male chauvinism and by reactionaries for lacking manliness.

Rousseau was more specific than has so far been indicated about the in-betweenness attributed to the bourgeoisie even now. The bourgeois exists between and beneath two types: natural man and the citizen. Natural man is simple, brutish, and asocial—human in potential rather than actuality, but possessed of a genuine wholeness and an innocent self-concern that is compatible with the rudiments of compassion; Rousseau can thus speak of "the natural goodness of man."[10]

The citizen stands in sharp contrast to natural man. He lives the life of wholehearted devotion to his city, whether that city be Sparta or Rome or Geneva. Immediately before the famous passage defining and castigating the bourgeois in *Emile*, Rousseau provides the reader with an example of a female citizen, drawn from Plutarch: "A Spartan woman had five sons in the army and was awaiting news of the battle. A Helot arrives; trembling, she asks him for news. 'Your five sons were killed.' 'Base slave, did I ask you that?' 'We won the victory.' The mother runs to the temple and gives thanks to the gods."[11]

Rousseau's example is apt because it is bound to strike his bourgeois readers as alien, most strange. They may well admire the Spartan citizen, but they will almost certainly be put off by her as well. (One might speculate that Rousseau himself shares this ambivalence.) Her conduct is cold and vaguely threatening. It strikes one as bizarre that she shows no concern whatever for what the helot, or anybody else, thinks of her preference for the fatherland over her own soul. The modern, or bourgeois, reader likes to think of himself as having more inwardness than the woman so starkly presented by Plutarch and Rousseau. That is in large part because of the overwhelming influence of Christianity in molding the modern soul. For Rousseau, and not only for Rousseau, the bourgeois is a Christian phenomenon.

III

When pondering the soul of the bourgeois, one does well to heed Allan Bloom's brilliant formulation, according to which the bourgeois "is the man who when dealing with others thinks only of himself and in his understanding of himself thinks only of others. He is a role player."[12] The bourgeois may indeed have a kind of inwardness that the citizen lacks, but it is an inwardness greatly decayed from, for example, the Christian inwardness portrayed in Augustine's *Confessions*. It is a crippled and crippling inwardness, the inwardness of other-directedness, of inauthenticity, of insincerity, of alienation.

At this point a serious objection may surface: the great target of Rousseau's loathing is not the bourgeois in particular but civilization in general. Rousseau seems to detest not just bourgeois man but modern man as such, and he even harbors few illusions about ancient man. He finds wickedness and depravity almost everywhere he looks, among nobles and workers, peasants and priests, the poor and the rich, libertines and ascetics. Hope is not Rousseau's strong suit; almost every book he wrote ends with gloom about today and despair about tomorrow.

Such an assessment is not so much wrong as incomplete. The bourgeois may be only one of Rousseau's many enemies, but he occupies a special place because the future belongs to this low human type. Civilized man may be bad as such, but some civilized men are worse than others. And the predominant type, the bourgeois, is surely more dangerous than others if only because this type of predominance threatens the existence of other types.

Before we leave Rousseau, that fountainhead of all subsequent modern thought, it may be useful to cull some additional generalizations from him about the bourgeois. First, the bourgeois is typically a city dweller; he is urban. He is therefore in significant ways closer to the citizen than to natural man, but he is also estranged from nature, natural rhythms, and the earth as such. Second, the bourgeois is a stranger to reverence, treading the thin line between being a Christian and being a post-Christian. He no longer has transcendent goals, devoting himself to self-preservation as defined by Hobbes or comfortable self-preservation as defined by Locke. The overwhelming importance of "making a living" comes to the fore.

The great enemy of self-preservation is, of course, death, and the most gruesome kind is violent death. Hence Hobbes, who can lay claim to being the first great bourgeois thinker, comes out for something close to peace at any price, though it may have to be peace with dishonor. Contrary to the claims of latter-day Marxists, the bourgeois will always prefer butter to guns.

Fourth, the fear of violent death yields quickly enough to the fear of death as such. (The analysis of Locke supersedes the analysis of Hobbes.) For the bourgeois the queen of sciences is medicine; he wants his son to be a doctor. And Nietzsche's last man—bourgeois man—has, as will be seen, a "due regard for his health."[13]

The fear of death that accompanies the whole life of bourgeois man makes him need a colossal amount of diversion, in Pascal's sense of diversion as man's avoidance of human mortality.[14] The avoidance, even denial, of death extends to bourgeois language; bourgeois man would rather speak of "passing away" than dying.

Finally, the bourgeois life is the life of commerce, as Hitler thought he well knew when he contemptuously referred to the British, modernity's exemplary bourgeois people, as a nation of shopkeepers.

IV

A discussion of the commercial aspects of bourgeois existence provides an ideal opportunity for a transition from Rousseau to his spiritual descendant Karl Marx. However, for reasons having much to do with terminology, it will be useful to tarry briefly with George W. F. Hegel.

Marx's philosophical journey—a journey that in his own self-understanding was to take him beyond philosophy altogether—can be said to have begun with his critique of Hegel's *Philosophy of Right*.[15] That critique takes the form of a loosely structured commentary that begins with paragraph 181 of Hegel's treatise. The starting point is by no means arbitrary. Marx picks up the thread of Hegel's argument when the latter moves from a discussion of the family to a discussion of *bürgerliche Gesellschaft*. That term *can* be translated "bourgeois society," but is also—and in Hegel translations virtually always— rendered as "civil society." In German it is difficult to retain Rousseau's distinction between bourgeois and citizen, since both terms can be rendered as *Bürger*. The problem is usually solved by turning a citizen into a *Staatsbürger*, literally a burgher or a citizen of the state. It is worth noting, especially when turning to Marx, that before him the usual term for bourgeois society (*bürgerliche Gesellschaft*) has no negative connotations. German does have a more pejorative term, *Spiessbürger*, but that is more accurately translated as "petit bourgeois" or even "a Philistine."

One must bear in mind that when Karl Marx dismisses bourgeois rights as claptrap he is attacking not only what we think of as *bourgeois* rights but what we think of as *civil* rights. Marx can be said to have radicalized Hegel, who wrote *The Philosophy of Right* to dissolve all possible tensions between civil rights and other human goods. He moves back from Hegel's solutions to problems that appear insoluble to Rousseau—only to advance solutions of his own.

The earliest text in which Marx can be said to have confronted the problem of the bourgeois is *On the Jewish Question*.[16] In this early work, Marx refers to *bürgerliche Gesellschaft* as well as to "bourgeois." Shortly afterward, by the time of *The Communist Manifesto*, he will decidedly favor the word "bourgeois."

One may well ask why Marx's first discussion of the problem of the bourgeois occurs in a confrontation of Bauer's views of the Jewish question, but the most preliminary reflections can make sense of this fact. The "Jewish question" in the nineteenth century centers on the desirability and possibility of emancipating the Jews to full citizenship. In modern states, however, a division occurs between the state and civil society, and therefore the full participation of Jews in the affairs of state might coexist with restrictions on them in civil—or bourgeois—society, so that political emancipation might coexist with utter rejection in the private sphere and thus be a hollow achievement.

Marx analyzes the split in modern life between the state and civil society, between a public and a private sphere, a split that is central to the fragmentation of the bourgeois observed by Rousseau. In the early Marx this fragmentation becomes known as *Entfremdung*, estrangement or alienation, a term the young Marx adopted from Hegel and the mature Marx no longer used except in disdain. The idea of alienation, however, remains very much with Marx in *Das Kapital*, where it has been transformed into "commodity fetishism" and other terms.[17]

Following the direction of Rousseau's thought, Marx maintains that modern man is not integrated. An inner split exists between his life in the state and his life in civil society. He lives a corrupt heavenly life—devoted to the general welfare—in the state and a real, earthly life that is private, privatized, in which other human beings are means to be exploited rather than ends in themselves. As Joseph Cropsey has pointed out, the rough equivalent of civil society in Marx is the market, or simply "the economy." It is the place of utter and utmost selfishness, masked as entitlements or rights.[18] This analysis is once more connected to the essay's title. The mercenary and exploitative character of civil society makes the bourgeois not so much a Christian as a Jewish phenomenon. *On the Jewish Question* is a decidedly anti-Jewish piece of work. Theologically, it dismisses the monotheism of Judaism as "the polytheism of many needs, a polytheism that makes even the toilet an object of divine law."[19] Socially, it looks forward to "the emancipation of society from Judaism."[20]

Turning from *On the Jewish Question* to *The Communist Manifesto*,[21] one finds that the growing radicalization of Marx's thought leads him to speak much more of simply the bourgeois or the bourgeoisie than of *bürgerliche Gesellschaft*, though the latter term does not disappear completely. The title of the first section bears the title "Bourgeois and Proletarians." Marx and Engels aspire to strict science, so they are not at all wary of formal definitions: in an 1888 footnote Engels defines the bourgeoisie as the class of modern capitalists, owners of the social means of production and the exploiters of wage labor.[22] By contrast, the proletarians are modern wage laborers who must sell their labor power in order to survive.

Instead of rehearsing all the charges Marx levels against the bourgeois, a few observations will suffice to show how Rousseau's analysis undergoes a change. Most obviously, and as the note cited above demonstrates, the bourgeois is subject in *The Communist Manifesto* and elsewhere to Marxism's tendency to engage in economic reductionism and determinism. Marx thereby gains simplicity but loses subtlety. In Marx, the bourgeois becomes a less immediately recognizable human type than he appears in such nineteenth-century novels as Flaubert's *Madame Bovary* or Stendhal's *The Red and the Black*. In turn such portraits, and those of Balzac, are more vivid than those of the Marxist Zola—a judgment concurring with that famous Marxist, Lenin.

Instead of an intricate psychology, the reader of Marx gets a series of economic predictions. At this point, even admirers of Marx encounter a difficulty. Marx claims to be a scientist, and one judges science in large part by the accuracy of its predictions. By this time, most of those predictions have been refuted by history. Thus the workday in countries with bourgeois economies grew shorter, not longer; the middle class expanded instead of contracting; capitalist countries managed to deal with their economic difficulties while socialist economies suffered decline. The problem of the bourgeois, in short, turned out to be anything but economic at its core.

In Marx's description of the bourgeoisie, the group also loses the character of in-betweenness assigned to it by Rousseau and others. The bourgeois tends to become simply the man on top with his boot on the neck of the worker. Two classes, and only two classes, constitute the scene: bourgeois and proletariat. Marx celebrates the latter as the agent of secular salvation, and he demonizes the bourgeois in spite of detailing the accomplishments of capitalism in the past. Marx regularly mocks moral standards, but in spite of this aspect of his work he depicts the bourgeois as the absolute oppressor who practices absolute exploitation—the incarnation of absolute evil. Individual capitalists may be decent, but individuality does not amount to all that much: the capitalist does evil because he participates in an evil system. He thus has no real redeeming features. It bears noting that this was not the case in Rousseau. For example, bourgeois marriage comes off surprisingly well. In *Emile*, where the family is considered a haven from a heartless world, a family is founded that seems in decisive respects a bourgeois family—or a nuclear family as it is sometimes labeled today.

Marx, then, lags behind Rousseau as a philosopher and differs from him in decisive respects, but he does inherit from Rousseau a strong sense of justice. Marx really loathed the bestiality of man to man, so one finds in him more than a bit of Rousseau's fervor and indignation. One can even argue that in one significant respect Marx exceeds Rousseau's concern for justice. Rousseau accepted nature and human nature as good in a denuded but real sense. Perhaps the most famous remark by Marx states: "The philosophers hitherto have interpreted the world in various ways, but what matters is to change it."[23] The world must be changed most radically because things at the root of the world are not as they should be. In Hobbes, Locke, and Rousseau, nature appears as primarily indifferent or stingy or shapeless. In Marx, by contrast, nature itself is accused of injustice. Unjust nature yields to human engineering, and perhaps even to human retribution. According to Rousseau, one can do no better than live with the problem of the bourgeois. According to Marx, history will solve that problem.

V

Marx's outcry against the injustice of the bourgeois finds no exact echo in the thought of Friedrich Nietzsche. To say the least, he does not necessarily disapprove of the oppression of the weak by the strong. He does not become indignant at exploitation and aggressive competition. Indeed, according to the doctrine of the will to power they are at the very heart and core of all human things, and ultimately of all things period.[24]

Nietzsche thinks of the recovery of irrational nature—nature "red in tooth and claw"—as humanity's task. He maintains that justice has been contaminated by a strict and ever stricter bourgeois identification of justice with equality; its purification requires that it be subjected to a transvaluation of all values. It reemerges from the process of transvaluation as a protective shield for the high, the strong, and the great, a shield necessitated by their inherent vulnerability and frailty. The new justice may well strike the bourgeois mind as being traditional *in*justice. With the appearance of Nietzsche on the scene, the bourgeois in a sense regains the quality of in-betweenness. Henceforth to be bourgeois means, in part, to be in between increasingly strident attacks from the Right inspired by Nietzsche and from the Left inspired by Marx. Sometimes the sources of attack can be almost impossible to distinguish. A number of passages by Marx might well have been written by Nietzsche, and a number of passages by Nietzsche might well have been written by Marx.

At times it almost seems that the descendants of Marx and Nietzsche have buried the hatchet and concentrated on the common ground between them. The Right has divested itself of its allegiance with royalty and religion. In time the Left has moved away from Marx's economism as a generation of latter-day Marxists and neo-Marxists arose who knew not surplus value or the immiseration of the proletariat. Both sides could, after all, agree in their opposition to the Center, also known as the bourgeois, also known as liberal democracy. Bourgeois bashing becomes all the rage and obliterates distinctions.

Nevertheless, the differences between Marx and Nietzsche are profound. Nietzsche, to repeat, does not concentrate on the battle against injustice as injustice had come to be understood. He dismisses Rousseau's moral fervor as decayed Christianity, and he understands himself to have moved boldly "beyond good and evil."[25] His charge against the bourgeois can be briefly summarized: it ushers in radical egalitarianism and is thus merely a prelude to communism. Nietzsche might agree with Tocqueville that one can conceive of a manly love of equality that consists in wanting to raise up the low, but that is not the variety Nietzsche sees around him. He observes instead the egalitarianism that wants to pull down the high. The bourgeois is the man who commits himself to combat against excellence and genius, even preferring stuttering to eloquence. It is worth mentioning that Nietzsche's love of and concern for greatness owes something to Rousseau, whom, incidentally, he acknowledges as one of the shapers of the modern image of man.[26] According to Nietzsche, Rousseau shares that honor with Goethe and Schopenhauer, and he tends to view them all as somehow incomplete Nietzsches.

The bourgeois does more than to attempt to level others; he levels himself. In Nietzsche's magnum opus *Thus Spoke Zarathustra*, his virtues are described as petty and sleepy, virtues that make people small and petty. The soul of the bourgeois is a flatland; the bourgeois is someone intent on thinking small rather than big. Zarathustra, who for present purposes can be understood as Nietzsche's spokesman, says in exasperation to his bourgeois audience: "Not your sin but your thrift cries to heaven, your meanness even in your sinning cries to heaven."[27]

Zarathustra provides the modern reader with the most chilling description of the bourgeois future in his short speech on the "last man." The basic event from which his passionate rhetoric proceeds is the death of God—primarily the Christian God but ultimately all gods. With the death of God, man will be forced to become either more than man, the superman, or less than man, the last man. He cannot remain man, because man has been defined by his reverence but now there is nothing left for him to revere. The audience Zarathustra addresses in the prologue of the book can fairly be called bourgeois, though Nietzsche does not use that term. It is both unimpressed by and uncomprehending of Zarathustra's vision of the superman, so he tries to awaken it to the horror of its alternative, the last man:

> Behold, I show you the last man. "What is love? What is creation? What is longing? What is a star?" thus asks the last man, and he blinks.
>
> The earth has become small and on it hops the last man, who makes everything small. His race is as ineradicable as the flea beetle. The last man lives longest.
>
> "We have invented happiness," say the last men, and they blink. They have left the regions where it was hard to live, for one needs warmth. One still loves one's neighbor, and rubs against him, for one needs warmth.
>
> Becoming sick and harboring suspicion are sinful to them: one proceeds carefully. A fool, whoever still stumbles over stones or

human beings! A little poison now and then: that makes for agreeable dreams. And much poison at the end, for an agreeable death.

One still works, for work is a form of entertainment. But one is careful lest the entertainment be too harrowing. One no longer becomes poor or rich: both require too much exertion. Who still wants to rule? Who obey? Both require too much exertion.

No shepherd and one herd! Everybody wants the same, everybody is the same: whoever feels different goes voluntarily into a madhouse.

"Formerly, all the world was mad," say the most refined, and they blink.

One is clever and knows everything that has ever happened: so there is no end to derision. One still quarrels, but one is soon reconciled—else it might spoil the digestion.

One has one's little pleasure for the day and one's little pleasure for the night, but one has a regard for health.

"We have invented happiness," say the last men, and they blink.[28]

Zarathustra speaks to his audience in the hope that though they are not *for* the superman they may at least be *against* the alternative. Instead the audience clamors for the last man. The bourgeois is not yet the last man, but he is in one respect worse: the last man is his ideal.

Nietzsche attacks the bourgeois on many levels and in many ways, but the attack at the deepest level is on bourgeois moderation, a virtue still honored by Rousseau because it is an indispensable virtue for a functioning political life. Moderation entails the belief that virtue is a mean between two extremes, but to Nietzsche virtue is an extreme. It is not a way of controlling the passions but itself a passion, a transfigured passion. It is a lavish squandering of energy and yearning. Nietzsche attempts to effect a transvaluation of values, in which justice reemerges with its ties to equality severed, courage turns into an intellectual as well as moral virtue, and wisdom develops into *wild* wisdom. Moderation, however, is evidently impossible to transfigure or even transform. By way of a pun[29] Nietzsche identifies it with mediocrity and dismisses it.

Nietzsche's war against moderation leads him into strange and dangerous regions that include the mockery of common decencies, the praise of cruelty, and a lust for a genuinely irrational politics. He thus becomes a precursor and ancestor of fascism.

VI

The mention of fascism brings us to this century, in which the attacks on the bourgeois leave the plane of theory and enter the plane of practice in the form of two mass movements, fascism on the Right and communism on the Left. These movements celebrated many triumphs against discredited bourgeois liberal democracy, but wherever they triumphed they made discredited democracy seem like a golden age.[30] They thus left honorable people with no choice but to become the defenders of bourgeois or liberal democracy.

Temporarily at least—and one hopes permanently—the threat to liberal democracy from without has ended, but the task of defending democracy persists because the attack from within persists. The charges against the bourgeois have not only continued but in some cases become more strident.

Much of that stridency directs itself at the moderation liberal democracies recognize as the political virtue par excellence. In doing so, bourgeois democracy becomes part of the great tradition of Western civilization. It becomes the heir, perhaps the sole surviving heir, of both Jerusalem and Athens. It is one thing to say that liberal or bourgeois democracy is the corrupted heir of that tradition, a charge to which it is forced to plead guilty. But it is another thing to say that it is the corrupt heir to a tradition that is itself corrupt because it is dominated by dead white European males, and because it was always defaced and disgraced by sexism, racism, homophobia, elitism, ethnocentrism, and other evils.

That *is* the charge against the bourgeois today, a charge that must be refuted. The bourgeois has become the image of evil itself. Those of us who have been teaching political philosophy a number of years saw the advent of this phenomenon. To teach the subject effectively, the teacher must explore the image of evil the students bring to class. Those of us born before, say, 1930, brought to our studies two splendid images, Hitler and Stalin. Slowly we witnessed the decline of the "relevance" of these images. Evil came to be equated with Scarsdale or Shaker Heights by students whose parents had the temerity to practice deferred gratification—a bourgeois virtue—so that their children could attend high-priced universities. Bourgeois life must be defended and is worth defending, but there seems to be no easy way to do it. Moderation, for one thing, resists glamorization. In addition, the defenders of the bourgeois have been "at it" for over 150 years, and their attempts to rectify the deficiencies of bourgeois life must so far be judged to be either most modest successes or most honorable failures. Bourgeois man is self-critical to a fault, but uncertain how to deal with the deficiencies he admits to having. That may be the ultimate problem of the bourgeois.[31]

By way of concluding our inquiry, let us glance at the three most prominent proposals for elevating the bourgeois.

VII

One of the recurring proposals seeks bourgeois improvement by means of art. That is the theme of Schiller's *Aesthetic Education of Man*,[32] and in a less schematic but more delicate way it runs through the works of Goethe. They both attempt to raise the taste of the bourgeoisie, to make it more aware of the high by making it more aware of the beautiful. The endeavor usually flounders. Poetry finds itself at a loss about overcoming the incurably prosaic quality of moderation. In art, the villains may well exert more appeal than the heroes, as Balzac and other great novelists realized. Salvation through art turns poets into not the unacknowledged but the acknowledged legislators of the human race. It thus may burden the poets with more weight than they are able to carry; it may lead them to forget about the ultimate foundation of their magic, providing people with pleasure.

A second proposal favors the elevation of the bourgeois by way of love, romantic love institutionalized in the family. But how well can the family perform this function? It stands or falls by its ability to tame eros, which can be done only to a modest extent. How appealing can bourgeois family life be made to seem? Jane Austen praises marriage, but her novels stop with the completion of courtship, and it is difficult to forget Nietzsche's dismissal of marriage as a sharing of bad moods and bad air. Goethe, to be sure, wrote a most beautiful epic poem about bourgeois love and marriage, *Hermann and Dorothea*, but few read it today. Goethe also wrote a novel called *Elective Affinities*. The doctrine of elective affinities—roughly that love is chemistry—is articulated in chapter 4, which contains a reference to the wellbeing of *bürgerliche Gesellschaft*,[33] civil or bourgeois society. In a sense, then, it is about self-preservation; the discussion begins with medicine and moves on to love and marriage. But the novel is not so much about the married bliss of the main characters as about their contemplation of adultery and their intention to commit it. Adultery points to the limits of marriage and the family.

Finally there is religion. Beginning with Rousseau, one finds wide agreement that religion is useful for bringing out the best and averting the worst in bourgeois man. Tocqueville is especially adept at developing this line of argument. But he does not excel in confronting the Nietzschean argument that God is dead and that the utility of religion is fatally damaged by a declining faith in the truth of religion.

This dilemma terminates our inquiry, since no proof can be advanced that God is not dead. We can rather lamely assert that the reports of his death have been exaggerated and that the Bible still offers wisdom as well as solace. We can do no more. Fortunately, as students and teachers we can parody Tennyson[34] and declare that ours is not to do or die, ours is but to reason why. And surely, in reasoning about the problem of the bourgeois, one could do worse than to think about the legacy of Rousseau.

Notes

1. In this connection the writings of Gyorgy Lukacs and the Frankfurt school, influenced by him, are of special interest. The best guide to their work, highly critical but fair, can be found in Leszek Kolakowski, *Main Currents of Marxism* (Oxford: Oxford University Press, 1981), 3:253–307, 341–95.

2. Karl Marx and Friedrich Engels, *Manifesto of the Communist Party*, in *The Marx-Engels Reader*, 2d ed., ed. Robert C. Tucker (New York: Norton, 1978), 487–88.

3. Friedrich Nietzsche, *Thus Spoke Zarathustra*, in *The Portable Nietzsche*, ed. and trans. Walter Kaufmann (New York: Viking, 1954), 124.

4. Karl Löwith, *From Hegel to Nietzsche: The Revolution in Nineteenth-Century Thought*, trans. David E. Green (New York: Holt, Rinehart and Winston, 1964), 235.

5. See Leo Strauss, *Natural Right and History* (Chicago: University of Chicago Press, 1953), 252–94 and idem, "On The Intention of Rousseau," in *Hobbes and Rousseau: A Collection of Critical Essays*, ed. Maurice Cranston and Richard S. Peters (Garden City, N.Y.: Anchor Books, 1972), 254–90. My debt to Leo Strauss, my teacher, is too far-reaching to be acknowledged in notes such as this.

6. See Allan Bloom, "Emile," in *Giants and Dwarfs: Essays 1960–1990* (New York: Simon and Schuster, 1990), 177–207, his chapter in this book, and *Love and Friendship* (New York: Simon and Schuster, 1993), 39–156. The lecture this essay is based on began with an informal tribute to my recently deceased friend. His influence on my

thinking about Rousseau, and not only about Rousseau, is second only to that of Leo Strauss.

7. Strauss, *Natural Right and History*, 252.

8. Jean-Jacques Rousseau, *Emile, or On Education*, trans. Allan Bloom (New York: Basic Books, 1979), 40, 482.

9. Alexis de Tocqueville, *Democracy in America*, ed. J. P. Mayer and Max Lerner, trans. George Lawrence (New York: Harper and Row, 1966), 7–8.

10. That is not only a phrase of Rousseau's but the title of a book to which I owe a great deal: Arthur M. Melzer, *The Natural Goodness of Man: On the System of Rousseau's Thought* (Chicago: University of Chicago Press, 1990).

11. *Emile*, 40.

12. Introduction to *Emile*, 5.

13. *Portable Nietzsche*, 130.

14. Blaise Pascal, *Pensées*, trans. A. J. Krailsheimer (Baltimore: Penguin Books, 1966). See especially fragments 132–46, pp. 66–74.

15. *Marx-Engels Reader*, 16–26.

16. The best available English edition can be found in *Writings of the Young Marx on Philosophy and Society*, trans. and ed. Lloyd D. Easton and Kurt H. Guddat (New York: Doubleday, 1967), 216–48.

17. See *Marx-Engels Reader*, 319–29.

18. Joseph Cropsey, chapter on Marx in *History of Political Philosophy*, 3d ed., ed. Leo Strauss and Joseph Cropsey (Chicago: University of Chicago Press, 1987), 807.

19. *Writings of the Young Marx on Philosophy and Society*, 245.

20. Ibid., 248.

21. *Marx-Engels Reader*, 469–500.

22. Ibid., 473.

23. Ibid., 145.

24. See Friedrich Nietzsche, *Beyond Good and Evil: Prelude to a Philosophy of the Future*, trans. Walter Kaufmann (New York: Vintage Books, 1966), aphorisms 9, 13, 36.

25. That, of course, is the title of the book cited above, Nietzsche's first after *Thus Spoke Zarathustra*.

26. See "Schopenhauer as Educator," in Friedrich Nietzsche's *Untimely Meditations*, ed. William Arrowsmith (New Haven: Yale University Press, 1989).

27. *Thus Spoke Zarathustra*, 126.

28. Ibid., 129–30.

29. Ibid., 282.

30. See Leo Strauss, *What Is Political Philosophy?* (Chicago: University of Chicago Press, 1988), 55.

31. I owe the insight into the importance of self-criticism for understanding the bourgeois to a conversation with François Furet.

32. Friedrich von Schiller, *On the Aesthetic Education of Man in a Series of Letters*, trans. Elizabeth M. Wilkinson and L. A. Willoughby (Oxford: Oxford University Press, 1967).

33. Johann Wolfgang von Goethe, *Elective Affinities*, in *Goethe: The Collected Works*, vol. 2, ed. David E. Wellberg, trans. Judith Ryan (Princeton: Princeton University Press, 1995), 110.

34. Alfred, Lord Tennyson, "The Charge of the Light Brigade," in *The Major Victorian Poets*, ed. William M. Marshall (New York: Washington Square Press, 1966), 157.

❦ 2 ❧

Rousseau and the Case against (and for) the Arts

CHRISTOPHER KELLY

Anyone who pays attention to contemporary debates over the public role of the arts cannot avoid being struck by the widely divergent claims raised by the participants in these debates. Critics of public support for the arts frequently argue that the artists who receive such support represent an elite, anti-American, privileged group whose artistic activities strike a blow at our political life by undermining the traditional values that hold our community together. Other critics, concerned with the effect of the arts on popular culture, claim they undermine personal autonomy by fostering a slavish conformism and concern for social approval. On the other side, defenders of the arts claim that artistic activity is the highest expression of our communal life, that our culture rather than our uninspiring political principles gives a deep and genuine sense of community. Other defenders argue that the arts are the vehicle for the development and expression of our unique individuality and that this function is far more important than any mere political or social concern. In short, the arts are bad because they promote individuality at the expense of society or because they promote society at the expense of individuality, or else they are good for precisely the same reasons. Because we usually see these claims raised by people who have very little in common, it can be unsettling to find them all put forward by the same person. Nevertheless, Jean-Jacques Rousseau makes every one of them, and he does so not because he is a singularly incoherent thinker, but because he is a coherent one. Furthermore, his coherence lends some insight into the sort of perspective on the arts and on politics that can give rise to such an odd mixture of competing claims.

The Political Case against the Arts

The best known part of Rousseau's argument is what could be called his political critique of the arts. This critique is an important part of the attack on

20

modern culture that suddenly made him famous upon publication of his *Discourse on the Sciences and the Arts* in 1751. This political critique—developed mainly in the *First Discourse*, in Rousseau's defenses of that work, and in the *Letter to M. d'Alembert on the Theatre*—has two basic elements. First, Rousseau argues that when the arts are esteemed in a society it is a symptom of an unhealthful political and social inequality. Second, he claims that the arts are incapable of lending support to morality in the ways that proponents of the arts think they can. The first of these attacks concerns the indirect effects of artistic activity, whereas the second more directly concerns the nature of our experience of the arts.

In the first place Rousseau argues that, from the standpoint of society as a whole, as a practical matter there is little that distinguishes artistic works from luxury goods such as jewelry, designer clothing, or wigs. When discussing the purveyors of such goods, Rousseau refers to "these important fellows who are called artists instead of artisans, and who work solely for the idle and the rich."[1] What hair stylists and jewelers share with painters, sculptors, and the like is that their clientele is made up of people who want to distinguish themselves from the crowd and are willing to pay to do so. This clientele is rather less interested in beauty than in distinction. For them and their societies the arts are merely tokens of inequality based on money or status.

Of course artists can be embarrassed by, or even disdain, the link between their world and the world of luxury even as they attempt to profit from it. No doubt artists who have had to seek patronage have always resented their prospective patrons' lack of artistic sensibility. Rousseau himself knew well from personal experience that wealth is a rare outcome of the pursuit of the artistic life. Accordingly, he acknowledges that artists are likely to be motivated by something other than the desire for wealth. As he says, "Every Artist wants to be applauded. The praises of his contemporaries are the most precious part of his reward."[2] Artists' interest in praise suggests that they can be flexible, adapting themselves to the various tastes of different audiences. From a political or moral perspective, one could try to separate those who ignobly pander to depraved tastes from those who help cultivate a more wholesome taste. However, Rousseau insists that even the most public-spirited artist contributes to the depreciation of civic virtue. This is so because even the most rigorous moralist will prefer an interesting and beautiful depiction of morality in a work of art to one that is equally moral but dull and homely. Thus, even when artists produce morally praiseworthy works, the praise they receive results more from their talent than from their morality. Even a society characterized by a wholesome taste encourages what Rousseau calls "the disastrous inequality introduced among men by the distinction of talents and the debasement of virtue."[3] In short, any praise given to artistic talent is subtracted from the amount that might be given to moral actions.

Rousseau does not stop here. The rewards given to those with a talent for pleasing an audience stimulate everyone to learn how to please. The high status of the arts tends to go along with a general concern for elegance and polished manners. Although defenders of politeness and elegance from the opponents of the *First Discourse* in 1751[4] to Miss Manners today argue that these things make life more pleasant, increase social harmony, and make people more humane, they must be prepared to admit that elegance and politeness are accompanied by a great deal of hypocrisy. Such people are fond of citing La Rochefoucauld's famous maxim, "Hypocrisy is an homage that vice pays to virtue."[5] Although they admit that politeness is not identical to good morals, they insist that it is superior to open bad morals and, furthermore, that it requires even immoral people to acknowledge morality as a standard to which they should submit.[6] Rousseau, however, responds that mastering the rules of polite social interaction allows the vicious to succeed and, even worse, makes them respectable. The unsophisticated may occasionally find themselves engaged in open hostility, but the appreciation of fine art and a veneer of politeness merely cover over this hostility rather than bringing it to a peaceful and humane conclusion. As Rousseau describes the hidden reality behind polite exchanges, "One says to the other deep in his heart: *I treat you like a fool and I laugh at you,* the other replies deep in his heart: *I know you lie shamelessly, but I return the favor as best I can.*"[7] The politeness fostered by the arts replaces a state of occasional war based on force with a state of constant war based on fraud. In Rousseau's view this substitution is a poor masquerade of a genuine peace.

This part of the case against the arts attacks their more or less indirect consequences, and Rousseau is quite ready to admit that the arts are the symptoms rather than the causes of these forms of corruption. He addresses himself most explicitly to the more direct moral effects of the arts when he considers one particular art, namely, the theater. This case is particularly important because its defenders can draw on a long tradition dating back to Aristotle claiming that theater is the clearest case of a type of art that can have a good moral effect. The most common assertion of Rousseau's contemporary defenders of the theater was derived from Aristotle's claim that it can support morality by purging the passions. To this they added that it could provide models of good behavior for imitation. These proponents knew that particular plays can have bad effects: they can stimulate the wrong passions and inspire the imitation of bad behavior. Consequently they tended not to oppose censorship in principle. They merely argued that a properly purified drama—like the French drama from the classical age on—could satisfy the most rigorous standards of any reasonable censorship.[8] Rousseau's position is more radical than any traditional pro-censorship position because he insists that censorship is not an adequate solution to the dangers posed by the theater. He insists that even a rigorously purified drama could not bring about the good effects its proponents claimed for it. Accordingly, in his debate with d'Alembert over the establishment of a theater in Geneva, it is Rousseau who argues against censorship on the grounds that it is an inadequate solution to the problems caused by the theater.

Rousseau does not deny that plays can have a moral content, although he is rather skeptical about the likelihood of this. Morality is not attained simply by giving villains an unhappy end; the ending of a drama is the least important contribution to its morality. A play in which a wicked man is presented as attractive and clever for four acts is not redeemed because he arbitrarily commits an implausible act of stupidity that leads to his undoing in the final scene.[9] When plays of a genuinely moral character are written, they are likely to be less interesting and therefore less successful than immoral ones because their authors have sacrificed the goal of pleasing an audience for the sake of tedious preaching.

To be sure, Rousseau does not deny that unusually gifted dramatists can combine the goals of entertainment and moral content. In fact he concedes that contemporary French dramatists were very successful in achieving this combination. Nevertheless, the essence of his political critique is that even a genuine moral content does not give art a moral effect. The heart of his criticism of the theater is found in his analysis of the way plays do inspire the audience to identify with good characters.[10] Rousseau is so far from denying the reality of this experience of identification that he insists that even the most notorious tyrants and coldhearted villains are frequently moved to tears at the sight of the misfortunes of good people portrayed in plays.[11] In fact Rousseau goes beyond many of his contemporaries by arguing that the experience of identification in the theater is more powerful than similar experiences in ordinary life. He claims that we identify with the characters in plays so strongly because our identification with them is pure, untainted by selfish concerns that adulterate our ordinary experiences of identification. When we enter the theater, we leave our own concerns at the door and are free to give vent to our most generous impulses. Nevertheless, precisely because Rousseau insists on the reality, strength, and purity of theatrical identification, he denies that it makes us better people. The very purity of the theatrical experience of identification makes it sterile.[12] A theatrical performance demands nothing of its spectators except that they abandon themselves to their pure and unadulterated emotion. This is why more tears are shed over plays about suffering than over solicitations from charities. Similarly, people frequently feel greater admiration for theatrical accounts of heroes' lives than they do for living heroes. The strength and purity of theatrical identification encourages an easygoing moral smugness, a false sense of having done one's duty simply by having identified with someone good. Because the members of the audience feel so purely in the theater, they congratulate themselves for possessing an exquisite sensitivity that is in fact acquired at no cost beyond the price of admission. The essence of Rousseau's political critique of the arts is contained in his remark, "People think they come together in the theatre, and it is there that they are isolated."[13] In short, the theater creates only an illusory sociability.

Rousseau's critique of the theater is particularly important because it contains an understanding of the nature of artistic experience that extends to other fine arts as well.[14] A survey of Rousseau's numerous writings on the arts shows that in his view identification with feelings is the essence not only of the theater, but of all experience of the arts, including those like music that do not obviously involve imitation. The distinctive character of Rousseau's understanding can be shown by comparing it with one contemporary presentation he was well acquainted with, given by Jean Le Rond d'Alembert in the Preliminary Discourse to Diderot's *Encyclopedia*, published in the same year as Rousseau's *Discourse on the Sciences and the Arts*.

D'Alembert's account indicates some of the dilemma of understandings of the fine arts in the eighteenth century. He embraces both a traditional doctrine that understands the arts as imitating nature[15] and a modern natural science whose account of nature provides little support for beauty. D'Alembert ranks the fine arts according to two criteria: how exactly the imitation resembles the original and how directly it appeals to the senses.[16] According to these criteria, painting and sculpture rank highest: they present accurate resemblances directly to vision. D'Alembert ranks poetry lower because it "speaks more to the imagination than to the senses." At the bottom of his hierarchy is music, which can imitate relatively few things when it tries to appeal to the senses with an exact simulation—for example, drums representing thunder or trumpets the neighing of horses. To d'Alembert's contemporary readers the precise order of this hierarchy would have been very familiar.[17]

There is, however, a certain tension in d'Alembert's account of poetry and music. Although the criteria of exactness and directness force him to place these at the bottom of the hierarchy, he expresses great admiration for these two arts. For example, he says that poetry "seems to create rather than to depict" its objects. As for music, he argues that it gains in scope to the extent that it abandons direct imitation. Most of his very brief discussion of music consists of an exhortation to composers and critics to perfect the poorly culti-vated resource of music, which can stimulate passions and even sensations in the absence of the objects that usually produce them. Thus, with a minimal amount of development, he introduces a new goal for music, one potentially sharply at odds with the criteria that serve as the basis of his hierarchy.

On reading this discussion Rousseau recognized its novelty and potential and wrote to d'Alembert to congratulate him on his observations about mu-sic.[18] In his own discussions of the arts he exploits this new perspective in a way that completely reverses the traditional hierarchy to which d'Alembert con-formed. Rousseau does so by arguing that appeal to the imagination rather than to the senses is what makes art genuinely imitative. This can be seen very clearly in his account of music. Rousseau agrees with d'Alembert that there are two types of music, one appealing directly to the senses and another appealing to the imagination. He calls the first "natural" music and suggests that its attraction comes less from the accuracy of its imitation than from the physical pleasantness of sounds.[19] Rousseau calls the other type of music, the type that is not natural, "imitative music." But if imitative music does not exactly simu-late the sounds of the things it represents, what does it imitate? According to Rousseau, music imitates human emotion rather than things. He says that a composer "will not represent things directly, but he will excite in the soul the same emotions we experience in seeing them."[20] Thus music does not so much imitate things as cause an imitation to take place in the listener's imagination. The purpose of music is not direct imitation, but excitement.

This power to stimulate the imagination gives music an extraordinary range and depth and makes it the foremost, not the least, of the arts and offers a new scope for the aspirations of musicians. As Rousseau says of the composer, "Not only will he agitate the sea at his whim, stir up the flame of a fire, make brooks stream, the rain fall, torrents swell, but he will increase the horror of a frightening desert, darken the walls of a subterranean prison, calm the storm, render the air tranquil, the Sky cloudless, and spread a new freshness over the groves from the Orchestra."[21] Rather than arguing that music should be measured by a standard of imitation set by the visual arts, Rousseau claims that the visual arts can rival music only to the extent that they use their ability to strike the eye as a means toward expressiveness, force, and vigor in their appeal to the imagination. In making this claim, he obviously gives an impetus to an understanding of the visual arts that ultimately abandons realistic representation of the external world in the name of expression.

In sum, in Rousseau's understanding the arts are imitative, but not of nature. Rather, they imitate human emotion, and they do this by inspiring emotion in members of the audience.[22] The way Rousseau links the experience of all the fine arts to what I have been calling theatrical or musical imitation causes him to push to the breaking point the link between the arts and nature still adhered to by d'Alembert. Therefore he says that painting is "closer to nature, while music is more closely related to human art,"[23] and in saying this he is praising music over painting.[24]

The Natural Case against the Arts

One does not expect to hear Jean-Jacques Rousseau, the apostle of nature, praising art at the expense of nature, and that he does so here indicates that the account given of the arts to this point is not his whole story. In fact, the break that Rousseau prepares for or makes between the fine arts and nature serves as the basis for his second critique of the arts. In this criticism he attacks the arts not because they make us unsocial, as he said about theater, but because they make us dependent and too social.

Even though it is not natural, according to Rousseau artistic imitation clearly has a natural root. When he refers to the weeping of tyrants at a tragedy, he uses this as evidence for the remnants of natural commiseration even in the most depraved of civilized humans. Rousseau identifies commiseration as one of the two fundamental principles of the human soul and calls it "a sentiment that puts us in the position of him who suffers."[25] Clearly, then, humans naturally possess the capacity to identify with feelings that is the distinctive characteristic of artistic experience. Although this capacity is natural, however, it requires development. In its primitive form it is simply "a natural repugnance to see any sensitive being perish or suffer."[26] Because natural humans can understand only physical suffering, they are unable to conceive of the suffering of, say, Oedipus when he discovers he has killed his father and slept with his mother. They certainly cannot understand Othello's jealousy or Macbeth's ambition. Although natural humans would be unmoved by Sophocles or Shakespeare, they would be affected by works that graphically show purely physical suffering. Such works, however, would barely qualify as imitative art in Rousseau's terms. Any genuinely imitative art must simulate emotions beyond physical pain and therefore depends on the acquisition of such emotions.

In sum, the imitative arts depend on two things: the ability to identify with others and the imagination to experience and recognize a complex range of emotions. The first of these is natural, the second is not. Furthermore, Rousseau presents the development of what we can call theatrical emotions such as ambition, vanity, desire for vengeance, jealousy, and so on as a threat to natural personal independence. These dramatic passions are passions that involve us with other people and make us dependent on them. Hence in the first half of *Emile*, Rousseau's description of an education meant to preserve natural independence, all the fine arts appear as threats to this independence. For example, Emile does learn to draw, but Rousseau says he does so "not precisely for the art itself, but for making his eyes expert and his hand flexible."[27] He will never draw without having the original in front of him, and will never substitute "bizarre and fantastic shapes for the truth of things." Every effort is made to suppress the development of what would today be called "creativity." Similarly, Emile is taught to sing in order to make his voice "exact, even, flexible, resonant," but Rousseau says, "above all, never a bizarre song, never a passionate one, and never an expressive one."[28] Here the "natural" criterion of exactness excludes the imitative criterion of emotional expressiveness. The young Emile is a natural artist and therefore not a genuine imitative artist in the full sense of the term.

The reasons for this restriction of the arts become more apparent in the context of Rousseau's attack on poetry in *Emile*. One aspect of his criticism of La Fontaine's fables is connected with the reader's tendency to identify with the character who gets the better of another rather than with the recipient of the lesson. On a deeper level, Rousseau's argument attacks identification altogether. Later, when he gives a qualified endorsement to the study of history and of Plutarch's *Lives* in particular, Rousseau says, "As for my Emile, if in these parallels he just once prefers to be someone other than himself—were this other Socrates, were it Cato—everything has failed. He who begins to become alien to himself does not take long to forget himself entirely."[29] Clearly the arts are even more likely than history to cause this alienation.[30] Rousseau's political attack on the arts claimed that they made us forget our neighbors and our duties and become too self-indulgent. Now it appears that his natural attack on the arts claims that they make us forget about ourselves and become too social.

The Political Case for the Arts

Rousseau's very different critiques from the perspectives of politics and nature are complementary, not contradictory. Naturally, humans are both radically independent and completely immune to the appeal of the arts, and furthermore, their independence results from their immunity to the arts. At the same time, their independence keeps them from being citizens. One of the most distinctive of Rousseau's claims is his argument that humans are naturally so self-sufficient that there is absolutely no reason for them to cooperate with each other in any sustained way. Moreover, he consistently argues that the rational calculation of what is in one's self-interest can lead only to fleeting attempts at cooperation with one's fellows and incites more permanent attempts at exploiting them. He claims that to attempt to base social ties on self-interest is in effect to say that performance of social duties can be bought at a price. But people who are offered a price for good citizenship can reasonably wonder whether they might get a better offer elsewhere. As Rousseau says, "There is no profit, however legitimate, that is not surpassed by one that can be made illegitimately."[31] Human beings can become citizens, then, only if they are given a social identity that makes them conceive of their self-interest in a collective way. Gaining this social identity means becoming imitative in the artistic sense. In essence, for Rousseau being social is essentially the same as being imitative.

This identity between sociability and imitation can be illustrated by Rousseau's treatment of the decisive step in acquiring a social identity, the acquisition of language, which he calls "the first social institution."[32] How this first institution originated is ultimately mysterious, but Rousseau is quite clear about its major precondition. He says, "As soon as one man was recognized by another as a sentient, thinking Being, similar to himself, the desire or the need to communicate to him his feelings and thoughts made him seek the means to do so."[33] Notice the peculiarity of this formulation. Rousseau does not say, "As soon as one man recognized another, he desired to communicate." What he says is, "As soon as one man was recognized by another he desired to communicate." The desire to communicate apparently depends on the awareness that someone else recognizes us as similar. We must be aware of other people as being aware of us. This entails a much deeper, more developed, and more complex identification with others than does the natural form of commiseration.

Note also that Rousseau identifies two different aims of language: the communication of thoughts and the communication of feelings. His definition of language as "the institution of sensible signs to express thought"[34] applies more to written than to spoken language. As he says, "One conveys one's feelings in speaking, and one's ideas in writing."[35] As the first social institution, language is much more bound up with communicating feelings as a means of identification with others than with communicating thoughts. Unlike Aristotle, for example, who regards the connection between language and rational deliberation as essential to the political nature of humans, Rousseau regards language as a means for communicating thoughts as secondary and also as inadequate to the demands of political life. In short, social life begins with the institution of the communication of feelings through what we have identified as artistic imitation. Genuine social life is coextensive with artistic life.

Rousseau makes this connection between social life and artistic life clear by asserting that the first language must have been sung rather than spoken. Just as music is the paradigmatic art for Rousseau, musical speech is the paradigmatic form of communication and indeed of social life. He argues that ancient legislators understood this truth, or at least acted as if they did.[36] He remarks that "in former times, all laws human and divine, exhortations to virtue, the knowledge of what concerned the Gods and heroes, the lives and actions of illustrious men were written in verses and sung publicly by Choirs to the sound of Instruments."[37] In short, the greatest ancient legislators could succeed in the art of legislation because they understood the importance of art for legislation.

The political importance Rousseau attributes to artistic imitation and to music in particular might well appear to be a Platonic element of his thought. After all, in the *Republic* the best city is founded on a musical education that looks like a prefiguration of Rousseau's principles in that it uses melody, harmonic modes, and rhythm to direct the souls of citizens in the proper way. Certainly Rousseau and Plato are the two philosophers who made the strongest argument for a connection between music and good citizenship. Yet there is nonetheless a very important difference in emphasis between the two of them. In the account in the *Republic* the ability of melody, harmony, and rhythm to channel passions is clearly secondary in importance to the need to subordinate these elements of song to speech and, furthermore, to subordinate speech to the reasonable demands of the city.[38] Briefly, Socrates suggests a hierarchy that descends from reason to speech to music. In modern music before Rousseau one can trace a Platonic inspiration based on this hierarchy running from Monteverdi through Lully.[39]

Rousseau, on the other hand, places far more importance on melody than on reason or articulated speech. To be sure, he does try to restore a connection between music and speech which had been severed in Rameau's music, or at least his theorizing about music.[40] Nevertheless, the connection he tries to restore is between music and the melodic accents of speech, not between music and the articulation of reasonable speech. Whereas Plato is interested in taming the power of music and submitting it to reason, Rousseau is interested in taking advantage of the untamed power of melody. Perhaps because he regards social life as unnatural, Rousseau thinks the full power of music is needed to socialize people. This is not to say that Rousseau would be unwilling to use reasonable argument to discuss what sort of music would be best for civil purposes. He did write an interesting essay, "On Military Music," and composed a pleasant march in accord with his principles. On balance, however, Rousseau turns on its head the Platonic order that gives primacy to reason over feeling.

Rousseau's first critique of the arts can now be put into proper perspective. Beyond his attack on the link between the arts and luxury, his precise complaint against the theater concerns the sterility of theatrical identification. This sterility comes from the very purity of the theatrical experience, in which spectators forget about their normal existence as citizens. Where citizenship is concerned, Rousseau's attack is against the sterility of this form of identification, not against identification as such. Genuine citizenship depends on finding a sort of identification that avoids this sterility and forgetfulness. Rousseau's two apparently opposite critiques of the theatrical and musical arts as they are cultivated by his contemporaries combine into the criticism that these arts are too imitative to preserve naturalness, but not imitative enough (or in the proper way) to support citizenship.

In the *Letter to d'Alembert* Rousseau gives qualified praise to the theater of ancient Greece for achieving this better form of imitation. He presents the Greek theater as superior to modern theater in numerous ways, including its taking place in the open air and having no admission fee. Both these factors mitigate its tendency to support inegalitarian display. Most important, Greek theater relied on political themes that invoked national traditions.[41] Furthermore, when the Greeks went to the theater they identified with citizens rather than with the unrealistic heroes, lovers, or corrupt sophisticates who walked the stage in classical French drama. Rousseau clearly regards the French Medea and Phaedra as artificial derivatives of the Greek originals.

Rousseau's attack on the moral sterility of classical theater has certainly been taken to heart by playwrights after him. A part of his artistic legacy is a series of attempts to overcome this sterility. Before writing the *Letter to d'Alembert,* he himself considered writing plays that would introduce the theme of civic republicanism to the French stage.[42] Perhaps because of his analysis of the limits of the theater, he abandoned this project. Even so, within the *Letter* he urges contemporary playwrights to turn their attention away from exalted themes and toward "simple suffering humanity."[43] In doing this he gives at least a partial endorsement to Diderot's project of a sentimental drama based on bourgeois heroes like those found in his plays *The Father of the Family* and *The Natural Son.* Furthermore, Rousseau's diagnosis of the intrinsic limits of drama is at least the remote inspiration for subsequent attempts, such as those in the twentieth century by Brecht and Artaud, to overcome those limits by breaking down the barriers between audience and actors.

In both its form and its content Greek theater minimized the distance between audience and actor. However, even the Greek theater does not earn Rousseau's unqualified praise. What he requires is a sort of entertainment in which the separation between spectator and actor is completely overcome. He recommends public festivals, competitions, and dances. Ultimately his goal is to make the entire community into a sort of constant spectacle in which the citizens are participants. He says, "Let the spectators become an entertainment to themselves; make them actors themselves; do it so that each sees and loves himself in the other so that all will be better united."[44] In the end, the problem with modern communities is not an excessive concentration on the arts, but a sterility resulting from the failure to understand exactly how far art is the foundation of community rather than simply its ornament, and how much it can serve as the basis of mutual identification rather than fostering pernicious inequality.

It is very tempting to regard Rousseau's analysis of the arts' failure to accomplish in modern society what they accomplished in ancient societies as a call to restore them to their proper importance. Certainly one of Rousseau's effects on the artists who followed him was to inspire them to attempt to recover the ancient connection between the arts and political life. He encourages them to see themselves as the genuine founders of communities rather than as the servants of the rich. Schiller found the inspiration for his *Letters on the Aesthetic Education of Man* in *Emile*, and one hears the echo of Rousseau in Shelley's assertion, "But poets, or those who imagine and express this indestructible order, are not only the authors of language and of music, of the dance and architecture, and statuary, and painting; they are the institutors of laws, and the founders of civil society."[45] It is no wonder Rousseau's name figures prominently in the poems of not only Shelley, but also Byron, Schiller, Hölderlin and other romantic poets who aspired to the goal of using art to construct a new culture.[46]

Rousseau himself was much more skeptical than his followers about the potential for a radical reconstruction of most modern societies. Nevertheless, he did consider numerous projects that would give the arts a more salutary role in contemporary society. Foremost among these projects was the impetus he gave the novel as a literary form that could indulge the unpolitical passions of modern peoples without leading them into the competitive display of the theater audience. Reading novels is a domestic rather than public activity, and good novels can help make domestic life a refuge from a corrupting public life.[47]

In Rousseau's opinion the greatest novelist was Richardson, and it is the key Richardsonian element of sensibility, or sentimentality, that Rousseau attempted to isolate and perfect. His one criticism is that Richardson does not place sufficient reliance on this element. In response to Diderot's praise of Richardson's ability to portray a great variety of characters and situations (and the implicit suggestion that Rousseau failed in *Julie*) Rousseau argued that surprise twists and wicked characters are cheap tricks used by the least talented novelists. His own novel succeeds without such devices by focusing on a relatively simple story and on the beautiful souls of its protagonists.[48] As Allan Bloom has shown, Rousseau's exploration of love set the agenda for most of the great novelists of the nineteenth century.[49] This agenda consists of ennobling private life in a corrupt world rather than reinstituting the healthy politics of antiquity.

In a second project Rousseau argued tirelessly against the predominant tradition of French music, which he saw as abandoning expressive power in the name of a purely technical expertise. In particular, he engaged in a lengthy and acrimonious debate with Rameau over the very nature of music.[50] One of the most interesting facets of Rousseau's treatment of music is his attempt to call attention to the music of other countries. This began with his championing Italian music in France and extended to his attempt to reproduce Chinese and South American music in his *Dictionary* and finally to his composition of a rather unusual tune, the "Chanson negre," to suit lyrics written in Creole. There are at least two reasons for Rousseau's interest. First, he wished to explore types of music that might recapture some of what had been lost in modern French music. Second, he attributed great importance to the encouragement of unique cultures.

The emphasis on what could be called primitivism and cultural diversity stems from his insistence that the artistic experience is not natural because the passions, feelings, and emotions we identify with in our experience of art are unnatural ones. Precisely because these feelings are unnatural, they are susceptible to an indefinite number of variations. They will vary from individual to individual and even more from nation to nation because of variations in temperament, climate, diet, historical accidents, and any number of other causes, of which some can be influenced by human activity and others cannot. As a result, different types of art will affect different cultures. To illustrate this point Rousseau refers to the traditional story that songs can cure tarantula bites. While provisionally accepting the fact of such cures, he denies that they have a directly physical cause. Rather, he asserts that the songs have an effect on the emotions, which in turn affect the body. Because of this he insists that each nation would require its own songs and concludes his account by saying, "Bernier's Cantatas are said to have cured a French musician of a fever; they would have given one to a musician of any other nation."[51] As many modern parents have found to their dismay, what is mere noise to one audience is to another music filled with profoundly moving associations.

Legislators must be aware of this variability in the power of the arts. They are not free to use any means whatever. They must learn to diagnose the artistic or cultural temperament of their own people and then use the means suited to channeling this temperament in the right direction. In a sense all happy political communities, like all happy families, are alike; that is, they are all founded on an artistic experience that makes citizens identify with each other, but this formal similarity is compatible with—and indeed requires—the maximum possible distinctiveness for each community.

Once again Rousseau had modest expectations for the practical effects of his analysis of contemporary music. He certainly hoped to rescue it from a wrong turn it had taken, but his two claims, that music must be based on the melodic character of language and that modern European languages were essentially unmelodic, made him more pessimistic than many of his followers.[52] In this case, as in numerous others, Rousseau imbued his followers with an acute sense that their own societies had gone desperately wrong. He was less successful in inculcating his pessimism about projects to set things right.

Independence and the Artistic Life

In sum, Rousseau's political critique of the arts as they are cultivated by his contemporaries ultimately leads him to a claim that, far from being in contradiction to the arts, healthy political life must be founded on an artistic basis. We can now ask whether his critique of the arts from the perspective of independence undergoes a similar reversal. To be sure, as indicated above, in its purer forms the natural life—either in the pure state of nature or in the more civilized life of the young Emile—is an essentially inartistic life. Naturally, the beautiful is reduced to the good, the good is reduced to the pleasant, and the pleasant is reduced to what pleases the senses. Good taste is literally identical to what tastes good. Although this sort of life is a possible one in that it is the truest expression of human nature, it is certainly not possible for humans in societies as we know them. We cannot go back to living in the forest with the bears, and even Emile cannot maintain his natural independence perfectly for long after he turns fifteen and discovers other humans.

Are there any other options for living a life of independence, or do the links Rousseau establishes among departure from nature, social dependence, and the arts mean that for us a life of independence is only an illusory dream? Traditionally, the life of independence could be identified with the philosophic life, which is understood in distinction from both artistic life and a life of political engagement. The classic statement of this position, of course, is the cave metaphor in Plato's *Republic*, in which the appeal of the philosophic life is presented largely in terms of independence or liberation from the chains that bind other humans and in which those chains are understood as being forged in large part by the arts, or poetry. There is very strong evidence that Rousseau's criticisms of the arts owe much to the Platonic account,[53] but his alliance with Plato stops with this critique precisely because he does not accept the view that philosophy ultimately has a more natural foundation than the arts do.

This is not to say that Rousseau does not understand philosophy at all in terms of independence or liberation. In fact, while speaking as a citizen, he frequently takes philosophers to task for destroying social bonds. This same process could be presented in a more positive light by saying that philosophy liberates from social bonds. Rousseau's answer to this is that philosophy represents only an incomplete liberation. Here is how he describes the way a philosopher looks at others: "By dint of reflecting on humanity, by dint of observing men, the Philosopher learns to appreciate them according to their worth, and it is difficult to have very much affection for what one holds in contempt. Soon he concentrates into his person all the interest that virtuous men share with their fellows: his contempt for others turns to the profit of his pride: his amour-propre increases in the same proportion as his indifference to the rest of the universe."[54] For Rousseau the characteristic mark of the philosopher is not the love of wisdom, but pride. To be sure, it is pride in one's freedom from the contemptible character of others, but this pride is not a total independence because it is based on a constant comparison. Thus, in the end philosophic activity is merely the most refined version of the characteristic vice of all nonnatural humans.

Rousseau does identify a natural source of the desire to know that can be distinguished from the unnatural pride-based one. The natural form of curiosity is based on the "innate desire for well-being,"[55] which leads to the desire to know everything connected to one's interest. Rousseau urges us to imagine "a philosopher relegated to a desert island." In an obvious reference to Newton, he says that this philosopher will lose all interest in things such as the system of the world, the laws of attraction, and differential calculus. Instead, he will explore every part of his island. This is not to say that this particular form of the desire to know cannot be extended indefinitely. After all, "the island of humankind is the earth and the most striking object to our eyes is the sun" and we may need to learn differential calculus, the laws of attraction, and more to understand how to use these things; but natural desire to know will always be based on the more or less clear connection between knowledge and our interests. Furthermore, these interests are defined in a material way rather than in terms of some presumed interest we may have in satisfying an erotic longing to know.

This leads to the question of how Rousseau understands his own philosophic activity. Is it based in pride or utility, or has something been left out of the account? A large part of the image of himself that Rousseau has left us is a picture of a solitary man who pursues activities that he loves, indifferent both to the opinions of others and to considerations of interest. Furthermore, some of these activities, such as the study of music or botany, look remarkably like philosophy in its traditional sense.

The best known of Rousseau's accounts of the satisfying character of non-utilitarian knowing occurs in his description of botany. Botanizing, as he describes it, is a contemplative pursuit that differs from both pride-based and interest-based philosophy. He pursues it by himself, without concern for other people's opinions. Most important, he insists that botany should not be pursued as a useful study. His botanical dictionary opens with the remark, "The first misfortune of botany is to have been regarded as a part of medicine since its birth."[56] This utilitarian approach has deformed botany by restricting it to a narrow field and by blinding those who study it to the genuine beauty of plants. That beauty is found by contemplating the structure or "organization" of plants. Furthermore, it can be appreciated only by study. One must be a knower in order to experience it.[57]

What causes the satisfaction Rousseau feels in contemplating the structure of plants? Does he recognize a beauty intrinsic to the plants and, in addition, one that points beyond plants to the beauty of the cosmos? Is the beauty of the structure of plants something like the forms or ideas of classical philosophy? The answer to these questions is somewhat complicated. In the first place, Rousseau makes only rather perfunctory efforts to link botany to ultimate concern about being. We can experience the structure of plants as beautiful without any reference to their connection with anything beyond themselves.[58] Even more important, he does not argue that the pleasure of botanizing increases in direct proportion to the knowledge gained. He describes his own intense pleasure by saying, "To wander nonchalantly in the woods and in the country, here and there to take up mechanically, sometimes a flower, sometimes a branch; to graze on my fodder almost at random, to observe the same things thousands of times, and always with the same interest because I always forget them, was enough for me to pass eternity without being bored for a moment. . . . I was, and my lack of memory ought to have always kept me at that fortunate point of knowing little enough about it so that everything was new to me and enough so that I was able to feel everything."[59] The pleasure of botanizing requires a degree of knowledge, but it consists more in the novelty of ever-renewed discovery of particular beauties than in the contemplation of eternal principles. Forgetting is at least as important an element in Rousseau's account as is understanding. In traditional accounts one does not find a bad memory this high on the list of qualities necessary for philosophic contemplation.

Finally—after sifting through much evidence and many qualifications—one must conclude that for Rousseau philosophy understood as the effort to understand the eternal truth about being is, to put it simply, boring at least to the extent that it succeeds in its aim. Contemplation as he liked to practice it resembles more an aesthetic activity, a pleasant stimulation of the imagination, a walk through an art gallery, admiring the beauty of one painting but moving on to another before the inevitable boredom can set in.

A large part of the reason for this need for novelty comes from the fact that in Rousseau's account the structure or organization of beautiful objects is more the occasion for the experience of beauty than it is the locus of beauty. As was argued above, the artistic experience is one of identifying with feelings, and those having the experience can identify only with feelings they are capable of recognizing or in some manner already have. A work of art or a natural object experienced as beautiful is only the medium for the stimulation of these feelings. As Rousseau says at least twice in quite different contexts, "Except for the single Being existing by itself, there is nothing beautiful except that which is not."[60] Because he insists that we have no access to this single Being existing by itself, this is the same as to say there is nothing beautiful except our experience of beauty. Because of this it would be a mistake to conclude from Rousseau's praise of botany that love of the beautiful is necessarily connected with an appreciation of the orderliness of nature. The disorder of tempests and the wildness of waterfalls can reflect the feelings of the soul as beautifully as can the structure of plants.

Throughout Rousseau's works there are numerous accounts of his experience of satisfaction with this new type of nonphilosophic contemplation. He gave his most comprehensive account in an attempt he made to explain that, contrary to what most of his acquaintances thought about him, he led a life of happiness rather than misery.[61] His description of a happy day has three stages. First, having left his home early to avoid pestering visitors, he observes the beauty of plants. Second, he imagines a society of friends and lovers to share his pleasure. An identification with even imaginary fellows is necessary to complete the pleasure. He shows how much even this pleasure comes from the act of imagining rather than from real company by saying, "If all my dreams had been turned into realities they would not have been enough for me; I would have imagined, dreamed, desired again. I found an inexplicable void in myself that nothing could fill." Naturally enough, this inexplicable void drives him to consider the traditional concerns of philosophy. His mind moves "to all the beings of nature, to the universal system of things, to the incomprehensible being who embraces everything." But when faced with these ultimate concerns he says, "I did not think, I did not reason, I did not philosophize." Instead he abandons himself to confusion and lets his imagination roam. He sums up this experience with a final antiphilosophic remark: "I believe that if I had unveiled all the mysteries of nature, I would have felt myself to be in a less delightful situation than that stupefying ecstasy to which my mind abandoned itself without reserve." Ultimate clarity is less delightful than stupefying ecstasy.

In what sense is this particular sort of independent life an artistic one in the precise sense of imitation or identification with human emotion? In the following way: Rousseau's peculiar form of confronting being is to see his own restless longing reflected in the universe itself. In contemplating the universe he identifies with his own feelings. The universe becomes a metaphor for himself. Thus Rousseau describes a life of self-sufficiency as the highest human happiness, but this is a life of aesthetic contemplation, imaginative creation, and stupefying ecstasy; it is a poetic rather than a philosophic life. Philosophy is at most instrumental to it.

What conclusion can be drawn from this survey of Rousseau's complex views of art, which see it as the source of both human dependence and independence, of both healthy and unhealthy social life? Perhaps the most significant practical outcomes of Rousseau's thought are the profound dissatisfaction it inspires with the current state of both the arts and politics and the enormous hopes it inspires about their possible future improvement. The arts as they are now cultivated destroy our autonomy and make us exploiters of each other; but the arts as they could be cultivated would fulfill us as individuals and unite us as fellow members of a community. This strange view raises artistic aspiration very high, but it is also easily fragmented into the different contentions about the arts that we see around us today.

NOTES

I thank the Camargo Foundation, the Earhart Foundation and the George A. and Eliza Gardner Howard Foundation for their support of the research for this chapter.

1. Jean-Jacques Rousseau, *Emile, or On Education*, trans. Allan Bloom (New York: Basic Books, 1979), 186. Eighteenth-century French does not always distinguish between artists and artisans, both of whom can be referred to as artists. Rousseau is going out of his way to make the distinction here.

2. *Discourse on the Sciences and the Arts*, in *Collected Writings of Rousseau*, ed. Roger D. Masters and Christopher Kelly (Hanover, N.H.: University Press of New England, 1990–93), 2:15. See also *Final Reply* in *Collected Writings*, 2:113. This same edition is cited throughout the chapter.

3. Jean-Jacques Rousseau, *First Discourse*, in *Collected Writings*, 2:18.

4. For the defenses of politeness, see in particular the *Refutation by Gautier*, in *Collected Writings*, 2:70–71, and the *Discourse on the Advantages of the Sciences and the Arts*, in *Collected Writings*, 2:100–101.

5. See *Observations by Jean-Jacques Rousseau of Geneva on the Reply Made to His Discourse*, in *Collected Writings*, 2:49.

6. Although Rousseau usually insists that he would prefer open to concealed wickedness, he occasionally concedes that "in a country in which it is no longer a question of honest people nor of good morals, it would be better to live with rogues than with brigands" (*Preface to Narcissus*, in *Collected Writings*, 2:196).

7. *Letter from J. J. Rousseau of Geneva to Mr. Grimm on the Refutation of His Discourse by Mr. Gautier*, in *Collected Writings*, 2:84.

8. On the debate over the theater leading up to Rousseau, see Moses Barras, *The Stage Controversy in France from Corneille to Rousseau* (New York: Phaeton Press, 1933).

9. See *Letter to M. d'Alembert on the Theatre*, in *Politics and the Arts*, trans. Allan Bloom (Ithaca: Cornell University Press, 1960), 28–29.

10. Rousseau does argue, however, that this is true only in the best cases. Frequently people will identify with brilliant success rather than goodness, particularly when they are seeing a comedy. See *Letter to d'Alembert*, 34–35, and *Emile*, 115–16.

11. See *Letter to d'Alembert*, 24–25. In an addition to the *Second Discourse* made after its original publication, Rousseau uses the same example to show that natural compassion does not die completely even in the most corrupt civilized humans. See *Collected Writings*, 3:36.

12. See *Letter to d'Alembert*, 24–25. One of the critics of the *Second Discourse* raised the question of why the populace "enjoys with such avidity the spectacle of an unfortunate dying on the rack." Rousseau responded with the same argument he gives in the *Letter to d'Alembert*, "For the same reason you go to the theater to weep and to see Seide kill his

Father or Thyeste drink the blood of his son. Pity is such a delightful feeling that it is not surprising that we seek to experience it" (*Collected Writings*, 3:125, 131). In this case, as in the *Letter,* Rousseau is far from denying the reality of the feeling of pity. Furthermore, he does seem to be implying that the populace feels no impulse to assist the victim of a public execution, any more than it feels an impulse to assist a victim in the theater. Because of this the feeling of pity is so pure that it brings about no result other than intense pleasure at a spectacle.

13. *Letter to d'Alembert*, 16–17.

14. Rousseau is not alone in promoting an understanding of all of the fine arts as somehow theatrical. See the excellent study of Diderot's art criticism by Michael Fried, *Absorption and Theatricality: Painting and Beholder in the Age of Diderot* (Berkeley: University of California Press, 1980). This is one of numerous cases in which Rousseau and Diderot made a very similar diagnosis of a problem and attempted to solve it in extremely different ways and in different fields. The intensely personal nature of their falling-out at the end of the 1750s has obscured the extent to which these philosophic differences of opinion fueled their disputes.

15. To avoid the problem posed by exact imitation of ugly things, d'Alembert appeals to the notion of *la belle nature,* which was a commonplace of French treatment of the beautiful in the seventeenth and eighteenth centuries. See Marian Hobson, *The Object of Art: The Theory of Illusion in Eighteenth-Century France* (Cambridge: Cambridge University Press, 1982), 159.

16. See Jean Le Rond d'Alembert, "Discours préliminaire," in *Encyclopédie, ou Dictionnaire raisonné des sciences des arts et des métiers* by Denis Diderot (Paris: Flammarion, 1986), 1:103.

17. For an identical statement of the hierarchy as dominant in accounts of music about 1700, see Etienne Haeringer, *L'esthétique de l'opéra en France au temps de Jean-Philippe Rameau,* Studies on Voltaire and the Eighteenth Century 279 (Oxford: Voltaire Foundation, 1990), 11.

18. See Rousseau's letter of 26 June 1751, in *Correspondance complète de J. J. Rousseau,* ed. R. A. Leigh (Geneva: Institut et Musée Voltaire, 1964–), 2:160. Hobson uses Rousseau's letter as evidence of the novelty of the position stated by d'Alembert. See Hobson, *Object of Art,* 283.

19. See the article "Musique," in the *Dictionnaire de musique* (Paris: Duchesne, 1768), 308. Translations from this edition are my own. The *Dictionnaire* has been translated into English as *A Complete Dictionary of Music,* trans. William Waring (New York: AMS Press, 1975). Citations to this edition will be added to citations to the French text. The passage concerning the distinction between natural and imitative music occurs at 258–59 in the English text. Consider also this remark from the article "Harmonie," "Harmony furnishes no principle of imitation by which Music, forming images or expressing feelings, can be elevated to the Dramatic or imitative genre, which is the most noble part of the Art, and the only energetic one. Everything that pertains only to the physics of Sounds, being very limited in the pleasure which it gives us, and having very little power over the human heart" (*Dictionnaire,* 242; *Dictionary,* 191–92).

20. "Imitation," in *Dictionnaire*, 251; *Dictionary*, 198–99.

21. "Opera," *Dictionnaire*, 350; *Dictionary*, 299.

22. "Entr'acte," in *Dictionnaire*, 201; *Dictionary*, 201–2.

23. Jean-Jacques Rousseau, *Essay on the Origin of Languages*, in *The First and Second Discourses Together with the Replies to Critics and Essay on the Origin of Languages*, ed. and trans. Victor Gourevitch (New York: Harper and Row, 1986), 287.

24. For an extensive account of the political importance of Rousseau's treatment of language and music, see Victor Gourevitch, "The Political Argument of Rousseau's *Essay on the Origin of Languages*," in *Pursuits of Reason: Essays in Honor of Stanley Cavell*, ed. Ted Cohen et al. (Lubbock: Texas Tech University Press, 1993).

25. See *Discourse on the Origin of Inequality*, in *Collected Writings*, 3:15, 37.

26. *Second Discourse*, in *Collected Writings*, 3:15.

27. *Emile*, 143.

28. *Emile*, 149.

29. *Emile*, 243.

30. Rousseau discusses the effect on himself of reading novels and lives in book 1 of the *Confessions*. See *The Confessions*, in *Collected Writings*, 5:7–8.

31. *Second Discourse*, in *Collected Writings*, 3:75.

32. *Essay on the Origin of Languages*, 240.

33. Ibid. I have altered the translation slightly.

34. Ibid., 240.

35. Ibid., 253. I have altered the translation slightly.

36. For an elaboration of this point see my "'To Persuade without Convincing': The Language of Rousseau's Legislator," *American Journal of Political Science* 31 (May 1987): 321–35.

37. "Musique," in *Dictionnaire de musique*, 311; *Dictionary*, 261.

38. See Plato, *Republic*, 398d and 400d.

39. On Monteverdi's use of Platonic authority for his claim that one should "make the words the mistress of the harmony and not the servant," see Gary Tomlinson, *Monteverdi and the End of the Renaissance* (Berkeley: University of California Press, 1987), 25. On the subordination of music to lyrics in Lully see Catherine Kintzler, *Jean-Philippe Rameau: Splendeur et naufrage de l'esthétique du plaisir à l'âge classique* (Paris: Le Sycamore, 1983). See also John Neubauer, *The Emancipation of Music from Language: Departure from Mimesis in Eighteenth-Century Aesthetics* (New Haven: Yale University Press, 1986), 22–23.

40. On this point see Kintzler, *Jean-Philippe Rameau*, 99–132.

41. *Letter to d'Alembert*, 33–34.

42. See *Confessions*, book 8, in *Collected Writings*, 5:331.

43. *Letter to d'Alembert*, 32.

44. *Letter to d'Alembert*, 126.

45. Percy Bysshe Shelley, "A Defense of Poetry," in *The Complete Works of Percy Bysshe Shelley*, ed. Roger Ingpen and Walter E. Peck (New York: Gordian Press, 1965), 7:112.

46. On Rousseau's importance for the mythmaking and culture-forming projects of

the English romantic poets see Paul A. Cantor, *Creature and Creator: Myth-Making and English Romanticism* (Cambridge: Cambridge University Press, 1984).

47. See *Letter to d'Alembert*, 82.

48. See *Confessions*, book 11, in *Collected Writings*, 5:456–57.

49. See Allan Bloom, *Love and Friendship* (New York: Simon and Schuster, 1993). It can also be argued that *Julie* helped bring to completion the agenda of the eighteenth-century novelists who preceded Rousseau. On this point see William Ray, *Story and History: Narrative Authority and Social Identity in the Eighteenth-Century French and English Novel* (Cambridge, Mass.: Basil Blackwell, 1990).

50. For an account of this debate, which lucidly explains the contrasting positions of Lully, Rameau, and Rousseau, see Kintzler, *Jean-Philippe Rameau*.

51. *Essay on the Origin of Languages*, 284.

52. For an account of Rousseau as a crucial step away from an older tradition to the romantic understanding of music as the paradigmatic art, see Neubauer, *Emancipation of Music from Language*.

53. Consider in particular his extract from the *Republic* and *Laws*—called *On Theatrical Imitation*—which was composed while he was working on the *Letter to d'Alembert*.

54. *Preface to Narcissus*, in *Collected Writings*, 2:192.

55. *Emile*, 167.

56. Jean-Jacques Rousseau, *Oeuvres complètes*, ed. Bernard Gagnebin and Marcel Raymond (Paris: Pléiade, 1959–), 4:201.

57. See *Confessions*, in *Collected Writings*, 5:537.

58. On this point see Paul A. Cantor, "The Metaphysics of Botany: Rousseau and the New Criticism of Plants," *Southwestern Review* 70 (summer 1985): 362–80.

59. *Confessions*, in *Collected Writings*, 5:537.

60. *Emile*, 447, and *Julie, ou, La nouvelle Héloïse*, in *Oeuvres complètes* 2:693.

61. This description is in the third of the "Letters to M. de Malesherbes." The quotations below are from this letter in *Collected Writings*, 5:579.

❧ II ❧
Nature, Culture, History

Rousseau, Kant, and the Beginning of History

SUSAN SHELL

I

We hear a lot these days about the end of history. It therefore seems to be a timely moment to consider history's *beginning*. By the beginning of history I do not mean the beginning of the natural world—a beginning that modern telescopes promise or threaten to bring eerily close; nor do I mean the beginning of the world in the original sense of *wer-eld*, literally "the age of man."[1] By the beginning of history I mean the moment when the flow of events as it pertains to human beings was first conceived as a self-sufficient "totality" or "whole." It is only history so understood that can reasonably be spoken of as "ending" in the Hegelian-Fukuyaman sense, a sense that implies neither the destruction of the earth nor the coming of the Messiah but something like the completion and hence the end of man's intelligibility to himself. After history, "life goes on." History in this radically modern sense is a story without mystery, the story of man made whole and therefore intelligible in that through it (uniquely) subject and object are or can be one. History so conceived is the union of the knower and the known, the actualization of its own "idea." As such it both answers and supplants the age-old question, What is truth? When Marx used "history" to "settle his accounts with philosophy," it is this sort of history he had in mind.

The first thinker to conceive of history as an "idea" and thus as a (potentially) self-sufficient whole was Immanuel Kant. Kant's elaboration of this idea in such essays as the *Idea for a Universal History from a Cosmopolitan Point of View* (1784), *Conjectural Beginning of Human History* (1786), and *The Conflict of the Faculties* (1798) is well known. Much less attention has been paid to earlier works that anticipate that idea in important and sometimes surprising ways. In what follows, I will examine some of these early works in hopes of shedding light on why this peculiar notion of history occurred to Kant and how Rousseau bears on that occurrence—a murky story that may, however modestly, restore some of the mystery to history.

*

Let me begin in media res with Rousseau (before the idea of history as such actually appears). A series of notes—the so-called *Bemerkungen* or "Remarks" on Kant's *Observations on the Beautiful and the Sublime*—furnish a detailed record of Kant's early reading of Rousseau and the responses it provoked. Scholars estimate their date of composition to be about 1764—two years after Kant's initial reading of *Emile*—a time long enough to allow for leisurely reflection, yet perhaps short enough to preserve the contours of Kant's first impression of Rousseau.

Two passages describe with special force Kant's estimation of Rousseau's importance. In the first, often quoted passage Kant writes:

> I am by inclination an inquirer. I feel in its entirety a thirst for knowledge and a desirous restlessness to come further in it, along with satisfaction with each acquisition. There was a time in which I thought that this alone could constitute the honor of mankind, and I despised the people, who know nothing. Rousseau brought me to rights. This blind prejudice vanished. I learned to honor human beings and I would find myself more useless than the common worker if I did not believe that this reflection could bestow a value on all else that establishes the rights of mankind. (20:44)[2]

In the second, less often quoted passage he calls Rousseau the Newton of the moral world:

> Newton was the first to see order and regularity bound up with the greatest simplicity, where before him disorder and badly matched manifoldness were to be met with, whereas since then comets travel in geometric course. Rousseau was the first to discover under the manifoldness of the available shapes [*Gestalten*] of mankind man's deeply hidden nature and the concealed law according to which providence through its observation is justified. (20:58–59)

What are we to make of these two statements, and how can they be brought together? Specifically, what was the misguided inclination that Rousseau corrected in setting Kant aright, and how do the hidden principles of human nature that Rousseau reveals bear on this correction?

To answer these questions, it is useful to look back to Kant's earlier works, of which perhaps the most helpful and revealing is the ambitious *Universal Natural History and Theory of the Heavens* (1755), written when Kant was about thirty.

The stated goal of the *Universal Natural History* is to account for the constitution and mechanical origin of the universe by means of Newtonian principles. Such a project was, of course, by no means altogether novel. Newton, out of piety or prudence, had assumed the placement of the planets as God-given. But Descartes (taking his clue from Lucretius) had already sketched out a mechanical history of the universe.

And yet when Kant at the beginning of his *Universal Natural History* echoes Descartes by boldly stating "give me matter and I will make a world from it" (1:230),[3] he is by his own account attempting something new. That something new essentially reduces to this: where earlier thinkers, in explaining the ultimate cause of things, resorted either to blind mechanism or to the will of God, Kant unites mechanics and theology in a novel way.

Kant, of course, was not the first to attempt such a mediation. His great predecessor Leibniz had given an account of the universe in which the ultimate cause or ground of things lies in the "optimizing" will of God. God wills the best world possible. Things happen as they do and the world is as it is because God's will is not omnipotent but must defer to a prior standard of compossibility. He cannot make everything perfectly good because some goods are incompatible with other goods. My winning the lottery, for example, is incompatible with your winning it, and Mabel's spending her life married to Sam is incompatible with spending her life married to John. At the same time, to make this reconciliation work, Leibniz is forced to argue that mechanical causation is merely a well-founded appearance or *phenomenon bene fundatum*. Substances or monads, the ultimate atoms of the universe, do not genuinely interact. Each, rather, reflects the universe internally, albeit from a unique point of view, as exemplified by the worldly consciousness of each human soul. Monads, as Leibniz liked to say, have no windows. Monads, as he also put it, are like individual clocks set to go off at the same time, or like singers who sing their individual parts without being able to hear the other members of the chorus. By Leibniz's account, only God hears the chorus. Only God knows the whole as it is because only in his intellect are its parts genuinely together. As individual monads we may approach God's vantage point (insofar as we reflect the whole internally) without being able to reach it.

47

The difficulty with Leibniz's ingenious doctrine, from Kant's point of view, is its thoroughgoing destruction of what we mean (or at any rate what he means) by the world as real. Confronted with the Cartesian question, Does the world as I perceive it actually exist? Leibniz is forced to admit that we have no thoroughly dependable way to distinguish between reality and a lifelong dream.[4] Metaphysically speaking, one could have a single dream that lasted a lifetime, for which the ordinary tests of internal consistency and predictability by which we usually distinguish dreams from waking states would not avail. But for Kant the deeper difficulty with Leibniz's teaching is the ultimate ideality of the world as such, whose monads—vis-à-vis each other—come together only in the mind of God. So conceived, the world seems indistinguishable from God's thought or dream. How can human understanding of the world be said to approach God's asymptotically when the limit of that approach is a state in which the difference between knowing and dreaming disappears? How can we know anything at all when the model of perfection in terms of which knowledge is defined is indistinguishable from fantasy?[5] Kant's *Universal Natural History,* as writings of the same period make clear, is at least partly devoted to resolving this larger question. Kant finds his clue to the structure of the world as a genuine whole in the peculiar necessity that connects its parts, a necessity expressed by Newton's "laws" of motion.

What, Kant wants to know, binds one factual event to another? And what distinguishes their connection from that of a logical syllogism on the one hand and an arbitrary fiction on the other?

Kant's answer is something like the following: The universe consists of matter in motion. But the motion of matter is governed by laws that God implanted in the elements at the moment of creation. The sort of necessity that informs the world and distinguishes it both from a product of blind chance and from immediate, arbitrary will has the character of law.

Let me be clear. Kant's mediating course between Lucretian atheism and divine interventionism is not merely a prudent attempt to make mechanical science palatable to revealed religion (though it is surely partially that). Rather, Kant sees in the mediation of science and religion a way to resolve the deeper question of how to grasp the world as a whole (which seems to presuppose our elevation beyond the world to something like the divine perspective) while still perceiving it as real (which seems to presuppose our submission to the lawful necessity that informs the world, and thus our submergence within it).

To be both of the world and beyond it—that is the challenge and dilemma with which the entire discourse of the *Universal Natural History* is bedeviled. To Kant the idea of lawfulness suggests both a metaphysical and a physical answer to this challenge.

Metaphysically construed, the notion of universal lawfulness suggests a reconciliation of the thoroughgoing unity of the universe with the individual integrity of the parts composing it. Where ancient and medieval thought looks to the regime, governed hierarchically by a ruling part, for an image of the cosmos, Kant's model calls to mind the reciprocal equality of civil or market society. Kant's "constitution" of the universe (the alternative title of his natural history) is thus closer to the liberal model of society than to a regime or "constitution" in the classical sense. (Kant's technical name for worldly connection is, revealingly enough, *commercium*.)

The form of metaphysical community lies not in a ruling part, but in the submission of each member to the same reciprocally determining law. But such reciprocal submission proves incomprehensible (for reasons we cannot here pursue) apart from the notion of a schema of God's interlocking purposes—a sort of plan or blueprint for creation. It is only in light of such a schema or idea, which reconciles the reality of each element with the reality of the whole, that worldhood is conceivable. To know nature fully is to think the divine schema or idea. The difficulty is that such a schema is, in the end, unavailable to man. God's plan reconciles infinite diversity and absolute unity only by transcending time. Man can comprehend the whole only in time, hence bit by bit or partially.

*

Kant's natural history is put forward with a view to these issues. Accordingly, Kant posits an "original state of nature" (the Hobbesian phrase is, I think, quite deliberate)—a first moment in which matter is dispersed throughout infinite space (1:263). This dispersal would immediately eventuate in static equilibrium (from which the world as we know it could never have evolved) but for the heterogeneity of the elements, which vary according to their own unique specific densities. Out of this diversity organized motion begins, as rarer matter "sinks toward" the more dense, governed by the universal law of attraction. To explain why some matter remains fixed in orbit rather than descending to the center of attraction, Kant posits a second force of repulsion, owing to which masses deflect each other in their downward path, and thus move sideward according to the principle of least reciprocal action. The upshot is a planetary system in which orbiting bodies radiate outward from a central vortex or "sinking point" according to their respective densities.

As with individual planetary systems, so with the universe as a whole. By positing a point in the universe of greatest density or attractive force, Kant imaginatively extends his understanding of the solar system to an "infinity of worlds." When we take our bearings from this cosmic sinkhole—this navel of the universe—the whole of creation appears to fall within our grasp.

But behind the bright sun of Kant's vision lurks an ominous—indeed monstrous (*ungeheuer*) cloud.[6] The whole thereby disclosed repels even as it attracts. The sun, source of both light and warmth, harbors a dark and ambiguous underside. Like a phoenix whose cycles of creation and destruction are echoed and repeated by the universe as a whole, the sun literally feeds on herself, monstrously breathing, to use Kant's striking language, "out of her own bowels" (1:326). (*Sonne*, as we will later have reason to recall, is in German a feminine noun.) Like the ambiguous fertility of nature herself, the sun attracts and animates only to destroy. Respectful (somehow) of the eternity of species, nature is indifferent to the fate of individuals. Unlike Leibniz's monads, who could count on their uniqueness to secure their necessary and hence eternal place in a nature that makes no leaps, for Kant individuals have no such claim on immortality. In the Kantian scheme of things the principle of plenitude, which ensures the eternal existence of all possible kinds, gives no guarantees to individuals. The forces of attraction and repulsion render all bodies vulnerable to a perpetual exchange of forces in which nothing (other than the eternal types) is permanent or secure.

Nature "exhibits her richness" in a sort of overflowing "prodigality": floods, earthquakes and pollution sweep whole nations from the earth—worlds and world systems are created and destroyed—without depleting nature's purse or diminishing her inexhaustible fecundity. Kant therefore urges us to accustom our eye to nature's terrible revolutions (*Umstürzungen*) and accept them as the normal ways of providence (1:318).

And yet confronted with the image of the universe he has created, Kant cannot quite bring himself to call it good. Man's place within the whole is especially doubtful, given the tumult of the elements that no human being can find fully satisfying. And yet if Kant cannot locate man within the whole—

cannot, that is to say, show how man's purpose and the purpose of the universe conjoin—his model of the whole as a divine schema of interlocking ends threatens to dissolve.

*

Hence the conjectural—and by current lights bizarre—appendix to the *Universal Natural History,* devoted to the inhabitants of other planets. Man's unhappiness, his failure to achieve the ends made manifest by his abilities, *can* be reconciled with the purposiveness of the whole, but only if we give up our geocentrism and view matters from an interplanetary perspective. If man is of all creatures the one who "least achieves his purposes," this need not count against the splendor and perfection of the whole. What seems to man to be a defect may from a higher standpoint prove to be a necessary shading.

The basis of that higher standpoint—that literally cosmopolitan perspective—is a novel theory that locates the stupidest beings on Mercury, the smartest on Saturn. Just as matter radiates outward from the center according to the principle of decreasing density, so, Kant speculates, does spirit radiate outward according to the principle of increasing intelligence. The reason is this: all intelligent creatures depend on a "bodily machine." The grosser that machine (the denser the matter it is composed of), the more sluggish the thought of the rational being dependent on it. The farther a rational being is from the sun, therefore, the finer is its bodily machine and the quicker its thought. Unlike Richard Wright, the English astronomer and divine whose writings on the Milky Way inspired Kant's universal history, Kant refuses to conflate the spiritual and material centers of the universe. What is materially most attractive is spiritually most repulsive. Whereas Wright locates the seat of virtue at the material center of the universe, Kant places it in God himself, who is equally near all who seek him and thus both everywhere and nowhere.

Kant's thesis about the placement of intelligent beings thus suggests a spiritual ladder of perfection inversely proportional to the physical ladder of increasing material density. At the center of the material system are spiritual beings sunk in such a torpor of physical grossness as to border on unreason. At the outer edges are beings whose vaporous rarity permits their thought to approach the instantaneousness of divine comprehension. Between these two extremes, earthbound man occupies a dangerous middle road. Halfway between reason and unreason, man is poised between the spiritual and physical centers of attraction. Man's perfection or end is thus uniquely indeterminate. Neither effortlessly drawn to the splendor of the divine center nor guiltlessly sunk into the torpor of the material center, he (alone) not only must struggle to achieve the dignity he is capable of, he also must assume the blame for his own failure.

None of this, of course, detracts from the perfection of the whole. There *must* be some point in the universe at which the inversely proportional spiritual and material ladders cross. Here neither the spiritual nor the material forces of attraction are (fully) determinative, and neither rational nor physical desire is fully authoritative. Man's freedom, however, does him no credit. Without the decisive victory of his higher nature, he is merely the defect or monster that nature in its plenitude also embraces.

But man's spiritual victory over his own monstrousness is achievable by few at best. Most men are content to "suck sap, propagate and die" (1:356), bringing about indecently what lower creatures manage with greater efficiency and decorum. Given the vegetative languor to which his lower nature predisposes him, man's situation might well seem hopeless were there no way to stimulate man's higher desire.

It is the ultimate intention of the *Universal Natural History*, I believe, to serve as such a stimulant. Kant's theory of the heavens is a sort of philosophical and spiritual aphrodisiac. If man is deflected from his higher path by its laboriousness, Kant's cosmic history shortcuts the task of uniting many into one and thus makes the journey relatively effortless. The achievement of Kant's universal system is thus as much psychological and spiritual as it is strictly scientific—or would be, if Kant could say with certainty that the world he has built *is* (or is like) the universe and is not merely a beguiling fantasy.

Thus we return to the problem we began with—how to consider the wholeness of the world without losing one's purchase on its reality. Kant can sustain the former, it seems, only by abandoning the latter (e.g., by an "impetuous *Schwung*" above the tumult of the elements (1:367). And yet without success in *both*, Kant cannot make the higher road compellingly attractive. The beckoning goal of rational knowledge is thus threatened by an undercurrent of repulsiveness. Like the physical sun, the spiritual center of attraction is shadowed by a certain monstrousness.[7] Yet it is precisely the *lack* of repulsiveness that is supposed to distinguish the spiritual goal of man's "higher nature" from the indecent if compelling goal of his "lower" one. Thus, in the end Kant is left without a stable principle of value on which to base his own elevation beyond nature's dismal economy. In the end, the difference between spiritual and natural attraction threatens to dissolve.

As a wavering (and erotically inconclusive) attempt to comprehend the whole, Kant's *Universal Natural History* is ambiguous in the most literal sense.[8] His argument takes the form, on the one hand, of a "mechanical" account of the formation of the heavens, an account whose novelty consists primarily in the opposition it posits between an all-penetrating force of attraction (*Senkungskraft*) and an equally crucial (although infinitely diffuse) impulse of repulsion (*Schwungkraft*), that is, a dualism *within* nature on which nature's organization is seen ultimately to rest.

The success of Kant's universal history hinges, finally, on an adequate definition of the relation between God and creation, or between the all-encompassing immediacy of the divine idea and its progressive propagation through an infinity of space and time. Worldly genesis involves a sort of "epigenesis," a development of "germs" implanted in matter by God in the beginning (1:263–66). To comprehend nature as a whole is thus to resolve the relation between the divine and natural procreative roles.

A principal source of instability in Kant's account arises from its failure to provide this resolution. Kant simultaneously locates the opposition of spirit (or male) and matter (or female) in the relation *between* God and creation, and *within* creation itself. Thus the curious role of so-called *geistige Materie* (spir-itous / spiritual matter) (1:265) and other manifestations of the all-important, but elusive, *Schwungkraft* that not only offsets the dizzying *Senkungspunkt* of nature but also empowers, rhetorically at least, the philosophic act itself. The spiritual nexus of mind and matter is inseparable from the problem, implicit in Kant's schema, of (male) eros generally. Kant's ambiguous ascent, both gradu-ally, via the principle of continuity, and all at once, by a single impetuous leap, never entirely frees itself from the awful fear and possibility of collapse.

A second aspect of Kant's history—openly speculative and deliberately reassuring—concerns the world of intelligences, in which we participate with-out the entangling complications that characterize our natural attachments. Here spiritual community replaces the community of matter, and a wholeness beyond space and time sustains the boundaries of individuality rather than— in the manner of nature's flux—perpetually threatening to dissolve them. As such, Kant's spiritual community anticipates the basic structure of his later "noumenal realm": each is an instance of imparted unity that somehow transcends the temporal/spatial flux of nature. In each case too, however, such unity is beyond the power of the human mind to represent as actual. Hence Kant's ultimate inability, in the *Universal Natural History*, to secure the boundary between truth and poetry.[9]

II

Kant's reading of Rousseau in the early 1760s opened a way out of these impasses, above all by emphatically linking morality and manhood. In so doing, Rousseau provides Kant with the basis for a new, radically egalitarian (if antifeminist) conception of nobility, as well as a new, morally grounded idea of spiritual community. The lack of a determining end, which Kant formerly treated as man's special problem, he now reckons as the very basis of human dignity. Freedom is no longer our monstrous undoing as a species but is our glory. And morality stands ready to replace metaphysics (with its wavering erotics) as the vehicle of human nobility.

Rousseau contributes in several ways to Kant's discovery of a thread leading out of the labyrinth of man's own (monstrous) duality. First, Rousseau's model of the general will gives Kant the clue he needs to reconceive spiritual manhood on a moral rather than metaphysical basis. Second, Rousseau's treatment of the power of the human mind to love its own illusions lays the foundation for Kant's new conception of ideas as self-projected "ends of reason" ("totality" in theory, the "highest good" in practice).[10] Stymied in its efforts to overcome theoretically the disorderly dualism of human consciousness, the mind discovers in its own systematic need a new way to rectify itself. Third, Rousseau's treatment of the relation between the sexes (especially in *Emile*) sets the stage for Kant's later systematic reliance on the feminine in its various guises as a sort of "missing joint," defining by its very incapacity the juncture of the intellectual and the material.

Rousseau convinces Kant that the end of reason lies not in knowing nature (a task that is, as Kant already suspected or feared, beyond our powers), but in striving morally to reform or transcend it.

The key to this redirection is a new configuration of will and law, and the transvaluation of freedom that it makes possible. At the heart of this new configuration stands Rousseau's general will, albeit interpreted in a peculiar way. It is this configuration that makes possible the discovery or construction of the new, explicitly "moral" world, one that answers to the demands of—and in the most crucial respect supplants—the intelligible world by whose nebulous light Kant earlier set his course.[11] The community of wills or will, in other words, points the way to a new sort of *moral* cosmology, one that no longer aims merely to comprehend the world (in [bootless] imitation of God's intellect) but rather attempts to enact it (in union with his will).

The interchangeability of will and wills here indicates the nature of the Rousseauian remedy. For what community of will(s) achieves is precisely the reconciliation of individuality and unity that Kant had previously reserved to God alone.[12]

One passage in the "Remarks" on *Observations on the Beautiful and the Sublime* illuminates with special force the structure of Kant's new moral universe:

> The single naturally necessary good of a man in relation to the will of others is equality (freedom) and with respect to the whole, unity. Analogy: Repulsion through which a body fills its own space as all others fill their own. Attraction, whereby all parts bind themselves into one. . . . The natural instinct of active benevolence toward others consists in love toward the [female] sex and children. That directed toward other men [*Menschen*] consists purely in equality and unity. There is unity in a . . . monarchical state but not equality. If unity is combined with equality it constitutes the perfect republic. (20:165–66)

In the constitution of the perfect republic individuals are connected to the whole through free submission to a common law.

Worldhood is at last made intelligible—as intelligible, that is to say, as it can be for man. Kant's earlier efforts to understand the world as a structure of reciprocal determination bear fruit in a moralized version of Rousseau's general will.[13] The mystery of worldly connectedness, which Kant earlier found himself unable to account for adequately, is resolved—as resolved, that is to say, as it can be—in the notion of the morally obligatory as a synthesis of freedom and necessity. The moral world, in short, fulfills Kant's old demiurgic ambitions in a novel way: not only does it supply the formula for individuality-cum-worldly membership that his earlier efforts vainly sought, it also dispels Kant's earlier concern to know the world as real by short-circuiting the very distinction between ideal and real.

The moral world transcends nature; hence it is in a certain sense unreal. But this does not make it a mere chimera. What distinguishes it from a chimera is the universally obligatory, hence objectively necessitating, status of its law.[14] Moral certitude replaces the theoretical certitude Kant previously despaired of. A "world" remains for Kant what it always was—a reciprocal community of self-subsistent elements. But this community is now grounded— not in divine intellect but in moral will. Philosophy can and must begin, in Kant's new moral universe, with a frank acknowledgment of its limitations. Membership in the moral community is assured, not through the vain pursuit of a supposedly divine schema, but by a feeling immediately available to all as free and equal beings.[15]

*

All, however, does not here mean everyone. Moral obligation (and the rectitude that accompanies it) are characteristically masculine functions for which women are naturally ill-equipped.[16] (This doubt about the capacity of most women for genuine moral action would never leave Kant.) The republic of virtue is a predominantly masculine community. The upright honesty of manly virtue that is embodied in the general will is explicitly distinguished from effeminate and ineffectual benevolence or softheartedness.[17] Genuine virtue, indeed, is saved from attraction to utopian, hence chimerical, visions, by its resistance to such softheartedness.[18]

But what happens to the principle of spiritual attraction Kant previously set such store by? The simple answer is that the distinction between spiritual and material attraction—a distinction that was never very stable—for all practical purposes disappears. Kant's earlier model of the human soul as the arena of a struggle between higher and lower centers of attraction gives way to the frank admission that the former does not differ in principle from—and hence cannot resist—the latter.[19]

Rather than attempting to quicken metaphysical desire (as Kant once thought), philosophy ought to provide the metaphysical version of a cold shower.[20] If this analysis is correct, Kant's later critical concern with the "purity" of reason bears a peculiar psychological weight, as Kant's sometime friend J. G. Hamann was perhaps the first to note.[21] Something, indeed, might be made of Kant's relations with Hamann around this time. Just prior to Kant's reading of Rousseau, Hamann, who is credited with having introduced Kant to the works of Hume, became a sort of religious mystic and avowed follower of Socrates. (A famous letter to Kant is full of half-mocking references to their allegedly Socratic or "Sapphic" mutual love.)[22] Kant renounces the principle of attraction, in both its male (or spiritual) and its female (or physical) forms, at the very moment that he discovers, via Rousseau, an explicitly masculine model of moral community.[23] It may be worth noting that Kant's mother, who died when he was thirteen, and to whose memory he remained devoted throughout his life, literally perished from her own good-heartedness, when in an effort to coax a lovesick female friend to take some medicine she put the sick friend's spoon in her own mouth. Kant was convinced that the ensuing fever that took his mother's life was brought about by this kind but thoughtless act of charity. Kant later credited his mother, whose simple piety and goodness he always praised, with first recognizing and nurturing his intellectual precociousness. Kant's few surviving statements about his father, a "common worker," emphasize his uprightness and honesty. In Rousseau, one might conclude, Kant found a way to thematize his father's honesty as *the* principle of genuine moral community. The ascendancy of practice over theory is firmly established in Kant's mind, one is tempted to say, only when the morality breaks free from its maternal "leading strings."[24]

But that is not all. Rousseau also furnishes Kant with a new understanding of ideas as spontaneous projections of the mind, an understanding that resolves the difficulty on which Kant's earlier model of spiritual attraction foundered. The soul, according to Kant's earlier model, remained—whatever the source of its attraction—dependently receptive, enthralled to a power beyond itself. And yet it was activity (as distinguished from passivity) that was supposed to differentiate the higher sort of attraction from the lower. After Rousseau, Kant is able to conceive the mind's relation to ideas as unambiguously active. Kant's newly conceived ideas, however, are more than the beautiful illusions ideas often seem to be for Rousseau. Kantian reason stimulates itself to labor, not to languid self-delight. Ideas are not objects of contemplation but goals that cannot be fully realized within the bounds of nature, limits on the infinite tasks that reason sets itself.

*

Obligation replaces attraction as the motive force of Kant's new moral universe. Moral community is an idea that demands its own realization. But how is it to be actualized? How can men, by nature rudely independent, become the virtuous citizens of a real republic? How can men, whose natural tendency is to flee each other and who thus exhibit a natural "repulsive force" analogous to that of spiritous matter, be brought together into genuine community? It is this question that gives rise to or calls for an idea of history. History is the cosmogony of Kant's new moral universe.

In answering the question of how the moral world is to be realized, Kant is forced to return to the principle of attraction, even as he acknowledges it to be the cause of man's degeneration from the rude but honest state of nature into his current condition of social and political degradation.[25] At the center of this attractive force is woman, the cause, through her seductive and deceitful charms, of man's entrance into society. Because of woman, man gives up his natural independence and manly pride and, enslaved by vanity, pursues the chimerical goods of wealth and preferment over others.

The corrupted desires of social man (which Kant especially associates with the effeminate excesses of courtly life) are in general reducible to the desire for limitless power over others.[26] The source of this desire, Kant claims, is mainly sexual.[27] Man wants to possess a woman exclusively; woman wants to be universally desired.[28] Thus arises the fatal dialectic by which man takes over woman's need and sacrifices his own independence for the sake of an illusory ideal of happiness.[29]

The answer is not a return to the suppression of women typical of more primitive and warlike times. For better or worse, the power of woman must be acknowledged and transformed from a necessary evil (the human race would not survive without it) to a positive good.[30] Not female seclusion but perfected domesticity becomes the vehicle of man's moral and spiritual salvation. Perfected domesticity—or romance within marriage—replaces the natural inequality of the sexes and its destabilizing dynamic with a genuine reconciliation of difference and equality.[31] Marriage so conceived restores man's natural self-sufficiency or completeness on a higher plane *within* society. Beyond the alternatives of female subjugation and female tyranny, Kant proposes one in which women rule domestically by inspiring men to virtue through their own goodness.[32]

Such idealized sexual pleasure, however, rests on deception: the object of man's desire must herself appear to be sexually indifferent.[33] But woman does in fact experience sexual need and is to this extent no goddess but a mere human being whose carnal attractions, once consummated, become repulsive.[34] The difficulty of maintaining ideal love in marriage stems from its connection with the unstable carnal cycle of desire and satiety. Wives, to be sure, can offset this repulsion by inspiring high esteem through the fact (or appearance) of their virtuous mastery of physical desire. The woman who is virtuously chaste—who, unlike the merely innocent maiden, knows all the pleasures of society and freely renounces them—is the most perfect woman, one who produces "the greatest impression that can befall the human heart."[35] Most women, however, are not capable of true virtue; nor need they be to win their husbands' love and esteem, for which the appearance of virtue seemingly suffices.

III

Kant's "Remarks" leaves us with two principles of worldly connection: a "physical" force of attraction rooted in sexual desire and a "spiritual" force associated with ideal citizenship. The first is destabilizing but also dynamic or timely; the second is bound up with the idea of a perfect and timeless moral whole. In the vexed relation between these two principles lies the germ of Kant's idea of history. In teaching virtue without herself being virtuous, woman bridges the fateful if not fatal gap between necessity and freedom, nature and morality. Seen in this light, an apparent evil, the root of all human suffering, becomes the source of all genuine good. But Kant, who never married, remained ambivalent about the value of a sexual romance in which truth is ultimately indistinguishable from fiction.[36]

Hence woman's mediation of the natural and moral worlds remains for Kant a stopgap measure. Woman as educator anticipates—but only anticipates— the role that Kant later reserves to history or culture proper.[37]

In a late work, Kant describes that role in the following terms: "Since man needs, for his moral education, good men who must themselves have been educated for it, and since none of these are free from innate or acquired corruption, the problem of moral education for the species remains unsolved in principle and not merely in degree."[38]

It is therefore only from "providence" that man can anticipate the education of the human race as a whole. By providence Kant means "precisely the same wisdom that we observe with admiration in the preservation of the species of organic natural beings, constantly working toward their destruction and yet always preserving them."

A key aspect of this providence is the "asocial sociability of man" by which we are unconsciously driven to attain the very civil constitution that morality demands, a constitution whose subsequent "internalization" through the moral conversion of its citizens is to realize (at last) the kingdom of ends on earth.[39]

The idea of history thus proves to be a humanized version of the divine schema to which Kant once futilely appealed. Through the idea of history, man himself makes the world intelligible. To the extent that each of us is consciously the end in itself that we are entitled to be, we ourselves realize the whole that ideally speaking we already are.[40] So interpreted, nature, whose seemingly purposeless destructive rampages repel and disgust us, becomes newly beautiful. As with all beauty, however, that of nature verges on the illusory, saved from "romance" only by the fact that the "idea" of history is or can become a self-fulfilling prophecy.[41]

Thus we have the birth of history as an idea whose time has come. Or rather as an idea that makes its own time come. Providence in Kant's later thought extends and replaces woman as the solution to the problem of moral education, the cure for Rousseauian "hypochondria" over the human condition.[42] (History, one is tempted to say, replaces her story.)

And yet the idea of history "with a cosmopolitan intention" remains "conjectural" at its source.[43] Forgetting or ignoring this conjectural character, later thinkers such as Hegel[44] and Marx made far more of history than Kant himself ever took it to be. Beguiled by the romance of a nature fully subservient to human ends, they forgot or ignored nature's ultimate threat and mystery.[45]

Kant's continuing fascination with this mystery makes visible, I think, the roots of his relatively modest expectations for political community—modest at least by the standards set by those who followed him.

"The organization of nature," he wrote to Schiller late in life:

> has always struck me as amazing and as a sort of chasm of thought; I mean, the idea of fertilization, in both realms of nature, always needs two sexes. . . . After all, we don't want to believe that providence has chosen this arrangement almost playfully. . . . This opens a prospect on what lies beyond the field of vision, out of which, however, we can unfortunately make nothing, as little as out of what Milton's angel told Adam about the creation: "Male light out of distant suns mixes itself with female for purposes unknown."[46]

At the same time, this fascination is always tinged for Kant with an undercurrent of abhorrence. Generation is his sticking point, a providential chasm out of which reason can "make nothing." Kant's continuing partiality to reason despite its impotence in this regard marks the limits of his kinship with Rousseau as well as later, less erotically encumbered thinkers whom Rousseau inspired.[47] It would no doubt be going too far to link Kant's political moderation—his refusal to conflate moral being and historical becoming—with his personal decision to remain a bachelor. Still, if Kant's moderation should prove to be anchored in a kind of cosmic misogyny—all of us (both men and women) may have reason to be grateful for it.

Notes

1. According to the *Oxford English Dictionary*, "world" derives from the Germanic *wer*, meaning "man," and *eld*, meaning "age."

2. References to the "Remarks" and other writings of Kant throughout are to *Kants gesammelte Schriften*, Prussian Academy edition (Berlin: Walter de Gruyter, 1902–) or, where possible, to an available English translation.

3. Cf. René Descartes, *Le monde*, chap. 6.

4. See Gotfried Wilhelm Leibniz, *New Essays on Human Understanding*, book 14, chap. 2, no. 14. (The *New Essays* were not published until 1765, and Kant read them around 1769.)

5. For Kant's early critique of Leibniz, see, for example, *Thoughts on the True Estimation of Living Force* (1746), 1:18–22; cf. *Universal Natural History*, 1:366–68. The problem of distinguishing genuine knowledge of the world from fantasy or "dreaming" is a thematically defining one throughout Kant's work.

6. See *Universal Natural History*, 1:303, 356–57.

7. Ibid., 1:323–27.

8. See Kant, *Nova delucidatio* (1756), 1:400. "Wavering" is the literal translation of the Latin *ambiguum*.

9. See especially 1:365.

10. For an incisive account of this transformation and its far-reaching implications, see Richard L. Velkley, *Freedom and the End of Reason: On the Moral Foundation of Kant's Critical Philosophy* (Chicago: University of Chicago Press, 1989).

11. See, for example, Kant's substitution of "pride that I am a man" for imitation of the intellectually more able Saturnians ("Remarks," 20:47).

12. See, for example, 20:129: "Obligation is communal selfishness in equilibrium."

13. See, for example, 20:104, 145: the general will contains the singular as much as it does the universal, and exhibits a "necessity" analogous to the laws of nature.

14. See 20:129, 139.

15. Compare, for example, 20:9, 33, 122.

16. See 20:36, 74, 98, 103, 110.

17. See, for example, 20:127–28.

18. See, for example, 20:9, 25, 45, 51, 56, 109, 127, 128, 135, 139, 145, 158.

19. See, for example, 20:120: "Correct knowledge of the world structure following Newton is perhaps the most beautiful product of inquisitive human reason. With regard to this Hume notes how easily the philosopher caught up in these delightful meditations can be disturbed by a little brown maid."

20. Such, at any rate, is the task of Kant's roughly contemporaneous *Dreams of a Spirit Seer*, a work he calls a metaphysical *catharcticon*. (See his letter to Moses Mendelssohn, 8 April 1766, 10:71.)

21. J. G. Hamann, "Review of Kant's *Critique of Pure Reason*," and "Metacritique of the Purism of Reason," in *J. G. Hamann: A Study in Christian Existence*, by Ronald Gregor Smith (New York: Harper Brothers, 1960), 207–21. I am indebted to Peter Fenves for drawing my attention to this work.

22. See his letter to Kant of 27 July 1759.

23. Goethe, perhaps, had something similar in mind when he praised Kant's "immortal service" to morality, in "[bringing] us all back from that effeminacy in which we were wallowing." (See his letter to Chancellor von Müller, 29 April 1818; quoted in Ernst Cassirer, *Kant's Life and Thought*, trans. James Haden (New Haven: Yale University Press, 1981), 270.

24. Cf. *Critique of Pure Reason*, B13; and *What Is Enlightenment?* in *Kant's Political Writings*, 2d ed., ed. Hans Reiss (Cambridge: Cambridge University Press, 1991), 54.

25. For a more detailed account of this process, see Susan Shell, "Kant's Political Cosmology: Freedom and Desire in the 'Remarks' concerning *Observations on the Feeling of the Beautiful and the Sublime*," in *Essays on Kant's Political Philosophy*, ed. Howard Williams (Chicago: University of Chicago Press, 1992).

26. See, for example, "Remarks," 20:55, 130, 161, 163.

27. See 20:164, 183.

28. See, for example, 20:174, 176.

29. See 20:74, 137, 175.

30. See, for example, 20:164, 188–99.

31. On the corresponding argument in *Emile*, see Allan Bloom's penetrating analysis in *Love and Friendship* (New York: Simon and Schuster, 1993), 39–156. As Bloom notes, the story of Emile and Sophie is an ideal history of the human species—a history that, unlike the real one charted in the *Discourse on the Origin of Inequality*, is consistent with man's natural wholeness. In short, it is the catastrophic history of man rewritten as a philosophic romance.

That Rousseau's expectations for the outcome of that romance were none too bright is suggested by the sequel to *Emile*, forebodingly titled "The Solitaries." The trouble—the discrepancy between natural and civil puberty—is that man remains (at least from a Platonic standpoint) erotically dysfunctional, with culture at best an unnatural ferment of ideas, an eau de vie distilled from the purification, as it were, of animal spirits. In short, sublimation as (in Bloom's words again) the making of the sublime out of the nonsublime. The effort of later thinkers to assimilate such soul culture with *Geist* or spirit in a traditional Christian sense cannot escape the ambiguity—which Kant was not the first to register—implicit in such a project. The attempt to rise above matter, as it were, on our own steam is powered by what Kant with some delicacy calls "spiritous matter" (*geistige Materie*) and others, less inspired or delicate, call wind. See in this regard Samuel Butler, *Hudibras* (1663), 2.3.773–76; as quoted in Kant, *Dreams of a Spirit Seer*, 2:348).

32. "Remarks," 20:3, 5, 62, 185, 188–89. On the relations between the sexes in Rousseau, see Joel Schwartz, *The Sexual Politics of Jean-Jacques Rousseau* (Chicago: University of Chicago Press, 1984).

33. See, for example, "Remarks," 20:61–62, 139–40: woman's "refusal is a kind of beautiful untruth"; her beauty is a kind of "permissible" deception (20:133–34).

34. See 20:133.

35. See 20:3, 185.

36. See 20:85, 95, 165.

37. See, for example, Immanuel Kant, *Idea for a Universal History from a Cosmopolitan Standpoint*, ed. Hans Reiss (Cambridge: Cambridge University Press, 1991), 44–51, and *Critique of Judgment*, trans. Werner S. Pluhar (Indianapolis: Hackett, 1987), 319. Cf. *Conjectural Beginning of Human History*: "[Female] *refusal* was the feat that brought about the passage from merely sensual to spiritual [*idealistischen*] attractions. . . . In addition, there came a first hint at the development of man as a moral creature." Kant attributes that development to woman's tendency to "conceal from others" that which might arouse "low esteem." As in Kant's earlier "Remarks," the transition from rude nature to morality turns on a permissible deception by which women make themselves seem more worthy than they are.

38. Immanuel Kant, *Anthropology from a Pragmatic Point of View*, trans. Mary J. Gregor (The Hague: Martinus Nijhoff, 1974), 188.

39. Kant, *Idea for a Universal History*, 44–49.

40. See, for example, ibid., 52.

41. Ibid., 51–53.

42. See Kant, *Anthropology*, 187–90.

43. It is not clear, for example, whether Kant intends his essay to provide such an idea, or whether he means merely to suggest what another writer (a "philosophic head" who is also "historically very artful") might be able to offer.

44. In the philosophic histories of Fichte and Hegel, woman reemerges in the crucial role of nonvirtuous educator to virtue of the human race. Woman so conceived is meant to solve what Bloom has called the problem of "sublimation," or the emergence of spirit out of nature. For Kant that emergence remains fundamentally mysterious to reason and is ultimately accessible only by way of the aesthetic. He is in this respect perhaps closer to the romantics Rousseau inspired than to Rousseau himself.

45. See, for example, Kant, *Anthropology*, 190: the progress of the human race is a "moral certainty" assuming that, Kant tellingly adds, "natural upheavals do not suddenly cut [that progress] short."

46. Letter to Schiller, 30 March 1795, 12:10–11.

47. Goethe comes immediately to mind here, though many later romantics might also be included. On Goethe's recovery of eros within the framework of modern science, I am indebted to Werner Dannhauser.

❧ 4 ❧
The Tension in the Beautiful: On Culture and Civilization in Rousseau and German Philosophy

RICHARD VELKLEY

I

The distinction between culture and civilization originates in certain modern attempts to define the highest cultivation of the human soul or spirit. Immanuel Kant and Wilhelm von Humboldt, in the age of idealist philosophy, first announced this distinction to define the idea of a moral culture; later Friedrich Nietzsche and Oswald Spengler developed it for very different purposes. At the start of this century the distinction of culture and civilization was of more than academic interest on both sides of the Atlantic. Many Germans with rather uncompromising ambitions used it to express what they supposed made German thought, politics, art, and customs superior to their Western democratic counterparts. The heroism and spirituality of German culture were contrasted with the low commercialism and utilitarianism of civilization in France, Britain, and North America. Although this German analysis was rooted more in a combination of national pride and intellectual orthodoxy than in a clearheaded evaluation of the world political situation, it could boast some profound philosophical sources.[1]

Similarly, the academic controversies of our day about the Western heritage take various stands on "culture" and "civilization" without examining the origins and meanings of this language. This criticism holds especially for the opponents of the "Western canon," who adopt a patently untenable position by claiming to have arrived at a standpoint beyond European traditions of thought. Their constant employment of the terms "culture" and "civilization" in fact betrays their dependence on eighteenth-century European philosophy and, not least, on Rousseau and his German followers. What is more, their critiques of the narrow and oppressive spirit of Western "logocentrism" have striking affinities with the attacks of German *Kulturphilosophie* early in this century on the "sterile intellectualism" of Western civilization, attacks ultimately derived from Rousseau via Nietzsche. But the current critiques of Western civilization are most immediately descended from Heidegger, whose profound attempt to move beyond all universalist and rationalist forms of thought is the ultimate outcome, one could say, of the German tradition of reflection on culture. Thus one does not need the present debates to make a case for the importance of this topic. To inquire about how culture was contrasted with civilization in modern efforts to surpass the classical understanding of culture is necessarily rewarding. This inquiry takes us into the innermost essence of the projects of later modern philosophy; at the same time, it brings to the fore the pivotal figure of Rousseau. I turn to the origins of the terms "civilization" and "culture," then to some important moments in the history of the distinction, in order to determine what Rousseau has contributed to this central aspect of recent history and thought, and what we might learn from it.

First a remark on some principles, mostly implicit and requiring full development in another context, that govern the historical reflections of this chapter. The modern stress on self-preservation is legislated to abolish the discord arising from the dialectic of reason concerning ultimate ends. Hence modernity's original goal is to achieve a certain kind of justice: the securing of universal foundations for the peaceful pursuit of happiness with no determinate content. The increase of power (mastery of nature) for attaining all possible "subjective" goods takes the place of the final good. Rousseau then observes that the justification of self-preservation does not satisfy the human need for wholeness or erotic fulfillment. His account of eros as the longing for prerational unity is the source of the later distinction between "culture" as the domain of erotic striving and "civilization" as the domain of mere self-preserving justice. Like Nietzsche after him, Rousseau envisions an irreconcilable conflict between eros and justice; thereby he also renews a classical (Platonic) theme.[2] At the same time, he uncovers a fundamental tension in the beautiful that is not solely between prephilosophic and philosophic accounts of the beautiful; it is a tension within the philosophic beautiful itself. (Here again Rousseau recollects a Platonic idea.) This latter tension can be described as the combination of dependence and opposition between philosophic wholeness (erotic knowing, contemplating, or reverie) and the legislation of moral life (justice). The philosopher's being necessarily drawn to both forms of the beautiful is a condition for approaching either one. This is the "contradiction" in philosophic efforts to attain a higher culture or to transcend civilization. The transcending is by means of civilization itself: the "cave" cannot be escaped except through taking the cave wholly seriously, since one discovers its limits only by seeking (at least "in speech") its unattainable perfection. Or as Nietzsche puts it, "the self-sublimation [*Selbstaufhebung*] of morality" defines the task of philosophic culture.[3]

II

Only about 1800 did our unreflecting practice of calling a society a "culture" or "civilization" become an acceptable form of speech. "Civilization" (French *civilisation*) in this sense has an eighteenth-century origin in the writing of the marquis de Mirabeau.[4] Napoleon uses it in revolutionary manifestos to describe France's mission: the propagation of the universal rights of man. "Civilization" is thus connected with early modern doctrines of natural rights and human equality, of scientific and technological progress, and their radicalization in the French Revolution. The term conveys the idea of the entire progress of humanity as culminating in the modern liberal state and its way of life, seen as inherently civil, polite, and pleasant. It was from the first universalist in intent and has largely remained so in France, where there has always been resistance to speaking of "civilizations" in the plural. There is but one civilization proper to the human species, and France happens by providential grace to be its spokesman. One should also note the relation of "civilization" to the Latin *civitas* and therewith the Greek *polis*.[5]

The term "culture," which originally meant the culture of the soul or mind, acquires most of its later modern meanings in the writings of eighteenth-century German thinkers, who are on various levels developing Rousseau's criticism of modern liberalism and Enlightenment. Thus a contrast between "culture" and "civilization" is usually implied in these authors, even when not expressed as such. Two primary meanings of culture emerge from this period: culture as the folk spirit having a unique identity, and culture as cultivation of inwardness or free individuality. The first meaning is predominant in our current use of the term "culture," though the second still plays a large role in what we think culture should achieve, namely the full "expression" of the unique or "authentic" self. Clearly there is considerable tension between the notions, although they are frequently advocated together without any regard for the tension. The common ground of the two is the idea, most profoundly developed in Rousseau, that human wholeness is achievable only through the recovery of or approximation to an original prediscursive or prerational natural unity. Rousseau is also the source of the bifurcation in the ways to reach such wholeness: either as the citizen in a society based on the true idea of nature, or as the natural individual who remains apart from the social order. Rousseau emphasizes the incompatibility of these ways of reaching wholeness and also stresses that the first way, citizenship, is much less natural and hence less satisfactory than the second way, natural freedom. Many central ideas of culture in German thought either confusedly blur this opposition or consciously seek to resolve it. The current primary usages of culture as folk spirit often consist in a blurring of the distinction in which the social order is ascribed attributes of spontaneity, individuality, and organic wholeness—attributes Rousseau concedes only to the life of the natural individual or to the earliest and simplest forms of human society, and then only guardedly. The Rousseauian spirit in current cultural thinking is all the same evident in its frequent preference for primitive or "developing" cultures.

Rousseau has been regarded as the source of a new moral outlook in which the *sentiment de l'existence* both "puts us in touch with an inner voice" and "connects us to a wider whole."[6] Although it is true that one finds the basis for such a moral outlook in Rousseau's writings, especially *Emile*, it has to be noted that in crucial respects for Rousseau this morality is an artificial construction. The original natural self is premoral, even prerational; its connection with wider wholes can be brought about only through an expansion of reason that compromises the original simplicity and unity of the self. The transition from premoral goodness to social virtue entails a loss. Indeed, social virtue is in Rousseau's account necessary only for an already fallen being that is in danger of further corruption. The German thinkers who follow Rousseau attempt to formulate notions of virtue that lack the defects of artificiality and the loss of unity and of wholeness. And these attempts are the heart of their accounts of culture. But as I shall argue, these German efforts are constantly troubled by conflicts between original wholeness and alienating reason. They repeatedly are made aware that they have not laid Rousseau's ghost to rest, and that the higher unity of natural wholeness and moral rationality they seek is difficult if not impossible to achieve. This underlying problem will be the chief theme in what follows.

There are two primary forms of the German efforts to show the necessary unity of what Rousseau thought to be only artificially combined: (1) the cosmopolitan notions of culture in early German idealism adopting a complementary stance toward liberal commercial civilization, and (2) the dialectical notions of culture in later idealism seeking to reconcile higher rational culture with the particular folk community having mythic and poetic origins. These are succeeded, first of all in Nietzsche's thought, by the tragic ideas of culture pitting the higher culture of great heroic individuals and folk spirits against the leveling and antispiritual tendencies of modern civilization. In some sense these ideas return to Rousseau's view that any harmony between the individual and social life is an artificial compromise, and they seek to recover or expose the sources for an original wholeness that necessarily eludes rational reflection and grounding. Toward the close of this chapter I will suggest how these proposals relate to "the tension in the beautiful."

III

To understand the origins of these notions one must return to the beginnings of modern philosophy. The career of modern "culture" begins linguistically and to an extent philosophically in the seventeenth century with Samuel Pufendorf's new application of the Ciceronian notion of *cultura animi*. Cicero in the *Tusculan Disputations* employs the agricultural term *cultura* to speak of the cultivation of the soul by philosophy; the term *cultura* then enters the modern European languages in the Renaissance with this sense.[7] Pufendorf, however, uses *cultura* to designate collectively the means for overcoming the inconveniences of the state of nature; he speaks of *vitae cultura* as overcoming the *status naturalis*. Culture then does not refer to a special education attaining a natural potential of the soul according to teleological conceptions like Cicero's. It rather refers to all the ways human beings overcome their original barbarism and through artifice become fully human. As in Hobbes's political philosophy, movement away from barbarism replaces movement toward perfection; thereby Pufendorf initiates our way of speaking of the entirety of social life as "culture."[8] This earliest modern notion of culture is based on a nonteleological view of nature, and as universal in application (for culture is not yet connected with a folk spirit) it reflects the universality of natural right.

In this connection we must also bear in mind the Baconian inauguration of the project "to extend the power and dominion of the human race over the universe" through the arts and sciences, which Bacon advertises as an ambition "more wholesome and more noble," because seeking the good of the "whole race of man," than political ambitions of producing civil benefits for particular states and peoples. The new project derives support from the judgments of former ages that accorded divine honors to authors of inventions and only heroic honors to founders, legislators, and saviors of cities and empires. Bacon would thus shift the focus of civilization from politics and civic virtue toward scientific and technological progress as the foundation for a universal human community overcoming the divisive forces of sectarianism and love of *patria*.[9] This account of civilization is crucial to the modern doctrines of culture retaining a universalist character, such as those of Pufendorf, Kant, and Wilhelm von Humboldt.

It is not such a large step from Pufendorf's view of culture as the universal artificial correcting (or supplementing) of nature to arguments that such artifice reflects the myths and poetry, as well as the climate and geography, of unique peoples and epochs. In the early modern accounts of human nature, universality and necessity reside in basic inclinations such as self-preservation. Higher constructions of culture employing reason, which has no end of its own and is only an instrument to satisfy the inclinations, will hence tend to be more particularized. Although Vico and Montesquieu offer some anticipations of the notion of culture as unique folk spirit, it first appears fully articulated in Herder. Only at this time does it become meaningful to speak of culture as European, African, or Asian, and to say that one is a "member of *a* culture."[10]

Herder's position also reflects, however, his absorption of Rousseau's thought, which is fundamentally an attack on earlier modern notions of nature. Whereas his predecessors stress the harshness and chaos of the natural state, Rousseau claims to find in that state the standard of human wholeness and unity. Accordingly, the idea of the best society must somehow recover or approximate that original wholeness. Hence culture does not attain a higher teleological perfection of our rational nature, and it does not conquer the destructive tendencies of nature; instead it preserves original, even prerational, wholeness. Herder's notion of cultures as natural organisms reflects Rousseau's thought while transforming it. According to Herder, culture is not simply the overcoming of nature but is itself an expression of nature, a nature that exists in the form of prereflective and predeliberative wholes. Nature qua culture is not centrally defined by legislation and education as conscious, rational, deliberative acts. The political suffers a demotion relative to the unconscious forces of poetry and myth, since these issue more immediately from the prerational or prediscursive wholeness identical with the character of a folk spirit and its first expression, language.

Herder's views on the naturalness of culture are surely at odds with what Rousseau says about any form of existence on the social level, which in Rousseau's view must always bear the marks of the artificial and antinatural. And at the same time Rousseau does not grant priority to folk poetry and myth over political deliberation, especially that of the great founding legislators, in spite of the importance he gives to particular traditions and customs in the framing of laws (cf. *Considerations on the Government of Poland*). Central to Rousseau's notion of the necessarily antinatural character of social life is his stress on the need for a certain patriotic exclusiveness in the spirit of the healthy political community. It should be noted that Herder introduces the later modern emphasis on the diversity and fundamental equality of all cultures as flowerings of native folk spirits. This gives an impetus to the replacement of both patriotic exclusiveness and universal rationality with the unrestricted openness of "pluralism"—a stance that tries to combine the advantages of exclusiveness and universalism. Accordingly, Herder regards the various cultures as parts of the progressive unfolding of a common humanity, while he attempts to endorse the incommensurability of the cultural perspectives and the beauty of their contributions to the whole. Yet the idea of a "common humanity" is originally a Western perspective, and the notion of universal progress implies the superiority of that perspective. The exclusiveness of non-Western societies is for a pluralist necessarily defective.[11]

Rousseau does not encounter this last difficulty, because he regards a primary attachment to one's own society as the necessary foundation for citizenship at all times and places, and because he does not subscribe to Enlightenment doctrines of the progress of the nations toward a common humanity. Cosmopolitan openness for Rousseau is therefore an attitude fitting only for philosophers, who moreover cannot be citizens in a genuine sense. Thus in the *Discourse on the Arts and Sciences* Rousseau questions whether progress in civilization addresses the need of society for the moral and civic education of its members. Thereby he sets up the problem Kant believes that he, unlike Rousseau, can solve in a satisfactory way: to reconcile progress and Enlightenment with the moral perfection of the human species. No more than Rousseau does Kant turn to the quasi-natural folk spirit as the key to this resolution. Kant's much greater sympathy for Rousseau than for Herder is unmistakable: although he contrasts the rational to the natural in a way that is unacceptable to Kant, Rousseau nonetheless maintains the fundamentally rational (if alienated) character of social life and its origins, unlike Herder. In sum, one can say that the notion of culture as folk spirit is more remote from classical notions of citizenship than any of the following: the modern idea of civilization, Rousseau's critique of such civilization, and Kant's effort to reconcile modern civilization with Rousseau's critique.

IV

To understand Rousseau's role in German ideas of *Bildung* as the cultivation of individuality, we must look more closely at Rousseau's criticism of modern philosophy. Again we shall see that whereas Rousseau stresses profound tensions or dichotomies, his German admirers use his thought to establish a true culture achieving ultimate unities or reconciliations. A primary purpose of the early modern founders of liberalism was to erect a secure bulwark against barbarism generated chiefly by religious fanaticism and intolerance. Of Rousseau it could be said that he regards the society grounded on modern principles as being only the securing of a new kind of barbarism, in the form of commmercial society with no place for virtue or goodness—no place for either the stalwart independence of the citizen or the simplicity of the natural individual. The consequence of the unlimited satisfaction of the passions is loss of original wholeness and unity, and ever greater servitude and self-dividedness. To the extent that civility, manners, taste, and the arts and sciences arise from and strengthen the passions (especially those of amour propre), Rousseau indicts them as deepening the dependence on the artificial. Rousseau of course reflects on how education might preserve natural unity and simplicity and foster a growth of reason compatible with maintaining wholeness. Such education attempts to direct the originally benign and prerational inclinations into a rational but nonetheless uncorrupted form of adult virtue. This is an artificial process, achieving a constructed telos, since the inclinations and reason do not by themselves tend toward this result.

Thus Rousseau's thought suggests three levels of human education: original naturalness, exposure to corrupting civilization, and true culture. The relation between the three stages is treated most comprehensively by Rousseau in *Emile*, which can properly be regarded as his magnum opus. Many German writers (most notably Kant) see in this work Rousseau's master plan for overcoming the opposition between citizen or moral virtue and natural freedom or individuality.[12] But it must be said that Rousseau has less sanguine expectations from this account of education. He surely does not regard the result of this education as identical with the truly free existence of the philosopher, and thus it cannot represent the most satisfactory solution of the human problems. This is one of several difficulties that Rousseau regards as intrinsic to the educational project of *Emile*.

Emile is educated to become an adult who lives self-sufficiently, although he partakes of the duties and pleasures of social life. He does not fracture and weaken himself by living according to the opinion of others; thus he does not develop the vices of social life (guile, hypocrisy, envy, avarice, etc.) that result from such fracturing and weakening. He nonetheless out of strength acts with beneficence and compassion. *Emile*'s notion of virtue as arising from inner unity and wholeness is the prime source of the great stress on "inwardness" in German conceptions of culture and the related idea of *Bildung*. Although Rousseau himself does not employ the contrast of "civilization" and "culture" in his argument, *Emile* is the most immediate source for the distinction in Kant and Humboldt between civilization concerned with the "external" refinement and regulation of human affairs and culture aiming at "inner" moral and spiritual excellence.[13]

Yet, as in the case of the folk spirit, there are great differences here between Rousseau and his German followers. In German accounts the inwardness of culture consists in its cultivation of self-unity based on freedom, or what Kant calls autonomy, which he sharply distinguishes from subservience to natural inclination. But inwardness for Rousseau is not grounded, as for Kant and his successors, in a "noumenal" or wholly nonsensuous faculty of spontaneous self-determination. It rests, rather, on a precarious harmony between the desires and human powers of satisfaction, a harmony quite easily disturbed by imagination and other developments of the perfectible human powers connected with reason: anxiety about the future and fear of death, communicating needs and persuading others to satisfy them, ability to make comparisons and judgments of merit. Since reason is the chief cause of disequilibrium, and since it has no autonomous power to rule the passions, it is wholly the educator's reason, not the pupil's, that must provide the structure and guidance in the delicate project of maintaining simplicity. The project of course must presume a virtuous and uncorrupted tutor, and such tutors are hard to find. Indeed, Rousseau himself cannot qualify, for fairly obvious reasons. Thus the "ideal" character of Emile's education could be described even as its "fictional" character; this work, we should recall, is a novel. Not only is *Emile* not the account of the most satisfactory life, even on its own level it is only an ideal whose realization is most unlikely. Rousseau's reservations are for the most part overlooked or rejected in German idealist transformations of his thought.[14]

V

A few remarks are needed on the importance of art and poetry to post-Rousseauian notions of culture. Generally one can say that the rise of the aesthetic and of aesthetic culture is related to the thesis that the human development of reason, or of civilization, tends to be in disequilibrium with human nature or inclinations, and that it thus tends to imperil human well-being—all of which Rousseau argued. The cultivation of imagination and sentiments connected with beauty becomes central to the project of creating and ensuring equilibrium. In the writings of Rousseau one sees three forms of this use of poetry: in the *Social Contract,* for the citizen in the celebration of the divine or heroic origins of the city; in the final book of *Emile,* for the ideally educated ordinary human being in the cultivation of romantic sentiments deepening marital bonds; and in the *Reveries of the Solitary Walker,* for the solitary thinker and kindred spirits, in sustaining the fleeting sense of harmony and natural unity. All these uses of poetry serve the aim of deepening the individual's attachments to some larger whole—be it city, family, or nature. And in Rousseau's view these attachments necessarily have, to some extent, an illusory and artificial character, since the individual human being is naturally centered only in the self—and in a prerational self at that. But since that self has expansive tendencies leading to corruption and loss of simplicity, the illusory wholes created by the philosopher-poet are necessary to prevent the worst forms of human alienation and civilized misery. It would be wrong to say that any one of these poetic illusions actually completes human nature as Rousseau conceives it.

When Kant and Schiller employ the aesthetic to further human unity, it is not on the premise that such unity rests on illusions, for they argue that the unified self is inherently rational by virtue of possessing freedom. Alienation by reason is less extreme in their doctrines than in Rousseau's. Kant and Schiller propose instead that aesthetic activity serves to refine the natural inclinations in such a way as to bring them into harmony with the moral demands of reason. Thus the aesthetic points to a true human perfection or completion. Yet the German authors find in Rousseau's thought an important source for this ideal of aesthetic culture because he renews the classical theme of the problem of human wholeness, neglected by earlier modernity. Rousseau thereby sets in motion the effort to emulate Greek antiquity on a new basis, without the Greek teleological account of the soul. The idealist conception of culture as individual wholeness through moral autonomy, resting on the supreme legislative power of reason, seems to rival in both comprehensiveness and elevation the Greek classical accounts of culture. It has the further attraction of resting on the modern principle of free subjectivity. Hence its enduring authority in Germany throughout the nineteenth century.

Yet the culture of moral autonomy does not resolve the tension between the two fundamental notions of culture. The folk spirit cannot attain the elevation and authority of individual *Bildung*. Indeed, it tends to remain on the plane of mere "civilization," as it does in Nietzsche's thought. This may be related to my earlier observation that culture as folk spirit gives dubious support to any notion of rational, deliberative, and prudent citizenship. And this points also to a difficulty on the side of individual *Bildung*. If a higher personal culture must rest on rational reflection on the human situation, then there can be no natural transition from the prerational folk spirit to such higher culture. Perhaps there can be only a divinely inspired transition through the overwhelming force of genius.[15]

The unresolved tensions in Rousseau and in German accounts of culture recall in some ways fundamental tensions within the classical approaches to culture. The latter start from common prephilosophic opinions about the way to human wholeness, such as immortal earthly glory or the rewards of the afterlife for good deeds; internal difficulties in these strivings then point to a philosophical resolution. Both the prephilosophic and the philosophic forms of wholeness can claim to be beautiful; hence classical culture discloses a tension in the beautiful. Rousseau, by contrast, does not start with the premodern opinions of the ultimate goods as glory and salvation, which no longer define the "common." The common assumptions have been transformed by modern philosophy into the goods of self-preservation primarily and of honor secondarily—and of honor chiefly as the instrument for securing self-preservation. The horizon of immortality or eternity has almost vanished from the picture. The starting point is the self-concerned individual. But Rousseau sees that this fails to offer human beings something genuinely beautiful and whole. The beautiful becomes the wholeness of presocial nature; the tension in the beautiful and its culture becomes that within a new kind of poetry celebrating a new kind of heroism (of which Rousseau himself is the prime exemplar).[16] Efforts to dramatize this wholeness tend to undermine it, by drawing it within the circle of corrupting social existence. In later terms the problem of culture is that it tends to become mere civilization. The chief effort of culture is to keep alive the recollection of original wholeness, or to point to a true autonomy that explodes the fascination with the empty glitter of civilization. Whereas the classical tension in the beautiful cultivates and transforms the desire for immortality present in pursuit of glory, the Rousseauian version of the tension cultivates and transforms the concern with selfhood—with wholeness qua individual being—present in self-preservation and in honor as derived from it.

In German idealism selfhood is still primary, but in the form of rational autonomy, at least until Hegel. It is Hegel's argument that the principles of the objective world of the folk spirit, or *Sittlichkeit*, and of subjective moral culture, or *Bildung*, are in the final analysis identical, and that their ancient tension has been overcome in the modern era's actualization of absolute wisdom. History brings full satisfaction to human eros; thus Hegel completes the idealist project of demonstrating the satisfaction of metaphysical eros through freedom. In other terms, his system is a theodicy that perfectly reconciles eros and justice and so resolves the tension in the beautiful.

VI

I turn now to Nietzsche, who renews the problem of culture and civilization in opposition to Hegel's claim to have definitively solved it. In so doing Nietzsche affirms the tension in the beautiful in its most radical form. Nietzsche exerts such a powerful attraction because he tries to combine the classical and the Rousseauian approaches to culture and human wholeness, while displaying a more genuine appreciation of the height and nobility of the classical world than any other modern thinker. Nietzsche's starting point is surely not just self-preservation, and he derides the British political philosophers for adopting this view of original nature. In a sense he starts from the classical concern with the noble, but it is no longer the political self-understanding of the noble the classics start from. Quite unlike Hegel, Nietzsche does not move swiftly to discredit the striving for glory of the hero or the master. Instead he tries to formulate a nobility the world has only anticipated and not yet seen. "Caesar with the soul of Christ" conveys only an approximate sense of this nobility. Although Nietzsche's restoration of the tension in the beautiful starts with something like the striving for immortal glory, it also incorporates a sense of the vanity of all human striving that exceeds in rigor the severest utterances of Hamlet.[17] Nietzsche by his own avowal owes much to

Christian heroism and to the radicality of Christian sacrifice to the divine.[18] The classical, the Christian, and the modern are combined in a complex fashion in his account of the noble and thus of culture.

Nietzsche constantly reminds his readers that there are higher human beings who have great capacities for erotic self-forgetting in the striving to create immortal and beautiful deeds and works, and who deserve the utmost gratitude and admiration. One simple way to think of Nietzsche's view of culture and civilization is this: Civilization seeks to secure the reign of the common or the "herd" against the threat posed to the common by the great creative human beings. Civilization must therefore be opposed so that the noble and heroic creators can flourish. This means that "culture" must encourage a certain cruelty that destroys the common, and that appears to the ordinary man as barbarism. Nietzsche writes that "the dissolving and necessarily decadence-producing means of civilization are not to be confused with culture."[19] In a short passage from the *Nachlass* titled "Culture contra Civilization," he goes further: "The highpoints of culture and of civilization are disparate: one must not be led astray about the abysmal antagonism between culture and civilization. From a moral point of view the great moments of culture were always times of corruption. And on the other hand the epochs of willful and forced *domestication* of man ('civilization') were times of frustration for the most spiritual and daring natures. Civilization desires something different from what culture desires, perhaps something quite opposed."[20]

In one sense of nature that Nietzsche uses often, civilization is hostile to nature, for civilization is the mere taming of nature that reduces it to the common and calculable. Nature, quasi-teleologically, attempts to produce organisms capable of a self-forgetting squandering of energy and talent to create the beautiful; such squandering is the expression of erotic drives that are prerational and do not conform to any conscious human sense of the rational, logical, or moral.[21] This is the Rousseauian element of prediscursive wholeness, what is distorted by social life and its reduction of the unique to the common. But of course for Nietzsche prediscursive wholeness is passionately full of conflict and striving, very unlike Rousseau's state of nature.[22] Civilization, however, is the common target of Rousseau and Nietzsche. Culture must make the heroic effort to recover or strengthen the individuality and independence of original nature, and to undo the weakening and socializing of genuine naturalness by civilization.

In another very interesting note from the *Nachlass* Nietzsche calls attention to his kinship with Rousseau: "The unsolved problem that I pose anew: the *problem of civilization*, the struggle between Rousseau and Voltaire about 1760."[23] Nietzsche is like Rousseau in raising the question of civilization, but he is clearly unsympathetic to Rousseau's understanding of nature. Indeed, Nietzsche has a high regard for the aristocratic, cheerful, and "healthy" Voltaire, the last representative of Renaissance *umanità* and *virtù* (Nietzsche uses the Italian), while he expresses disdain for the plebeian, resentful, and "sickly" Rousseau, the founder of romanticism. The objectionable character of Rousseau is summed up in his "pure fantasy" of man's natural goodness. But Nietzsche cannot simply take the side of Voltaire, who did not grasp the depth of the problem of civilization. Rather, the argument between these two great figures must be restated in more radical terms. Neither of Nietzsche's predecessors saw the "fundamental contradiction in civilization and in the elevation of man."[24]

The effort to strengthen or recover nature is opposed by nature itself, since erotic squandering entails the self-sacrifice of the individual to the beautiful work, and nature includes the tendency to seek the preservation of individuals as well as the tendency to squander them.[25] This is the natural ground of civilization, which favors self-preservation and seeks to avenge itself on any manifestation of natural self-squandering. In civilization human consciousness was developed as a tool to communicate needs and to aid the human as the naturally "most endangered animal."[26] Nietzsche's dualistic account of nature combines problematically a modern conception of reason as overcoming a harsh nature with a more ancient view of nature as aiming at the noble, beautiful, and useless. The essential product of nature in the first sense is morality, understood as the organized vindication of the herd of servile self-preservers against the free and noble self-squanderers. But the problem of culture and civilization is not just one of external antagonism. A higher human being must incorporate a certain revenge within himself, since he must overcome the tendencies within himself toward the calculable, the common, and the self-preserving, and not least toward resentment of an existence made difficult by the possession of refined sensibilities and intelligence. A creative human being is constantly engaged in a self-overcoming or cruelty to self that is the inversion of the revenge of the civilized moralist, since it is directed at destroying what the moralist tries to preserve. Much of Nietzsche's writing is devoted to presenting this internal struggle within the souls of the great human beings of the past. And for the most part Nietzsche sees the struggle as ending in a tragic betrayal of true nobility.

In other terms, all efforts at creating a higher culture, or elevation of the human type, tend to be self-contradictory. Human life needs self-restricting illusions (or traditions) in order to rise to the creation of beautiful forms and "the grand style" in manners, politics, and art. Yet these same illusions tend to become stifling and "antinatural" dogmas and moralities that turn against the noble, creative, and independent forms of life. And in fact modern civilization has apparently reached a point of exhaustion where human beings can no longer sustain the tension of the beautiful. The higher natures that are able to transcend moralism and to create the form-giving and hierachical illusions of a beautiful culture, for the enhancing of life and not for narrow self-advancement, seem to be disappearing. Dogmatic egalitarianism is increasingly the only virtue. The lower aspect of nature, the merely self-preserving drive, seems to be stronger than the higher in the long run.[27]

VII

At this point the Christian element of radical self-sacrifice enters the account. Nietzsche holds that the noble and free human beings (and he says that some still exist) will be the most generous self-squanderers by performing the most difficult sacrifice that has ever been made in human history: the sacrifice of God. This is equivalent to the sacrifice of all notions of "truth" transcending the will, in favor of the creative (and not merely human) will as the sole truth. That sacrifice is a necessary condition of recovering an extramoral perspective and so also of grounding a noble culture. In this way those who are the "heroes and fools of the passion for knowledge" will embody the supreme virtue, for their sacrifice of everything hitherto sacred and transcendent is the ultimate self-overcoming. Yet they assume that this sacrifice, which is equivalent to uncovering the ultimate superficiality of all consciousness and reason, is an expression of a higher fate—a law of nature, if one will, that has no regard for the good as moral or "humane." Such knowing is a vehicle whereby erotic nature (or "will to power") squanders and overcomes itself. The knowers believe, or rather will, that their disclosure of "truths" is part of a larger comedy and tragedy of existence that nature itself is performing through the human species. Thus in spite of the danger of nihilism, they discover a new basis for gratitude to fate, nature, or existence.[28]

Nobility in this utterly novel sense will be the possession of philosophers who are certainly very different from classical philosophers. It is the one form of nobility left after the devastations of political and cultural life wrought by Christianity, modern science, and Enlightenment. But it is also the highest possibility in nobility. As a radicalization of Enlightenment it owes much to modernity, so the new nobility has reasons for gratitude to all of history and to every culture of the past. The apparently utterly self-defeating character of human history is not the last word on it. Civilization seemed to result only in the impossibility of any further beauty of action or thought; a destructive resentment against all time and history seemed to be the only prospect for human beings who had any spirit left in them. So it seemed, until Nietzsche exposed the liberating thoughts of his philosophy.

The nobility that vindicates history needs a new kind of poetry to celebrate its insights and virtues, and to provide the education for a new kind of culture. As in the case of Rousseau's new poetry celebrating natural wholeness, this poetry contains an internal tension. All foundings of cultures by poets, thinkers, and legislators tend to degenerate into the common, the familiar, the merely civilized. The praise of the new kind of nobility bears within it the likelihood, indeed the necessity, that it will be misunderstood as something either merely moral or basely egoistic. Clearly Nietzsche does not suppose that true culture can guarantee its own continuance, for his notion of true culture contains nearly as much subtlety, complexity, and resistance to universalization as the classical notions. What is most problematic about Nietzsche's conception is what relates him most to Rousseau.[29] The rational is only the artificial: it is the superficial and constructed ordering of primordial drives that invariably jeopardizes the vitality and uniqueness of those drives.[30] Culture therefore is never fully distinguishable from contemptible civilization, or a vital culture is always becoming an ossified civilization, as Spengler later maintains. Therefore the cruelty directed at mere civilization cannot be moderated from the standpoint of a higher rationality. The erotic self-squandering that is necessarily self-cruelty must be turned, in a Dionysian intoxication combining destruction and creation, against any culture that begins to be rational.[31] Any common way of life that claims to be "culture" must be opposed, for the "common" is inherently hostile to culture. How then is true culture recognizable or even describable, as a common possession of the noble?[32] How can the noble style be established? The intransigent stance that the common is always low only serves to ensure that the low alone remains common.[33]

VIII

Briefly and inadequately, I wish to close with an indication of how Heidegger's critique of Western rational civilization relates to earlier ones. In Heidegger's view the universalist pretensions of Western philosophy have robbed human life of its depth, which must come from a profound attachment to the temporally finite and contingent grounds of human existence. Hence Heidegger undertakes an interpretation of the Western question of Being so as to show that the horizon of intelligibility (Being) giving man access to beings is not an eternal order of ideas and principles. Instead the horizon comes into "presence" as the unique fates of particular languages, folk spirits, and historical epochs.[34] The great poets and thinkers who proclaim a horizon or dispensation of Being are the oracles for a folk spirit or epoch, although they are at the same time alien and lonely creators out of step with their age.[35] This duality in their relation to their age is Heidegger's version of the Rousseauian tension of the beautiful. As a poet Heidegger is rooted in the present moment and its experience of the flight of the gods and the longing for their return. As a thinker he claims to have an almost godlike vision of the whole fate of Western humanity and to see well beyond the limits of his present moment. But what enables him to see beyond those limits and to develop his critique of the West? How can he as poet assert the overwhelming power of the immediate and at the same time as thinker reflect on it from a distance? Insofar as Heidegger gives an account of the general structure of Being as "presencing" itself in particular epochs, does he not ascend to the universal? Heidegger wishes to point beyond "philosophy" as the Greeks understand it (the seeking of the Logos of "enduring presence") to a new pious "thinking" that attentively responds to the unfathomable demands of history. But is he not still a philosopher who retains distance on his historical fate through his powerful analysis of *what it is* (*ti estin*) to have a fate?[36] This problem is akin to the problems that Rousseau and Nietzsche face as the heroes of prediscursive wholeness: Can they proclaim that wholeness in philosophical speech and at the same time preseve its purity?

NOTES

1. For accounts of the German literature on culture and civilization in the early twentieth century, see Fritz K. Ringer, *The Decline of the German Mandarins: The German Academic Community, 1890–1933* (Cambridge: Harvard University Press, 1969); Jeffrey

Herf, *Reactionary Modernism: Technology, Culture and Politics in Weimar and the Third Reich* (New York: Cambridge University Press, 1984); Richard Wolin, *The Politics of Being: The Political Thought of Martin Heidegger* (New York: Columbia University Press, 1990); and Pierre Bourdieu, *The Political Ontology of Martin Heidegger*, trans. Peter Collier (Stanford: Stanford University Press, 1991). Spengler gave currency to what was often called "the German theory of culture," according to which "civilization is to culture as the external to the internal, the artificially constructed to the naturally developed, the mechanical to the organic, 'means' to 'ends'" (from *Der grosse Brockhaus*, cited in Ringer, *Decline of the German Mandarins*, 89).

2. See also Joel Schwartz, "Rousseau and Freud on Sexuality and Its Discontents," chapter 5 in this volume, for Freud's account of eros and its relation to Rousseau's.

3. See Friedrich Nietzsche, *Morgenröte*, 1886 preface, sec. 4.

4. Victor de Riquetti Mirabeau, *L'ami des hommes, ou Traité de la population* (1756); also the entry in *Dictionnaire de Trévoux* (Paris, 1771), which cites Mirabeau. The noun formed earlier in the century from *civiliser* had a juristic meaning (the rendering of a criminal process into a civil one) before Mirabeau and others connected it to "sociability." F. Rauhut, "Die Herkunft der Worte und Begriffe 'Kultur,' 'Civilisation,' und 'Bildung,'" *Germanisch-Romanische Monatschrift* 34 (April 1953): 81–91; J. Moras, *Ursprung und Entwicklung des Begriffs der Zivilisation in Frankreich (1756–1830)* (Hamburg: Seminar für Romanische Sprachen und Kultur, 1930); L. Febvre, E. Tonnelat, et al., *Civilisation: Le mot et l'idée* (Paris: Centre Internationale de Synthèse, 1930); Ernst Robert Curtius, "The Conception of Civilization," in *The Civilization of France*, trans. O. Wyon (New York: Random House, 1962), 3–34; Jean Starobinski, "The Word 'Civilization,'" in *Blessings in Disguise, or The Morality of Evil*, trans. Arthur Goldhammer (Cambridge: Harvard University Press, 1993), 1–35. It should be noted that "civilization" in this early modern universalist sense designates an unfinishable process rather than a completed entity— unlike the later plural "civilizations."

5. Characteristic is the definition of M. Block, *Dictionnaire générale de la politique* (Paris, 1873), s.v. *"Civilisation"*: "Civilization is civil and political society among humans, opposed to natural dispersion and barbarism. As the ideal end of the civilizing process, the goal that humanity is destined to pursue indefinitely, it is also the perfection and the extension of civil and political society. In other terms it is the establishment of human solidarity and fraternity."

6. See Charles Taylor, *The Ethics of Authenticity* (Cambridge: Harvard University Press, 1991), 25–29, 81–91.

7. "Philosophy is the culture of the soul"; Marcus Tullius Cicero, *Tusculanae disputationes*, 2.4.

8. Samuel von Pufendorf, *Eris Scandica, qua adversus libros de jure naturali et gentium objecta diluuntur* (1686): "In a second way we have considered the natural state of man, insofar as it is contrasted to that culture which human life has acquired through the help, industry, and inventions of other men, by means of their own reflection and labor or divine instruction" (My translation from Rauhut, "Die Herkunft," 83).

9. See Francis Bacon, *The New Organon*, 1:129, and René Descartes, *Discourse on Method*.

10. See the discussion in Isaiah Berlin, *Vico and Herder: Two Studies in the History of Ideas* (New York: Random House, 1976).

11. See Charles Taylor, *Multiculturalism and "The Politics of Recognition,"* with commentaries, ed. Amy Gutmann (Princeton: Princeton University Press, 1992), for an argument that "multiculturalism" necessarily presupposes some notion of a common humanity, contrary to the express intent of many of its advocates.

12. Immanuel Kant, "Anmerkung," in *Mutmasslicher Anfang der Menschengeschichte*.

13. Immanuel Kant, *Idee zu einer allgemeinen Geschichte in weltbürgerlicher Absicht* (1784), seventh thesis, in *Kants gesammelte Schriften,* Prussian Academy edition (Berlin: Walter de Gruyter, 1902–), 8:26. Humboldt employs the "external" and "internal" contrast to amplify Kant's distinction, with somewhat less stress on the moral content of culture: "Civilization (*Zivilisation*) is the humanizing of the nations in their external organization, and in the spirit and temper to which this is related; to this elevation of the social situation, culture (*Kultur*) adds science and art" (quoted in Curtius, *Civilization of France,* 5–6). The contrast of inner and outer also owes much to Leibniz and his account of the substantial monad as a unique individual, all of whose states are expressions of an inner essence and not the result of external interaction. This Leibnizian dynamic is an important factor in the critiques of Newtonian mechanistic science in Goethe, Schelling, and Hegel. It is decisive for Goethe's concept of the natural "daimon" governing the individual's life through a certain inner teleology, and more generally for the Goethean notion of "inner productive powers." See the "Orphic" poems "Dämon" and "Notigung," and also "Natur und Kunst." But more Rousseauian is the internal connection in Goethe between study of nature (botany), lyric poetry (reverie), and exemplary individuality (confession).

14. A possible exception here is Goethe's treatment of education in *Wilhelm Meister,* a work that follows *Emile* closely in preserving the distinction between *le citoyen* and *l'homme naturel.* I have been instructed on this by remarks of Professor Wilhelm Vosskamp, University of Cologne.

15. See the discussions of genius as the unity of unconscious forces of nature and rational communicability in Kant, *Kritik der Urteilskraft,* and Friedrich Schelling, *System des transzendentalen Idealismus.* By way of Hölderlin, genius is central to Heidegger's conception of the historical missions of poets and thinkers.

16. See Christopher Kelly's fine discussion in *Rousseau's Exemplary Life: The "Confessions" as Political Philosophy* (Ithaca: Cornell University Press, 1987).

17. For a learned and thoughtful account of *Hamlet* as a study of the struggle between Christian and classical heroisms, see Paul A. Cantor, *Shakespeare: Hamlet,* Cambridge Landmarks of World Literature (New York: Cambridge University Press, 1989), to which I would add reflection on how Hamlet wishes for a godlike existence denied to him by the Christian views of this world and the next. In Nietzsche's account Hamlet resembles "the Dionysian man"; see *Die Geburt der Tragödie,* sec. 7. Hamlet's rage at being denied divinity (not merely at being denied the crown of Denmark) also relates

him to Pyrrhus, the murderer of Priam; compare 2.2.301–19 and 456–529. There is an important connection between Shakespeare's Pyrrhus and Nietzsche's Dionysus (whose rapture causes "annihilation of the ordinary bounds and limits of existence").

18. Friedrich Nietzsche, *Die fröhliche Wissenschaft*, 344.

19. Friedrich Nietzsche, *Werke in drei Bänden*, ed. K. Schlechta (Munich: Carl Hansa, 1966), 3:810.

20. Ibid., 3:837.

21. It therefore is misleading to assign to Nietzsche the Neo-Kantian account of the object as the "thing in itself" that is wholly "chaotic and meaningless" until "man's creative acts" endow it with meaning (see *Die fröhliche Wissenschaft*, 354, concluding paragraph). To say that human beings can know only interpretations of the world is not to say that "man is the measure of things," since "interpreting" is not a distinctively human activity; the greatest error is precisely to regard human will and reason as the meaning of things. Nietzsche speaks of the "ridiculous immodesty that would be involved in decreeing from our (human) corner that perspectives are permitted only from this corner." See Friedrich Nietzsche, *Jenseits von Gut und Böse*, 9; *Die fröhliche Wissenschaft*, 346, 374; "Die vier grossen Irrtümer," in *Götzendämmerung*, esp. 7–8. The human will is itself only a created "fiction," and as such it cannot be identified with the creative ground of all fictions; this insight is the basis of a new "infinite" perspective. Even so, the consequences Nietzsche wants to draw from his critique of anthropocentrism are first and foremost of human significance, since they should result in an elevation of human life.

22. See "Streifzüge eines Unzeitgemässen," in *Götzendämmerung*, 48: "*Progress in my sense.*—I too speak of 'return to nature,' although it is properly not a going back, but an ascent—upward into the high, free, even frightful nature and naturalness which plays with great tasks, which is *permitted* to play with them."

23. Nietzsche, *Werke in drei Bänden*, 3:507–9.

24. Ibid., 3:493. Rousseau has, unlike Voltaire, the crucial insight into the historical character of human rationality and is thus the true philosophical predecessor of Nietzsche's view of the artificiality and superficiality of all rational civilization. But unlike Rousseau, Nietzsche seeks to build an aristocratic culture based on the "historical sense."

25. Nietzsche, *Die fröhliche Wissenschaft*, 110.

26. Ibid., 354.

27. See "Streifzüge eines Unzeitgemässen," 14 ("Anti-Darwin").

28. Compare *Die fröhliche Wissenschaft*, 1, 107, 276, 324, 343, 382.

29. It is the search for prerational wholeness that links both Rousseau and Nietzsche to Hamlet, from whom Shakespeare maintains a critical and magisterial detachment. Unlike Shakespeare and Goethe, Nietzsche was unable or unwilling to free himself from Christianity's radicalism. Had he done so he would have been less inclined to proselytize for its destruction.

30. *Die fröhliche Wissenschaft*, 110–12.

31. Heidegger considers Nietzsche's "Dionysian" critique of civilization to be the

deepest authority for the "fundamental mood of our present situation," as expressed in contemporary *kulturphilosophisch* writers like Spengler, Klages, and Scheler. See lectures of 1929–30 titled *Die Grundbegriffe der Metaphysik: Welt-Endlichkeit-Einsamkeit; M. Heidegger Gesamtausgabe*, pt. 2, vols. 29–30 (Frankfurt: Klostermann, 1983), 105–16. In Nietzschean fashion such writers contrast mere logical intellect or *Geist* with the deeper intuitive forces of life or *Seele*; this distinction is often put in term of civilization versus culture. See Oswald Spengler, *The Decline of the West*, trans. Charles Francis Atkinson (New York: Knopf, 1986), 1:31–36 and 351–64. Heidegger, though sympathetic to this "mood" and analysis, seeks a more fundamental ontological account of their basis. Needless to say, he does not correct the analysis from the standpoint of a "traditional" account of rational culture. He replaces the naturalistic or biologistic critique of *ratio* or intellect with a critique arising from the authentic experience of Being as the overpowering abyss.

32. For Nietzsche's awareness of this problem see, for example, *Die fröhliche Wissenschaft*, 381.

33. Nietzsche's contempt for the common seems to place him at the opposite pole from Kant, who identifies both nobility and the task of culture with universal justice. But Nietzsche also is in the end concerned with justice: the new nobility will justify history. And so his philosophy is, like Kant's, a "theodicy." See *Zur Genealogie der Moral*, third essay, secs. 24, 27–28, and the 1886 preface to *Morgenröte*. Nietzsche speaks of his "aesthetic justification of existence," which at one point he relates to the central tradition of German philosophy; see Nietzsche, *Werke in drei Bänden*, 3:496. See also Heidegger, "The Word of Nietzsche: 'God Is Dead,'" in *The Question concerning Technology and Other Essays*, trans. William Lovitt (New York: Harper and Row, 1977), 88–93 (on certainty, justification, and Nietzsche's "metaphysical concept of justice," with an important reference to Kant).

34. Heidegger rejects Nietzsche's account of primordial drives (will to power) as the source of the profound perspectives of higher creators overcoming the superficiality of logical-calculative reason. Heidegger instead grounds the critique of reason in the fated particularity of historical horizons of intelligibility. These are the "events" that give human life its only access to the beings and endow life with its only possible depth, and that require the assistance of great thinkers and poets for their "arrival." In this way Heidegger criticizes the "naturalist" element in Nietzsche that still ties the latter's thought to the metaphysical tradition of focusing on beings rather than on the elusive ground of intelligibility (Being). This is the theme of Heidegger's great seminar series on Nietzsche, whom Heidegger acknowledges to be his closest precursor.

35. See Martin Heidegger, *An Introduction to Metaphysics*, trans. Ralph Manheim (New Haven: Yale University Press, 1959), a 1935 lecture series first published in 1953: The great creators and men of action are "preeminent in their historical place but at the same time *apolis*, without city and place, lonely, uncanny, without issue in the midst of beings as a whole, also without statute and limit, without structure and order, because they *as* creators must first ground all of this" (152–53; translation slightly modified).

36. This tension is evident in Heidegger's way of rethinking the claims of Plato and Aristotle that philosophy begins in the *pathos* of wondering (*to thaumazein, das Erstaunen*): "In wondering we restrain ourselves (*être en arrêt*). We step back, as it were, from what is—from the fact that it is as it is and not otherwise. . . . As this stepping-back and self-restraining, wondering is at once forcibly drawn toward and, as it were, enthralled by that from which it retreats." At the conclusion of the same lecture Heidegger speaks of the necessity of discussing the relation between thinking and poetic making (*Denken und Dichten*), between which there is a "secret kinship" although the thinker and poet "dwell on the most widely separated mountains." See Martin Heidegger, *What Is Philosophy?* (lecture of 1955 held in France), trans. William Kluback and Jean T. Wilde (New Haven: College and University Press, 1958), 85 (translation modified).

❧ 5 ❧

Rousseau and Freud on Sexuality and Its Discontents

JOEL SCHWARTZ

Rousseau and Freud are the two greatest writers about human sexuality and its impact on our psychological and social lives. Although I will focus on their many disagreements, it is important to realize that they had much in common, both in their subject matter and in their approach to it. Both are scientific materialists. Both seek to understand human nature by examining its origins; both do so by making conjectures about primitive or protohumans who existed before the dawn of civilization and also by examining the behavior of infants and children. Both Rousseau and Freud criticize civilization for the ways it hampers and inhibits human happiness. Both of them focus on love and sexuality as the surest, indeed the only, natural force capable of binding individual human atoms into any sort of coherent and cohesive social unity. Both also emphasize the plasticity of the human sex drive, its capacity to be channeled (in Freud's term, "sublimated") from its obvious physical outlet into more spiritual directions. Both Rousseau and Freud, in other words, suggest that morality and art can be understood in some sense as outgrowths of human sexuality.

Yet these affinities do not result from any direct influence Rousseau might have had on Freud. Freud does not appear to have known Rousseau's work at all well. We know the contents of Freud's library, and Rousseau's books formed no part of it.[1] Freud's works include only five or six scattered references to Rousseau; to judge from them, the only work by Rousseau that he may have known well was the *Confessions*—a book that should surely have been required reading for someone like Freud, who was so eager to map the terrain of sexual perversions.

In any case, the differences and disagreements between Rousseau and Freud are ultimately more profound and more significant than their affinities. To understand these disagreements, we can begin by noting that Rousseau harshly criticized doctors, and that Freud was equally unimpressed by philosophers. Rousseau describes medicine as "this lying art, made more for the ills of the mind than for those of the body"; he goes on to argue that medicine "is no more useful for [our mental illnesses] than for [our physical ailments]" (*Emile*, 54).[3] Note also that Rousseau speaks scornfully of those who "get an odious pleasure out of seeking for sinister interpretations of everything" (*Emile*, 237), and that the Savoyard Vicar attacks what he calls an "abominable . . . philosophy—one which is embarrassed by virtuous actions, which [must] fabricat[e] base intentions and motives without virtue" (*Emile*, 289). Perhaps we can view these judgments as Rousseau's critique of psychoanalysis before the fact.

For his part, Freud denounced philosophers for creating grand theoretical systems that ignore empirical reality.[4] Nevertheless, Freud was clearly an unusual physician, and Rousseau was an equally uncharacteristic philosopher. For this reason it requires a bit of a leap to assume that Rousseau's critique of physicians generally would apply to Freud in particular (and that Freud's critique of philosophers generally would apply to Rousseau in particular); I intend this to be a hypothesis to explore, not a postulate whose truth is unquestioned. But if the general critiques were to apply to Rousseau and Freud's specific cases, we could suggest that Freud might criticize Rousseau for paying too little attention to behavioral phenomena that need to be explained,while Rousseau might criticize Freud for focusing on medical phenomena and slighting moral ones, and also for propounding a doctrine of human nature that cannot really account for human excellence. These at any rate are the propositions I will explore: I will focus first on childhood, where I think that Freud more plausibly accounts for some aspects of children's behavior; then I will consider adulthood, where I think Rousseau raises important moral considerations that are slighted by Freud.

Sexuality, Independence, and the Child

Perhaps the most obvious disagreement between Rousseau and Freud concerns their understanding of infants and children; Freud contends, and Rousseau denies, that they must be understood, both physically and emotionally, as sexual beings. This momentous disagreement masks an underlying similarity: both agree that the first emotional attachment is tremendously consequential for one's later life. They simply differ over when that first emotional attachment occurs: in infancy or upon the adolescent's first experience of romantic love. Rousseau speaks of "the invincible influence" of the adolescent's first romantic attachment "on the rest of his life" (*Emile*, 318), and Freud, speaking of the baby at the mother's breast, claims he can give us "no idea of the important bearing of this first object upon the choice of every later object."[5]

This disagreement is important because it bears on Rousseau's great claim, which Freud would contest—the claim that human beings are by nature whole, unified, independent of others, untroubled by internal conflicts.

Thus Rousseau criticizes civilization by arguing that it introduces an unnatural split or division into the human soul. In contrast to the primeval man, who Rousseau contends was naturally independent—that is, not dependent on others—Rousseau argues that civilized man is a walking self-contradiction, or a "double m[a]n" (*Emile*, 41). Civilized man is double because he appears to be concerned with the welfare of others (and is actually concerned to win their approval), while chiefly being concerned only to advance his own interests by exploiting others. Now by nature, Rousseau would argue, we are indeed inclined to benefit ourselves. By nature, however, he insists, we do not want to or need to exploit others, to take advantage of them, because we do not depend on others. In Rousseau's view, civilization is to blame for causing us to depend on one another, and hence for leading us to exploit one another.

But is the dependence Rousseau deplores really unnatural? Might not human interdependence instead be a necessary and not obviously regrettable fact of life? An obvious objection to Rousseau's view, as he was well aware, would seem to emerge when one considers infancy and childhood. Aren't children naturally dependent on their parents? And doesn't their dependence suggest that by nature we are indeed social or interdependent creatures?

That is the objection to which Rousseau must respond. To do so, he argues that the child is by nature free, not dependent on others. He must, of course, concede that children's "freedom is limited by their weakness," so that they "enjoy only an imperfect freedom, similar to that enjoyed by men in the civil state" (*Emile*, 85).[6] But Rousseau then introduces a distinction that is crucial for understanding his thought—the distinction between dependence on people and dependence on things. His claim is that children are essentially dependent only on things—things such as food and shelter. The child is only instrumentally dependent on his parent or guardian (in the case of the subject of Rousseau's educational novel *Emile*) as the means to the necessary end of attaining those things.[7] The claim, in short, is that the child is at least emotionally independent of others (even though physically dependent on them for sustenance); the child does not really love anyone else and is indifferent to receiving love. Rousseau argues for the radical isolation and independence of the child, most notably in the following remarkable passage:

> The child raised according to his age is alone. He knows no attachments other than those of habit. He loves his sister as he loves his watch, and his friend as his dog. He does not feel himself to be of any sex, of any species. Man and woman are equally alien to him. He does not consider anything they do or say to be related to himself. (*Emile*, 219)[8]

The contention that children are naturally dependent only on things and not on people is crucial for Rousseau's argument in *Emile*. It underlies the great division in the book, in which hunger for food is the motivator for the education conveyed in the first half, and sexual desire (at first as transformed into compassion and piety) is the motivator in the second half. It is because the young Emile is fundamentally unconcerned about other humans that he can be whole or undivided: he does not care about the opinion of others and therefore can live—like primeval natural man—"within himself," and never—unlike corrupt civilized man—"outside of himself" (*Second Discourse*, 179).[9]

Two passages in Freud's works helpfully restate what seem to be the premises underlying Rousseau's conception of childhood. In the first Freud argues that the essential characteristic of dreams—that they are the fulfillments of wishes—can most readily be seen in children's dreams, because many of the wishes children have are not yet repressed by the psychic censorship that distorts adult dreams and makes the interpretation of dreams both difficult and imperative. Freud observes that these uncomplicated, uncensored dreams of children often are motivated by children's wish for food. He illustrates this claim by recounting a dream his daughter Anna had when she was nineteen months old:

> [she] had had an attack of vomiting one morning and had consequently been kept without food all day. During the night after this day of starvation she was heard calling out excitedly in her sleep: "Anna Fweud, stwawbewwies, wild stwawbewwies, omblet, pudden!" At that time she was in the habit of using her own name to

express the idea of taking possession of something. The menu included pretty well everything that must have seemed to her to make up a desirable meal.[10]

The image we have here is of a child with very uncomplicated desires, desires that tend not to raise difficult moral issues because they are desires for things (food) and not for control over human wills, desires that abstract from love, hate, and the whole messy web of interpersonal and intrafamilial relations. These desires, and these alone, are the desires that in Rousseau's view naturally characterize childhood.

In the second passage, Freud comments on a story penned by an Austrian writer, Josef Popper-Lynkeus. The story told "of a man who could boast that he had never dreamt anything nonsensical."[11] Freud observes:

> Translated into my manner of speech this meant that in the case of this man no dream-distortion occurred; and the reason produced for its absence put one at the same time in possession of the reason for its occurrence. Popper allowed the man complete insight into the reasons for his peculiarity. He made him say: "Order and harmony reign both in my thoughts and in my feelings, nor do the two struggle with each other. . . . I am one and undivided. Other people are divided and their two parts—waking and dreaming— are almost perpetually at war with one another.[12]

The character in Popper-Lynkeus's story is "one and undivided"— precisely the goal Rousseau aims to realize in the education of Emile (*Emile*, 41). Other people, however, are "divided" into "two parts—waking and dreaming" that "are almost perpetually at war with one another." The dividedness Popper-Lynkeus speaks of is not a bad capsule description of Freud's notion of the unconscious and its significance for our entire emotional life. Nor is it a bad capsule description of Emile's education to suggest that Rousseau's goal is to have Emile dream the dreams of this fictional character; put differently, Rousseau's goal in *Emile* is to produce a man who lacks the unconscious desires Freud speaks of.

Now this goal, of course, is in Freud's view impossible. And it is impossible, Freud would argue, because Rousseau's depiction of childhood is necessarily wrong: the child is not naturally alone and unconflicted; instead he is necessarily confronted with enormous and insuperable conflicts, both with his parents and with his siblings.

Neuroses and Infantile Sexuality

But before we turn to Freud's vision of the child, we must briefly consider his picture of the mind. Freud rejects the possibility of harmonious psychic unity for which Rousseau argues. Freud rejects it because—unlike Rousseau—he denies that our desires are naturally limited and moderate. For this reason Freud contends that the "mind . . . is no peacefully self-contained unity. It is rather to be compared with a modern State in which a mob, eager for enjoyment and destruction, has to be held down forcibly by a prudent superior class."[13] The conflict Freud speaks of here can be understood to pit what he variously called mental censorship (the faculty that brings about the distortion of our dreams) against our infantile wishes, the ego against the id, or the instincts of self-preservation against the sexual instincts. This conflict is the cause of what he calls neuroses. Crucially, neuroses (along with civilization) are for Freud unique to human beings; they are the characteristics that distinguish us from our animal brethren. Whereas Rousseau argues that primeval natural man was whole or nonneurotic because he was essentially an animal, Freud contends that man, akin to the animals in so many respects, is unlike them in his capacity for mental conflict and hence neurosis.[14]

We have already seen that Freud, unlike Rousseau, regards infants and children as sexual creatures. And it is noteworthy that infantile sexuality lies at the heart of both our unconscious wishes and our resultant neuroses. Whereas Rousseau argues for the existence of natural harmony and natural moderation, Freud contends that the infantile wishes he speaks of are "repugnant to morality"; he also claims that they "have been forced upon us by nature."[15] Because of their existence, true psychic harmony of the sort Rousseau argues for and that is embodied in the Popper-Lynkeus character cannot exist: "Even where psychical health is perfect, the subjugation [of the unconscious wishes by the force that represses them] is not complete: the measure of suppression indicates the degree of our psychical normality."[16]

As is well known, in describing these infantile wishes Freud chiefly emphasizes their Oedipal character: he makes much of the child's supposed desire to kill the father and to sleep with the mother. But even if Freud wrongly focuses on the Oedipal wishes, wrongly harps on them so consistently as the not-very-illuminating explanation of everything, there is still much to Freud's argument that children are naturally immoderate—an argument Rousseau needs to rebut. To put this differently: there are not many psychologies one can think of compared with which Freud's might be considered commonsensical. But Rousseau's psychology—at least his psychology of children—may be one of them; whatever its exaggerations and shortcomings, Freud's psychology in many respects seems to correspond more closely to childhood experience.[17]

To begin with, consider Freud's arguments about the physical and emotional characteristics of children that lead him to regard them as sexual creatures. Freud argues that children seek physical pleasure in ways that are analogous to adults' quest for sexual pleasure; he points, for instance, to the sensual pleasure the child takes in sucking his thumb.[18] Consider also this piece of evidence that Freud brings forward: "No one," he argues, "who has seen a baby sinking back satiated from the breast and falling asleep with flushed cheeks and a blissful smile can escape the reflection that this picture persists as a prototype of the expression of sexual satisfaction in later life."[19]

Of even greater importance, in Freud's view, is the immoderation of the child's quest for love, his attempt to monopolize love. Much of Freud's discussion focuses on the rivalry between siblings for the love of their parents. (By contrast, Rousseau attempts to stack the deck in *Emile*, so to speak, by eliminating rivalry. Emile is an orphan, raised alone, without siblings.)

Freud emphasizes the competition between children for parental love: "What the child grudges the unwanted intruder and rival [its younger sibling] is . . . all the . . . signs of maternal care. It feels that it has been dethroned, despoiled, prejudiced in its rights; it casts a jealous hatred upon the new baby. . . . [W]e rarely form a correct idea of the strength of these jealous impulses. . . . A child's demands for love are immoderate, they make exclusive claims and tolerate no sharing."[20]

Elsewhere Freud notes that "children are completely egoistic; they feel their needs intensely and strive ruthlessly to satisfy them—especially as against . . . other children, and first and foremost as against their brothers and sisters."[21] Needless to say, Freud is not issuing a moral condemnation of children here; instead he speaks of the younger child "meet[ing] his oppressor with the first stirrings of a love of liberty and a sense of justice",[22] and he notes that "we do not on that account call a child 'bad,' we call him 'naughty.'"[23] Freud illustrates his argument with a nice example of a former only child who, when his mother gave birth to a baby boy, was told that the stork had brought the new baby. The elder child responded: "The stork can take him away again!"[24]

One important aspect of infantile sexuality to which Freud calls attention is its perversity. As he points out, infantile sexuality must by definition be perverse: "If a child has a sexual life at all it is bound to be of a perverse kind; for, except for a few obscure hints, children are without what makes sexuality into the reproductive function. . . . [T]he abandonment of the reproductive function is the common feature of all perversions."[25] We know from the *Confessions* that Rousseau had personal experience of many varieties of perverse sexuality. Nevertheless, in the *Second Discourse* (197) he asserts that perverse sexuality is unnatural, in the sense that it is the product of corrupted civilization; by contrast, Freud sees perverse sexuality as the natural base from which reproductive adult sexuality emerges only later, and at times with great difficulty.

One form of perverse sexuality Freud speaks about is anal sexuality, which frequently involves a small child's play with his feces. In this context Freud argues for the great importance of toilet training for the subsequent development of the child's (and later the adult's) character. Freud's argument here may pose serious difficulties for Rousseau's understanding of childhood. I say this while recognizing that on a commonsense basis one can argue that Freud makes far too many mountains out of these particular unsavory molehills. Rousseau, however, is probably not in a very good position to dismiss the importance of toilet training, for Freud notes that toilet training "must be the first occasion on which the infant has a glimpse of an environment hostile to his instinctual impulses,"[26] which is to say, in Rousseau's terms, the first occasion on which the child confronts a will (and not a thing) opposing his own will. Rousseau nowhere speaks of toilet training in *Emile*, and he emphatically asserts that the child must never come to be aware of opposition from an alien will (*Emile*, 89). But as Rousseau himself acknowledges (*Emile*, 94–95), it is barely conceivable that a child could avoid encountering wills opposing his own.

The Emotional Dependence of the Child

But the issue between Rousseau and Freud goes beyond the question of wills in conflict with one another. It also involves the extent of the child's emotional dependence on the parent or guardian. In this context it is interesting to compare Rousseau's and Freud's discussions of children's fear of the dark. Rousseau considers it at some length (*Emile*, 134–38); he indicates that fear of the dark is in some sense natural but that it can be overcome by habituation, in that children can grow accustomed to being in the dark. He ascribes great importance to overcoming this fear, and it is clear why he does so: fear of the dark relates to the human tendency to be superstitious, to be subjected to irrational religious passions that preclude human self-sufficiency. In short, fear of the dark is important because of its evident link to what Hobbes referred to as the "fear of power invisible."[27]

Now Freud, a dogmatic atheist, was no more sympathetic to superstition than Rousseau; but his discussion of children's fear of the dark is suggestive, because it shows that the threat to human self-sufficiency that concerned Rousseau stems from a second, this-worldly source that cannot be eradicated as easily as superstition. Freud understands fear of the dark as a manifestation of infantile anxiety caused by the absence (the invisibility) of the loved one. He defends his explanation with a very pertinent anecdote:

> For this explanation of the origin of infantile anxiety I have to thank a three-year-old boy whom I once heard calling out of a dark room: "Auntie, speak to me! I'm frightened because it's so dark." His aunt answered him: "What good would that do? You can't see me." "That doesn't matter," replied the child, "if anyone speaks, it gets light." [Freud then comments:] Thus what he was afraid of was not the dark, but the absence of someone he loved; and he could feel sure of being soothed as soon as he had evidence of that person's presence.[28]

Children are naturally in need of love, naturally anxious in the absence of the loved one; the emotional self-containedness of the child that Rousseau argues for is in Freud's view unattainable, probably inhuman. Nor does Freud's view here seem at all implausible.

In arguing that children are naturally self-contained, Rousseau ascribes to them two additional characteristics. He contends first that properly raised children would not fantasize, would not imagine themselves to be other than they are: "The foundation of imitation among us comes from the desire always to be transported out of ourselves. If I succeed in my enterprise, Emile surely will not have this desire" (*Emile*, 104). In addition, Rousseau asserts that the properly raised child "does not know what routine, custom, or habit is. What he did yesterday does not influence what he does today" (*Emile*, 160).

Freud would take exception to both these claims, and again I think he would be right. Freud notes that children are anything but creatures ignorant of "routine, custom, or habit." Instead, much of children's play is characterized by endless repetition of the same game, endless pleas for daddy and mommy to sing the same song in the exact same way, tell the same story in the exact same way, play hide-and-go-seek in the exact same way. Children "repeat everything that has made a great impression on them" in their play, Freud notes,[29] because doing so helps to acclimatize them, to familiarize them with their environment. Freud makes a second observation that is more interesting, one that Rousseau would clearly need to deny. Freud notes that children's play "is influenced by a wish that dominates them the whole time—the wish to be grown-up and to be able to do what grown-up people do."[30]

Freud repeats this observation in his discussion of children's imaginary lives—of the fantasizing that Rousseau regards as unhealthy. Freud asserts that "[a] child's play is determined by his wishes: in point of fact by a single wish—one that helps in his upbringing—the wish to be big and grown up."[31]

That is a large and significant claim. Freud may overstate his case here; I doubt that all children's play is about being grown up. Nevertheless, much of it surely is. And to say that children wish to be grown up is to contradict Rousseau's view of childhood. Rousseau would completely agree with Freud's claim that "a happy person, never [fantasizes], only an unsatisfied one."[32] But Rousseau would argue that childhood can be truly happy because it is self-contained: childhood is a good in itself, and it should not and must not be understood as a station on the way to adulthood (*Emile*, 79–80).

Here Freud would disagree with Rousseau. He would argue that childhood is from the child's perspective (as opposed to that of a sentimental adult) necessarily unsatisfying; childhood is, as it were, teleologically directed toward adulthood. The child's fantasies of being an adult testify to the necessary shortcomings of his existence, to the way childhood points beyond itself. Peter Pan's song "I won't grow up" was written by adults—it was not and probably would not be written by children.

The Nature of Sexuality

Thus far I have argued that Freud's focus on infantile sexuality in particular (and his understanding of childhood generally) offers a useful corrective to Rousseau's views. Now, however, I wish to suggest that Rousseau offers an equally useful corrective to the deficiencies in Freud's vision of adulthood and adult sexuality. To do so I begin by considering another respect in which Freud's thinking is teleological.

In speaking of female sexuality, Freud notes that "nature takes less careful account of its demands than in the case of masculinity." He continues by saying, "And the reason for this may lie—thinking once again teleologically— in the fact that the accomplishment of the aim of biology has been entrusted to the aggressiveness of men and has been made to some extent independent of women's consent."[33]

Here Freud restates an argument that Rousseau advanced in *Emile*. Rousseau says the male must "will and be able," the female need only "put up little resistance." Rousseau notes that "this is not the law of love," but he claims that "it is [the law] of nature, prior to love itself" (*Emile*, 358). Note that Rousseau, but not Freud, distinguishes between love and nature; Freud's failure to do so points to a serious defect in his thought, to which I will return shortly.

It is also important to realize that Rousseau goes on to develop his argument in a way that has no counterpart in Freud's account. Rousseau argues that male sexual desire must be supplemented by male amour propre, the male's desire to think well of himself because he is thought well of by others. It does not suffice for the normal male simply to satisfy his lusts with a female partner; it is also important to him that his partner think well of him. Because the male wants to deserve his partner's good opinion, Rousseau observes that the male is actually as dependent on the female as she is on him. This is so, Rousseau declares, because of "an invariable law of nature" (*Emile*, 359–60).

One conclusion to be drawn from this comparison of the two thinkers is that the issue of sexual equality is far more important for Rousseau than for Freud. But I want to focus instead on two larger theoretical questions that divide Rousseau from Freud. One, to which I have already alluded, concerns the status of nature in their respective understandings of sexuality. The other relates to the emphasis that Rousseau, as opposed to Freud, places on amour propre: Rousseau, but not Freud, argues that if the sexual act is to be performed, our physiology must be supplemented by the psychological factor of amour propre, the desire for self-esteem, the desire to win the good opinion of others. Freud has little to say about amour propre, and this omission points to an important weakness in his view of sexuality—and also in his psychology generally.

These two questions—which concern the status of nature and the importance of amour propre—relate to one another in important ways. Rousseau argues that by nature human sexuality is a moderate and hence a peaceful force. Natural sexuality—meaning the sexuality of primeval protohumans, who existed before the human family had been created—did not bring males into conflict with females, nor did it bring them into conflict with one another in competition for females. The human sex drive may appear to be stronger than that of the animals, in that the human sex drive is not periodic: animals are in heat only at certain times of the year, but our sexuality is unrestricted as to season. In fact, however, Rousseau argues, this lack of periodicity points to the weakness of the human sexual drive: if everyone is always in heat, so to speak, a sexual partner is always available, so competition for sexual partners will be weak or even nonexistent. In effect, Rousseau makes an economist's argument here: the large supply of potential partners outstrips the demand for them, so the price of a partner (hence the reason to fight for one) will be low (*Second Discourse*, 134–37).

It is the rise of amour propre—a faculty that for Rousseau is unnatural— that changes things. Amour propre particularizes and hence strengthens sexual desire. Just any partner is no longer good enough; it now has to be this particular partner, so that I can win her esteem (or win the esteem of others, who will be impressed that she has preferred me to them). Amour propre is a very ambiguous phenomenon for Rousseau; it can raise us above primitive amoral protohumans (in part by moralizing our sexual drive), or it can lower us beneath them (by making us immoral exploiters of others). The crucial point to observe, however, is that amour propre strengthens the previously weak force of natural, unamplified sexuality. For Rousseau, natural sexuality is weak; it is only civilized sexuality, sexuality driven by amour propre, that is strong.

Freud, by contrast, does not think seriously enough about what sexuality is by nature. He does not consider the Rousseauian argument that human sexuality is by nature weaker than animal sexuality. Like Rousseau, he notes that human sexuality "has almost entirely overcome the periodicity to which [sexuality] is tied in animals"; but the conclusion he draws is that sexuality is therefore "probably more strongly developed in man than in most of the higher animals."[34]

Sexuality and Amour Propre

Freud is famous for attacking the ways civilization harmfully restricts the expression of human sexuality. He claims that "the injurious influence of civilization reduces itself in the main to the harmful suppression of the sexual life of civilized peoples . . . through the 'civilized' sexual morality prevalent in them."[35] But unlike Rousseau, Freud fails to consider the ways civilization or amour propre not only may unnaturally restrain sexuality, but also may unnaturally strengthen or exacerbate it.

Nor is this simply a theoretical issue: it also means that Freud has nothing to say about certain important sexual phenomena that Rousseau calls our attention to. Rousseau notes, for instance, that much sexual promiscuity results less from the strength of the sex drive than from the desire to keep up with the sexual Joneses, to "score," to brag to our buddies in bars, in locker rooms, on golf courses. Rousseau is substantially correct in noting that "*amour-propre* produces more libertines than love does" (*Emile*, 331).[36] That is an important psychological (and moral) observation, and it is not one to which Freud leads us.

Freud is not simply oblivious to the phenomenon of amour propre; the interpretations he offers of his own dreams are replete with indications of his desire to think well of himself, to be thought better than others. Still, it is noteworthy that all these dreams (or at any rate, all Freud's interpretations of them) have to do with Freud's personal and professional ambitions, not with his erotic life.[37] As I have already noted, Freud seems not to take sufficient account of the impact of amour propre on our erotic lives.[38]

To digress for a moment, one can argue that guilt is in some respects a Freudian equivalent of amour propre. In the final evolution of Freud's psychological views, after he introduced the concept of the superego, the question of guilt becomes exceedingly important to him. Freud goes so far as to say that the sense of guilt is "the most important problem in the development of civilization."[39] Freudian guilt resembles Rousseauian amour propre in that both presuppose our concern with the opinion of others: for Rousseau, the man obsessed with amour propre demands that others think well of him; for Freud, the man obsessed with guilt lives in fear lest his parents (whose views he has internalized) think ill of him.

Freud writes about what he sees as a guilt-ridden society, in which young people in particular are too hard on themselves, faulting themselves for failing to comply with excessively harsh moral strictures, strictures that they wrongly believe all others obey.[40] People feel guilty, Freud suggests, because they are unaware of social hypocrisy. But here too Rousseau's account of our social experience is preferable: instead, Rousseau would say, people feel little or no guilt because they are so very well aware of social hypocrisy, of the fact that a strict moral code may be preached but is virtually never practiced (*Emile*, 116, 330). In this respect Rousseau's vision of eighteenth-century Paris seems far more compelling and persuasive as a description of, say, twentieth-century Washington than does Freud's vision of twentieth-century Vienna.

Rousseau's emphasis on amour propre is of particular importance for his treatment of sexual morality. His distinction between natural and civilized love is also a distinction between what he calls "physical" and "moral" love (*Second Discourse*, 134); and it is Rousseau's attention to amour propre that enables him to give a deeper, more thoughtful account of sexual morality than Freud does.

In one sense, Freud's understanding of the love we should aim for is very much akin to Rousseau's. Freud speaks of the need to unite what he calls "the affectionate and the sensual current[s]."[41] In short, we should love (that is, idealize or admire) those we physically desire. Rousseau could not agree more; but it is striking how much more Rousseau has to say about that admiration and idealization. Freud says virtually nothing about the affectionate current, except to observe that it somehow derives from the infant's desire for his mother.[42] This in turn implies that the affection is somehow misplaced (since the new love object is not, of course, the mother). And Freud says precisely this: "The final object of the sexual instinct is never any longer the original object but only a surrogate for it."[43]

Rousseau very much agrees with Freud that the lover idealizing his beloved sees something in her that is not objectively there (*Emile*, 329). But at the same time, Rousseau's notion of amour propre enables him to give more content than Freud does to the idea of the affectionate current. Amour propre can be understood as the unreasonable desire to have others prefer us to themselves (*Emile*, 214). By contrast, love can be understood as a healthier, because mutual, variant of amour propre: I think well of myself because you think well of me, but at the same time I think well of you, which leads you to think well of yourself. Rousseau would add that we love another for the good qualities the other incarnates (*Emile*, 214, 430–31). This argument points to a moral component to love that Freud tends to ignore.[44] It is not that Freud is opposed to moral love, or that he does not believe in it; it is just that he has little to say about it, which makes his account of love less comprehensive than Rousseau's. Freud was fond of quoting this remark: "As for morals, that goes without saying."[45] But morality does not go without saying. It is possible (as Rousseau well knew) to talk a lot about morality while being thoroughly immoral, and also to be thoroughly moral while never speaking of morality; but it is hard to get others to take morality seriously when you suggest (as Freud does) that morality is a surface phenomenon about which there is little to say.

The (Unsuccessful) Quest for Sexual Pleasure

I have noted that Freud's understanding of sexuality is teleological, and its teleology is evident in another important respect. Freud argues that infantile masturbation can be understood as a manifestation of nature's grand design: "We may expect that nature will have made safe provisions so that [the infant's] experience of [masturbatory] satisfaction shall not be left to chance."[46] What Freud suggests here, of course, is that by nature the sex drive is directed not just toward procreation (or as Rousseau would argue, to pleasure in the service of procreation); instead, it is directed from the outset to pleasure as an end in itself.

Freud's argument is an important and immensely influential one, which I would not dispute. It is worth pointing out, though, that for all his emphasis on sexual pleasure, and more generally on what he calls the pleasure principle, Freud somehow does not make sex seem very pleasant. Consider, for instance, this remarkable passage: "If one makes a broad survey of the sexual life of our time and in particular of the classes who sustain human civilization, one is tempted to declare that it is only with reluctance that the majority of those alive today obey the command to propagate their kind; they feel that their dignity as human beings suffers and is degraded in the process."[47]

By contrast, consider Rousseau's very different analysis of a similar phenomenon, where he speaks of the desire "to perform a useless act [sexual intercourse] so as always to be able to start over again, . . . to turn to the prejudice of the species the attraction given for the sake of multiplying it" (*Emile*, 44).

It is striking that it is Rousseau and not Freud who speaks of people engaging in sexual activity divorced from the end of procreation, purely for the sake of pleasure. Obviously the two thinkers lived in different times and were describing different places; conceivably each accurately observed conditions in his own time and place. Nevertheless, Rousseau's analysis seems to speak better to our own situation today than does Freud's, for all that Freud is so much closer to being our contemporary.

Still, one must ask: Why does Freud think so many people find sex repulsive? Surprisingly, and significantly, it is not just—or even primarily—because social conventions restrict and inhibit what would otherwise be the free and harmonious flowering of our sexual lives. Instead, Freud suggests, "We must reckon with the possibility that something in the nature of the sexual instinct itself is unfavorable to the realization of complete happiness."[48] Or as Freud elsewhere observes, "Nature . . . appears to us to be . . . inconsistent."[49]

To understand the source of our sexual discontents, Freud would say, one must remember that normal adult procreative sex is far narrower than is the infantile sexuality (described by Freud as "polymorphously perverse")[50] out of which adult sexuality develops. We have already seen that infantile sexuality is incestuous, in that the mother is the initial object of desire. Thus in later life this initial object choice is replaced, in Freud's words, "by an endless series of substitutive objects."[51] None of these replacements, Freud goes on to say, "brings full satisfaction."[52]

In addition, the passage out of childhood involves giving up not only incestuous objects, but excremental ones.[53] Freud knows full well that excrement is objectively disgusting; nevertheless, on some level, he argues, renouncing the infantile capacity to play with excrement is perceived as a restriction, a loss.[54] To repeat, normal adult sexuality is narrower, more limited than perverse or infantile sexuality; adult sexuality is therefore unsatisfactory, Freud indicates, because the emergence out of childhood means we can never again be sexual in all possible ways.

Rousseau's understanding is far different. On one level, he obviously makes sex seem far more appealing than Freud does. Rousseau's depiction of moralized, reciprocal sexual love is intentionally romantic, whereas nothing could be less romantic than Freud's clinical observations. To see this, consider first Freud and then Rousseau on kissing. In the following passage, it is hard to be certain whether Freud is posing as a scientific straight man or instead as a very droll scientific comic: "[A] man who will kiss a pretty girl's lips passionately, may perhaps be disgusted at the idea of using her toothbrush, though there are no grounds for supposing that his own oral cavity, for which he feels no disgust, is any cleaner than the girl's."[55] An interesting contrast is offered by Rousseau's account of Emile's kissing his fiancée, Sophie, for the first time, when they are making up after she has taken offense at his taking the liberty of kissing her dress: "Emile . . . tremblingly approaches Sophie's face. She turns her head away and, in order to save her mouth, exposes a rosy cheek. The tactless boy is not satisfied. She resists feebly. What a kiss . . . !" (*Emile*, 427). Freud's air of scientific detachment, as though he were an anthropologist from some other planet observing our quaint earthling customs, is light-years apart from the tone of vicarious, voluptuous, voyeuristic enjoyment that we see as Rousseau describes with such relish the courtship of Emile that Rousseau himself stage-manages.

Similarly, in treating the sense of smell in relation to our sexuality, Rousseau characteristically describes a lover being made to "quiver by the smell of the flowers on his beloved's bosom" (*Emile*, 157); equally characteristic is Freud's focus on the "strong smell" of human excrement that brings about what he calls the "'organic repression'"—a repression caused by nature and not by social convention—of "anal erotism." [56]

Sexuality, Independence, and Sublimation

In contrast to Freud, Rousseau was the great advocate of or publicist for the belief that moralized monogamous sexuality was the likeliest route to human happiness. Nevertheless there is another equally important side of Rousseau in which he, like Freud, appears as a great critic of human sexuality. Like Freud, Rousseau has his own theory to explain the discontents that human sexuality occasions; significantly, however, Rousseau's theory differs greatly from Freud's.

For Rousseau, the problem with sexuality is that it endangers our independence, our self-sufficiency. To minimize that danger he insisted on the asexuality of the child, and (in the *Second Discourse*) on the unnaturalness of the family. It is because sexuality seems to suggest that we are in fact by nature sociable animals that *Emile* is replete with references to sexual desire as "the most violent, the most terrible" of our needs (165), to "the new perils" and "the enemy" (318). Consider in particular this remarkable statement:

> The senses are awakened by the imagination alone. Their need is not properly a physical need. It is not true that it is a true need. If no lewd object had ever struck our eyes, if no indecent idea had ever entered our minds, perhaps this alleged need would never have made itself felt to us, and we would have remained chaste without temptation, without effort, and without merit. . . . [T]he more I reflect on this important crisis and its near or distant causes, the more I am persuaded that a solitary man raised in a desert, without books, without instruction, and without women, would die there a virgin at whatever age he had reached. (*Emile*, 333)

Rousseau suggests that sexual desire is an artificial need, created (as opposed to merely being extended) by our imaginative capacity; he further suggests that the hypothetical experiences of a solitary man on a desert island may disprove that in some way we are by nature sexually directed toward one another. These statements make sense only if one believes, as I think on some level Rousseau did, that sex is a threat because it calls into question our individual self-sufficiency—as, of course, it clearly does.

I have already noted Freud's belief that we are discontented with sex because as adults we are unable to be sexual in all ways at all times; Rousseau's very different view is that our discontents are occasioned by the fact that we are compelled to be sexual in some ways at some times, hence to relate to others, to depend on others, to lose the self-sufficiency that supposedly characterized primeval man. For Rousseau, on one level, even moralized and mutual heterosexual interdependence is less attractive than the amoral (I would say inhuman) asexuality that seems to be the prerequisite of true individual independence or self-sufficiency.

There is one further respect in which the views of Rousseau and Freud can fruitfully be compared. Both emphasize the plasticity of the sexual drive, its capacity somehow to be sublimated or spiritualized; for both thinkers, the transformation of sexual energy makes possible phenomena such as sociability, morality, and art. Neither Rousseau nor Freud is able to explain how these transformations occur. It may be helpful, though, to point to one very characteristic difference in emphasis.

Thus, in one of Freud's discussions of sublimation he says the following: "There is to my mind no doubt that the concept of 'beautiful' has its roots in sexual excitation and that its original meaning was 'sexually stimulating.'"[57] That claim is interesting if true, but in general it is striking how little beyond that Freud has to say about what characterizes beauty and art (or for that matter politics and morality). It is almost as though their material and efficient causes were the only things of interest about them. Rousseau, by contrast, has infinitely more to say about such phenomena in their own terms. He provides us, for example, with richly nuanced discussions of the beauty and appeal of works of art,[58] of the harms that can be caused by works of art, of the crucial distinctions among artistic genres (novels as opposed to plays). Similarly, Rousseau's discussions of the character of competing social orders (pagan republics, Christian monarchies, oriental despotisms) are infinitely rich in comparison with the bland uniformity of Freud's wholly abstract notions of the social order.

These remarks may seem like harsh criticism of Freud, and in one sense they are meant to be. At the same time, it is worth noting that Freud himself was aware of, and in a curious sense proud of, the limitation of his thought to which I call attention here. Consider this passage from a letter by Freud to the psychoanalyst Ludwig Binswanger: "I have always lived on the ground floor and in the basement of the building—you maintain that on changing one's viewpoint one can also see an upper floor housing such distinguished guests as religion, art, and others. You are not the only one; most cultivated specimens of *homo natura* think likewise. In this respect you are the conservative, I the revolutionary" (letter of 8 October 1936).[59]

Freud's view to the contrary notwithstanding, Rousseau is the more comprehensive thinker, in that he gives us a better sense of the penthouse as well as the basement. On the other hand, to continue this analogy, Freud has the merit of recognizing that we naturally live in the family room; there is in Rousseau a disturbing and implausible vision suggesting that we might be better off as isolated, asexual, thoroughly independent beings, each of us living apart from all others in some sort of single room occupancy hotel.

NOTES

1. See Harry Trosman and Roger Dennis Simmons, "The Freud Library," *Journal of the American Psychoanalytic Association* 21 (1973): 646–87.

2. Sigmund Freud, *Three Essays on the Theory of Sexuality* (1905), in *The Standard Edition of the Complete Psychological Works of Sigmund Freud* (hereafter *SE*), vols. 1–24, ed. James Strachey, Anna Freud, and Alan Tyson (London: Hogarth Press, 1953–74), 7:193; idem, *Delusions and Dreams in Jensen's "Gradiva"* (1907), in *SE*, 9:36.

3. Jean-Jacques Rousseau, *Emile, or On Education*, trans. Allan Bloom (New York: Basic Books, 1979).

4. Sigmund Freud, *The Ego and the Id* (1923), in *SE*, 19:36; idem, *Inhibitions, Symptoms and Anxiety* (1926), in *SE*, 20:96.

5. Sigmund Freud, *Introductory Lectures on Psycho-Analysis* (1916–17), in *SE*, 16:314.

6. Consider Rousseau's development of this analogy: because men in the civil state are "no longer able to do without others," they become "weak and miserable." The analogy might therefore seem to suggest that all children are necessarily weak and miserable; but since it is "the rich, the nobles, [and] the kings" in particular whom he compares to children, Rousseau presumably means only that spoiled children—those who depart from the natural order—are weak and miserable.

7. One can, however, wonder whether the child's dependence can really be limited in this way. Rousseau claims that the child must never sense in his governor the existence of a will that can possibly oppose his own will; but that claim is immediately brought into question by Rousseau's statement that the child should receive the gover-

nor's "services as a sort of humiliation" (*Emile*, 86). Can the child be humiliated by his governor's assistance without seeing the governor as a second, rival, and possibly opposing will?

8. See also *Emile*, 222: "[Emile] has neither felt nor lied. Before knowing what it is to love, he has said, 'I love you,' to no one. . . . Indifferent to everything outside himself like all other children, he takes an interest in no one."

On the other hand, Rousseau also says that "the child ought to love his mother before knowing that he ought to" (*Emile*, 46), that as between the child and the governor, "it is very important for each to make himself loved by the other" (53), that the governor must not "turn [the child] away from loving [him]" (91). These passages seem to suggest that emotional dependence on others both is and ought to be an inescapable aspect of childhood; it is not clear that they are compatible with Rousseau's statements that appear to deny the reality (or at any rate the desirability) of that dependence.

9. Jean-Jacques Rousseau, *Second Discourse*, in *The First and Second Discourses*, ed. Roger D. Masters, trans. Roger D. Masters and Judith R. Masters (New York: St. Martin's Press, 1964).

10. Sigmund Freud, *The Interpretation of Dreams* (1900), in *SE*, 4:130.

11. Sigmund Freud, "My Contact with Josef Popper-Lynkeus" (1932), in *SE*, 22:222.

12. Ibid., 223.

13. Ibid., 221.

14. Freud, *Introductory Lectures on Psycho-Analysis*, 414. The sort of mental conflict Rousseau attributes to civilization is for Freud built into the human mind itself. See *Interpretation of Dreams*, 142, where Freud contends that dream censorship—through which we soften or disguise our unconscious wishes, especially our unconscious hatreds—can be analogized to "the politeness which I practice every day," which "is to a large extent dissimulation." Rousseau would blame hypocrisy of this sort on the corruption caused by civilization; Freud claims that such dissimulation is part of our innermost nature.

15. Ibid., 263.

16. Ibid., 580–81.

17. In *Emile* Rousseau remarks that "none of us is philosophic enough to know how to put himself in a child's place" (115), and that "a judicious man" ought "to give us a treatise on the art of observing children" (199). I do not claim that Freud is the judicious observer Rousseau hoped for; nevertheless, Freud does make a number of observations about children that seem to me to be correct, important, and in conflict with Rousseau's views.

18. Sigmund Freud, *Three Essays on the Theory of Sexuality*, 179–83.

19. Ibid., 182.

20. Sigmund Freud, *New Introductory Lectures on Psycho-Analysis* (1933), in *SE*, 22:123.

21. Freud, *Interpretation of Dreams*, 250.

22. Consider the analogous discussion in *Emile*, 66, where Rousseau recounts his

observation of an infant who had been struck by his nurse: "The unfortunate [child] was suffocating with anger; he had lost his breath; I saw him become violet. A moment after came sharp screams; all the signs of the resentment, fury, and despair of this age were in his accents. If I had doubted that the sentiment of the just and the unjust [was] innate in the heart of man, this example alone would have convinced me."

Freud commonsensically assumes that children will inevitably encounter oppressors, or wills in conflict with their own wills; Rousseau, by contrast, wishes to argue that an environment can be created for the child in which he will never encounter wills (like that of the irascible nurse) opposing his own. The child cannot avoid being burned by "a live ember" (a part of the natural order and a thing devoid of a will), but he need not be the recipient of a "blow" (delivered by a human possessing a will).

23. Cf. Thomas Hobbes, *De Cive*, in *Man and Citizen*, ed. Bernard Gert (Garden City, N.Y.: Doubleday, 1972), preface, 100, for exactly the same argument: "Yet are [children] free from guilt, neither may we properly call them wicked; first because they cannot hurt; next, because wanting the free use of reason they are exempted from all duty." Hobbes goes on to say that "a wicked man is almost the same thing with a child grown strong and sturdy"; for Rousseau's critique of this view, see *Emile*, 67.

24. Freud, *Interpretation of Dreams*, 251.

25. Freud, *Introductory Lectures on Psycho-Analysis*, 316.

26. Freud, *Three Essays on the Theory of Sexuality*, 187n.

27. Thomas Hobbes, *Leviathan*, ed. Michael Oakeshott (London: Collier, 1962), chap. 6, p. 51.

28. Freud, *Three Essays on the Theory of Sexuality*, 224n.

29. Sigmund Freud, *Beyond the Pleasure Principle* (1920), in *SE*, 18:17.

30. Ibid.

31. Sigmund Freud, "Creative Writers and Day-Dreaming" (1908), in *SE*, 9:146.

32. Ibid.

33. Freud, *New Introductory Lectures on Psycho-Analysis*, 131.

34. Sigmund Freud, "'Civilized' Sexual Morality and Modern Nervous Illness" (1908), in *SE*, 9:187.

35. Ibid., 185. Note that Freud puts the word "civilized" in quotation marks to underscore the question he raises about the value of civilization.

36. See also Jean-Jacques Rousseau, *Julie, ou La nouvelle Héloïse*, in *Oeuvres complètes*, vol. 2, ed. Bernard Gagnebin and Marcel Raymond (Paris: Pléiade, 1964), pt. 2, letter 26, 294–97, where Saint-Preux confesses to Julie that he has slept with a prostitute. A group of libertines (young army officers) bring him under false pretenses to a whorehouse and get him drunk. When Saint-Preux realizes what is happening he does not complain, because he fears that the officers would only make fun of him if he did.

37. Consider, for example, Freud's interpretation in *The Interpretation of Dreams*, 96–121, of what he calls his specimen dream (the dream through which he first illustrates his theory of dream interpretation). In the dream a female patient of his, Irma, is given an injection. Freud signally fails to offer what might ordinarily seem to be the most "Freudian" explanation of what that injection might represent. He also notes (105n)

that he intentionally does not bring forth "the *complete* interpretation" of any of his dreams.

38. See, however, Sigmund Freud, "On the Universal Tendency to Debasement in the Sphere of Love" (1912), in *SE*, 11:185, where Freud speaks of many men's "need for a debased sexual object." In such cases (and Freud thinks they are extremely common), potency is possible only where the man feels contempt for—a sense of superiority to—the sexual object.

But even if this passage indicates that amour propre does play a role in Freud's psychology of sex, Freud's treatment of amour propre is narrower than Rousseau's in that Freud focuses only on this unhealthy aspect of it; he does not sufficiently consider the plasticity of amour propre, the wide range of outcomes (healthy and unhealthy, moral and immoral) it can produce in our sexual lives. Both Freud and Rousseau pay great attention to human pathology, and both agree that the vast majority of humans are pathological; but Rousseau has more to say than Freud when it comes to depicting a standard of health according to which pathology can be judged and found wanting.

39. Sigmund Freud, *Civilization and Its Discontents* (1930), in *SE*, 21:134.

40. Ibid., 134n.

41. Freud, "On the Universal Tendency to Debasement in the Sphere of Love," 180.

42. Freud, *Three Essays on the Theory of Sexuality*, 200, 207.

43. Freud, "On the Universal Tendency to Debasement in the Sphere of Love," 189.

44. On one hand, Freud insists on a continuum that includes both sensual and affectionate (or moral) love: "The nucleus of what we mean by love naturally consists . . . in sexual love with sexual union as its aim. But we do not separate from this . . . love for parents and children, friendship and love for humanity in general" (Sigmund Freud, *Group Psychology and the Analysis of the Ego*, in *SE*, 18:90). But on the other hand, Freud also suggests that sexual and affectionate love are in large measure mutually exclusive: "Each sexual satisfaction always involves a reduction in sexual overvaluation" (ibid., 113); that is, in the lover's idealization of the beloved. Thus the union of physical and moral love is in Freud's view necessarily precarious.

45. Sigmund Freud, "On Psychotherapy" (1905), in *SE*, 7:267.

46. Freud, *Three Essays on the Theory of Sexuality*, 184.

47. Sigmund Freud, *Leonardo Da Vinci and a Memory of His Childhood* (1910), in *SE*, 11:96–97.

48. Freud, "On the Universal Tendency to Debasement in the Sphere of Love," 188–89.

49. Sigmund Freud, "Contributions to a Discussion of Masturbation" (1912), in *SE*, 12:247.

50. Freud, *Three Essays on the Theory of Sexuality*, 191.

51. Freud's German term is *Ersatzobjecten*, which suggests that the replacement objects are not only substitutes for the original, but also inferior to it.

52. Freud, "On the Universal Tendency to Debasement in the Sphere of Love," 189.

53. Ibid.

54. On another level, it is the disgustingness and not the attractiveness of excrement that poses a problem for sexual development; thus Freud argues that the proximity of the genitalia to the organs of excretion accounts for "a primary repelling attitude . . . towards sexual life" (Freud, *Civilization and Its Discontents*, 106n). Compare this passage with *Emile*, 217: "Follow the spirit of nature which, by putting in the same place the organs of the secret pleasures and those of the disgusting needs, inspires in us the same cares at different ages, now due to one idea, then due to another; in the man due to modesty, in the child due to cleanliness." Unlike Freud, Rousseau characteristically assumes that the development from childhood to adulthood is (at least in principle) reasonably smooth and unproblematic; far from posing a problem, the physical link between excretion and procreation offers a solution.

55. Freud, *Three Essays on the Theory of Sexuality*, 151–52.

56. Freud, *Civilization and Its Discontents*, 100n.

57. Freud, "'Civilized' Sexual Morality and Modern Nervous Illness," 156n.

58. Consider in this context Richard Velkley's discussion in chapter 4 of this volume of Rousseau's understanding of the various ways the love of poetry can serve the end of human wholeness.

59. Sigmund Freud, *The Letters of Sigmund Freud* (1960), ed. Ernst L. Freud, trans. Tania Stern and James Stern (New York: Basic Books, 1975), 431.

❧ 6 ❧
Rousseau and the Rediscovery of Human Nature

ROGER D. MASTERS

The legacy of Jean-Jacques Rousseau includes a central contribution to the natural and social sciences: his insistence that early modern political thought, whether in the Anglo-Saxon version stemming from Hobbes and Locke or in the Continental tradition derived from Spinoza and Descartes, had failed to understand "human nature." Rousseau's challenge to his predecessors, implicit in the *First Discourse,* became explicit—and explosive—in the *Discourse on the Origin of Inequality:* the task of philosophy is to discover the "nature" of man, hidden beneath the transformations of history and society over the "multitudes of centuries" separating contemporary humans from their animal ancestors.

In antiquity, it was widely thought probable that humans had evolved from an animal existence that was prepolitical. Machiavelli clearly endorsed this pagan tradition in his critique of the Christian view of human nature, but Hobbes and Locke replaced the ancient account with a model of what they called the "state of nature." Rousseau retained the modern conceptualization but attempted to reestablish much of the ancient content, and in so doing he provided a major impetus that contributed to the emergence of evolutionary biology.

It is impossible to assess this scientific legacy of Rousseau without attempting to relate natural science and political philosophy. These subjects were once less distinct than in today's universities (as is illustrated by the now obsolete term "natural philosophy"). Although few contemporary philosophers have challenged the divorce between what C. P. Snow called "the two cultures," Leo Strauss and some of those strongly influenced by his teaching (including Allan Bloom and Leon Kass), have pointed to the ultimate need to confront the teachings of political philosophers with the findings of contemporary scientists.[1] Such a confrontation is particularly fitting in an assessment of Rousseau's thought because, notably in the *Second Discourse* and *Essay on the Origin of Languages,* he could be seen as a precursor of the historical or evolutionary approach that, since Darwin, has produced profound changes in our knowledge of the origins and nature of the human species.

There is great irony, however, in confronting Rousseau's account of human nature with today's scientific approach to the questions he proclaimed would be suited to the "Aristotles and Plinys of our century."[2] While research in the life sciences shows that Rousseau's theoretical assumptions are superior to those of Hobbes and Locke, this evidence also challenges a crucial aspect of Rousseau's understanding of human nature. Rousseau saw the "goodness" of man in the pure state of nature as that of an animal with "positive" sentiments but without the "negative" emotions associated with amour propre or social comparison (or in Freud's terms, an individual with eros but not thanatos). Recent scientific research in ethology, neuroscience, and behavioral ecology leads to a paradoxical criticism of Rousseau: humans are innately social animals whose psychology and politics are more clearly understood by the ancient tradition of Plato and Aristotle than by modern political philosophy.

Rousseau's Scientific Legacy

It is not widely enough realized that Rousseau has had an immense *scientific* as well as philosophic influence. Rousseau's vigorous insistence on a historical approach to human nature antedated Darwin's *Origin of Species* by a century and (through the intermediary of Charles Bonnet and other naturalists) contributed to the awareness that traditional biology—or "natural history," as it was then called—could not explain the origins and transformation of animal species. As a result, Rousseau's questions stimulated the scientists of his own day and remain of immense importance in fields ranging from psychology, anthropology, and linguistics to human ethology and behavioral ecology.

The strictly scientific legacy of Rousseau's thought has been overshadowed by the attention devoted to his philosophic, political, and literary influence on the Western tradition. This tendency is unfortunate, for Rousseau's persistent focus on human nature and the mechanisms (as well as the limits) by which it could be reshaped was motivated as much by the quest for the truth of science as by the critique of moral corruption: his attempt to combine *verité* and *vertu* necessarily transcends the divisions that characterize contemporary universities.[3]

To understand Rousseau and relate his thought to our own time, it is therefore important to consider scientific analyses of human origins and social behavior that are all too often ignored by intellectual historians. In the remarks that follow, I shall survey the principal features of Rousseau's theory of human nature and indicate how it is supported, modified, or contradicted by contemporary work in the natural and social sciences.

Such an examination confirms Rousseau's critique of the modern individualist or bourgeois tradition exemplified by Hobbes and Locke: human nature is neither as selfish nor as capable of a rational calculus of cost and benefit as would appear from the laissez-faire economists, rational-choice theorists, and philosophic liberals who continue to elaborate the Lockean view of human nature. Paradoxically, however, contemporary research has also challenged Rousseau's own "system," leading to renewed interest in the classic or Aristotelian view of our species as "the political animal." To see how this could be, let us begin by restating the principles of Rousseau's political and social theory before summarizing contemporary research that addresses the themes he so clearly articulated.

Rousseau's "System" and the Natural Man

Rousseau's critique of early modern philosophy and political life first attracted public attention in 1750 when the Academy of Dijon awarded its prize to the *Discourse on the Sciences and Arts*. To explain why conformism, deception, and vice had followed the spread of enlightenment in Western societies, Rousseau claimed that this process reflected an irreversible historical change that could be observed in all societies that have cultivated science and literature. Humans, although now subject to "chains," were once good and free.

Rousseau's dream of transparency, which has been so well articulated by Jean Starobinski,[4] thus reflected a vision of human history:

> Before Art had molded our manners and taught our passions to speak an affected language, our morals were rustic but natural, and differences of conduct announced at first glance those of character. Human nature, basically, was no better, but men found their security in the ease of seeing through each other, and that advantage, which we no longer appreciate, spared them many vices.[5]

Although it emphasizes the importance of changes in the human condition, this passage fails to indicate the precise historical process, which we today call hominid evolution, by which humans have moved away from the "lovely shore, adorned by the hands of Nature alone." As we can confirm from such texts as the *Préface d'une seconde lettre à Bordes*, Rousseau chose not to present his theory of human history until the publication of the *Discourse on the Origin of Inequality* (*Second Discourse*) in 1755.[6]

Rousseau's celebrated image of equality and freedom in the state of nature in the *Second Discourse* provides the theoretical model of natural man that underlies his critique of the moral corruption of modern society in the *First Discourse*. Originally, each human was an animal "wandering in the forests, without industry, without speech, without domicile, without war and without liaisons, with no need of his fellows, likewise with no desire to harm them, perhaps never even recognizing anyone individually."[7] In short, original human nature was very much like—and perhaps even identical to—that of the chimpanzees or orangutans observed by Europeans traveling in Africa and Asia.

This image of human origins permits Rousseau to discover the difference between the passions natural to humans and those resulting from historical change and social institutions.

> Amour-propre and love of oneself, two passions very different in their Nature and their effects, must not be confused. Love of oneself is a natural sentiment which inclines every animal to watch over its own preservation. . . . Amour-propre is only a relative sentiment, artificial and born in Society, which inclines each individual to have a greater esteem for himself than for any one else. . . . in our primitive state, in the genuine state of Nature, amour-propre does not exist.[8]

Human evil, then, can be traced to the emergence of new passions that were not originally present in our species.

Given this radically historical analysis of human nature, Rousseau had to postulate a long process of transformation leading to the emergence of language, stable social institutions, and moral as well as political corruption. In this transformation, the condition that was both most durable and "best for man" was "savage society"—the so-called primitive way of life encountered as Europeans conquered and colonized Africa and the New World.

Rousseau is aware, therefore, that the savages of North America or black Africa were separated from the "pure state of nature" by an evolutionary process over "multitudes of centuries." Despite those transformations, savage society had not yet succumbed to the vices Rousseau denounces in the *First*

Discourse and can therefore serve as a model of human freedom and goodness: "As long as men were content with their rustic huts . . . they lived free, healthy, good, and happy insofar as they could be according to their Nature, and they continued to enjoy among themselves the sweetness of independent intercourse."[9] Although individual autonomy—the absence of the "personal dependence" characterizing civilized societies—is the principal attribute of savage society, humans at this stage of history also have psychological characteristics that differ from those of civilized men.

In the pure state of nature, individuals were motivated primarily by self-love (*amour de soi*). In this original human condition, although the actions contributing to self-preservation may have been qualified by vague feelings of pity at the sight of another's suffering, such other-directed sentiments depend on a power of imagination that would have been impossible; even when compassion arose, moreover, it could not overpower the more urgent demands of self-interest. Hence the goodness of the pure state of nature is primarily based on the combination of narrow self-interest and stupidity rather than either the rationality of the natural law tradition or the pity or compassion Rousseau himself attempted to use as the ground of sociability.

Rousseau's theory of human nature therefore treats social feelings as the product of hominid evolution; all society is in this sense radically conventional. Pity is the first other-directed sentiment not only because it is a prerational passion that does not require calculation and thought, but also because it can be traced to self-interest: as soon as humans can imagine themselves in the position of another who is suffering, assistance to relieve the suffering can arise as a means of generating one's own feelings of happiness.

For Rousseau, therefore, the analysis of human nature requires a radical reexamination of self-regarding and other-regarding feelings on the assumption that the latter must necessarily be unnatural products of historical development. If self-love is a pleasant or positive feeling, in itself inconsistent with intentionally harming others, Rousseau had to explain the origins of social competition and the aggressive selfishness of Hobbes's warlike state of nature. Rousseau does so by emphasizing the difference between self-love and such passions as vanity or pride (amour propre), which lie at the root of competition and the quest for power over others.

Rousseau's understanding of this difference was ultimately derived from reconsidering Locke's distinction between passive responses to external stimuli ("sensation") and the active transformations of these sensations by the human mind ("reflection").[10] Late in life, Rousseau articulated his understanding of the connection between the "active" or "moral" capacity of the human mind and the social passions arising from amour propre as follows:

> There is a purely passive physical and organic sensitivity which seems to have as its end only the preservation of our bodies and of our species through the direction of pleasure and pain. There is another sensitivity that I call active and moral which is nothing other than the faculty of attaching our affections to beings who are foreign to us. This type, about which study of nerve pairs teaches nothing, seems to offer a fairly clear analogy for souls to the magnetic faculty of bodies . . . depending on the nature of these relationships it sometimes acts positively by attraction, sometimes negatively by repulsion, like the poles of a magnet. The positive or attracting action is the simple work of nature, which seeks to extend and reinforce the feeling of our being; the negative or repelling action, which compresses and diminishes the being of another, is a combination produced by reflection. From the former arise all the loving and gentle passions, and from the later all the hateful and cruel passions. Please recall at this point, Sir, along with the distinctions made in our first conversations between love of oneself and amour-propre, the manner in which each of them acts on the human heart.[11]

In short, to understand Rousseau's view of human nature, it is necessary to make two fundamental distinctions: first, the passive responses characteristic of the pure state of nature came to be supplemented by active, other-directed feelings and thoughts; second, these active or "moral" feelings can be either positive, producing pleasurable bonds with others, or negative and competitive. The latter, as a "combination produced by reflection," is unnatural; it is also the source of pride, competition, and moral evil.

On this basis, Rousseau develops a theory of human nature in which there are no fewer than three distinct situations that are positive or desirable: the natural goodness of the pure state of nature and its residue in the savage societies of North America and Africa (still dominated by passive sentiments), virtuous civilized societies like ancient Sparta and Rome (dominated by the positive moral sentiment of patriotism), and the artificial return to goodness of the solitary walker (who voluntarily chooses to retreat to the passivity that Rousseau describes in his *Reveries*).

It is neither possible nor necessary to articulate here the way these three peaks of human excellence relate to each other or to Rousseau's theory of human nature: that is the task of interpretations of the coherence of Rousseau's "system."[12] Instead, let us turn to the contemporary scientific findings that address the questions Rousseau thought essential to an adequate understanding of human behavior and society.

Rousseau's Theory in the Light of Contemporary Science
THE "CRY OF NATURE": ETHOLOGY, EMOTION, AND NONVERBAL BEHAVIOR

Although other eighteenth-century thinkers like Hume and Adam Smith also emphasized the feelings or passions as powerful limitations on human rationality, Rousseau's historical or evolutionary approach to human nature led him to connect these individual feelings with the communication of emotion to others. Hence, when Rousseau asserts that the "cry of nature" is the first communicative act, he admits that such nonverbal signals are an animal "language" that must have been shared by the earliest humans.[13] He thus understood that the expression of emotion is the basis of *social* interaction as well as the visible sign of an *individual's* "sentiments" or passions.

This relation between emotions or subjective feelings and the organization of social interaction became a central issue for Charles Darwin, whose *Expression of Emotion in Animals and in Man*[14] showed how the approach of evolutionary science could transform what had long been merely philosophical speculation about human nature. More recently, Darwin's approach to the nature of human feelings and nonverbal communication has been explored by scientists in three disciplines: ethology (the observation and analysis of animal behavior, especially in "field" or naturalistic settings), social psychology (the study of human responses, particularly in controlled laboratory experiments), and neuroscience (the exploration of the structure and function of the brain, which has revolutionized our knowledge of the biological foundations of thought and emotion over the past decade).[15]

These extensive studies confirm Rousseau's insight that there is a natural language of the emotions arising from the fundamental difference between "positive" (pleasurable or hedonic) and "negative" (competitive or agonic) feelings. Although some social psychologists developed the theory that emotions are naturally undifferentiated responses whose positive or negative direction or "valence" depends on the cognitive assessment of the stimulus, it is now increasingly evident that these two systems of response are naturally distinct. Not only are the positive and negative feelings processed by different structures in the brain, but the nonverbal displays of animals differentiate sharply between hedonic behaviors associated with pleasure or bonding and agonic cues of threat or flight. Among nonhuman primates, moreover, these two dimensions of emotion are communicated by nonverbal cues that are highly similar to those of humans.[16] The study of individual emotion and the way it is communicated in social interactions has thus become a central means of understanding human nature from a scientific perspective.

What Rousseau called amour propre—social comparisons leading to competition for dominance—is an innate characteristic of the monkeys and apes who provide evidence of our animal origins. On the one hand, since Konrad Lorenz and Niko Tinbergen developed scientific methods for studying animal behavior, ethologists have repeatedly shown the critical role of displays of threat and dominance behaviors in other species; on the other, neuroscientists have confirmed Paul MacLean's "triune" model of the brain, in which the limbic system regulates emotions and social behavior among mammals. Hence it is impossible to understand such species as wolves, cats, and dogs without recognizing the natural origins of sociability.[17]

Although social structures among primates vary from the asociality of the orangutan (so strikingly similar to the individual isolation in Rousseau's image of the pure state of nature) to the highly structured groups of hamadryas baboons and rhesus monkeys (in which dominant males seem to regulate access to food and females), the combination of agonic and hedonic display behavior is innate to all primates—and indeed to mammals more generally. Human beings can no longer pretend that their emotions and sentiments are unrelated to those of animals. Far from being an unnatural acquisition due to society, therefore, the feelings and behaviors associated with social competition and dominance are as natural as those underlying pleasure and bonding.

"The Study of Nerve Pairs": Neuroscience, Modularity, and the Social Brain

Although confirming Rousseau's insight that one cannot understand human emotions without studying the "cry of nature" in other animals, contemporary scientific research contradicts his theory in other important respects. Rousseau's understanding of the distinction between "active" and "passive sensitivity" can no longer be sustained. The "study of nerve pairs"—now called neuroscience—explains the way the human brain "sometimes acts positively by attraction, sometimes negatively by repulsion" in a very different way: not only is what Rousseau called "physical or organic sensibility" *active* rather than passive, but both the "loving and gentle passions" and those he considered "hateful and cruel" are perceived and expressed by innate structures in the mammalian central nervous system.

In the eighteenth century, the dominant understanding of the human brain was derived from Locke's *Essay Concerning Human Understanding*, which postulates a sharp distinction between the "sensation" (which is "passive") and "reflection" (in which the mind is "active"). According to Locke, who in this respect follows Hobbes,[18] sensation occurs when "the senses . . . from external objects convey into the mind what produces there those perceptions" or "ideas," a process in which the mind is passive. In contrast, reflection is the active process consisting of "the perception of the operations of our own mind within us, as it is employed about the ideas it has got;—which operations, when the soul comes to reflect on and consider, do furnish the understanding with another set of ideas, which could not be had from things without."[19] As is clear from the analysis of sensation and thought in book 2 of *Emile*, this distinction between an active process of reflection or thought (generated internally within the conscious mind of a human being) and the passivity of sense impressions is the foundation of Rousseau's understanding of the passions cited above.

Neuroscientists today have more direct means of studying the actions of "pairs of nerves" than were accessible to Locke (who participated in dissections of the brain) or Rousseau (whose personal theological beliefs led to a preference for a dualist view of the mind).[20] Even the simplest sensory perception is now viewed as an active, "self-organized dynamic process" in which the brain itself constantly generates and modifies "activity patterns."[21] Conversely, much of the information processing that Locke called active "reflection" (arising from "the different actings of our own minds;—which we being conscious of, and observing in ourselves") now appears to be unconscious or preconscious.[22]

To see how the recent transformation in the scientific understanding of the brain has occurred, it is necessary to relate discoveries in neuroanatomy to the analysis of perception, emotion, and thought. Broadly speaking, there are three principal structures in the human or mammalian central nervous system, which has been conceptualized by Paul MacLean as the "triune brain": the brain stem or "R-complex" (the structures, already developed in the reptiles, controlling simple consummatory behaviors of copulation, eating, and dominance), the limbic system (which first emerged in mammals and controls emotion), and the cortex (whose greatest enlargement is seen among the primates, and which controls both information processing and complex social and communicative behavior).

Each of these structures is itself a highly complex system. Far from the tabula rasa of Locke and the empiricists, the central nervous system is a highly structured array of neurons in which localized sections of the cortex are pre-programmed to respond to very specific cues in the environment. In the visual cortex, for example, there are precisely localized neuronal structures that respond to color, movement, or shape; the functional capacities of each specialized structure or "module" can be traced to computational algorithms that are linked to form a complex parallel processing system. Neuroscientists therefore speak of the "modular" structure of the brain and have developed "connectionist" models to explain how these specialized local modules are linked in a complex parallel processing system.[23]

These characteristics of the brain are directly related to social behavior. For example, several distinct pathways lead from the retina to the visual cortex (at the back of the brain), the neocortex (where information is processed and compared with memory), and the limbic system (where the stimulus elicits emotional responses associated with pleasure, pain, and survival). One of these pathways ("dorsal")—which leads from the retinal cells (the eye) to a specific type of neuron in a structure known as the lateral geniculate and thence to structures in the cortex on the sides of the brain (the inferior temporal lobes)—differentially processes the shapes of objects; corresponding to this perceptual pathway is an area in the frontal cortex devoted to working memory, which is also specialized in the processing of the shape of objects (the "inferior prefrontal convexity"). Recent studies have shown that in primates, approximately 10 percent of the neurons in the inferior temporal lobes respond *only* to the faces of other individuals of the same species; among these cells, moreover, some fire only in response to specific movements of the face (e.g., an upward movement that is often associated with displays of threat, the head tilt associated with reassurance, etc.). This innate preprogramming of the brain is, moreover, not limited to perception, since a similar proportion of the neurons in the object-recognition structure of the prefrontal cortex are also specialized in the perception of faces.

Such studies show that, contrary to the assertions of the empiricist philosophers, there are indeed "innate ideas" in the brain. Happiness and reassurance are social cues that correspond to preprogrammed perceptual and motor responses in the human infant. Not only are similar nonverbal displays perceived as signs of happiness and reassurance in the most diverse cultures, but infants respond differentially to these cues; the displays in question can hardly be learned, for even blind infants exhibit similar displays as expressions of the corresponding emotions. And—consistent with Rousseau's understanding of our primate origins—it should not be surprising to discover that though there are cultural differences in emotional expressions, the specific cues forming the human repertoire of facial displays are common to primates more generally.

The human central nervous system can thus be called a "social brain" in at least three senses. First, the brain has inborn structures that are preprogrammed to perform a diversity of functional capacities, which then need to be integrated like the behaviors of individuals in a "social" system.[24] Second, the innate capacities of the brain include schemata of social behaviors; Konrad Lorenz seems to have been correct when he spoke of a "parliament of instincts" that includes reassurance, bonding, aggressiveness, and flight.[25] Finally (though this point is still controversial), the enlargement of the *human* brain cannot be explained by the supposed advantages of increased intelligence: the large human brain may be the consequence—not the cause—of social cooperation. Not only do nonhuman primates have many of the cognitive capacities long considered unique in humans, but the enlargement of the brain occurred *after* the transition to bipedal stature and tool use. Even more important, since the change to bipedal stature rendered childbirth much more dangerous for the human female than for chimpanzees or other primates, it seems likely that natural selection worked *against* increases in brain size rather than in favor of them.

While this last point confirms Rousseau's claim that human ancestors could have survived in the "pure state of nature," it suggests the radical hypothesis that the enlargement of the human brain some 500,000 years ago would have been impossible without social cooperation, especially between the pregnant woman and other females of the band. If true, this would mean that the role of midwife was essential in the emergence of the large-brained species known as *Homo sapiens sapiens*.[26] Even if this interpretation is called into question, it cannot be denied that the human brain is a *social* organ to a degree that not only Rousseau, but modern philosophy more generally, has failed to appreciate.

SOCIAL DISPLAYS, DECEPTION, AND
SELF-CONSCIOUS THOUGHT
Nonhuman Primates and the Origins of Morality

In a long and very important note to the *Second Discourse* (usually numbered XI or J, depending on the edition),[27] Rousseau called for the scientific study of those animals like chimpanzees and orangutans who might hold the key to understanding human nature. Over the past generation, the pioneering observations of Jane Goodall, Dian Fossey, and Biruté Galdikas have been supplemented by numerous long-term studies of both wild and captive groups. It is now evident that primates differ in the precise patterns of social behavior not only between one species and another, but from one population or even one individual to another. What Rousseau called the "moral" acquisitions due to "society"—or, in contemporary terms, "culture"—are not uniquely human.

Only recently, for example, have the patterns of tool use and social behavior been compared among all known groups of chimpanzees. The results call into question the neo-Marxian assumption that the making and use of tools is constitutive of human as distinct from animal behavior, and demonstrate that apart from the use of verbal language, chimpanzees meet all the conventional criteria for cultural variability.[28] Speech may indeed differentiate humans from other animals, but as Rousseau pointed out, this difference does not permit us to assume that monkeys or apes lack intentionality or purpose in their behavior.[29]

Careful observations of the social displays of nonhuman primates provide evidence that, at least among chimpanzees and other great apes, there is a degree of intentionality. For example, chimpanzees not only form shifting alliances as a way of competing for dominance but exhibit reciprocity in grooming behavior and the sharing of food, both favoring others who have previously cooperated and punishing those who fail to do so.[30] Among the best indications of this emerging capacity to modify behavior are social interactions in which one chimpanzee uses nonverbal cues to mislead another.

Two examples described by Frans de Waal indicate not only that primates are capable of a degree of intentionality long thought to be uniquely human, but that these instances of social deception often arise in the context of competitive or agonistic relationships (or what Rousseau described as the "negative sentiments" supposedly due to human society). In one case a dominant male chimpanzee being challenged by a coalition of two others was sitting with his back to them; hearing a threat call by one of the rivals, the dominant male exhibited the facial expression of fear (what Jan van Hooff has described as the "silent bare teeth scream face"), put his hands to his mouth to remove the telltale grimace, and—once composed—turned to face the challengers. In another situation, on seeing a sexually receptive female, a subordinate male exhibited the display inviting copulation (sitting back with legs spread to show a penile erection)—only to see the dominant male come into sight; since dominant males typically prevent copulations between subordinate males and females, using threat displays and even physical attacks, the subordinate male reacted to the sight of the dominant by covering his penis with his hands.[31]

Although evidence of consciousness is widespread in other animals, these instances of apparent intentionality reflect three capacities: an awareness of the likely effect of one's own behavior on others, some conception of the results of the others' response to that behavior, and—-to avoid these consequences— manipulation of one's own behavior to change the outcome. In short, the evidence is now very strong that even the corrupting effects Rousseau attributed to amour propre can be seen in at least one other species that lacks verbal language and human civilization.

What Rousseau described as "moral relationships"—intentional or active behaviors of competition and cooperation based on the individual's assessment of the relative worth of others—exist among other animals. Although perhaps less fully developed in chimpanzees than in humans, the intentional manipulation of the "negative" or competitive sentiments was likely to have been present at the origin of hominid evolution. Now that biologists have described and explained the importance of "moralistic aggression" among animals,[32] it is no longer possible to accept Rousseau's claim (cited above) that "in our primitive state, in the genuine state of Nature, amour-propre does not exist."

Rousseau's view of the state of nature as a condition of perfect "transparency" in which positive sentiments were unsullied by the negative feelings of competition and pride is thus no longer tenable. What Arthur Melzer has called the "cult of sincerity" in his contribution to this volume is more precisely understood—and its possibility more fully challenged—when analyzed in the light of the scientific research that, in this century, has fulfilled Rousseau's injunction to subject the similarities and differences between human and non-human primates to the most rigorous study.

SELF-DECEPTION AS A MEANS OF DECEPTION:
EVOLUTIONARY BIOLOGY, REASON, AND MORALITY

Human nature is thus more complex than Rousseau expected. Not only is there a natural language of the emotions that humans share with other animals (as he well understood), but the ability to manipulate nonverbal communication points to the importance of dominance, subordination, and deception among the nonhuman primates who provide our best insights into human origins. What do these discoveries teach us about the roots of social behavior and evil?

Among other animals, the effectiveness of deception is limited by the difficulty of controlling the outward expression of the individual's actual emotion. Although a chimpanzee may successfully hide displays of fear or sexual invitation, typically the emotions or motivations being hidden will "leak" through in other behavioral manifestations. A classic example is described among vervet monkeys by Cheney and Seyfarth. When a previously unaffiliated mature male sought to join a group of vervets, a subordinate male whose status would have been further lowered by the newcomer's arrival gave the species' warning display for a dangerous snake; the potential rival fled in terror—but the deceptive vervet then nonchalantly walked across the clearing where the snake supposedly lay (much as a child might leave cookie crumbs on his chin while vehemently denying having touched the cookie jar).

Such leakage of actual or "true" motivations is probably due to the very close neurological relation between the centers of the brain that regulate the emotions and the motor coordinations for expressing them. At the neuroscientific level, this automaticity of emotional display is well demonstrated among humans as well as nonhuman primates. When actors produce the facial display associated with an emotion, one muscle at a time, they elicit within themselves the physiological correlates of the feelings displayed. When citizens watch a political leader on television, the sight of the leader's facial display instantaneously activates the muscles producing a similar emotional expression in the viewer, whose emotional responses (as later reported verbally) correspond to these feelings; though the viewer's consciousness can modify the intensity and direction of the response, humans seem naturally predisposed to perceive and express socially relevant feelings.[33]

It follows that the most reliable way of deceiving another is to engage in self-deception. Since an expression of emotion that would be contrary to one's self-interest can most safely be hidden by experiencing the expected or socially "appropriate" feelings, the most effective strategy for cheating others is to be convinced that one's own intentions are "pure." Although a long philosophic tradition followed Rousseau's view that deception is produced by an "active" or conscious intention to mislead, the evolved system of emotional expression constantly undermines such behavior in all but the most accomplished liars.

In one sense this consequence of scientific studies of emotion reinforces Rousseau's skepticism concerning reason. Much human manipulation of social behavior seems to be preconscious or unconscious. The neuroscientist Michael Gazzaniga has shown experimentally that there is a center in the brain capable of inventing missing information to produce congruence among apparently discrepant facts; called the "interpreter module," this function—localized in the left hemisphere—is not associated with language and consciousness.[34]

It should be no surprise that the consciously expressed "reasons" for behavior are often rationalizations for motivations of which we are dimly aware or which we have consciously repressed. Much human learning lies beneath conscious awareness. Indeed, there are many skills (such as athletic performance at a high level of proficiency) which are seriously disturbed if one attempts to be fully conscious of what is being done. In place of the Freudian unconscious, contemporary neuroscience has discovered a "modular" brain in which a broad array of active information processing and emotion lies beyond the normal reach of consciousness and language, becoming accessible to speech only when attention is focused on introspection rather than action. The very structure of the human brain points to the embarrassing fact that speech and language are often devices for deceiving ourselves as well as—and perhaps even more successfully than—deceiving others.

This challenge to the equation of rationality and morality is reinforced by a second line of research, based on the latest techniques by which images of the brain reveal the precise structures involved in perception, feeling, and thought. As these detailed studies have confirmed, the capacity for moral behavior depends on the activation of those centers of the brain that integrate emotions and cognitive planning (including the frontal cortex and temporal lobes).[35] For diverse reasons, some people—known as "primary psychopaths"—lack the capacities for empathy and emotional arousal apparently required for moral judgement; such individuals have abnormal emotional responses associated with distinct patterns of brain function.[36] In short, not only do some humans lack moral standards, but in extreme cases immoral behavior is associated with deficits in feeling, not an inability to reason. As a result, such psychopaths often engage in elaborate plans and self-deception in the process of harming others.

The capacity for evil—intentionally harming others for one's own benefit—can thus be substantially *enhanced* by the development of human language and rationality. Even though nonhuman primates engage in comparisons with others, competing for social dominance and access to resources, this evidence is consistent with Rousseau's attack on reason as a means of "isolating" individuals from the feelings of others and thereby as a source of violence, crime, and immorality. Whatever the shortcomings of Rousseau's theory of natural sensibility, his critique of Hobbesian rationality cannot be easily dismissed.

Nature's "Invincible Empire": Behavioral Ecology, Human Nature, and History

As Rousseau argued, the transformations of human nature over the course of history have been extraordinary. Although today we take such an evolutionary account for granted, Rousseau—writing a century before Darwin—faced readers who were more likely to believe in the biblical account of creation. To avoid theological controversy when explaining human evolution in the *Second Discourse*, Rousseau therefore focused on the faculty of "perfectibility" as the source of the property, social inequality, slavery, violence, and misery observed in civilized societies. Although the concept of perfectibility allowed Rousseau to leave open the "metaphysical" question of whether these changes were due to the free will of an immortal soul, today some commentators have erroneously concluded that, according to Rousseau, nature places no limitations whatever on the malleability or openness of human society.

In Rousseau's thought, nature imposes two different limitations on human civilization, one formal and the other substantive. Formally, the legitimacy of civil society is constrained by the necessity that political institutions conform to the "nature of law"—the logic of obedience elaborated in Rousseau's "principles of political right" (and notably in his celebrated doctrine of the general will). Substantively, the content of a civilized society's regime must conform to the nature of its size, geographic situation, and history. Whereas the first of these constraints has been the subject of an enormous literature, the second—derived from Rousseau's reading of Montesquieu and elaborated at even greater length in the *Social Contract* (from book 2, chapter 8 through book 3, chapter 18)—has unfortunately been ignored by political scientists.

According to Rousseau's explicit assertion, the political institutions of any given society must conform to the necessities of its material situation. Failure to respect these limits will, he states emphatically, lead to conflict and instability "until nature regains her invincible empire."[37] Far from being free to produce any social and political institution at will, humans as a species are as limited by nature within civil society as they were in the state of nature. Or to put it the other way around, nature remains a standard within civil society, although the consequence of human perfectibility is that the natural characteristics and constraints impinging on civilized politics differ from those in the pure state of nature.

Confusion can easily arise in this regard because in describing the pure state of nature, Rousseau focused on the nature of the individual (on the assumption that the primitive "regularity" of the original human condition precluded substantial differences from one population to another), whereas human history has introduced linguistic, economic, political, cultural, and even physical variations from one people to another. As a result, the natural constraints on entire societies concern the relation between economic, political, or cultural institutions and the environment—that is, the type of "natural" factors that can be used to explain the difference between one species of animal and another (rather than differences between one individual and another).

Contemporary natural and social scientists have explored natural constraints on social behavior at this level. In cultural anthropology, a field that some (e.g., Claude Lévi-Strauss) have traced directly to Rousseau, such explanations of the nature of society sometimes emphasize the relation between a people's mode of livelihood and its institutions of kinship, social behavior, or law.[38] More recently, in the field of behavioral ecology, similar principles have been used to account for differences in the social behavior of nonhuman species.[39]

It is therefore instructive to reconsider briefly the three main stages of human evolution outlined in the *Second Discourse* from the perspective of behavioral ecology and related approaches in anthropology. In so doing, I will rely heavily on a major new work that integrates the study of nonhuman primates and human cultures: *The Social Cage: Human Nature and the Evolution of Society*, by Alexandra Maryanski and Jonathan Turner.[40] How, then, do contemporary scientists understand the stages of human history that Rousseau called the "pure state of nature," "savage society," and "civil society" (or "the state")?

Freedom and Equality among the Hunter-Gatherers

Although direct evidence of the social life of our earliest hominid ancestors is inaccessible to us, three lines of evidence point to life in small bands of between twenty-five and one hundred scavenger-gatherers or hunter-gatherers. First, the nonhuman primates that have been observed over the past generation form groups of this scale, suggesting limits to the likely social structure of what Maryanski and Turner call the "last common ancestor" between humans and apes. Second, studies of the differences between australopithecine and hominid fossils as well as of the environment in which this evolution took place indicate that our ancestors must have modified earlier modes of livelihood during the transition to fully bipedal stature and enlarged cranial capacity. And finally, surviving populations of hunter-gatherers, like the San of the Kalahari, provide evidence of the viability and characteristics of band organizations of this scale living in comparable ecological settings.

The resulting picture of hominid origins differs from the "pure state of nature" of Rousseau's *Second Discourse* in several important ways. Our earliest ancestors were forced to adapt to a savanna habitat that would have precluded asocial foraging like that among the orangutans (who live in a forest environment of abundant food and few predators); although the solitude Rousseau attributed to "natural man" exists among a few other primates, it was not likely to have been characteristic of early hominid social life. Before the invention of stone tools, scavenging may have been more important than hunting, but since even chimpanzees use tools and on occasion hunt, early hominids were omnivores who were probably more sophisticated in their mode of food acquisition than Rousseau imagined. A lasting pair bond, though not necessarily lifelong monogamy (found in gibbons but not in other apes), was likely between males and females.

Some elements of dominance or leadership in the band seem inevitable, since these social relations are so ubiquitous in nonhuman primates, though such roles entailed limited authority and could be filled by either males or females. Group membership need not have been rigidly fixed, since individuals probably left one band to join another (not only at puberty, when female apes leave their natal band, but perhaps even later in life). Decisions were likely to have been based on consensus.

Maryanski and Turner summarize the likely social structure of the last common ancestor of nonhuman primates and early hominids as a network of "loose ties" in which individuals have a high degree of autonomy. Unlike Old World monkeys, in which groups are typically structured around more rigid dominance patterns and tighter bonds, both surviving ape species and contemporary hunter-gatherers are highly egalitarian and provide broad opportunities for individual variability. Hence in chimpanzees, as in humans, the foraging group varies from day to day, individuals exhibit markedly different types of personality, and bands establish strikingly varied "cultural" traditions.

Paradoxically, these findings confirm Rousseau's emphasis on equality and freedom in the pure state of nature even though they contradict many of the details of his account. Rousseau was aware, of course, that "savage man" could well have lived in groups, much like those of the "monkeys and crows" whose nonverbal communication (the "cry of nature") is described as the model for early human language; such a band is, moreover, described as engaged in hunting deer in part 2 of the *Second Discourse*. Even if Rousseau underestimated the extent and complexity of social life among our earliest ancestors, his main point is that without verbal language, agriculture, and complex social or political institutions, humans would have been far more independent and egalitarian than in any civilized human society.

"Savage Society," Morality, and the Cage of Kinship

For Rousseau, although the "savage societies" of the indigenous peoples of Africa and the New World had undergone substantial changes from the pure state of nature, this stage of human evolution was "best for man": not only were the savages still free and independent, but their social systems had more stability, morality, and decency than the civilized societies of Europe. Indeed, even before writing the *First Discourse*, Rousseau was unusual in siding with the "savages" against the colonial conquests that followed Columbus's discovery of the Americas.[41]

Contemporary research on the transition from the early hominid way of life to what Rousseau called "savage society" presents a second paradox: whereas Rousseau seems to have underestimated the social behavior likely in the pure state of nature, he probably overestimated the individual autonomy of the members of most savage societies. To be sure, North American or African tribes frequently were "stateless societies," often described by anthropologists as segmentary lineage systems in which voluntary cooperation is limited to kin groups; compared with civilized societies, there is much greater equality and individual freedom in such tribes, since leaders have little power to command

and there are no government institutions capable of enforcing the law. When members of a band or village feel that outsiders have done them wrong or injustice, the group relies on self-help.

Stateless societies are thus typically characterized by feud if not "warfare" between groups, with the level of violence depending on the geographic distance and kinship relations between them. In some respects these peoples resemble Hobbes's state of nature, in which the "concord" of family or kin-based groups is based on "natural lust"; like international relations between sovereign states, as Hobbes pointed out explicitly, the natives of North America were thus their own judges whenever a conflict broke out. Rousseau understood this well enough, admitting that among the savages "terror of revenge" took the place of law,[42] but he seems to have been unaware of a critical difference between most such societies and the pure state of nature.

It now appears that one of the biggest transformations in human evolution took place with the origin of stabilized food supplies in the form of horticulture (domesticated plants) and pastoralism (domesticated animals). Associated with these changes was what has been described as the domestication of the human species itself. In a careful study of this crucial transition, Peter J. Wilson has suggested that the change was related to the capacity to describe social and kinship relations in terms of formal, mutually exclusive linguistic categories (perhaps as the result of the establishment of fixed homesites in which rudimentary architecture included the construction of distinct spaces or rooms with functionally distinct purposes).[43]

Whatever the explanation, as soon as savage societies began to exploit horticultural or pastoral modes of livelihood, groups were organized in terms of kinship relations that placed far greater constraints on the individual than were likely to have existed in earlier hominid epochs. The complex rules of marriage, descent, and dispute settlement which have been the focus of cultural anthropology during this century differ dramatically from the loose and fluid social arrangements of hunter-gatherers. Above I cited Rousseau's claim that "as long as men were content with their rustic huts" (i.e., assuming savages have already developed sedentary villages) "they lived free, healthy, good, and happy" because they "continued to enjoy among themselves the sweetness of independent intercourse."[44] The reality was probably rather different.

It is true that, among the savages living in stateless societies relying on horticulture, individuals can leave the village or band at any time. But it seems a serious mistake to call this "the sweetness of independent intercourse": in many cases an individual left the group as a consequence of ostracism, particularly when clan elders and fellow kinsmen disapproved of behavior. When someone was viewed as a "bad lot" or unsociable, frequently causing trouble for others, more or less explicit consensus led to ostracism (which could take place simply by forcing the unpleasant individual to go to the fields alone): in a situation of more or less permanent feud with rival villages or clans, such ostracism could often be tantamount to a death sentence.[45]

The principle of "an eye for an eye" (or as Rousseau put it, the savage practice of "revenge") is thus associated with an intensification of social bonds within the group. Maryanski and Turner describe the result as the "cage of kinship," when humans *lost* the autonomy of the flexible hunter-gatherer group as stabilized food supplies were made available from horticulture or pastoralism. Whereas Rousseau attributes the loss of natural freedom to the emergence of private property, agriculture, and the division of labor, leading to conflict and the formation of centralized states, this process apparently took place in two distinct stages. The establishment of horticulture or pastoralism, along with settled homesites, elaborate kinship systems, and formalized religion (complete with rituals, taboos, and witchcraft), clearly occurred long before the development of agricultural production based on irrigation made possible the establishment of centralized states, governments, and written laws.

The reduction of individual freedom in savage society coincides with the increased social inequality made possible by the beginnings of wealth. Although leadership is still generally informal and dependent on the consensus of the village, the "head man" or "chief" of the horticultural or pastoral band often has several wives as well as greater than average wealth (whether in the form of larger herds, sacred "medicine bundles," or other valued goods). The transformation of the highly egalitarian, fluid groups of primitive hunter-gatherers into stable, stratified societies was probably a slow process in which—as Rousseau admitted—no single moment marked the formation of property and the end of the state of nature. If so, however, it needs also to be added that Rousseau's description of savage society—however salutary as a corrective to the ignorance of human origins among his contemporaries—had the result of somewhat romanticizing the precivilized tribes of North America and Africa.

Agriculture, the State, and the Cage of Power

Whatever these corrections of detail, the main outlines of Rousseau's account are clearly confirmed by the past century of anthropological research.

Humans have evolved from an apelike animal without speech, without government, and without the extensive obligations and social inequalities observed in all civilized societies. The centralized state not only was a late development in human history but has been accompanied by rigid class distinctions, social inequality, and the loss of individual freedoms characteristic of earlier phases of society. Moreover, civilized societies are inherently unstable: no known state system has failed to collapse, whether as a result of overexploiting its resource base, of environmental catastrophe, or of foreign conquest.

The form of society we take for granted is thus unnatural in the sense that it was not characteristic of the original "human nature" and depended on a radical shift in our mode of livelihood. In this regard, perhaps the biggest scientific modification of Rousseau's account has been due to contemporary archaeological research into the conditions of state formation. Virtually everywhere that sites of early states have been examined, scholars have found an epoch in which centralized communities depended on the construction of "public works" which provided the infrastructure for social agglomerations of hitherto unknown size. Although in many cases the collective goods took the form of irrigation systems capable of regulating the water supply, sometimes the principal common investments have been in systems of roads making possible trade as well as in centralized grain storage and distribution facilities.[46]

These findings suggest two paradoxes of importance in any reconsideration of the scientific adequacy of Rousseau's political thought. First, while confirming Rousseau's emphasis on the common good as the foundation of civil society, the evidence of the actual origins of early states contradicts the "social contract" theory he shared with Hobbes, Locke, and other moderns. Far from originating in an epoch of conflict, early states seem to have grown in a pacific era which only later gave rise to conflict as populations grew, states began to compete with each other, and natural resources were overexploited or diminished by environmental change. Hence even if Rousseau's conclusion is sound, his premises have been called into question.

Second, and even more surprising, is Maryanski and Turner's conclusion that the urbanized, commercial, and industrialized societies whose advent Rousseau so violently condemned come closer to fulfilling the needs of human nature than did either savage societies based on kinship or early states based on agriculture. They point out—as if confirming Rousseau's central point in the *Second Discourse*—that humans evolved for millennia in apelike social groups composed of networks of "loose ties"; hence, by nature, human nature seems adapted to a high degree of individual autonomy and flexibility in small-scale social groups. While retaining the scale of the face-to-face band or village, kin-based tribes of horticultural or pastoral peoples led humans into what Maryanski and Turner call "the cage of kinship"; the rise of the central-ized agrarian state constituted an even more rigid "cage of power," generating additional obligations and constraints on individual autonomy. In contrast, they suggest, the industrialized urban societies of the twentieth century provide for a degree of autonomy that humans have not known since domestication and sedentary villages began to transform our hunter-gatherer mode of liveli-hood over the past 20,000 years.[47]

Such an interpretation is, it needs be added, still controversial. Other scholars point to the tensions that industrialized society creates for the human primate accustomed to life in a small band of extended kin.[48] But such diverse interpretations need not be mutually exclusive: some theory is needed that can explain *both* the alacrity with which humans everywhere have chosen to flee the supposedly bucolic pleasures of small-scale agrarian villages for the prospect of wealth and independence in industrialized, capitalist cities *and* the often ex-pressed frustration of those (including many with wealth and independence) living in the industrialized societies that have resulted.

Rousseau's political and social thought provides insight into this paradox, if only by forcing us to reconsider overly simplistic models of the social contract (or more recent versions of a similar cost-benefit calculus, like the prisoner's dilemma) in the context of human nature and the evolution of human soci-ety.[49] But as we have seen, recent scientific research calls into question Rous-seau's understanding of human nature and the evolution of human society on many critical points. Any assessment of the legacy of Jean-Jacques needs to consider the implications of these discoveries in such fields as evolutionary biology, primatology, neuroscience, anthropology, and archaeology.

Rousseau's Legacy: Freedom, Sexuality, and the Discontents of Civilization

Rousseau's legacy—symbolized by his motto *vertu et verité, verité et vertu* (see note 3)—suggests the need to confront theories of human nature with the findings of natural science. A century and a half after Darwin, the project set forth in the *Second Discourse* is even more necessary than in Rousseau's own time: as biologists discover hitherto unsuspected complexities in human ge-netics, neuroscience, and the evolution of behavior, the gap between science and political philosophy has never seemed greater or more problematic. On scientific grounds, we can no longer view humans either as *merely* animals (like other primates in all respects), *or* as having become unique if not specially created merely because our species has developed attributes of language, cultural variability, and self-conscious deception not found in other primates. From a biological point of view, one can no longer treat individual human beings as *either* naturally sociable *or* naturally selfish or self-sufficient, isolated individuals.

What are the theoretical implications of abandoning Rousseau's dichotomy between nature and sociability now that his explanation of amour propre has been demolished by primatological observation, neuroscientific research, and psychological experimentation? How do contemporary accounts of human nature explain the dynamics of human social behavior—and the persistent inequality, violence, and injustice that seem to characterize human civilization as contrasted with the societies of nonhuman primates or human hunter-gatherers (whose so-called primitive cultures have been studied by anthropologists seeking a better understanding of what Rousseau called "savage society")?

To summarize the scientific findings described above, Rousseau failed to see that humans—like nonhuman primates—are naturally social animals. Positive (hedonic or "attracting") and negative (agonic or "repelling") emotions are mediated by different innate structures in the mammalian brain, which is preprogrammed to perceive and express distinct nonverbal cues of bonding, attack, and flight. And because the brain is constantly "active," reorganizing the input of modules or centers whose neurons are innately specialized in distinct perceptual or motor responses, contemporary neuroscience flatly contradicts Locke's tabula rasa and the models of environmental determinism or social conditioning built upon it by both behaviorist psychologists and Marxists.

Contrary to Rousseau's view, the state of nature was social—as is the newborn human infant. Moreover, the process of normal child development is necessarily social: a human—or a monkey or an ape—that is reared apart from others is seriously disturbed and does not mature into a functional adult. As can be demonstrated by neurochemical as well as behavioral similarities, dominance and subordination are as natural to humans as to other primates, from rhesus monkeys to chimpanzees.

Because Rousseau's understanding of human nature is contradicted on many points by contemporary science, it useful to contrast his psychology with that of Freud (as Joel Schwartz has done so incisively in this volume). From the neuroscientific perspective, Freud's theory corresponds more precisely to Mac-Lean's "triune" model of the brain, since what Freud called the ego, superego, and id could be taken to stand for the cortex, limbic system, and midbrain or "R-complex," respectively. Unlike Rousseau, moreover, Freud's duality of eros and thanatos captures the innate dualism of hedonic and agonic emotions and behavior (thereby avoiding Rousseau's romantic presumption that the latter is an artifact of human society).

From a scientific point of view, however, Freud's thought is as vulnerable as Rousseau's. Whereas Freud saw unconscious or repressed sexuality as the basis of mental illness and dysfunction, neuroscientists and psychologists have now demonstrated the necessity of unconscious or preconscious information processing. Given the brain's modular organization and parallel distributed processing system, discrepancies between perceptions or emotions elicited by the same event are apparently regulated by what Gazzaniga calls the "interpreter module"—an inborn, localized structure whose nonverbal, preconscious function accounts for the ubiquity of rationalization whenever humans try to explain reactions of which they themselves are not fully aware.

Because Freud used the term "eros" to describe all positive or hedonic emotions, moreover, he was led to a theory of infantile sexuality that greatly distorts human behavior. Contrary to Freudian theory, the pleasures of bonding, food, and sex are distinct (as indicated, for example, by distinct inborn structures in the brain for perceiving and regulating the behaviors and emotions associated with each "consummatory activity"). Not only is the infant asexual—as Rousseau taught—but the mother-infant bond or a functionally similar substitute is essential for normal development—as Rousseau also understood.

From an ethological perspective, the Oedipus complex could be reinterpreted as the normal result of paternal dominance over male offspring. Among nonhuman primates, incest between mother and son is usually inhibited by such behavioral mechanisms as the dominant male's aggressive interference with attempted copulations between estrous females and subordinate males; as the adolescent matures, threat displays by the dominant male often drive him to the periphery of the group (except when this outcome is prevented by a close mother-child bond). A student of animal behavior must then ask whether what Freud called the Oedipus complex really reflects the infant's subconscious, guilty desire to kill the father in order to have sexual relations with the mother, or whether it merely results from the father's normal use of threat behavior to force the maturing child to engage in social relations with peers. Or, as psychoanalytic critics have asked, did Freud convert his patients' memories of actual events of childhood sexual abuse (which some ethologists relate to misplaced aggressive drives) into sexual fantasies in order to fit their symptoms to his poetic theories?

If Freud is Rousseau's principal contender as a modern theorist of human nature, the least one could say is that neither theory has been fully confirmed by scientific research. Indeed, of the two theories, Rousseau's comes somewhat closer to an adequate account of the "discontents" of civilized man: an animal who lived for millennia in loose, egalitarian face-to-face groups has been led, through the course of human history, to live with increased cultural restraints based on kinship and power. Rousseau's denunciation of "personal dependence" as the great evil, destroying the freedom and equality of the state of nature, reflects the profound and very real transformations of society under the impact of horticulture, agriculture, and the rise of centralized states—though, ironically enough, it may be the very anonymity of the modern industrial city which has created a modicum of space for the autonomy Jean-Jacques so earnestly sought.

Rousseau follows Hobbes in explaining civil society as the result of a social contract between asocial or hedonistic individuals. For Hobbes, these individuals were naturally warlike, but *homo homini lupus est* now has the ironic implication of stressing the social and moral cohesiveness of the wolf pack.[50] For Rousseau the individual was a naturally isolated, stupid, and asocial animal like a chimpanzee, but recent studies of chimpanzees reveal intelligent social animals whose behavior includes dominance and leadership, cultural variability, and a degree of self-consciousness long claimed to be uniquely human.

Ultimately, consideration of Rousseau's scientific legacy has the paradoxical effect of suggesting a return to the ancient naturalism of Plato and Aristotle in preference to modern theories of human nature. Like Freud (and unlike either Hobbes or Rousseau), Plato articulates a psychology that correctly distinguishes between the three principal structures of the human brain; unlike Freud (not to mention Hobbes or Rousseau), Plato shows how the conflicts between desire, guilt, and reason underlie human politics. And even more important, Aristotle's biology points to an understanding of humans as the *zoön politikon*, deriving the uniquely human dimension of experience from speech and verbal language as distinct from the psychological mechanisms empha-sized by Hobbes, Rousseau, or Freud.[51]

Unlike Nietzsche, whose attempt to return to the pagan view of human nature led toward poetry rather than scientific knowledge, Rousseau insisted that the science of human nature and history should be the ground for judging poetry. That a serious reconsideration of Rousseau's attempt to combine moral virtue and scientific truth points to the need to return to the classic or Socratic view will seem to many puzzling if not absurd. Yet it was Rousseau who, perhaps more insistently than any modern before Leo Strauss, reminded us that the conflict between modern natural science and ancient political philosophy has become the central issue of our civilization. At a time when biological science is making *Brave New World* a practical possibility, we dare not ignore the human implications of this tension and Rousseau's warning that we can easily be enslaved or destroyed by the dangerous dream of conquering the "invincible empire" of nature.

NOTES

1. The central statement of Leo Strauss, who was my teacher as well as Bloom's, is perhaps the introduction to *Natural Right and History* (Chicago: University of Chicago Press, 1953), esp. 7–8. Bloom's comments in part 2 of the *Closing of the American Mind* (New York: Simon and Schuster, 1987) have received less attention than they deserve. At the risk of immodesty, I might also mention Bloom's remark that "those who are concerned with what science teaches about life and about what life should teach scientists" need to connect "the tradition of political philosophy" with "the just claims of modern natural and social science"; although the words are part of a comment on the dust jacket of my *Nature of Politics* (New Haven: Yale University Press, 1989), there is no reason to assume that friendship led Allan to dishonesty. See also Leon Kass, *The Hungry Soul: Eating and the Perfection of Our Nature* (New York: Free Press, 1994).

2. Jean-Jacques Rousseau, *Second Discourse*, preface, in *Collected Writings of Rousseau*, ed. Roger D. Masters and Christopher Kelly (Hanover, N.H.: University Press of New England, 1991–), 2:13. See also the tasks he claimed were suited to "a Plato, a Thales, a Pythagoras" (ibid., n. *8, 85) as well as "a Montesquieu, Buffon, Diderot, Duclos, d'Alembert, Condillac, or men of that stamp" (ibid., 86). Note that the three crucial studies proposed by Rousseau are "experiments" (including the possible cross-breeding of chimpanzees and humans—what today would be called genetic analysis of species-specific traits), observation of primate behavior (ethology), and cross-cultural analysis (anthropology and behavioral ecology). Although this note is listed in conventional editions of the *Second Discourse*, as either note XI (e.g., Pléiade) or note j (e.g., Vaughan), Heinrich Meier has shown the importance of the fact that Rousseau's original text had a combination of letters and numbers: see his critical edition of the *Second Discourse:*

Diskurs über die Ungleicheheit (Paderborn: Schöningh, 1984; 2d ed., 1990). For this and many substantive insights I am deeply indebted to his edition.

3. This point deserves emphasis because, in his replies to critics of the *First Discourse,* Rousseau emphatically stated his goals to be *vertu et verité, verité et vertu*—that is, a combination of moral criticism and scientific truth. See *Letter to Raynal,* in *Collected Writings of Rousseau,* 2:27.

4. Jean Starobinski, *Jean-Jacques Rousseau: Transparency and Obstruction,* trans. Arthur Goldhammer (Chicago: University of Chicago Press, 1988).

5. *First Discourse,* pt. 1, in *Collected Writings,* 2:6.

6. See *Collected Writings,* 2:184–85.

7. *Second Discourse,* pt. 1, in *Collected Writings,* 3:40.

8. *Second Discourse,* n. *12, in *Collected Writings,* 3:91.

9. *Second Discourse,* pt. 2, in *Collected Writings,* 3:49.

10. See below, 118.

11. *Rousseau Judge of Jean-Jacques,* dialogue 2, in *Collected Writings,* 1:112).

12. See Arthur Melzer, *The Natural Goodness of Man: On the System of Rousseau's Thought* (Chicago: University of Chicago Press, 1990); Roger D. Masters, *The Political Philosophy of Rousseau* (Princeton: Princeton University Press, 1968).

13. *Second Discourse,* pt. 1, in *Collected Writings,* 3:31; pt. 2, 3:45.

14. First published in 1872, Darwin's work continues to be relevant and in print (Chicago: University of Chicago Press, 1962).

15. For example, Robert Plutchik, *Emotion: A Psychoevolutionary Synthesis* (New York: Harper and Row, 1980).

16. Masters, *Nature of Politics,* chap. 2.

17. For recent illustrations, see Elizabeth Marshall Thomas, *The Hidden Life of Dogs* (Boston: Houghton Mifflin, 1993), as well as Vicki Hearne, *Adam's Task* (New York: Viking, 1987), and Konrad Lorenz, *Man Meets Dog* (New York: Penguin, 1988). Cf. Rousseau's discussion of the "moral" awareness of dogs in *Emile,* bk. 4, trans. Allan Bloom (New York: Basic Books, 1986), 286–87.

18. See *Leviathan,* pt. 1, chaps. 1–3.

19. John Locke, *Essay on Human Understanding,* 2.1, sec. 3, ed. Alexander Campbell Fraser (New York: Dover, 1959), 1:12–23. For a critical analysis of Locke's epistemology from the perspective of contemporary neuroscience, see Roger D. Masters, *Beyond Relativism: Science and Human Values* (Hanover, N.H.: University Press of New England, 1993), 118–23.

20. For the "Profession of Faith of the Savoyard Vicar," see Bloom's edition of *Emile,* 266–94. For interpretations, compare Roger D. Masters, "Rousseau and the 'Illustrious Clarke,'" in *Jean-Jacques Rousseau et son temps,* ed. Michel Launay (Paris: Nizet, 1969), 37–50, with John T. Scott, "The Theodicy of the *Second Discourse:* The 'Pure State of Nature' and Rousseau's Political Thought," *American Political Science Review* 86 (1992): 696–711, and idem, "Politics as the Imitation of the Divine in Rousseau's *Social Contract,*" *Polity* 24 (1994): 473–501.

21. "The idea that perception . . . is caused by the stimulus or can be explained as

the sum of responses to stimuli, is no longer acceptable. Our model tells us that perceptual processing is not a passive process of reaction, like a reflex, in which whatever hits the receptors is registered inside the brain. Perception does not begin with causal impact on receptors; it begins within the organism with internally generated (self-organized) neural activity that, by re-afference, lays the ground for processing of future input. In the absence of such activity, receptor stimulation does not lead to any observable changes in the cortex. It is the brain itself that creates the conditions for perceptual processing by generating activity patterns that determine what receptor activity will be accepted and processed. Perception is a self-organized dynamic process of interchange inaugurated by the brain in which the brain fails to respond to irrelevant input, opens itself to the input it accepts, reorganizes itself, and then reaches out to change its input." Christine A. Skarda and Walter J. Freeman, "Chaos and the New Science of the Brain," *Concepts in Neuroscience* 1 (1990): 279.

22. For example, see Pawel Lewicki, Thomas Hill, and Maria Czyzewska, "Nonconscious Acquisition of Information," *American Psychologist* 47 (1992): 796–801. In no area is this more decisive than in what is usually called "creative" thought. For an insightful analysis of the contribution of connectionist models in artificial intelligence to a deeper understanding of human thought, see Margaret A. Boden, *The Creative Mind: Myths and Mechanisms* (New York: Basic Books, 1992).

23. For recent surveys, see Stephen M. Kosslyn and Olivier Koenig, *Wet Mind: The New Cognitive Neuroscience* (New York: Free Press, 1992); George Johnson, *In the Palaces of Memory* (New York: Vintage, 1991); and *Mind and Brain*, a special edition of *Scientific American* for September 1992. On the philosophic implications of neuroscientific research, see Masters, *Beyond Relativism*, esp. chap. 5.

24. Michael Gazzaniga, *The Social Brain* (New York: Basic Books, 1982).

25. Konrad Lorenz, *On Aggression* (New York: Harcourt, Brace, and World, 1966).

26. For the evidence in support of this hypothesis, see Masters, *Nature of Politics*, chap. 1. Aristotle's claim that "man is more of a political animal than bees or any other gregarious animals" (*Politics*, 1.1252a–b) may be valid to a far deeper extent than has been realized by modern philosophers and social scientists.

27. See note 2 above.

28. William C. McGrew, *Chimpanzee Material Culture* (Cambridge: Cambridge University Press, 1992).

29. See Rousseau, *Second Discourse*, n. *8, in *Collected Writings*, 3:83.

30. Frans de Waal, *Chimpanzee Politics* (London: Cape, 1982), and idem, *Peacemaking among Primates* (Cambridge: Harvard University Press, 1989).

31. De Waal has described both events in detail in numerous conference presentations in addition to the accounts in the works cited in note 30. For a fuller survey of evidence for primate intentionality, see Glendon Schubert and Roger D. Masters, *Primate Politics* (Carbondale: Southern Illinois University Press, 1991), conclusion.

32. For example, Robert Trivers, *Social Evolution* (Menlo Park, Calif.: Benjamin/Cummings, 1983).

33. See Paul Ekman, R. W. Levenson, and Wallace V. Friesen, "Autonomic Ner-

vous System Activity Distinguishes among Emotions," *Science* 221 (1983): 1208–10; Gregory J. McHugo, John T. Lanzetta, Denis G. Sullivan, Roger D. Masters, and Basil G. Englis, "Emotional Reactions to Expressive Displays of a Political Leader," *Journal of Personality and Social Psychology* 49 (1985): 1512–29; Gregory J. McHugo, John T. Lanzetta, and Lauren Bush, "The Effect of Attitudes on Emotional Reactions to Expressive Displays of Political Leaders," *Journal of Nonverbal Behavior* 15 (1991): 19–41.

34. Gazzaniga, *Social Brain.* In these studies, split-brain patients (individuals whose left and right hemispheres have been dissociated) have no verbal memory of responses that were entirely produced by the nonverbal right hemisphere; when asked to explain drawings controlled by the right hemisphere, the patients imagine causal sequences that are consistent with events that actually occurred in the left hemisphere but which had nothing to do with the experimental stimulus. See also Michael Gazzaniga, *Nature's Mind* (New York: Basic Books, 1992), 124–37.

35. See Antonio Damasio, *Descartes' Error: Emotion, Reason, and the Human Brain* (New York: G. P. Putnam's, 1994). Damasio's work provides a summary of recent research on the neuroanatomical localization of brain function with particular emphasis on moral judgment; as such, it is of particular relevance to the philosophic reader.

36. Robert Hare, *Without Conscience: The Disturbing World of the Psychopaths among Us* (New York: Pocket Books, 1993).

37. *Social Contract*, 2:11, in *Collected Writings*, 4:164.

38. For example, Marvin Harris, *Cannibals and Kings* (New York: Random House, 1977).

39. For the theoretical principles, see Trivers, *Social Evolution*, or David Barash, *Sociobiology and Behavior*, 2d ed. (New York: Elsevier, 1982). For applications to human societies, see Napoleon Chagnon and William Irons, eds., *Evolutionary Biology and Human Social Behavior* (North Scituate, Mass.: Duxbury Press, 1979); William H. Durham, *Coevolution: Genes, Culture, and Human Diversity* (Stanford: Stanford University Press, 1991).

40. Alexandra Maryanski and Jonathan Turner, *The Social Cage: Human Nature and the Evolution of Society* (Stanford: Stanford University Press, 1992). Because this work came to my attention after the first presentation of the present argument, it could be said to provide an interesting confirmation of the central thesis that contemporary research on human nature provides vitally important insights on the assessment and continued relevance of Rousseau's thought.

41. See his early play *La découverte du nouveau monde* and compare the scene depicted in the frontispiece of the *Second Discourse* (in *Collected Writings*, 3:xxx, 92–93).

42. *Second Discourse*, pt. 2, in *Collected Writings*, 3:48.

43. Peter J. Wilson, *The Domestication of the Human Species* (New Haven: Yale University Press, 1987).

44. *Second Discourse*, pt. 2, in *Collected Writings*, 3:48.

45. See Margaret Gruter and Roger D. Masters, eds., *Ostracism: A Social and Biological Phenomenon* (New York: Elsevier, 1986).

46. See Masters, *Nature of Politics*, chap. 6.

47. In addition to Maryanski and Turner's *Social Cage,* compare Irenäus Eibl-Eibesfeldt, *Human Ethology* (New York: Aldine-Atherton, 1989).

48. For example, Lionel Tiger, *The Manufacture of Evil: Ethics, Evolution, and the Industrial System* (New York: Harper and Row, 1987).

49. The popularity of "explaining" social competition and cooperation with the game theoretical model of the prisoner's dilemma—e.g., Robert Axelrod, *The Evolution of Cooperation* (Cambridge: Harvard University Press, 1983)—reflects the persistent appeal of the social contract as a model of complex human behavior. Even among those who specialize in such rational-choice theories of behavior, however, awareness of something like Rousseau's distinction between private wills or private interests and the general will or common good has been recognized as essential: e.g., Howard Margolis, *Selfishness, Altruism, and Rationality* (Cambridge: Cambridge University Press. 1982).

50. For a convenient account, see Thomas, *Hidden Life of Dogs,* or Lorenz, *Man Meets Dog.*

51. For a fuller account of the *scientific* reasons to return to an ancient approach to nature as well as to human nature, in addition to works cited above, see my *Machiavelli, Leonardo and the Science of Power* (Notre Dame: University of Notre Dame Press, 1996).

❧ III ❧
Our Politics: General Will, Revolution, Nation

Rousseau's Critique of Liberal Constitutionalism

ALLAN BLOOM

At the moment the Framers wrote "We the people of the United States
. . . ," the word "people" had been made problematic by Jean-Jacques Rousseau.[1] How do you get from individuals to a people, that is, from persons who
care only for their particular good to a community of citizens who subordinate
their own good to the common good? The collective "we" in the Preamble
might well be the voice of a powerful and wealthy few who coerce and deceive
the many and make their consent meaningless. Or the many who consent to
the use of "we" may do so innocently, not realizing how much of their "I" they
must sacrifice, or corruptly, intending to profit from the advantage of the social
contract and evade the sacrifice it demands. It is difficult beyond the belief of
early modern thinkers, so Rousseau teaches, to turn men free and equal by
nature into citizens obedient to the law and its ministers. "Man was born free.
Everywhere he is in chains," he observes. Rousseau's task is not to return man
to his original condition but to make the results of force and fraud legitimate,
to persuade men that there is a possible social order both beneficial and just.

Based on these preliminary remarks, it should be evident that Rousseau
begins from an overall agreement with the Framers and their teachers about
man's nature and the origins and ends of civil society. Man is born free, that is,
able to follow his inclinations and to do whatever conduces to his preservation
or comfort, and equal, that is, with no superiors who have a valid claim to
command him. He has no obligations. Government is therefore not natural
but a construction of man, and the law is a thing strictly of his making. The
natural state is wholly distinct from the civil state, and the only way from the
one to the other is consent. All other titles of legitimacy, divine or human,
derived from appeals to the ancestral or exclusive wisdom, are neither binding
nor believable. In *the state of nature* rights are primary; duties are derivative and
become binding only after *the social contract* is freely made.

All this and much more provides the common ground of modernity where
Rousseau walks arm and arm with his liberal predecessors and contempor-

aries. He does not reject the new principles, but he radicalizes them by thinking them through from the broadest of perspectives. In his eyes the epic battle of his Enlightenment fellows against throne and altar, which had lasted for two centuries, had simply been won. Monarchic and aristocratic Europe was, he correctly predicted, on its last legs. There would soon be great revolutions, and it is the visage of the political orders that were to emerge that concerns him. He could even afford a few generous gestures of recognition toward the defeated nobles and kings (though rarely the priests) whose moral and political greatness was hardly recognized by those who had been locked in battle with them. The new world would be inhabited by individuals who know they are endowed with rights, free and equal, no longer treading the enchanted ground where rights and duties were prescribed by divinities, now recognizing no legitimacy with higher sources than their own wills, rationally pursuing their own interests. Might they become the victims, willing or not, of new despotisms? Might they not become as morally questionable in their way as the unthinking patriots or fanatic believers who were the special objects of modern criticism and whose place they were to take?

Rousseau's reflections had the effect of outflanking the Framers on the Left, where they thought they were invulnerable. Their enemies were the old European orders of privilege, supported by the church and monopolizing wealth and the ways of access to it, and their revolution was the movement from prejudice to reason, despotism to freedom, inequality to equality. This was a progress, but not one that was to be infinite, at least in principle. The dangers were understood as coming from the *revanchisme* of throne and altar in various forms. There were many opponents of Enlightenment and its political project—in the name of tradition or the ancestral, in the name of the kings and the nobles, even in the name of the ancient city and its virtue. But Rousseau was the first to make a schism within the party of what we may call the Left. In so doing he set up the stage on which the political drama has been played until this day. The element that was so much more extreme in the French Revolution than in the American Revolution can be traced, without intermediaries, to Rousseau's influence on its principal actors. And it was by Rousseau's standard that it was judged a failure and only a preparation for the next, and perhaps final, revolution. The camp of radical equality and freedom has very few clear political successes to show for itself, but it contains all the dissatisfactions and longings that put a question mark after triumphant liberalism.

Rousseau gave antimodernity its most modern expression and thereby ushered in extreme modernity. It is a mistake to treat him as only the genius of the Left. His concentration on the people, the corporate existence of individual peoples, provided the basis for the religion of the nation in the nineteenth and twentieth centuries. His assault on cosmopolitan civilization prepared the way for the assertion of national cultures, unique and constitutive of their individual members. His regret of the lost happy unity of man was the source of the romanticism that played at least as much of a role on the Right as on the Left. His insistence on the centrality of religion to the life of the people gave a new content to theology and provided the impulse for the religiosity that is one of the salient traits of the nineteenth and twentieth centuries. The contempt for the new man of liberal society that Rousseau articulated lent itself to the projects of both extremes of the political spectrum, and his Left informed the new Right, which constituted itself on the intellectual shambles of the old Right. His influence was overwhelming, and so well was it digested into the bloodstream of the West that it worked on everyone almost imperceptibly. Even the mainstays of democratic liberalism were affected by Rousseau; they were impressed by his critique of the harshness of the political and economic relations characteristic of the modern state and sought to correct them on the basis of his suggestions. The influence was direct on Alexis de Tocqueville, indirect, by way of Wordsworth, on John Stuart Mill. The Thoreau who for America represents civil disobedience and a way of life free from the distortions of modern society was only reenacting one part of the thought and life of Jean-Jacques.

Rousseau's presence is ubiquitous, and often where conservatives or leftists would least like to recognize him. He is the seedbed of all these schools and movements that enrich, correct, defend, or undermine constitutional liberalism. His breadth and comprehensiveness make it impossible to co-opt him completely into any single camp. The schools that succeed him are all isms, intellectual forces that inform powerful political or social movements with more or less singleness of purpose. Rousseau resists such limitation. For him the human problem is not soluble on the political level; and though he, unlike Socrates, suggests practicable solutions, they are tentative and counterpoised by other solutions and temptations. One can always find in him the objections to each school that depends on him. Therefore Rousseau did not produce an ism of his own, but he did provide the authentically modern perspective. His concern for a higher, nonmercenary morality is the foundation of Kant's idealism. His critique of modern economics and his questions about the legitimacy of private property are at the root of socialism, particularly Marxism. His emphasis on man's origins rather than his ends made anthropology a central discipline. And the history of the movement from the state of nature toward civil society came to seem more essential to man than his nature—hence historicism. The wounds inflicted on human nature by this process of socialization became the subject of a new psychology, especially as represented in Freud. The romantic love of the beautiful and the doubt that modern society is compatible with the sublime and pure in spirit gave justification to the cult of art for art's sake and to the life of the bohemian. The longing for rootedness and for community in its modern form is part of Rousseauian sensibility, and so is the love of nature and the hatred for nature's conquerors. All this and much more flows from this inexhaustible font. He possessed an unsurpassed intellectual clarity accompanied by a stirring and seductive rhetoric.

The Bourgeois

The bourgeois is Rousseau's great invention, and one's disposition toward this kind of man determines one's relation to modern politics, inasmuch as he is the leading human type produced by it. The word has a strong negative charge, and practically no one wants to be *merely* a bourgeois. The artists and the intellectuals have almost universally despised him and in large measure defined themselves against him. The bourgeois is unpoetic, unerotic, unheroic, neither aristocrat nor of the people; he is not a citizen, and his religion is pallid and this-worldly. The sole invocation of his name is enough to legitimate revolutions of Left and Right; and within the limits of liberal democracy, all sorts of reforms are perennially proposed to correct his motives or counterbalance them.

This phenomenon, the bourgeois, is the true beginning point of Rousseau's survey of the human condition in modernity and his diagnosis of what ails it. The bourgeois stands somewhere between two respectable extremes—the good natural man and the moral citizen. The former lives alone, concerned with himself, his preservation, and his contentment, unconcerned with others, hence wishing them no harm. The latter lives wholly for his country, concerned solely with the common good, existing only as a part of it, loving his country and hating its enemies. Each of these two types, in his own way, is whole—free of the wasting conflict between inclination and duty that reduces the bourgeois and renders him weak and unreliable. He is the individualist in

146

society, who needs society and its protective laws, but only as means to his private ends. This need does not provide sufficient motive to make the extreme sacrifices one's country sometimes requires. It also means that he lies to his fellow countrymen, making conditional promises to them while expecting them to abide by their promises unconditionally. The bourgeois is a hypocrite, hiding his true purposes under a guise of public spiritedness. And hence, needing everyone but unwilling to sacrifice to help others reciprocally in their neediness, he is psychologically at war with everyone. The bourgeois's morality is mercenary, requiring a payoff for every social deed. He is incapable of either natural sincerity or political nobility.[2]

The cause of this dominant new character's flaws is that he took a shortcut on the road from the state of nature to civil society. Rousseau's thinking through of the new political science, which taught that man is not by nature political—a thinking through that led much further in both directions, nature and society, than his predecessors had believed necessary or possible—proved to him that natural motives cannot suffice for the making of social man. The attempt to use man's natural passions as the foundation of civil society fails while it perverts those natural passions. A man who never says "I promise" never has to lie. One who says "I promise" without sufficient motive for keeping his promise is a liar. Such are the social contracts proposed by Hobbes and Locke, requiring binding promises from their participants, who are concerned solely with their own well-being and whose contracts are therefore conditional on calculations of self-interest. Such social contracts tend toward anarchy or tyranny.

In essence, Rousseau's bourgeois is identical to Locke's rational and industrious man, the new kind of man whose concern with property was to provide a more sober and solid foundation to society. Rousseau sees him differently— from the perspective of morality, citizenship, equality, freedom, and compassion. The rational and industrious man might be an instrument of stability, but the cost of relying on him is human dignity. This contrast between two ways of seeing the central actor in modernity summarizes the continuous political debate of the past two centuries.

The Enlightenment and Virtue

Rousseau's earliest formulation of this critique of modernity was in his *Discourse on the Arts and Sciences,* which exploded on the European scene with a force hardly credible to us today. In it he made the first attack on the Enlightenment based on the very principles that motivated Enlightenment. Simply put, he argued that the progress and dissemination of the sciences and the arts, their emancipation from political and religious control, are noxious to decent community and its foundation, virtue. By virtue he appears to mean the republican citizen's self-forgetting devotion to the common good, a common good established and preserved by freemen, which protects the equal concern for and treatment of all the citizens. In this definition of virtue, Rousseau follows Montesquieu, who calls virtue a passion and says it was the principle, or spiritual mainspring, of ancient democracies, as fear is of despotism or honor is of monarchies. Virtue, of course, was not a passion in any ancient account of it, and it was certainly not especially connected to democracy. Rousseau apparently accepts Montesquieu's account of virtue because he, like the rest of the moderns, believed that passion is the only real power in the soul and that there is nothing in it capable of controlling the passions. Passion must control passion. Virtue must be understood as a special kind of complex passion. However that may be, Rousseau comes out squarely in defense of those ancient "democracies," early republican Rome and especially Sparta, in opposition to Montesquieu, who in harmony with the general tendency of Enlightenment favored the commercial republic or monarchy (with some in-difference as to the choice between the two) because he thought the price for ancient virtue too high. Rousseau chooses patriotism, a motive tinged with fanaticism, because it alone can counterpoise the natural inclination to prefer oneself over everyone else, an inclination much intensified and perverted by man's social condition, where men are interdependent and self-love turns into amour propre, the passion to be first among them, to be esteemed by them as he esteems himself. Patriotism is a sublimated form of amour propre, seeking the first place for one's country. Without such a counterpoise society turns into a struggle for primacy among individuals or groups who unite to manipulate the whole.

Thus it is as the solvent of patriotism that Rousseau objects to Enlighten-ment. The fabric of community is woven out of certain immediate habits of sentiment. They are vulnerable to reason, which sees clearly only calculations of private interest. It pierces veils of sentiment and poses too powerfully the claims of preservation and comfort. Reason individualizes. In this Rousseau picks up the old assertion of classical political philosophy that there is a tension between the theoretical and practical lives that renders their coexistence at best uneasy. Or to put it otherwise, Enlightenment proposed a parallelism between intellectual and moral or political progress, which the ancients regarded as very doubtful, a doubt recapitulated and reinforced by Rousseau, who expresses the opposition in the contrast between Sparta and Athens. He, of course, categorically preferred the former. Enlightenment wished to convert the selfishness of man in the state of nature into the enlightened self-interest of man capable of joining civil society rationally on the basis of the natural and dependable natural passions. It is this conversion that Rousseau regarded as noxious and as the source of moral chaos and the misery of man. He first comes to light as the defender of the old moral order against the spirit of philosophy to a degree unparalleled by any previous philosopher, doing so perhaps because modernity had more systematically attacked the moral order than had any previous thought. Rousseau is the first philosopher to appear as morality's defender *against* reason. He insisted that the movement from the natural state to the social one could not be made in the direct and almost automatic way Enlightenment claimed.

More concretely, the arts and sciences can flourish only in large and luxurious countries, which means from the outset that they require conditions contrary to those required by the small, austere, tightly knit communities where moral health prevails and the individuals have no objects of aspiration beyond those of the community. For some to be idle, others must work to provide the surplus necessary for them. These workers are exploited for the sake of the few privileged who no longer share their condition or their concerns. The fulfillment of unnecessary desires, begun as a pleasure, ends up being a necessity; the true necessities are neglected and their purveyors despised. Desire emancipated becomes limitless and calls forth an economy to provide for it. The pleasures are exclusive and are pleasant in large measure because they are exclusive. The sense of superiority follows from the practice of the arts and sciences and is also part of the reason they are pursued. Following from the general principles of modernity, it may be doubted that the intellectual pleasures are natural rather than affects of vanity. They almost always have some of the latter mixed in with them, which suffices to render them antisocial. The spirit of Enlightenment philosophy, perhaps of all philosophy, is to denigrate the simple feelings of common humanity that cause men to forget their self-interest.

In fine, the arts and sciences tend to increase inequality and fix its throne more firmly within society. They give more power to the already powerful and make the weak ever more dependent on the powerful without any common good uniting the two parties. The effective freedom of the state of nature, where man could choose what seems to him good for himself, has been replaced by the imposition of arbitrary authority over him, which has no concern for his good. Freedom was the first and most important of the natural goods, as means to live as one pleases, also as end in itself. Equality meant that in right nobody can command another and in fact nobody wished to do so because men were independent and self-sufficient. The civil condition means, in the first place, mutual dependence, physically and spiritually, but without order, each struggling to maintain the original freedom, failing to do so as relations of force or power take the place of freedom. The purpose of life becomes trying to find an advantageous place in this artificial system. Freedom is lost, not only because there is mastery and slavery but mostly because it becomes absorbed in commanding or obeying, in moving the wills of others rather than in fulfilling the objects of one's own will. The loss of freedom is best expressed in the fact of inequality, that some men are strong, others weak, some are rich, others poor, some command, others obey. The primary fact of the state of nature as described by all teachers of the state of nature is that men are free and equal. But the bourgeois state, which in speech affirms the primacy of natural freedom and equality, in practice does not reflect that primacy. Natural right, as opposed to merely conventional right, demands the continuation or restoration of the original equality of man.

In this all regimes fail, but Rousseau judges that the ancient city came closest of all to real equality and collective freedom. Although the ancient city looks, with all its restraints, traditions, austerity, harsh duties, and so on, to be much further away from the natural state than does a liberal society where men apparently live pretty much as they please, it comes close to the essence of what really counts for man. The study of the state of nature permits Rousseau to see that essence, but such study cannot result in a plan for building a civil state that protects that essence. That must be a purely human invention, and the easy solutions that seem to preserve or to be most faithful to nature are specious. Rousseau's analysis leads to a much stricter insistence on freedom and equality within civil society than the thought of Locke or Montesquieu. Against their moderation, Rousseau adds a dose of extremism to modern politics from which it cannot easily recover. What began as an attempt to simplify politics ends up as a program for reform more complex and more imperative than anything that had preceded.

Rousseau introduced the taste for the small, virtuous community into the modern movement toward freedom and equality. Here freedom becomes less a matter of each one doing what he pleases than of each equally taking responsibility for making and preserving the law of the city. Ancient politics used freedom as the means to virtue; Rousseau and his followers made freedom, the natural good, the end and virtue the means to it. But in any event, virtue, morals, and character become central again to politics and cannot, as the moderns would have it, be peripheral to the machinery of government, to institutions that channel men's passions instead of educating, reforming, or overcoming them.

Property

This point is made most forcefully in Rousseau's reflections on economics or, to put it more precisely, on property, the cornerstone of modern politics. "Ancient political writers spoke constantly about morals and virtue; ours speak only about commerce and money."[3] A man's attachment to his property, always threatened by the poor and the rapacious, is the special motive used by Locke and his followers to get his consent to the making of a social contract and the establishment of government. This is the means of achieving mutual recognition of property rights as well as protection for them from a whole community capable of punishing aggressors. The rational and the industrious who provide for themselves by labor rather than by war are the foundations of civil society, and its purposes are elegantly defined and limited by their needs. They preserve themselves comfortably, following their most powerful inclinations, and produce peace and prosperity for the whole. Their wills assent to the arrangement that their reason determines is best for their interest. This is so manifestly superior to the condition of war that prevails before the contract that it fully engages the hearts and minds of those who profit from it.

The right to property is society's golden thread, the right that emerges as the ground of consensus of the free and equal. "Work and you shall enjoy the fruits of your labors." For Hobbes, whose civil society emerges out of fear of death alone, property rights are left to the prudence of the sovereign, who can arrange them in whatever way seems fitting for the most secure establishment of peace. But for Locke, who taught that property is the true means to peace, property rights are more absolute, and the economic system governing the increase of property, what is now called the market, must as much as possible be respected by the sovereign. Government protects the individual best by protecting his property and leaving him as free as possible to care for it. The naturalness of property and government's special concern for the protection of the pursuit of it are Locke's novelties and become the hallmark of the serious projects for the reform of governments.

For all the plausibility and even practical effectiveness of this scheme, Rousseau observes, there is something immediately shocking about the assertion that equal men should freely consent to great inequalities of property. The rich have lives that are so much freer, so much easier, so much opener to the enjoyment of life. They are so much more powerful. They can buy the law, and they can buy men. Why should the poor accept this willingly? No, the poor must have been forced to agree, or they must have been deceived. This is not natural right. The property relations that prevail in the nations are so many acts of violence against the poor, which they are too weak to prevent. There is no legitimacy here. The opposition between Locke and Rousseau is measured by the fact that the establishment of private property is for Locke the beginning of the solution to the political problem, whereas for Rousseau it is the source of the continuing misery of man.[4]

This does not mean Rousseau is a communist or that he believed it is possible or desirable to do away with private property. He is far too "realistic" to follow Plato's *Republic* and abandon the sure motive of love of one's own things. It does mean, however, that he strongly opposes the emancipation of acquisitiveness and that he argues against laissez-faire. For him the business of government is to supervise the pursuit of property in order to limit the inequality of fortunes, to mitigate the harshness of economic competition, and to moderate the increase of desire among the citizens. Adam Smith's book *The Wealth of Nations*, which is very much in the spirit of Locke, is in large measure a presentation of the iron laws of the increase of property. Rousseau's book *Political Economy* is a treatise devoted to moral education. A modern reader who picks up *Political Economy* finds himself at sea, wondering what in the world this has to do with economics. The science of economics as we know it is predicated on the emancipation of desire, an emancipation Rousseau is concerned to prevent. In no point does Rousseau's analysis of the meaning of freedom and equality differ so much from Locke's as in the property question. The most practically radical opposition to liberal constitutionalism comes from this direction. The property right, which Locke wished to establish solidly, becomes the most doubtful of all things.

Again, though, this difference begins in an initial important agreement between Locke and Rousseau. Property is in its most primitive form that with

152

which a man has mixed his labor. Neither God nor nature gives man directly what he needs. He must provide for himself, and his appropriation of things necessary for preservation is an extension of the original property that all have in their own body. The man who has planted beans and wishes to eat them is universally recognized to have a better right to do so than the one who without planting takes away the other's beans. There is an original of simple justice here, accessible to men of good sense. And Locke follows it through its fullest development and most complicated expressions in commercial societies. The reciprocal recognition of this right to what one has worked for constitutes property, and this solution unites self-interest with justice. The ancient view that property is constituted by a combination of what one has worked for with what one can use well is reduced to the single principle, for the classical formula implies that property is based on political determinations that can be regarded as subjective and arbitrary.

Rousseau parts company with Locke on the question of scarcity. The man who has no beans concerns him. The economist responds, "He didn't plant any, so he doesn't deserve them." But his hunger obliterates his recognition of the property right of the other, and the essence of the right is in the recognition. This malcontent can be controlled by the union of those who have provided themselves with beans, or who have inherited them, and wish to live in security from attacks by him and his kind. So force must be introduced to compel the idle and contentious to keep away from other's property and to work to provide for themselves. The civil union is really made up of two groups: those who freely recognize one another's property rights and those who are forced to comply with the rule of the property owners. The latter are used for the collective private interest of the former. *Class* is decisive in civil society, and there is no common good without radical reform.

Thus the liberal view is that society consists in the opposition between, to repeat, the rational and industrious and the idle and quarrelsome. The former produce peace and prosperity for all, the latter produce penury and war. Rational men must recognize and consent to the order that favors the dominance of the propertied. Rousseauian economics, however, views the social opposition as existing between the selfish, avaricious rich, exploiting nature and men for the sake of the increase of their personal wealth, and the suffering poor, unable to provide for their needs because the land and the other means of production are monopolized by the rich. As the perspective shifts, those who were once objects of execration become objects of pity.

Locke found the source of prosperity in the transformation by labor of the naturally given. This labor is motivated by need, by desire for comfort, and by anxiety for the future. For the satisfaction of all that man might possibly want, there is never enough. Once the imagination has been opened out beyond the merest physical need, the desire for acquisition becomes infinite. Rousseau concludes from this that those who are ablest at getting land and money end up possessing all the means of gaining wealth. They produce much wealth, but they do not share. For those who do not succeed, there is ever greater scarcity, and they must live their lives at the mercy of the rich. In the beginning their simple needs did not require much for their satisfaction, but that little disappears, for example, when all the land is enclosed and they have no place to plant their beans. The best they can do is sell their labor to those who have land in return for subsistence, which depends no longer on their own efforts but on the wills of the rich or the impersonal market. The scarcity that Locke asserts existed at the beginning was really, Rousseau asserts, a result of the extreme extension of desire, and Locke's solution increases scarcity within wealth, a scarcity that could be corrected by moderation—a return to a simple economy directed to real needs. The expanding economy can never keep up with the expansion of desire or of longing for the means of satisfying future desire. The economy that was instituted to serve life alters the purpose of life, and the activity of society becomes subservient to it. The present is sacrificed to a prosperous future that is always just beyond the horizon. Actually nature was not such a stepmother as the moderns thought, and it is not so unreasonable to seek to live according to nature as they teach.

As politics turns into economics, the qualities requisite to the latter come to define the privileged human character. Selfishness and calculation have primacy over generosity and compassion. Dealings among men are at best contractual, always with an eye to profit. Differences of talent at acquisition do exist; but, Rousseau asks, does a decent society privilege them at the expense of differences in goodness and decency? The social arrangement of property that he asserts should follow from the study of man's natural condition is not that of commercial societies but that of agricultural communities, where production requires only simple skills, where the division of labor is not extreme, where exchange is direct and the virtuosos of finance play little role, where inequalities of land and money are, if not abolished, limited, where avarice has little opportunity for activity, and where the motive for work is immediate necessity. The scale should not become such that men are abstractions while money is real. A modest sufficiency of goods and a moderate disposition, not the hope of riches and their perpetual increase, should be the goal of political economy. The natural equality of man can tolerate only a small amount of the inequality produced by society.

Rousseau confronts Locke's assertion that liberal economies make all members of society richer, and therefore, palpably better off than they were in the natural condition, with the counterassertion that freedom can never properly be put in the same balance with riches and comfort. Perhaps the day laborer in England is better clothed, housed, and fed than a king in America. Unimpressed by the moral qualities Locke finds in the English day laborer, Rousseau turned back toward the proud dignity and independence of the king. Locke took it that his argument is sufficient to persuade the rational poor to accept the inequalities present in society in preference to the neediness of the state of nature. Rousseau uses the same argument to make men rebel against the state of dependence and anxiety caused by the economies of civilized society. He goes further. In depicting the degradation of the bourgeois, the new kind of ruler, in comparison with the greatness of the ancient citizen, he makes the life of the advantaged in liberal society appear to be as despicable as the life of the disadvantaged is miserable.

The delegitimation of property's emancipation from political control, that is, from the will of all, was one of the most effective and revolutionary aspects of Rousseau's thought. His great rhetoric was used to make compassion for the poor central to relations among men and indignation at their situation central to political action. With all the freshness of original insight, before this kind of analysis became routine and tired, he outlined all that is negative about excessive concern for self-preservation and the means of ensuring it. But for all that, Locke was simply right in one decisive aspect. Everybody, not just the rich, gets richer in a system of liberal economy. Gross inequalities of wealth persist or are encouraged by it, but the absolute material well-being of each is greatly enhanced. Rousseau, followed by Marx, taught that the inner logic of acquisition would concentrate wealth in fewer and fewer hands, completely dispossessing the poor and alienating them from the means of becoming prosperous. Locke's great selling point has proved to be true. Joining civil society for the sake of protection and comfort is a good investment. This fact has been widely accepted by Americans for a long time; it is only now becoming fully recognized by Europeans. Intellectuals committed to the revolution are the last to resign themselves to the facts. The grinding sense of necessity has been alleviated, and with it most of the revolutionary fervor. One may continue to believe, as somber critics still do, that the way of life of such a society is repulsive and that the motives for association are inadequate and corrupt. But that is not quite the same as the progressive impoverishment and enslavement of mankind at large. Most of all, the poor, the many, the masses—however they are now qualified—become supporters of "the system," out of crass self-interest, and that destroys the revolutionary movements. The humanness of life may be lessened, but that is not accompanied by starvation.

Locke taught that the protection and increase of property guaranteed by government based on consent are both efficient and just. The justice is harsh natural justice—the protection of unequal natural talents for acquisition from the depredations of the idle, the less competent, the envious, and the brutal. The argument for efficiency remains; but since the full effect of Rousseau penetrated the bloodstream of Western thought, hardly any of the economists who are capitalism's most convinced advocates defend the justice of the inequalities it results in. It is at best an effective way of increasing collective and individual wealth. Rousseau's arguments for the primacy of natural equality have proved persuasive. The construction of civil society based on inequalities of property-producing gifts is seen to be a contradiction of what is most fundamental. As a matter of fact, natural inequalities of any sort—whether of strength, beauty, or intelligence—must not have any privileges in civil society because they did not in the state of nature. This is a step away from the sway of nature that Rousseau was the first to make. Nature mandates political inventiveness for the attainment of equality in civil society. Coarse pragmatism can live with a system that "works," as long as it works. But we find ourselves, at least partly because of Rousseau, in the interesting situation where we do not entirely believe in the justice of our regimes.

The General Will

Since man is naturally free, for Rousseau the only political solution in accordance with nature is one where man governs himself.[5] This does not mean that man consents to let others govern for him. Practically, he cannot accept the dictates of other men. He experiences them merely as wills opposing his will. Other men may force him to act against his wishes, but this is force, not right. Law is not essentially force. For law to be law, the one who obeys it must do so with the assent of his will; and in the absence of a fully wise and just ruler, other men cannot be trusted. The human law worthy of obedience is the law one has made for oneself. Only this formula combines freedom with obligation. Self-legislation is the true meaning of a decent political order.

This Rousseau contrasts with the liberal formula that one gives up a bit of freedom to enjoy the rest undisturbed. This leaves everything unresolved. Just how much is this bit? How is the ever-present possibility of opposition between what the individual wants and the demands of the collectivity to be mediated? The arrangement contains no element of morality or obligation, only contingent calculations of immediate interest. Utilitarian morality is no morality at all. Analysis reduces it at best to long-range self-interest. Real duty, the unselfregarding moral deed, becomes a will-o'-the-wisp. The struggle between inclination and duty, obstinate and irreconcilable, is the psychological price paid for the liberal social contract. Only the man whose private will wills only the common good would experience no tension between his individuality and society, freedom and duty.

This analysis is the source of the general will, Rousseau's most famous innovation, his attempt to establish a moral politics that does not degrade man or rob him of his freedom.[6] The will of individuals is by definition individual and is therefore not concerned with the good of others. But man is capable of generalizing. His rationality consists in it. The simple operation of replacing "I want . . . " by "we want . . . " is typical of reasoning man. The man who wills only what all could will makes possible a community of shared, harmonious wills. The society of men who generally will together dissolves the virtual war of all against all with respect to which liberal society is only a truce. General will is the common good.

Man's dividedness is not overcome by the general will, but its character is transformed. It is no longer experienced as an opposition between self and other, inside and outside. The struggle is now between one's particular desire and one's general will, a will recognized as nonarbitrary and good. Selfovercoming is the essence of the moral experience, and it is this capacity that Rousseau believed he had discovered, a discovery only dimly perceived by ancient politics and entirely lost in modern politics. Willing generally constitutes a new kind of human freedom—not the satisfaction of animal inclination but real choice. It is the privileged and profound form of rationality as opposed to the calculation of personal benefit. It is a transformation of nature that preserves what is essential about nature. Obedience to the general will is an act of freedom. This is the dignity of man, and a good society makes possible and encourages such dignity.[7]

The passage from the particularly willing savage to the generally willing citizen is the triumph of civilization, and it is man's historic activity to construct the bridge between the two. The distance is great. The soul has no such natural order, and its development is not a growth but a willful making, a putting in order of man's disordered and incoherent acquisitions during the course of time. Education is this activity of construction, which Rousseau presents in all its complexity and richness in his greatest work, *Emile*. Putting this education into political practice is really the work of the legislator, who must be an artist. Beginning from the first needs and desires of a limited and selfish being, passing through all the experiences requisite to learning how to preserve itself, he ends with the man who thinks of himself as man simply, controlling his wishes by the imperative of their possibility for all men.

All this is abstract. For such a man really to exist, there must be a community into which he is woven so tightly that he cannot think of himself separately from it, his very existence formed as part of this whole. The public business is identical to his private interest, and he thinks of it when he wakes in the morning and when he goes to bed at night. It does not suffice that he be an unquestioning part of a traditional society governed by ancestral ways. He must understand himself as guiding his own destiny, as a lawmaker for his city and thereby for himself. Every decision, act, or decree of the city must be understood to be the result of his own will. Only in this way is he autonomous and does he maintain his natural inalienable freedom. The citizen as understood by Rousseau combines the competing charms of rootedness and independence.

It follows immediately that the citizen must choose to practice the severest virtues of self-control, for if his private bodily needs or desires are imperious, he will be too busy tending to them. Moderation for the sake of freedom is his principle. This is different from the bourgeois' delay of gratification, which still has as its motive the private needs of the individual and looks toward infinite increase as the end. The citizen's efforts are connected with present satisfactions that constitute their own reward. Concern with public business in the assembly of citizens is the core of his life. He works and cares for his property with a view to maintaining a modest competence, setting aside great private indulgences and personal anxieties about the future. The whole organization of community life inclines him toward generality in a substantial way. The choice of individuality would be difficult to make, whereas in a commercial society the public-spirited way of life has no support. Rousseau's city provides little opportunity for private consumer expense and imposes severe sumptuary taxes on itself.

The simplest political requisite of healthy politics is therefore a small territory and a small population.[8] The whole body of citizens must be able to meet regularly. Moreover, they must know one another. The extension of human sentiments is limited, and caring requires acquaintance. Love of country and one's fellows cannot be abstract; they must be continuously experienced. Perhaps the most remarkable difference between Rousseau's politics and the politics of Enlightenment concerns this question of size. The commercial republic tends to favor large territories and large populations. Large markets encourage production and exchange, hence increase of wealth. Moreover, only large countries can counterbalance large and powerful enemies. And they offer all kinds of advantages for the machinery of modern governments that rely less on the good character of men than on various counterpoising forces, on checks and balances. What is sacrificed, according to Rousseau, is autonomy and human connectedness. Concentration on local community and responsibility is part of Rousseau's legacy, a concentration that goes against all the dominant tendencies of commercial republics in modernity. Rousseau connects large size with despotism. As Montesquieu looked to great nations like England as the models for modern regimes directed to freedom, Rousseau looks to modern cities like Geneva as well as to Sparta to demonstrate the possibility of what he prescribes.

Small size is also necessary to avoid the modern democratic device of representation, which for Rousseau epitomizes the halfway modern solution to the problem of freedom.[9] Without transforming natural freedom into civil freedom—that is, without abandoning the habit of living as one pleases and doing what is necessary to become a part of a sovereign body—men hope that others will take the responsibility of governing for them while remaining loyal to their will. The effort of determining general wills is to be left to the representatives without having a citizen body that wills generally. This is a prescription for interest politics or the compromising of particular, selfish wills. The idea of the common good disappears, and the conflict of parties takes its place. Worst of all, representation institutionalizes divided modern man, no longer really free, hopelessly dependent on the wills of others, believing himself to be master but incapable of the effort of moral autonomy.

Thus, in broad outline, Rousseau rejects most of the elements of modern constitutionalism including those that make up the United States Constitution. In his view the principles of enlightened self-interest as well as the machinery of limited representative government only exacerbate the tension between individual and society and lead to ever greater egotistical individualism accompanied by dangerous arbitrary abuses of centralized governmental power. The very notion of checks and balances encourages the selfishness of partial interests. Good institutions in this sense are predicated on the badness of men. Whether the institutions function or not, they give way to and encourage moral corruption.

The foundings of government Rousseau wishes to encourage are those that make the virtue of all the citizens necessary to their functioning, and they are very complicated affairs. In most modern political philosophy after Machiavelli, there is little talk of founders or legislators. Lycurgus, Solon, Moses, Theseus, Romulus, Numa, and Cyrus were previously the common currency in discussion of the origins of political regimes. It was taken for granted that the union of disparate individuals into a community of goods and purposes is the most difficult of political deeds and requires men of surpassing greatness to achieve it. A way of life that engages all the members had to be instituted. But the new political discoveries seemed to indicate that the foundation of civil orders was more like the striking of a business contract, where all that is required is individuals who are clear about their personal interests and where they intersect with those of others. The transition into the civil state was understood to be almost automatic, certainly not requiring common agreement about the good life. This hardly perceptible transition indicated the naturalness of the new politics. All that was necessary to the founding of a political order was enlightenment or an instruction manual. Hobbes thought that the advantages of the civil order could be made evident to men before its establishment. The ancients thought that the most far-seeing statesmen alone could know those advantages and that the individual citizens could know them only afterward. The foundings require persuasion, deception, and force as well as an elaborated plan for a way of life adapted to the particular people that is to be founded. The ultimate goals of justice may be universal, but the ways to them are almost infinitely diverse. The legislator must combine particular and universal, taste and principle. Prudence rather than abstract reason is his instrument. Such was the view of ancient politics, and Rousseau partially returns to it, though further encumbering the legislator with the abstract demands of modern legitimacy. All of this underlines Rousseau's view of the great distance between the natural state and the civil state.[10]

This treatment of the legislator may be useful in thinking about the American Framers, whose position is anomalous in modern political thought. Their role was at least halfway between the Enlighteners and Rousseau. Their founding activity was not based on any explicit teaching about founding in the philosophies of Locke or Montesquieu. They were, as is Rousseau's legislator, without authority, acting as they did before the legislation that founds all authority, and their task was almost limitless. Surely they thought not only of the abstract contract but of how it would fit the people they were founding. And they reflected—individual members of the founding group more or less coherently—on the moral character of the citizens and the national life requisite for the success of their project. They were for a time and in their way almost princes, legislating for egalitarian rule, preparing their own extinction, acting out of motives of a vastness and selflessness far transcending those they expected of the citizens. All this is discussed by Rousseau, and it provides a link between the petty egotism Rousseau attributed to the classical liberal model of politics and the sublime morality he sought and insisted on.

Conclusion

Rousseau's description of what the legislator must accomplish might make the modern reader think he is speaking of culture rather than politics. The very word "culture," first employed in the modern sense by Kant, stemmed from an interpretation of Rousseau's intention. He was looking for a harmony between nature and civilization, civilization meaning all the historically acquired needs and desires of man and the means of satisfying them discovered by him. Civilization had shattered man's unity. Although the foundation of civil societies and the discovery of the arts and sciences might appear to be simply a progress, if progress is measured by actual happiness rather than the production of the means for the pursuit of happiness, the advantages of civilization become doubtful. The restoration of the unity of man is the project of politics taken broadly. Politics in its narrow modern sense concerns the *state*, the minimal rules for human intercourse, not the happiness of man. Culture is where we think man as a whole lives; it frames and forms man's possible ways of life and his attainment of happiness. It is thought to be the deeper phenomenon. Rousseau appears to us to combine the concerns of culture and of politics. For him they are really not separable. The nineteenth-century idea of culture was completely separated from politics. It ceased to be understood as a conscious founding within the power of men to construct. It came to be understood as a growth, a result of the mysterious process of history. But however far the notion moved from its roots in Rousseau, it continued to express his concern for the "organic" character of human association. The habitual way of using the word "culture"—as something admirable, as opposed to mere cosmopolitan, superficial "civilization"—reflected and still reflects Rousseau's contempt for bourgeois society and modern liberal constitutionalism as well as the critique of civilization he launched with the *Discourse on the Arts and Sciences.*

So it is perhaps helpful for us to describe Rousseau's legislator as the founder of a culture, and this makes more evident the magnitude of the task imposed on him by Rousseau. To succeed he must charm men with at least the appearance of divine authority to make up for the human authority he lacks and to give men the motives for submission to the law that nature does not provide. He not only needs authority from the gods, he must establish a civil religion that can support and reward men's willing the common good. What is called the sacred today and is understood to be the summit of culture finds a place in Rousseau's project more central than the very ambiguous one it has in liberal legislation, where religion may be understood to be unnecessary or even dangerous to the civil order. As one looks at what the legislator must do, it is hard to resist the temptation to say it is impossible.[11]

This impression was confirmed for Western consciousness by one highly visible experiment, the legislative activity of Robespierre, or the Terror. The attempt to institute citizenship was a bloody business, which was sufficient to repel most observers. As Locke and Montesquieu were the presiding geniuses of Adams, Madison, Hamilton, and Jefferson in their moderate founding, Rousseau was the presiding genius of the excesses of the French Revolution. Edmund Burke's overwhelming description of the events and Rousseau's influence on them is unforgettable.[12]

In spite of Rousseau's dangerous impracticality, he could not be put aside as just another failure. His articulation of the problem of democratic politics was simply too potent. His views about what effect his thought should have on practical politics are difficult to penetrate. Locke and Montesquieu would certainly in general have approved of the handiwork of their great pupils, and

Rousseau would just as certainly have disapproved of Robespierre. Although his teaching is full of fervent aspiration, it is also full of bleak pronouncements about the possibility of correcting the tendencies of modernity. Whether he thought his kind of city could actually come into being is uncertain. But if it were possible, it would be so only in a few small places with very special circumstances, like Corsica. The universal applicability and possibility of actualization that is the hallmark of modern political science disappears in Rousseau. In this again he is more like Plato and Aristotle than a modern. But Plato and Aristotle made a distinction between the just regime and acceptable ones that permitted men to live with the less than perfect, whereas Rousseau insists that only the simply just regime is legitimate, thereby making almost all real political life unacceptable. He somehow combines the high standards of the ancients with the moderns' insistence on actualization of the good regime, thus producing the ultramodern political disposition.

The origins of this are in Machiavelli's turning away from the imaginary cities of the old philosophers toward the way men really live. He intended to reduce the disproportion between the is and the ought, in favor of the is, so as to achieve the modest goals given by men's real needs. A lowering and simplification of the understanding of man's nature would make the satisfaction of that nature possible. But somehow this moral reductionism does not work. Man's longing for justice and dignity will not accept it, and with Rousseau the old tension reasserts itself in the form of the opposition between the real and the ideal. The state-of-nature teachings, which were elaborations of Machiavelli's intention, taught that man is naturally a brute concerned exclusively with his preservation. Civil society was in those teachings only a more prudent way of realizing the most primitive goals. Its establishment is a progress in that sense alone, not in the sense of a movement from brutishness to humanity. Freedom in the state of nature was only the means to preservation, and equality was only the absence of the authority of any man over any other man to prevent the exercise of his freedom. Civil society uses freedom and equality merely as means to the basic end of comfortable self-preservation. Therefore they could be greatly attenuated in the service of that end. Freedom and equality could be signed over to civil society, which adopts the responsibility for the more effective fulfillment of the goal for which they were the imperfect natural instruments. So it seems. But experience and reflection teach that, once man knows himself to be naturally free and equal, it is impossible to avoid the demand that men in society be free and equal in the most absolute sense.

The freedom of man is recognized to be his essence, and civil freedom is not possible without factual equality. In practice, all of society's laws remain doubtful until they can really be understood to be self-imposed, and every inequality appears intolerable. The easygoing solution of the satisfaction of the basic needs is overturned by constant demands for greater freedom and equality. They become insistent in practice as men are informed of their natural rights and act as perpetual goads to reform and revolution. What later came to be called a dialectic was set in motion, and natural freedom tends to civil freedom. Only when law is the expression of rational universality and all men are equally recognized by all as moral agents and as ends in themselves is the process complete. The chapter in the *Social Contract* where Rousseau describes the difference between natural animal freedom and moral freedom describes the two terms of the process.[13]

Whatever the consequences, once the principles appear to be self-evident, this aspiration toward ever greater freedom and equality follows, tending to challenge all prudential stopping points or efforts to counterpoise it by other principles or by traditions. The problem can be epitomized by the idea of social contract. All thinkers are in agreement that consent is requisite to the establishment of laws. But, Rousseau argued, none of them before him found any kind of rule of consent that binds the individual when he believes the law to be contrary to his interest—in the extreme case, his life, liberty, and property. Only Rousseau found the formula for that, distinguishing self-interest from moral obligation, discerning an independent moral interest in the general will. He discovered the source of moral goodness in modern political principles and provided the flag democracy could march under. So, at least, it was understood. Regimes dedicated to the sole preservation of man do not have the dignity to compel moral respect.

Although the attempt to incarnate the moral democratic regime in a modern nation appeared worse than quixotic to sober men after the French Revolution, they all agreed that Rousseau had to be taken account of, that his thought had to be incorporated into the theory and practice of the modern state.[14] Kant and Hegel are only the two most notable examples of this, giving an account of moral dignity in freedom based on Rousseau while using it to reinterpret and sublimate bourgeois society. Thus they hoped to reconcile Rousseau with the reality of modernity rather than permitting the impulse he transmitted to lead to ever greater extremes in rebellion against triumphant modernity. Failing that reconciliation, Rousseau's persuasive depiction of humanity shattered and fragmented by the apparently irresolvable conflict between nature and society authorizes many different kinds of attempts to pick up the pieces: on the political Left, new revolutions and new terrors to install the regime of democratic virtue; on the Right, immersion in the rootedness of local cultures without the justification of rational universality; then there are those who, like Thoreau, flee the corruptions of society in an attempt to recover natural self-sufficiency.

Taking Rousseau seriously, however, does not necessarily mean despising and rejecting the regime of the United States Constitution, as is proved by the example of one of the most serious of those thoughtful men influenced by Rousseau. That is Alexis de Tocqueville, whose very obvious Rousseauism is masked to contemporary eyes by his conservative admirers, who refuse to admit he could have any connection with Rousseau, the leftist extremist. He turned from the spectacle of European egalitarian disorder to the United States, which he saw as the model of orderly liberty. He affirmed without hesitation the justice of equality over against the unjust privileges of the past. He interpreted the United States as a vast educational undertaking, instructing citizens in the political exercise of their rights. He treated the Founders as men whose characters expressed a higher morality that may not have been contained in their principles. He, of course, could not believe that the United States simply solved the political problem. His view of American democracy is tinged with the melancholy that Rousseau induces when one looks at real political practice. He casts respectful glances at American savages and at the great souls of some aristocratic men. He recognized the danger that the regime might tend toward materialism, to mere self-interest on the part of the citizens, and to atomizing individualism. He concentrated on the importance of local self-government, which approximated the participation of the independent city, and saw the New England town as the real foundation of American freedom, the core around which the larger government aggregated. Moreover, he introduced compassion, a sentiment alien to Locke and Montesquieu, as the corrective to the harshness of economic relations in the commercial society. Compassion he took to be the core of democratic feeling and the ground for something more than connections of interest among men. He also concentrated as liberals did not on the connectedness between man and woman and their offspring as constituting an intermediate community, a bridge between individual and society. He simply reproduces Rousseau's reflections on the family in *Emile*. And he looks to a gentle, democratic religion to mitigate the

American passion for material well-being. Rousseau makes Tocqueville alert to the dangers of liberal society and allows him to reinterpret it in such a way as to encourage the citizen virtues that can emerge out of the principles of freedom and equality rightly understood.

I have adduced the example of Tocqueville to indicate the kind of meditation about politics that men of Rousseauian sensibilities might have. Rousseau's specific projects were quickly exploded. But he infected most of us with longings for freedom and virtue that are difficult to get over. He is that modern thinker of democracy who had the depth and breadth in his vision of man found in Plato and conspicuously absent in those who propounded our principles. He does not simplify man to get results. He can talk about love and God and the sublime in revealing the fullness of the human potential. Most of all Rousseau concentrates not so much on what threatens life as on what makes life worth living, taking his orientation from the positive rather than the negative. More than any of his predecessors, he tried, based on what moderns believe to be true about man, to describe and recover the fundamental sweetness of existence. This complicates things but proves irresistible to all who seek for the good. This generation must come to terms with his understanding of our democratic life, as have all those who lived since he wrote.

Above all, Rousseau's criticism of liberalism must be tested against the original and authentic voices of liberalism to see whether they can meet his objections. Is Rousseau perhaps like Machiavelli, who subtly parodied Plato and made him appear to later ages to be an idealist? Is liberalism as coarsely materialistic as Rousseau alleges, or did Locke, Montesquieu, and the *Federalist* anticipate his objections? Did triumphant liberalism forget its own profound moral sources and replace them with oversimplified arguments in favor of itself, leaving itself open to Rousseau's assault? Have we not adopted Rousseau's characterization of us and thereby weakened our self-respect? This confrontation between Rousseau and the great liberals will enhance our self-awareness and make us recognize the profundity of the antagonists and the richness of Rousseau's influence. He may be a charm to be overcome, but to do that, his charm must first be experienced.

NOTES

1. Jean-Jacques Rousseau, *On the Social Contract*, bk. 2, chaps. 8–10.
2. *Social Contract*, bk. 1, chap. 6 note, and *Emile, or On Education*, trans. Allan Bloom (New York: Basic Books, 1979), 39–41.

3. Jean-Jacques Rousseau, *Discourse on the Origins of Inequality*, pt. 2; compare *Social Contract*, bk. 1, chap. 9.

4. Jean-Jacques Rousseau, *Discourse on the Arts and Sciences*, in *Two Discourses*, ed. Roger Masters and Judith Masters (New York: St. Martin's Press, 1964), 51.

5. *Social Contract*, bk. 1, chap. 6.

6. Ibid., chap. 8.

7. Ibid.

8. Ibid., bk. 2, chap. 9; bk. 3, chap. 12.

9. Ibid., bk. 3, chap. 15.

10. Ibid., bk. 2, chap. 7.

11. Ibid., bk. 2, chap. 8. Compare "Profession of Faith of the Savoyard Vicar," in *Emile*, 266–313.

12. Edmund Burke, "Letter to a Member of the National Assembly," in *Selected Writings and Speeches*, ed. Peter J. Stanlis (Garden City, N.Y.: Doubleday, 1963), 511–13.

13. *Social Contract*, bk. 1, chap. 8.

14. There were strands of utopian socialism that still looked toward the establishment of small communities of the kind Rousseau prescribed. Their most notable expression was the kibbutzim in Israel, founded by Russian Jews influenced by Tolstoy, a most ardent admirer of Rousseau.

❈ 8 ❈
Rousseau and the French Revolution

FRANÇOIS FURET

I

The urge to cast Jean-Jacques Rousseau as the author whose ideas presaged and directed the course of the French Revolution is as old as the event itself. It was already felt by the actors of the Revolution, many of whom from 1789 on continually referred to him as their great inspiration. Beginning with the Constituent Assembly, praise of Rousseau and especially of the *Social Contract* was frequent.[1] In October 1790 the bust of the famous man was installed in the Assembly Hall, alongside a copy of that no less famous work, and in December the deputies passed a motion to bestow public honors on Rousseau. Nothing can be more inexact than to date the French revolutionaries' official consecration of Rousseau to 1792—to what one might call the second period of the Revolution. True, that was when the name and face of Rousseau acquired a particular aura linked at least in part to the mounting influence of Robespierre over the course of events. The head of the Jacobins wielded his power by means of an ideological authority in which the cult of Rousseau figured not only centrally but almost exclusively. In his celebration of the author of the *Social Contract*, Robespierre, unlike the men of 1789, was no longer paying tribute to one of the greatest figures of the Enlightenment; on the contrary, he was honoring the only individual who had given voice to Virtue and Reason in a corrupt century and who had, for that very cause, been persecuted by a coalition of the government and his fellow philosophes.[2] Rousseau was the intellectual patron of the Festival of the Supreme Being: the *Savoyard Vicar* followed upon the *Social Contract*.

After 9 Thermidor, Rousseau's glory would survive for a time even beyond the fall of his greatest disciple. The decision to transfer Rousseau's remains to the Pantheon, taken by the Convention in the spring of 1794 at the height of the Terror, was carried out only in October, and then it was at the initiative of Lakanal and the "Thermidorians" who had triumphed over Robespierre.[3] By then, heaven knows, the reign of Virtue was over. Rousseau was "pantheo-nized"—as was Marat at about the same time—because the machinery had already been set in motion to do so. But that decision had lost its meaning in the current political context: the victors of Thermidor were the very men who would go on to oppose the alleged influence of the *Social Contract* on the Revolution. During the constitutional discussions of the year III they contin-ued to pay homage to the memory of the great Jean-Jacques, but more from habit and rhetorical expediency than from any authentic feeling of kinship with Rousseau. Sieyès, moreover, during this same debate of July and August 1795, was the first to question the excessive if not superstitious respect the French had maintained since 1789 for the unlimited sovereignty of the people along the model of that possessed by the kings.[4] In this he was seconded by Madame de Staël and Benjamin Constant, who had just arrived from Switzer-land. The intellectuals close to the regime of the year III, known as the "Ideologues"—men such as Destutt de Tracy, Cabanis, and Volney, would also deplore Rousseau's baneful influence on the course taken during the Robespierrist years.

At the end of the Revolution, in the last years of the eighteenth century, the spirit of the age turned not against Rousseau the great man of letters, but against the supposed role his political philosophy had played in the failure of the Revolution. Witness the utterance of Bonaparte (recounted by Roederer) during a visit to Jean-Jacques's room at Ernonville in 1800: "He was a real lunatic, your Rousseau; it was he who led us to where we are now."[5] The brutality of this statement is diametrically opposed to the adulation Rousseau enjoyed among the Jacobins in 1793, but it evinces the same diagnosis of the Revolution as inspired by Rousseau.

That diagnosis was shared not only by participants in the Revolution but also by interpreters at the time and throughout the following century. As an example of a contemporary observer, no one is better than Burke, who was already incriminating Rousseau at the end of 1790.

> The paradoxes of eloquent writers, brought forth purely as a sport of fancy to try their talents, to rouse attention and excite surprise, are taken up by these gentlemen, not in the spirit of the original authors, as means of cultivating their taste and improving their style. These paradoxes become with them serious grounds of ac-tion upon which they proceed in regulating the most important concerns of the state. . . . Mr. Hume told me that he had from

Rousseau himself the secret of his principles of composition. That acute though eccentric observer had perceived that to strike and interest the public the marvelous must be produced; that the marvelous of the heathen mythology had long since lost its effect; that the giants, magicians, fairies, and heroes of romance which succeeded had exhausted the portion of credulity which belonged to their age; that now nothing was left to the writer but that species of the marvelous which might still be produced, and with as great an effect as ever, though in another way; that is, the marvelous in life, in manners, in characters, and in extraordinary situations, giving rise to new and unlooked-for strokes in politics and morals. I believe that were Rousseau alive and in one of his lucid intervals, he would be shocked at the practical frenzy of his scholars, who in their paradoxes are servile imitators, and even in their incredulity discover an implicit faith.[6]

By means of his attack on Rousseau as a man of letters, Burke was really raising the issue of the abstract ambitions of the French Revolution. The guiding principle of the men of 1789 was the reverie of a writer in search of something witty to say about man in general. As Maistre would put it later on (inspired, incidentally, by Burke), the revolutionaries saw themselves as legislating not specifically for the French people—in the light of their history, their political and moral habits, the state of their mores—but for humanity.[7] Humanity, however, is merely an abstract concept that does not exist from a political standpoint. Because their goal was so nebulous, the revolutionaries could only enact the conditions for a catastrophe.

In his own particular language, Hegel would say much the same thing in his chapter in the *Phenomenology of Spirit* addressing the Terror. That discussion begins with a critique of the *Social Contract*. According to Hegel, the goal of the *Social Contract* was the absolute unification of private wills in the concept of the general will. It was by virtue of that concept that Rousseau clearly saw that the key problem of modern society was how it could exist as a stable whole while founded upon a multiplicity of private interests. But in the *Social Contract* Rousseau does not reconcile the universal and the particular except in a formal, abstract way exclusive of any mediation. The general will thus lacks concrete institutions to attach it to private interests and remains incapable of resolving the problem of governing. It issues only in a negation of the singular and the particular and thus in the death of everyone. The Terror is thus described as dealing "the coldest and meanest of all deaths, with no more significance than cutting off a head of cabbage or swallowing a mouthful of water."[8]

To understand how far the interpretation of the French Revolution has revolved around the *Social Contract*, we must turn to the French political debates of the first half of the nineteenth century and more particularly to those around the time of the revolution of July 1830. In line with Benjamin Constant[9] and Madame de Staël, Guizot quite early on tried to found Orleanism upon a revision of the revolutionary tradition that would be conducive to a stable bourgeois government. In that revision, which Guizot began working on in the early 1820s when he was combating the ultraroyalist movement, the critique of the *Social Contract* holds, as if by accident, a central position. An entire chapter of the *Essai sur l'histoire du gouvernement représentatif*,[10] a collection of Guizot's lectures given at the Sorbonne in 1821–22, is devoted to Rousseau's idea of the general will. Guizot viewed that idea as no less false than the notion of absolute sovereignty, even if it issued from the people, because individuals can never conform to it in their private lives—for example, within their own families. Pure democracy leads only to anarchy, as shown by 1789. All modern society can do is to extract from itself, by means of representative government, its share of Reason, that is, a semblance of the superior order of justice between men.

After 1830, in reaction to Orleanism, the opposite tendency appeared. If the critique of Rousseau was the banner of those who would have liked to revise 1789 according to better principles, the celebration of Rousseau was one of the favorite themes of those who objected to the bourgeois expropriation of the revolution of July 1830. The battle of ideas around Rousseau became ever more a political struggle over the contradictory heritage of the great ancestors of the Revolution. The *Social Contract* was the test. Those critical of Rousseau affirmed 1789 while rejecting 1793. Disciples of Rousseau favored 1793 over 1789.

Opposed to Guizot were Buchez and Louis Blanc. Buchez represented the crossroads of two traditions he tried to reconcile: the critique of bourgeois individualism that originated with the St. Simonians, and "republican" loyalty to Robespierrist Jacobinism. From Rousseau, Buchez would borrow the concept of the sovereignty of the people, imbuing it with a religious foundation and so transforming the national community into an "organic" one, sheltered from the hazards inseparable from individual wills.[11] For whereas the men of

1789 had wished to create a society of individuals, those of 1793 had aspired (albeit with only partial success) to found a true community. After Buchez, Louis Blanc would place these two opposed periods of the Revolution under the names and patronage of the greatest French philosophers of the century: the revolution of Voltaire, thinker of the bourgeoisie, and that of Rousseau, philosopher of the people.[12] The general will was the promise of both democratic and strong government, and the *Savoyard Vicar* superimposed on it a civil religion of fraternity between citizens.

Quinet wrote his history of the French Revolution largely against the socialist prophets who had drawn upon both Rousseau and Robespierre; it was marked by a liberal if not libertarian bent. But Quinet had no disagreement with the socialists' diagnosis that from 1793 on Rousseau had become "the book and the law of the Revolution." He, however, saw this as a great danger. "The more the Revolution evolved, the more it seemed to be an incarnation of Jean-Jacques, and immediately the Revolution was in danger. To found a society upon Jean-Jacques: Is that not like building a city on the crater of Aetna?"[13] Thus we can see that for the whole of the nineteenth century Rousseau was at the heart of the interpretation of the Revolution for both its admirers and its critics. It was as if the ideas of the *Social Contract* or *Emile* could have enabled one to predict the radicalization of the French Revolution from 1789 to 1794 and could promote an understanding of what had happened and dictate, depending on one's viewpoint, a celebration of the grandeur or a denunciation of the failure of those events. Finally, a new chapter has been added to this long tradition of debate over the Rousseauism of the French Revolution, this one linked to the political experience of the twentieth century. After the Second World War, Jacob Talmon cast French Jacobinism as the matrix of what he termed "totalitarian democracy."[14] Thus the Rousseau of the *Social Contract* now stands accused as the inspiration not only of the French Revolution, but also of the Communist revolutions of the twentieth century.

II

Let us leave the domain of the interpretation of the Revolution and ask what lessons the French revolutionaries themselves drew from Rousseau's thought and in what respect they were most faithful to it. Since Rousseau went to the trouble to write a political treatise, we can make a fairly precise comparison between the *Social Contract* and the successive regimes of the revolutionary years.

Our first and fundamental observation is that the revolutionaries were quite unfaithful to the *Social Contract:* between 1789 and 1800, they devoted all their energy to founding a representative government, the very type Rousseau had declared intrinsically corrupt, since the will of the people could not be transferred and therefore could not be represented. It is true that he retreated from this absolute condemnation of representation when considering countries such as Poland, whose size and population prohibited the exercise of direct democracy. But he modified his concession to the necessity of representation by requiring binding instructions that would subject the representatives to the will of their constituents. The men of 1789, in contrast, forbade binding instructions, which they viewed as an institution of the ancien régime. They had hardly been elected and had just assembled when, in order to declare themselves a Constituent Assembly and appropriate the king's constituent sovereignty, they had to break the contract of subordination to their constituents that underlay the entire system of the Estates General during the French monarchy.[15] As a relic of the ancien régime, binding instructions were completely out of place in the new one.

Sieyès, one of the most influential men of 1789, was also the theoretician who, on this issue, most opposed the thought of Rousseau. He distinguished between democratic government—by which he meant the direct democracy of classical times—and representative government, a necessary feature of modern states. For the vast and populous states created by modern monarchies faced obstacles to the collective exercise of power by all their citizens besides the circumstantial impediments of geographical size and population.

> Modern European peoples bear little resemblance to the ancient ones. All we can think about is trade, agriculture, factories, and so on. The desire for wealth seems to turn all the states of Europe into great workshops; there one cares a great deal more for consumption and production than for happiness. Today's political systems are also exclusively based on labor; the productive capacity of man is everything. . . . We are thus obliged to see the vast majority of men as mere machines for working. Nonetheless you cannot deny the status of citizen and civic rights to that uneducated multitude that is entirely absorbed in forced labor.[16]

According to Sieyès, the solution to this dilemma lay in the representation of the less enlightened by the more enlightened, a political form of the division of labor. "Without alienating their rights," he continued, "citizens may delegate their exercise." One could not have come up with a doctrine more foreign to Rousseau, more contradictory to the *Social Contract.* Jean-Jacques had proposed classical methods of organizing the city to the moderns because he saw only corruption in the modern view of man as a being defined by acquisitive activity and the division of labor. The revolutionary abbé, to the contrary, imbued with the ideas of the Anglo-Scottish Enlightenment, adopted the division of labor as the guiding principle of both the exercise of citizenship and the choice of forms of government under modern conditions.

It is true that after Sieyès opted for representative government over "pure democracy," he still attributed almost absolute power to the representatives of the people—as if, from his constitutional perspective, the sovereignty of the National Assembly was as unified and complete as the sovereignty of the people in Rousseau's thought. But there are two problems with this ascription of representative sovereignty to Rousseau's influence. The first is that it remains to be demonstrated that the majority of the National Assembly felt it possessed such sovereignty. The second is that it is not certain the doctrine granting a unitary character to the representative exercise of sovereignty originated solely or even principally in Rousseau's "general will."

The first constitution of the Revolution, that of 1791, did eventually grant the king a position along with the National Assembly as representative of the nation, that is, a cosovereignty in the making of laws. I say "eventually" because this particular feature was not voted until August 1791, during the period of "reaction" that followed the restoration of Louis XVI to the throne after his flight to Varennes. The earlier form of the text, voted in 1789, had not accorded him the dignity of "representative of the nation." Nonetheless, even at that time, against the advice of Sieyès, the Constituent Assembly had vested in the king the right of veto suspending for two legislative sessions the validity of laws passed by the Assembly. This was the proof that though the elected representatives did indeed have the last word, Louis XVI retained the all-important prerogative of sending a given decision back to the Assembly, thus making the nation the last arbiter of any disagreement.

Whatever juridical interpretation the men of 1789 gave to this arrangement, it was obviously incompatible with Rousseau's insistence in the *Social Contract* on the formation of the law by the general will. The designation of the king as representative of the nation in the constitution of 1791 departed still further from this principle. It remains true, however, that from 1789 on many of the French revolutionaries endowed the idea of sovereignty with such a powerful aura of respect and invested it with such strong passions that they could hardly divide its exercise: thus the right of veto that the constitution of 1791 had granted to Louis XVI was never actually exercised by him, except in 1792 when it was finally taken away.

Even if the revolutionaries did sometimes borrow the vocabulary of the *Social Contract* and speak of the general will, their respect and passion for undivided sovereignty drew on other sources as well. One of the central traditions of French Enlightenment philosophy was that of political rationalism, according to which the state was to be organized along the lines of Reason—that is, in the form of a cascade of deductions issuing from the sovereign conceived as Reason in action. Such a system resembled a cohesive clockwork rather than a system of checks and balances. Sovereignty implied unity for Turgot[17] no less than for Rousseau, though now assumed to represent reason as well as will.

There is, however, an explanation of a different nature for why the French of the revolutionary period were so receptive to a unitary idea of sovereign power: quite simply, the influence of the prerevolutionary political tradition. For the France of 1789 was also the France of absolutism. It was, after all, a nation that little by little had been unified by its kings, who had mostly sought to weaken or extinguish local initiatives. France was the cradle of what is known as absolute monarchy, a regime that, as Tocqueville demonstrated, constituted in itself a first revolution that was the necessary condition for that of 1789. Tocqueville analyzed with unequaled profundity the subversive effect of the activities of the centralized administrative state on the traditional order in the seventeenth and eighteenth centuries. In book 2, chapter 6 of the *Ancien Régime* on the methods of administration, he further suggested that absolutism had been even more present in people's imaginations than in actual practice.[18] In other words, long before 1789 the French were already used to thinking of a sovereign state above them, driven by a central government and represented by bureaucrats directly dependent on that government. Their experience of absolutism led directly to a unitary concept of sovereignty.

Experience and the habits it bred were surely more compelling than the effects of reading the *Social Contract*—which had hardly been a best-seller.[19] What measure of influence could a few thousand readers of an abstract, obscure treatise have wielded compared with the political reflexes of a people? In the end, merely by replacing the king with the representatives of the people,

in what looked like a radical rupture, the revolutionaries were able to perpetu-
ate the idea of undivided sovereignty without missing a beat. The notion of the
general will, drawn from the *Social Contract,* was perhaps but a bit of window
dressing on that transfer. Throughout human history, the greatest books may
have been those that engendered the greatest misunderstanding.

It remains for us to examine whether the year II, as so many witnesses
and commentators believed, brought with it a greater fidelity to the *Social
Contract.*

The king fell in August 1792 and would be guillotined the following January. France was now a republic, but this was neither necessary nor sufficient to
reconcile the Revolution with Rousseau's political teachings. For according to
Rousseau, the existence of a king is perfectly compatible with political legitimacy should he be an executive agent of the general will: this eventuality is
discussed in book 3, chapter 18 of the *Social Contract.* Conversely, a republic can
be organized in such a way as to usurp the sovereignty of the people. Such was
the case, indeed, with the first French Republic, in which the sovereign power
of legislation was exercised by representatives rather than by the people. That
Republic did not view representation as opposed to democracy (that is, the
power of the people). On the contrary, the establishment of universal suffrage
in August 1792 tended to reinforce, in the imagination of the second revolutionary generation, the idea of a potentially perfect correspondence between
the people and its representatives. Nevertheless, the elections to the Convention in that month showed that this reform had not altered the functioning of
the political system. There were circumstantial reasons: these elections took
place in an atmosphere of terror, hardly favorable to voter participation. But
there were also more basic problems, including the indirect election in two
tiers provided for since 1789, something the legislators had carefully preserved
despite pressure from the Jacobin Club and the Commune of Paris. Under this
scheme, the departmental electoral college became the key to the outcome of
the election. Although elected by primary assemblies, it was completely independent of them and thus rather easily manipulated by the activists of the
clubs and popular societies.[20] Since the beginning of the French Revolution,
there had been no elections more contrary to the spirit of Rousseauism than
those of 1792. In Paris, for example, a scant 1,000 departmental electors
representing 160,000 voters were brought together in the very confines of the
Jacobin Club, where they proceeded by voice vote and were thus subject to

public intimidation. It is hardly surprising that the Paris representatives to the Convention formed a homogeneous delegation.

In contrast, the constitution that Condorcet proposed to the Convention in February 1793, favored the rights of the people and sought to restore their ability to monitor their representatives. Every citizen, as long as he had the support of his primary assembly, was to enjoy the right to appeal any proposed law, as well as to bring new laws before the legislators. Condorcet's project would not outlast the Girondin period of the Convention, however, and when a new constitutional debate took place in June, the Jacobin orators opposed any attempts to limit parliamentary sovereignty. After the "purge" of the Convention (the forcible expulsion of the Girondins carried out under threats from the armed Parisian *sections*), the curbing of the sovereignty of the national representation was no longer in the interest of the left wing of the Assembly.

Thus the concessions made to direct democracy by the men who would constitute the dictatorship of the year II were more tactical than philosophical. Robespierre illustrates this well. Though the will of the people was always on his tongue, what he meant by it varied widely according to circumstance.[21] He first built his reputation on his critique of the poll tax system conceived by the Constituent Assembly; without specifically calling into question the idea of representation, he nonetheless defended the principles of direct democracy, by emphasizing the right of the people's *sections* to recall their deputies. The legitimation of 10 August 1792 was to be the apogee of his electoral Rousseauism, since the people then reestablished their rights in opposition to their disloyal representatives. He would trot out the same argument on 2 June 1793 in favor of the expulsion of the Girondins. From then on, however, the Jacobin chief would unceasingly defend the national representation against any popular intervention, and his notion of the dictatorship of public safety, which he exercised by virtue of powers granted by the Convention and only the Convention, no longer resembled in any way the ideas of the *Social Contract*. Nor is there the slightest reference to Rousseau in his famous speech of December 1793 on revolutionary government: "The theory of revolutionary government," he declared there, "is as new as the Revolution that created it. It is as pointless to seek its origins in the books of the political theorists, who fail to foresee this revolution, as in the laws of the tyrants."[22]

Can we say that though the *Social Contract* does little to explain Robespierrist politics, it did at least inspire the sansculottes, those activists of the Parisian *sections* and champions of direct democracy? Even this cannot be taken for granted. For those popular militants made no demands for binding instructions. What they wanted was constantly to supervise and direct their representatives, maintaining them at their mercy by making their positions revocable at any moment and liable to be superseded by violent action should the necessity arise. They constantly invoked Rousseau, but as Bernard Manin has shown,[23] they drew their inspiration from sources other than the *Social Contract.* For their very policy of surveillance of elected officials implied that those officials have the right to legislate in their own names, without any sanction by the people they represent. It did not evince Rousseau's doctrine of the radical illegitimacy of the will expressed by representative officials.

III

In the final analysis, there is not much of the *Social Contract* in the French Revolution. There is not a single leading participant in the Revolution, including Robespierre, whom we might consider a reliable interpreter of that difficult text. Each drew what he wanted from it, without attempting to penetrate its complexities and extraordinary abstraction, and none really tried to apply its program. In the end, the *Social Contract* provided catchwords like the general will but no constitutional formulas.

Was the relation of the *Social Contract* to the French Revolution merely a gross misunderstanding perpetuated by a borrowed vocabulary? Certainly not. For if Rousseau's political program was not present in the Revolution, his spirit certainly was, especially if we extend our inquiry beyond the *Social Contract.* Let us consider the *First Discourse* (*Discourse on the Arts and Sciences*), which marked Rousseau's entry onto the literary scene, or *Emile.* No one had a better sense of the corruption of modern man than Jean-Jacques. History, celebrated by so many Enlightenment authors as the agent of "civilization"— that is, progress toward the social state of greater civility and sociability, increased wealth, and gentler mores and laws—was for Rousseau a process of moral degradation and degeneration from natural man. Natural man had been solitary and self-sufficient, feeling only a vague compassion for his fellow-man. Social or historical man, although he retains the happy egoism of the natural man when among his fellow citizens, lacks his self-sufficiency. He is a citizen, but a bad one, a divided man, devoting all his energy to the satisfaction of his amour propre by constantly comparing himself with others. To become a good citizen, man must be "denatured" by having his most essential tendencies transformed to be in keeping with the moral life of man-in-society. "He who in the civil order wants to preserve the primacy of the sentiments of nature does not know what he wants. Always in contradiction with himself, always floating between his inclinations and his duties, he will never be man or citizen. He will be good neither for himself nor for others. He will be one of these men of our days: a Frenchman, an Englishman, a bourgeois. He will be nothing."[24]

The men of 1789 adopted this Rousseauian image of humanity degraded. The cause was the ancien régime, and the remedy was regeneration. No sentiment was more intense at that moment than the feeling that a breach had opened up in time, that there had been a rupture in the usual order of things. Subjectively, what the French had begun calling "the Revolution" in the spring of 1789 was precisely the peculiar consciousness that they were living through the watershed that divided past from future. The past was the ancien régime, the epoch of man corrupted by society, and in destroying it the Revolution opened up the way to regeneration.

The word "regeneration" was vague enough to encompass a variety of meanings ranging from a return to the classical city of citizens to the spiritual renaissance of humanity in Jesus Christ, including the modern utopia of a universal pedagogy of virtue. But all these definitions shared a fundamental repudiation of the course of French history up to 1789. Even—or perhaps especially—the complexity of that history was suspect. For it was a history composed of three curses superimposed on one another: the aristocracy, the sacerdotal power, and the monarchy. None of these could serve the task of regeneration. It was in their rejection of the past and the radicalism of the tabula rasa they imagined that the men of 1789 showed their affinity with the spirit of Rousseau. Like him, they wished to educate an entire people for happiness in and by liberty—an undertaking that, like the one articulated in *Emile*, was without precedent either in its ambition or in its universality.

It is by virtue of the project of regeneration that the Revolution belongs to Rousseau. Like him, the revolutionaries wished to create a new man. It was in pursuing that project that the Revolution underwent successive liberal and illiberal periods that mirrored the ambiguity in Rousseau between the egalitarian process of republican politics and the authoritarian method of creating the new man. For in the *Social Contract*, the notion of sovereignty exercised by society over itself exists alongside the Plutarchian idea of the sage-legislator, the enlightened founder of institutions destined to force the people to be free. And like the tutor of *Emile*, the great legislator is not above using tricks to persuade the people to adopt his system of mores and laws. Regeneration cannot be obtained through the will or consent of individuals who have been corrupted by history; a sage must stand ready to persuade or constrain them to virtue.

Approaching the question of Rousseau's influence on the French Revolution from another angle, one could show not how the Revolution appeared to have reproduced the scenario of the founding of society conceived of by Rousseau as indispensable to the existence of the modern citizen, but how the Revolution exposed the passions whose force and internal economy had been analyzed in the *Second Discourse* and *Emile*. In Rousseau, it is the sentiment of pity[25] that links man in a state of nature to his fellows. Society awakens reason, thereby weakening pity; henceforth social man begins ceaselessly comparing himself with others and spends his life the victim of his amour propre, the prisoner of his own perception of how others regard him. He continues to identify himself with other men, but his compassion has lost the tranquil character it had in the state of nature and is tinged with anxiety. The imagination, that privilege or curse of social man, has superimposed a feeling of difference on the sentiment of common humanity. Henceforth compassion will be subordinate to amour propre. It therefore tends to be less a participation in the suffering of one's fellows than a way of feeling exempt from those sufferings. The rich isolate themselves from the poor, fueling their envy and thus jeopardizing the very existence of the social bond. The psychology of amour propre thus finds its arena in social inequality. It will in the end place the blame on the rich and powerful, who are incapable of compassion and consequently unworthy of receiving it. This is Rousseau's contribution to the discourse of the French Revolution, radicalizing it by extending to the bourgeois the condemnation of the "aristocrat" pronounced by the men of 1789. As Hannah Arendt so clearly perceived, the theme of compassion as constituting the "social question" is one of the essential elements of the revolutionary rhetoric.

Almost a century before Marx, Rousseau's works constitute a critique of the liberal postulate of the social character of the natural man: natural man must be denatured to produce social man. The corruption of modern man must be wiped clean and the individual rid of all interests and amour propre to provide the tabula rasa on which can be inscribed the citizen—the only acceptable participant in the social contract. The French revolutionaries continuously circled that ambition, which is why their entire project from 1789 on resembles a fragment of the history of philosophy. This is so true that we can read the unfolding of the Revolution like a book that describes the contradictions of that project and the political impasses it collided with, above all the impossibility within liberal institutions of forming a citizen who thinks in terms of something other than utility or of maximizing his private interests. The contradiction inherent in the abstract attempt to constrain modern man to subordinate everything to the public good led to the Terror.

From a very early date, the course of the French Revolution lent itself to being decoded philosophically—both as a striking manifestation of liberal individualism and as the attempt at an *Aufhebung* or overcoming of that liberal individualism. The easiest way to understand the torrential event that concluded the eighteenth century is still to come to the Revolution from philosophy, to approach Mirabeau and Robespierre from Rousseau. Jean-Jacques may not have left the revolutionaries any political formulas, but his writings remain indispensable to the interpretation of their experience.

I can borrow my conclusion from one of those revolutionaries, Joseph Lakanal, a member of the Convention in charge of reporting in the spring of 1795 on Rousseau's installation in the Pantheon. "It is not the *Social Contract* that brought about the Revolution. Rather, it is the Revolution that explained to us the *Social Contract*."[26]

NOTES

1. The reference to Rousseau and to the *Social Contract* is found in the first great constitutional debate of the Constituent Assembly, from the end of August to the beginning of September 1789. Cf. Roger Barny, "J. J. Rousseau dans la Révolution française, 1787–1791," 5 vols. (doctoral diss., University of Paris X, Nanterre, 1976); Marcel Gauchet, *La révolution des droits de l'homme* (Paris: Gallimard, 1989); Keith Baker, "Sovereignty," and Bernard Manin, "Rousseau," in *A Critical Dictionary of the French Revolution*, ed. François Furet and Mona Ozouf, trans. Arthur Goldhammer (Cambridge: Harvard University Press, 1989).

2. Maximilien Robespierre, *Discours du 18 floréal an II (7 mai 1794) à la Convention sur les rapports des idées religieuses et morales avec les principes républicains et sur les fêtes nationales,* in *Oeuvres,* ed. E. Déprez et al., vol. 10 (Paris, 1960–67).

3. Joseph Lakanal, *Rapport sur J. J. Rousseau fait au nom du Comité d'Instruction publique, 29 fructidor an II* (15 September 1794), *Moniteur* 21:770 (June–September 1795).

4. Emmanuel Sieyès, *Discours du 2 thermidor an III* (20 July 1795) in Sieyès, *Oeuvres,* vol. 3, no. 41 (Paris, 1989).

5. Louis Roederer, "Relations particulières avec le premier consul" (28 August 1800), in *Oeuvres, 1854,* vol. 3 (Paris: Firmin Didot, 1853–59), 336.

6. Edmund Burke, *Reflections on the Revolution in France*, ed. J. G. A. Pocock (Indianapolis: Hackett, 1987), 150.

7. Joseph de Maistre, *Considerations on France*, chap. 6 in *The Works of Joseph de Maistre*, trans. Jack Lively (New York: Schocken, 1971), 80.

8. G. W. F. Hegel, "Absolute Freedom and Terror," in *The Phenomenology of Spirit*, trans. A. V. Miller (Oxford: Oxford University Press, 1977), 360.

9. Benjamin Constant, *Ecrits et discours politiques* (1851), ed. O. Pozzo di Borgo (Paris: J. J. Pauvert, 1964), 2 vols., vol. 2, lecture 10, pp. 27–145.

10. François Guizot, *Essai sur l'histoire du gouvernement représentatif, 1820–22*, 129–53.

11. Philippe-Joseph-Benjamin Buchez, *Histoire parlementaire de la Révolution française*, 40 vols., vols. 1 and 2 (Paris: Paulin, 1834–38).

12. Louis Blanc, *Histoire de la Révolution française*, vol. 1 (Paris, 1847–62).

13. Edgar Quinet, *La Révolution* (1856), 2 vols. (Brussels, 1856), vol. 2, bk. 14, chap. 4.

14. Jacob Talmon, *The Origins of Totalitarian Democracy* (New York: Praeger, 1960).

15. François Furet and Ran Halévi, introduction to *Les orateurs de la Révolution français* (Paris: Gallimard, 1989), lxv–lxvii.

16. Emmanuel Sieyès, *Discours du 7 septembre 1789 à l'Assemblée nationale*, in Sieyèyes, *Oeuvres*, vol. 2, no. 12.

17. See the critique of American bicameralism by Turgot in his letter to Richard Price, which impelled John Adams to write his *Defense of the Constitutions of the United States*. The letter was published in 1785 at the end of Richard Price, *Observations on the Importance of the American Revolution and the Means of Making It a Benefit to the World*. It can be found in *Richard Price and the Ethical Foundations of the American Revolution*, ed. Bernard Peach (Durham, N.C.: Duke University Press, 1979), 215–24.

18. Alexis de Tocqueville, *The Old Regime and the French Revolution*, trans. Stuart Gilbert (New York: Doubleday, 1955, 1983), 61–72.

19. Louis Trénard, "La diffusion du *Contract social*," in *Etudes sur le "Contrat social" de J. J. Rousseau*, publications of the University of Dijon 30, Les belles-lettres (Dijon: University of Dijon, 1964).

20. Patrice Gueniffey, *Le nombre et la raison* (Paris: Ecole des Hautes Etudes, 1993).

21. Patrice Gueniffey, "Robespierre," in Furet and Ozouf, *Critical Dictionary of the French Revolution*.

22. Maximilien Robespierre, "On Revolutionary Government" (25 December 1973), in *Robespierre*, ed. George Rudé (Englewood Cliffs, N.J.: Prentice-Hall, 1967), 58.

23. Manin, "Rousseau."

24. Jean-Jacques Rousseau, *Emile, or On Education*, trans. Allan Bloom (New York: Basic Books, 1979), 40.

25. See Clifford Orwin, this volume, chapter 14.

26. See Lakanal, *Rapport*.

❧ 9 ❧

Rousseau and the Origins of Nationalism

MARC F. PLATTNER

Nationalism is one of many contemporary doctrines whose origins can be illuminated by turning to the writings of Jean-Jacques Rousseau. In this chapter I examine those teachings of Rousseau that helped give birth to modern nationalism and explore their uneasy coexistence with another, much more cosmopolitan side of Rousseau's thought. This is not a question I had thought much about until quite recently. When, under the tutelage of Allan Bloom, I devoted several years of concentrated study to Rousseau during the early 1970s, I had been preoccupied with those aspects of Rousseau's thought that both profoundly influenced the New Left's critique of liberal democracy and shed continuing light on it. From that perspective, I had explored the antinomy in Rousseau's work between individualism and collectivism, as well as that between nature and society.[1] Though the issue of nationalism is implicated in both these antinomies, I paid it little heed in the course of my work on Rousseau.

Today, of course, as a glance at the news on virtually any day will confirm, the question of nationalism has thrust itself back into the center of contemporary politics. It is an especially salient issue for someone like me whose day-to-day work focuses on the fortunes of democracy around the world. In the late 1980s nationalism rather suddenly emerged as a crucial ally of the new democratic movements seeking to liberate the non-Russian republics from the yoke of Soviet communist rule. Still more recently, however, nationalism has come to be viewed as a source of deadly strife and as one of the gravest obstacles hindering the consolidation of democracy in the postcommunist countries.

Now it is true, of course, that nationalism, though it seemed to be waning in most of the West, had remained a potent force in the Third World throughout the Cold War era. Yet Third World nationalism typically clothed itself in the language of anticolonialism and anti-imperialism. In part because of its overriding hostility to the liberal West, and in part because right-wing nationalism had been largely discredited by the enormities and the decisive defeat of

Nazism, postwar nationalism in the Third World was a phenomenon of the Left and thus usually understood itself as a stage on the way to a more egalitarian and cosmopolitan future. In the former Soviet bloc, however, nationalism, even when manipulated by erstwhile communists, inevitably has been pretty much immune to the cosmopolitan charms of the Left. Postcommunist nationalism, therefore, is a much more powerful, free-floating, and indeterminate phenomenon.

The present-day resurgence of nationalist passions cannot help but lead to renewed interest in the origins and foundation of nationalism. If one turns to some of the leading works of modern scholarship on the nature and rise of nationalism, one learns a number of interesting things.

First, nationalism comes to light as a distinctively modern phenomenon, whose origins can be found in the latter half of the eighteenth century and whose flourishing coincided with the rise of such other distinctively modern phenomena as industrialization and democratization. To be sure, human beings had always been divided into peoples united by common language, ancestry, and territory, which often produced strong bonds of mutual attachment; human beings also had in many cases displayed strong loyalty to the political regime that governed them. But in earlier eras it was rare among civilized peoples for ethnic divisions to coincide with political ones. Political units might be smaller than national units, as in the case of the Greek cities, or more commonly, larger than national units, as in the case of the empires that ruled numerous subject peoples both in the Orient and in much of Europe. The object of people's devotion might be their city, their king or emperor, or their religion; almost never was it their nation. Nationalism, by contrast, implies that political boundaries and national divisions should coincide and that the resulting nation-state should be the sole locus of political loyalty.

Another thing one learns from the literature on nationalism is that the thinker perhaps most commonly identified as the key source of the nationalist idea is none other than Jean-Jacques Rousseau. Hans Kohn, in *The Idea of Nationalism*, credits Rousseau with having "provided the modern nation with its emotional and moral foundations" and with preparing the "modern basis" of "the identification of nation and state."[2] And a 1939 volume titled *Nationalism*, issued by a study group of the British Royal Institute of International Affairs under the chairmanship of historian E. H. Carr, offers the following assertion: "The importance of Rousseau's thought in the development of the idea of nationalism can hardly be exaggerated. . . . Rousseau provided the theoretical foundations upon which alone the nationalism of the nineteenth century could be built."[3]

In the light of my own previous reading of Rousseau, I could not help but find rather surprising this identification of him as the intellectual father of nationalism. This is not merely because the individualistic and cosmopolitan aspects of Rousseau's thought seem to be clearly at odds with the spirit of nationalism, but also because even the emphatically political or civic side of Rousseau's teaching seems to hark back to the political theory and practice of classical antiquity and to be marked by a clear and often repeated preference for the small republic (or polis) as opposed to the larger political units associated with nationalism.

In the opening pages of book 1 of *Emile*, Rousseau provides one of his most powerful presentations of the gap that separates the natural man from the citizen. His examples of the public-spiritedness and selflessness of the citizen are all taken from Sparta and republican Rome. With respect to his own time, he states that "where there is no longer a fatherland [*patrie*], there can no longer be citizens" and adds that the very words *patrie* and *citoyen* "should be effaced from modern languages." And he says of a man educated in a manner that seeks to preserve the primacy of his natural sentiments in the midst of the civil order: "Always in contradiction with himself, always floating between his inclinations and his duties, he will never be either man or citizen. . . . He will be one of these men of our days: a Frenchman, an Englishman, a bourgeois. He will be nothing."[4] Rousseau thus clearly seems to suggest that belonging to a modern nationality is no equivalent of or substitute for true citizenship.

So before we explore the antinomy between nationalism and cosmopolitanism in Rousseau's thought, it is first necessary to analyze the more fundamental antinomy between *patriotism* (or citizenship) and cosmopolitanism. Only then will we be in a position to see how the concept of nationalism fits—or fails to fit—into the civic or patriotic side of Rousseau's teaching.

Cosmopolitanism versus Patriotism

Let us begin by looking briefly at the cosmopolitan side of Rousseau— those elements of his thought that seem to run counter to the notion that man's highest duties and deepest loyalties should be bound up with his role as a citizen of his fatherland. In the first place, we must consider here Rousseau's favorable treatment of what might be called subpolitical or prepolitical man, especially in the *Discourse on Inequality*. It is true that Rousseau's praise of the most primitive men or of the savage is typically juxtaposed to a critique of the artificial, hypocritical, and selfish men of his own time and is sometimes even accompanied by praise of Sparta or republican Rome. Yet a careful reading makes it clear that this praise of the primitive or natural individual is ultimately at odds with his praise of the genuine citizen.

Thus in the *Second Discourse* Rousseau favorably contrasts the savage, who "breathes only repose and freedom," and "wants only to live and remain idle" with the "citizen, always active, [who] sweats, agitates himself, torments himself incessantly in order to seek still more laborious occupations; he works to death, he even rushes to it in order to get in condition to live, or renounces life in order to acquire immortality." Rousseau explains "the true cause" of these differences as follows: "the savage lives within himself; the sociable man [and this must include the genuine citizen as well], always outside himself, knows how to live only in the opinion of others; and it is, so to speak, from their judgment alone that he draws the sentiment of his own existence."[5]

This criticism of the citizen from the point of view of the independence and self-sufficiency of the savage can be found implicitly even in some of Rousseau's writings that are most devoted to the praise of citizenship. Thus in the *First Discourse* Rousseau writes: "While government and laws provide for the safety and well-being of assembled men, the sciences, letters and arts, less despotic and perhaps more powerful, spread garlands of flowers over the iron chains with which men are burdened, stifle in them the sense of that original liberty for which they seemed to have been born, make them love their slavery, and turn them into what is called civilized peoples."[6] From the standpoint of "original liberty," Rousseau appears to identify all government and laws— which is to say, political society as such—with chains, despotism, and even slavery. Similarly, in the *Social Contract,* citizenship is clearly opposed to natural liberty and independence: "Man was born free, and he is everywhere in chains"; a true *patrie* based on the social contract can do no more than render those chains "legitimate."[7]

 Next, one must take account of Rousseau's favorable references—as we will later see, there are also many unfavorable ones—to the suprapolitical man, the cosmopolitan in the true sense. Though one might also speak of the unique type of individual that Rousseau portrays in his autobiographical writings, I will confine myself here to his discussion of the philosopher. In the *First Discourse,* he expresses his scorn for those who are "subjugated by the opinions of their century, their country, their society" and praises philosophers like

Bacon, Descartes, and Newton as "the preceptors of the human race."[8] In the *Second Discourse*, where he presents himself as a philosopher using "a language that suits all nations" with "Plato and Xenocrates for judges, and the human race for an audience," he refers to "a few great cosmopolitan souls who surmount the imaginary barriers that separate peoples and who, following the example of the sovereign Being who created them, include the whole human race in their benevolence."[9]

This passage is directly followed by Rousseau's strongest statement on the evils occasioned by the division of humanity into separate peoples:

> The bodies politic, thus remaining in the state of nature with relation to each other, soon experienced the inconveniences that had forced individuals to leave it; and among these great bodies that state became even more fatal than it had previously been among the individuals of whom they were composed. Hence arose the national wars, battles, murders, and reprisals which make nature tremble and shock reason, and all those horrible prejudices which rank the honor of shedding human blood among the virtues. The most decent men learned to consider it one of their duties to murder their fellow men; at length men were seen to massacre each other by the thousands without knowing why; more murders were committed on a single day of fighting and more horrors in the capture of a single city than were committed in the state of nature during whole centuries over the entire face of the earth. Such are the first effects one glimpses of the division of the human race into different societies.[10]

In the *Discourse on Political Economy*, moreover, Rousseau notes that the general will of a particular state is no longer general with respect to other states and their members. He goes on to speak of "the great city of the world" (*la grande ville du monde*) as "the body politic of which the law of nature is always the general will, and diverse states and peoples are only individual members" and holds that the duties of man come before those of the citizen.[11]

Yet far from advocating that political societies should cultivate a cosmopolitan outlook in their citizens, Rousseau's political teaching calls for the greatest possible attachment of the citizen to his own particular *patrie:*

> It seems that the sentiment of humanity evaporates and weakens in extending itself across the globe, and that we are incapable of being touched by the calamities of Tartary or Japan as much as by

those of a European people. It is necessary in some manner to limit and compress concern and compassion in order to render them active. But as this penchant of ours can be useful only to those with whom we live, it is good that humanity, concentrated among fellow citizens, gains new force from the habit of living together and the common interest that unites them. It is certain that the greatest prodigies of virtue have been produced by love for the fatherland [*patrie*].[12]

Another emphatic statement expressing Rousseau's preference for patriotism over cosmopolitanism appears in the opening pages of *Emile:*

Every particular society, which is narrow and unified, is estranged from the all-encompassing society. Every patriot is harsh to foreigners. They are only men. They are nothing in his eyes. This is a drawback, inevitable but not compelling. The essential thing is to be good to the people with whom one lives. Abroad, the Spartan was ambitious, avaricious, iniquitous. But disinterestedness, equity, and concord reigned within his walls. Distrust those cosmopolitans who go to great length in their books to discover duties that they do not deign to fulfill around them. A philosopher loves the Tartars so as to be spared having to love his neighbors.[13]

Rousseau's political teaching thus abjures the charms of cosmopolitanism in the name of virtue, understood as love for the *patrie*. And far from seeking to weaken the chains that bind men to the political order so that they may retain a greater share of their original liberty, it calls for expunging natural liberty in favor of civil liberty, understood as complete submission to the general will of a properly constituted *patrie*. Rousseau holds that "good social institutions are those that best know how to denature man."[14] The great task of the legislator, he explains in the *Social Contract*, is to change human nature, to transform natural man into a true citizen who in some sense derives his life and being from the *patrie* to which he belongs:

The nearer men's natural powers are to extinction or annihilation, and the stronger and more lasting their acquired powers, the stronger and more perfect is the social institution. So much so, that if each citizen can do nothing whatever except through cooperation with others, and if the acquired power of the whole is equal to, or greater than, the sum of the natural powers of each of the individuals, than we can say that law-making has reached the highest point of perfection.[15]

The successful transformation of men into citizens requires that they be totally subordinated to the law, which is the expression of the general will. For the empire of the law to be effective, the wills of the individual citizens must be to the greatest extent possible in conformity with the general will. This in turn, Rousseau argues, can best be achieved not through institutional mechanisms of reward or punishment but by implanting in the hearts of the citizens a love for the *patrie* and its laws. Through the inculcation of appropriate mores, customs, and opinions, the power of habit can take the place of cruder forms of authority in leading the citizens to pursue the good of the *patrie*. Thus, harking back to the view of the ancient lawgivers and political philosophers, Rousseau insists on the central importance of public education to a good political order.

For similar reasons, Rousseau argues that the good political order must be relatively small. In his dedication to the Republic of Geneva preceding the *Second Discourse*, he praises the land of his birth as

> a society of a size limited by the extent of human faculties—that is, limited by the possibility of being well-governed . . . a state where, all the individuals knowing one another, neither the obscure ma- neuvers of vice nor the modesty of virtue could be hidden from the notice and judgment of the people, and where that sweet habit of seeing and knowing one another turned love of the fatherland into love of the citizens rather than love of the soil.[16]

The small size of the state also makes it easier to convoke the periodic assem- blies of the sovereign people that Rousseau so strongly insists on in the *Social Contract*. To those who raise the difficulty of convening such assemblies in states composed of many cities, Rousseau responds that "it is always an evil to unite several cities [*villes*] in one body politic [*cité*]," and he adds that "it is no use complaining about the evils of a large state to someone who wants only small ones."[17]

The Shaping of Nations

Our examination up to this point has confirmed that Rousseau's posi- tive political teaching manifestly puts very great—one might even say unprecendented—emphasis on the importance and desirability of patriotism, but so far there has been no indication that such patriotism in any way takes on a specifically nationalist form. Indeed, in arguing for the superiority of small republics that encompass no more than a single town, Rousseau seems opposed to any notion that political boundaries should coincide with those of nationalities.

Let us then approach the problem from a somewhat different angle and inquire into what Rousseau says directly about the nation. This is not an easy task, for he never systematically analyzes the concept of nationhood. Nor does he explicitly define the term *la nation* or seem to use it with the same care and rigor as such terms as *la patrie* or *le citoyen*. So far as I can discern, Rousseau appears to employ *la nation* more or less interchangeably with *le peuple*— "nations" are the equivalent of "peoples." And both of these terms sometimes seem to refer to what are clearly political units, whereas in other cases they designate prepolitical groupings of men.

In the *Second Discourse*, where Rousseau presents a history of the development of the human race from its original condition of primitive isolation, the formation of nations clearly precedes that of political societies. After the advent of the family and the introduction of language, men, "having adopted a more fixed settlement, slowly come together, unite into different bands, and finally form in each country a particular nation, unified by customs and character, not by regulations and laws but by the same kind of life and foods and by the common influence of climate."[18] In the *Essay on the Origin of Languages*, Rousseau asserts that it is language that distinguishes one nation from another, and he adds that "speech, being the first social institution, owes its form solely to natural causes."[19] He then goes on to trace the distinct origins of northern and southern languages, which he attributes to regional differences in climate and soil.

In the *Emile* (and also in note J of the *Second Discourse*), Rousseau laments the fading of national differences that has occurred in modern times. He attributes this to the much greater contact among modern nations, to large-scale migrations and intermingling of peoples, and to the transformations of the land made by Europeans, all of which have prevented distinctions of climate and soil from having their full effect. He adds that one must go to remote provinces rather than capital cities to "study the genius and the morals of a nation," claiming that "the English are more English in Mercia than in London, and the Spanish are more Spanish in Galicia than in Madrid." It is in the hinterlands "that a people reveals its character and shows itself as it is without admixture," Rousseau says, and it is also "there that the good and bad effects of government are more strongly felt."[20] This suggests, however, that not only natural or material causes but also political ones shape the character of nations.

The same ambiguity arises in the *Social Contract*, where in book 2, chapter 7, the great legislators who "appeal to divine intervention and . . . attribute their own wisdom to the Gods" are called the "*founders* of nations," and Rousseau states that religion serves as an instrument of politics in the "*birth* of nations."[21] In the following chapter, however, peoples are said to be teachable only in their youth, to which Rousseau adds, "Youth is not childhood. For nations as for men there is a time of youth, or, if you prefer, of maturity, which they must reach before they are made subject to laws."[22] He then goes on to criticize Peter the Great for having given the Russians laws before they were ready: "He tried to turn them into Germans or Englishmen, instead of making them Russians."[23]

Two chapters later Rousseau explains the apparent contradiction: "Which people, then, is fit to receive laws? I answer: a people which, finding itself already bound together by some original association, interest, or agreement, has not yet borne the yoke of law; a people without deep-rooted customs or superstitions; . . . a people in which every member may be known by all; . . . and lastly, one which combines the cohesion of an ancient people with the malleability of a new one."[24] It appears, then, that though such factors as climate and soil may shape the human material that composes a nation, it is the work of the legislator that gives it its real form.[25]

Corsica and Poland

To gain a clearer sense of Rousseau's understanding of the role of nature, history, and laws in shaping a nation, we must turn to the two works in which he proposes a plan of legislation for nations of his own era—his *Project of a Constitution for Corsica* and his *Considerations on the Government of Poland*. In each case, Rousseau's work was written in response to a request from the people in question, though with respect to Corsica that request was prompted by Rousseau's reference in the *Social Contract* to this island as the one country in Europe fit to receive legislation.[26] Corsica and Poland did share certain significant similarities—each had recently displayed great bravery in defending its independence against a foreign power, each had a rather unfixed or anarchic form of government, and each was relatively primitive economically and culturally. In other respects, however, they differed enormously. Corsica was a small island in the Mediterranean ruled by the general who had led its fight to regain its independence, and Poland was a vast kingdom with a northern climate, a powerful nobility, and an elective monarchy.

To be sure, Rousseau's proposed legislation for these two countries differs in many significant ways. He proposes a much more egalitarian system for Corsica, whose old institutions had been largely effaced in the course of its struggle against Genoese domination, than for Poland, whose ancient institutions he suggests be modified only with great circumspection. And in the case of Corsica he speaks of the importance of topography and climate, though in suggesting that it look to Switzerland as a model, he puts greater stress on the poverty caused by its long subjugation and frequent wars than on the fertility of its soil and the mildness of its climate.[27] What is most striking, however, is how similar is the spirit of the legislation proposed in the two works. Both call for a simple way of life based on agriculture, for minimizing the importance of money and commerce, and for emphasizing the separateness and singularity of the nation and patriotic devotion to it.

Echoing language in the *Social Contract* about the importance of modifying legislation to suit local habits and conditions, Rousseau says in the essay on Corsica, "The first rule we have to follow is that of national character." He immediately adds, however: "Every people has or ought to have a national character, and if it lacks one, the first step must be to give it one."[28] Similarly, in the foreword to this essay he writes that, rather than forming the government to fit the nation, it would be much better for the lawgiver to form the nation to fit the government.[29] In the essay on Poland, Rousseau emphasizes that the only defense for Poland against its more powerful Russian neighbors lies in "the virtue of its citizens, their patriotic zeal, and the particular form that national institutions can give to their souls." "It is national institutions," he says, "that form the genius, the character, the tastes, and the customs of a people, that make it be itself and not another, that inspire it with that ardent love of the fatherland [*patrie*] founded on habits impossible to uproot."[30] National character, then, is above all an *effect* of legislation.

Rousseau goes on to say that "today there are no longer Frenchmen, Germans, Spaniards, or even Englishmen . . . there are only Europeans. All have the same tastes, the same passions, and the same customs, because none has received a national form through a particular legislation." He urges that Polish souls be given "a national physiognomy that will distinguish them from other peoples" and thus prevent them from becoming mingled with or finding pleasure among other peoples.[31] They must love their *patrie* with all their hearts. "With this sentiment alone," Rousseau asserts, "legislation, even if it were bad, would produce good citizens."[32] In the same spirit, encouraging the Poles to resist the European penchant for adopting French tastes and customs, he calls for the revival of ancient usages and the introduction of new ones that are purely Polish. Even if these usages are bad in some respects, he adds, "they would still have the advantage of giving Poles greater affection for their country and a natural repugnance toward mingling with foreigners."[33]

To give the souls of the citizens a national bent and to make them passionate patriots is the task of education:

> Every true republican imbibes with his mother's milk the love of the *patrie*, that is of the laws and of liberty. This love constitutes his entire existence; he sees only the *patrie*, and lives for it alone; the moment that he is alone, he is nothing; the moment that he no longer has a *patrie*, he is no more, and if he is not dead he is worse than dead. National education belongs only to free men; it is they alone who have a common existence and who are truly bound together by the law.[34]

Such men can be formed only by the most rigorously national education. The studies of young Poles should focus on the literature, the history, the laws, and the glorious deeds of their nation, and they should have only Poles as their teachers: "When a Pole reaches the age of twenty, he must be a Pole, and not some other kind of man."[35]

From these and similar passages from the essay on Poland, it is not hard to see why Rousseau is regarded as a founder of nationalism. But how does this square with his preference for the small ancient republic? This is a question that Rousseau confronts directly in chapter 5 of the essay on Poland, titled "The Radical Vice." Reforming the government of Poland, he acknowledges, poses the perhaps impossible task of endowing the constitution of a large kingdom with the stability and vigor of that of a small republic. Proclaiming that the "largeness of nations and the vastness of states" is "the principal source of human misfortunes," Rousseau suggests that Poland should begin the reform of its government by retrenching its borders. As an alternative, however, he proposes that it adopt a federal system, dividing the nation into as many as thirty-three smaller units and increasing the powers of the local assemblies (or dietines) in each of them.[36]

Yet Rousseau makes it clear that these smaller units must remain bound by common legislation and subordinate to the "body of the republic." In short, it is still Poland that its citizens will regard as their *patrie*, the primary object of their devotion, and the source of their common education. The ancient Spartan was a Greek, but he was first and foremost a citizen of Sparta. By contrast, a Pole or a Corsican educated under the legislation proposed by Rousseau would regard himself as a citizen not of the town or province where he lives but of Poland or of Corsica.

Notwithstanding the almost insuperable barriers to making freedom and virtue reign in large states, Rousseau nonetheless urges the Poles to adopt legislation aimed at this end. This presents a puzzle to which I am not sure I can provide a good answer. Perhaps one might begin to address it in the following way. For Rousseau a legitimate political order must be based on the general will, which is to say on the sovereignty of the people who compose it. For the general will to prevail, as Rousseau indicates in the *Discourse on Political Economy*, the individual wills of the citizens must correspond to it as much as possible.[37] It is precisely this conformity of the individual will to the general will that constitutes virtue, and the best way to promote this conformity is by inculcating the love of the *patrie*. Thus the only way to sustain a legitimate political order where the general will prevails is to make freedom and virtue reign.

Now it is true that in the *Social Contract* Rousseau affirms Montesquieu's principle that "freedom is not a fruit of every climate, and it is not therefore within the capacity of every people."[38] He likewise follows Montesquieu in arguing that political institutions should be modified to suit the local conditions and national characters of different peoples. But the consequences of this recognition of the importance of diversity are much more limited in the thought of Rousseau, who also asserts that "all legitimate government is republican"[39] and that the goal of every system of legislation should be freedom and equality. Thus, although Rousseau endorses the reasoning that led Montesquieu to establish virtue as the principle of small republics, he faults him for having "failed to see that, since the sovereign authority is everywhere the same, the same principles should have a place in every well-constituted state."[40] I take this to mean that, since the people are sovereign in any legitimate state, virtuous citizens are required in every legitimate state, whatever its size or its climate.

Nationalism and the Sovereignty of the People

Citizenship in Poland at the time Rousseau proposed his plan for reform was restricted to the nobility. But while the nobles constituted the entire body politic, they obviously constituted only part of the nation. As Rousseau puts it, "The Polish nation is composed of three orders: the nobles, who are everything; the middle class, who are nothing; and the peasants, who are less than nothing."[41] Though the reforms he proposes largely stay within this aristocratic framework, he also argues that in the long run the people must count for something if Poland is to have real strength and stability:

> Although everyone feels how harmful it is for the republic that the nation is in a certain fashion confined to the noble order, and that all the rest, the peasants and the middle class, have no part in the government or in legislation, that is Poland's ancient constitution. It would at this moment be neither prudent nor possible to change it all at once; but it would be possible to bring about this change gradually, and without any perceptible revolution to see to it that the most numerous part of the nation becomes tied to the fatherland [*patrie*] and even the government with bonds of affection.[42]

By gradually admitting the middle classes and the peasants to citizenship, Rousseau concludes, it would be possible to "revivify all the parts of Poland and to bind them together in such a manner that they would constitute a single body whose vigor and strength would be at least ten times what it can be today."[43] It is clear that the concept of the nation Rousseau espouses in the essay on Poland ultimately has an egalitarian character.

Whatever Rousseau's deepest intentions or hopes for the political future of Europe may have been, without question his thought played a crucial role in laying the foundations of modern nationalism. His doctrine of the sovereignty of the people helped explode the traditional claim to rule of the monarchs and despots who held sway over large realms often containing diverse peoples. With the discrediting and eventual downfall of such rulers, only the people can legitimately decide how and under what laws they will be governed in the future. In other words, there must be self-determination. But what defines and constitutes a people that has the right to make this determination for itself? Clearly, the subjects of the Hapsburg or Ottoman or Soviet empire did not regard themselves as a single people. The most obvious available criterion for filling this void is the principle of nationality, which at least provides a certain common bond among many of those who will constitute the new political units. The existence of such a common bond becomes especially important when it is no longer merely a question of subjects to be governed, but of citizens who will have a right to participate in political life and a duty, if need be, to fight and to die for their country.

An attempt to delineate the nature and the diverse manifestations of modern nationalism—perhaps one should say nationalisms—would take us far beyond the scope of this chapter. In concluding, however, there is one crucial point that must be stressed. Far from being invariably based on a common ancestral language and way of life, modern nationalism often enlists wider loyalties whose origin lies in more recent historical and political factors. Nationalism, then, is not identical with ethnicity. Thus what is commonly called nation building in the Third World typically involves transforming various ethnic or tribal groups into a people conscious of belonging to a single nation, and in a number of places this effort has been quite successful. To take another example, the French nationalism, partly inspired by Rousseau, that erupted during the French Revolution required overcoming the older and more parochial loyalties of the peoples of Brittany, of Provence, or of Languedoc. Precisely because nationalism involves an attachment that extends far beyond the place where one lives and the people one knows, it requires something not unlike the education in the literature, history, and geography of one's country that Rousseau prescribes for the Poles.

In this sense, by expanding men's horizons beyond their direct and, so to speak, natural attachments, nationalism can even be viewed as a step on the road to cosmopolitanism. It is worth noting in this connection that Rousseau, for his role in reworking and presenting to the public the abbé de Saint-Pierre's project for "perpetual peace" through a confederation of the sovereigns of Europe, has also been regarded as one of the founders of modern internationalism.[44] Perhaps one might say that modern nationalism, unlike the patriotism of the ancient city, does not *necessarily* entail harshness to foreigners. Indeed, a Georgian political thinker, Ghia Nodia, has argued that "the idea of nationhood is an idea of membership in humanity" and points out that the United Nations, based on the principle of respect for national sovereignty, is the first political organization to embrace virtually the whole world.[45] Thus it may not be so entirely paradoxical as it first appears that Jean-Jacques Rousseau might be viewed simultaneously as a founder of both modern nationalism and modern internationalism.

NOTES

1. Marc F. Plattner, *Rousseau's State of Nature: An Interpretation of the Discourse on Inequality* (DeKalb: Northern Illinois University Press, 1979).

2. Hans Kohn, *The Idea of Nationalism: A Study in Its Origin and Background* (New York: Macmillan, 1944), 251, 23.

3. E. H. Carr et al., *Nationalism: A Report by a Study Group of Members of the Royal Institute of International Affairs* (London: Oxford University Press, 1939), 27. See also 30: "It was Rousseau, therefore, who not only laid the foundations of a coherent and systematic theory of nationalism, but also established the association between nationalism and democracy which gave such a powerful stimulus to the nationalist movements of the early nineteenth century."

4. Jean-Jacques Rousseau, *Emile, or On Education*, trans. Allan Bloom (New York: Basic Books, 1979), 39–40.

5. Jean-Jacques Rousseau, *Second Discourse*, in *The First and Second Discourses*, ed. Roger D. Masters, trans. Roger D. Masters and Judith R. Masters (New York: St. Martin's Press, 1964), 179.

6. Jean-Jacques Rousseau, *First Discourse*, in *The First and Second Discourses*, ed. Roger D. Masters, trans. Roger D. Masters and Judith R. Masters (New York: St. Martin's Press, 1964), 36.

7. Jean-Jacques Rousseau, *The Social Contract*, trans. with an introduction by Maurice Cranston (Baltimore: Penguin, 1968), bk. 1, chap. 1, p. 49.

8. *First Discourse*, 33, 63.

9. *Second Discourse*, 103, 160–61.

10. Ibid., 161.

11. Jean-Jacques Rousseau, *Discours sur l'économie politique* (Discourse on political economy), in *Oeuvres complètes*, 5 vols., ed. Bernard Gagnebin and Marcel Raymond (Paris: Gallimard, Bibliothèque de la Pléiade, 1959–95), 3:245, 246; translation mine.

12. Ibid., 254–55.

13. *Emile*, 39. Consider also the following passage from the unpublished first version of the *Social Contract:* "We conceive the general society [of mankind] on the model of our own particular societies; the establishment of little republics makes us think of the all-encompassing one, and we do not properly begin to become men until after having been citizens. Thus one can see what should be thought of those pretended cosmopolitans who, justifying their love for the fatherland [*patrie*] by their love for the human race, boast of loving the whole world in order to have the right to love no one." Jean-Jacques Rousseau, *Du contrat social (première version)*, in *Oeuvres complètes*, vol. 3, bk. 1, chap. 2, p. 287; translation mine.

14. Ibid., 40.

15. *Social Contract*, bk. 2, chap. 7, p. 85.

16. *Second Discourse,* 79.

17. *Social Contract,* bk. 3, chap. 13, p. 138.

18. *Second Discourse,* 148.

19. Jean-Jacques Rousseau, *Essai sur l'origine des langues* (Essay on the origin of languages) (Paris: Bibliothèque du Graphe, 1969), 501; translation mine.

20. *Emile,* 468. As Donald Forbes emphasizes in his essay in this volume (chapter 11), Rousseau's political teaching is hostile to "multiculturalism," or the mixing of diverse ethnic groups within a single political unit.

21. *Social Contract,* bk. 2, chap. 7, pp. 87, 88 (emphasis added).

22. Ibid., bk. 2, chap. 8, p. 89n.

23. Ibid., p. 90.

24. Ibid., bk. 2, chap. 10, p. 95.

25. Anne Cohler offers the following useful formulation: "Rousseau advocates building on a pre-existing group, the nation, but he does not pretend that the political order to be formed on the nation will leave it the same as before. . . . To build a political order on a nation alters the nation irrevocably." See Anne M. Cohler, *Rousseau and Nationalism* (New York: Basic Books, 1970), 34. This book contains a number of valuable insights, but it fails to confront the disjunction between the classical small republic and the large modern nation-state.

26. Ibid., 96.

27. Jean-Jacques Rousseau, *Projet de constitution pour la Corse* (Plan of a constitution for Corsica), in *Oeuvres complètes,* 3:914–15.

28. Ibid., 913; translation mine.

29. Ibid., 901.

30. Jean-Jacques Rousseau, *Considérations sur le gouvernement de Pologne* (Considerations on the government of Poland), in *Oeuvres complètes,* 3:960 (chap. 3); translation mine. As Richard Velkley points out in his essay in this volume (chapter 4), it is Rousseau's emphasis on the role of the legislator in shaping culture that separates him from "Herder's notion of cultures as national organisms."

31. Ibid., 960.

32. Ibid., 961.

33. Ibid., 962.

34. Ibid., 966 (chap. 4).

35. Ibid.

36. Ibid., 970–71 (chap. 5).

37. *Discours sur l'économie politique,* 252 ff.

38. *Social Contract,* bk. 3, chap. 8, p. 124.

39. Ibid., bk. 2, chap. 6, p. 82.

40. Ibid., bk. 3, chap. 4, p. 113.

41. *Considérations sur le gouvernement de Pologne,* 972 (chap. 6).

42. Ibid., 1024 (chap. 13).

43. Ibid., 1028.

44. Jean-Jacques Rousseau, *Ecrits sur l'abbé de Saint-Pierre* (Writings on the abbé de

Saint-Pierre), in *Oeuvres complètes*, 3:563–600. On the *Ecrits sur l'abbé de Saint-Pierre* and the internationalist aspect of Rousseau's thought, see Pierre Hassner's essay in this volume (chapter 10). Beginning from a different starting point, Hassner comes to some conclusions similar to those expressed here regarding Rousseau's views on nationalism, patriotism, and cosmopolitanism.

45. Ghia Nodia, "Nationalism and Democracy," *Journal of Democracy* 3, no. 4 (1992): 12. Reprinted in Larry Diamond and Marc F. Plattner, eds., *Nationalism, Ethnic Conflict, and Democracy* (Baltimore: Johns Hopkins University Press, 1994), 3–22.

❧ 10 ❧
Rousseau and the Theory and Practice of International Relations

PIERRE HASSNER

The short answer to the question of what Rousseau thought about the theory and practice of international relations is "very little." Both were to be avoided as much as possible—the theory because it was useless, the practice because it was harmful.

About the theory of international relations Rousseau could be quite dismissive. "Nothing could be more frivolous than the political science of courts. Since it has no certain principles, no certain conclusions can be drawn from them; and all this fine theorizing about the interests of princes is a child's game which makes sensible men laugh."[1] It seems a safe bet that Rousseau would find our fine theorizing about the "national interest" of contemporary states conceived as "rational actors" no less laughable than "the political science of courts." Although his views on the selfishness of rulers and on the weakness of common interests mark him as an ancestor of contemporary "realism," he would deride the rationalistic presuppositions and scientific pretensions of realists, neorealists, behaviorists, and functionalists alike.

More important for our purposes is Rousseau's attitude toward the practice of international relations. Here again he could hardly have been more negative. To the Corsicans, the nation besides the Poles that sought his advice, he counsels distrust of all foreign powers. "No one who depends on others, and lacks resources of his own, can ever be free. Alliances, treaties, gentlemen's agreements, such things may bind the weak to the strong, but never the strong to the weak. . . . Leave negotiations, then, to the powers and depend on yourselves only. . . . Pay no more attention to foreign powers than if they did not exist."[2] For nations as for individuals, relations entail dependence and division, whereas freedom and unity require self-reliance and isolation.

Shocking as Rousseau's advice may be to ears used to both the realities of interdependence and the pieties of cooperation, it reminds one of the classical prescription for a healthy city according to which it should seek an impregnable location far from the sea and pass laws limiting its citizens' foreign travel.

Closer to home it reminds us of American isolationism, as well as of contemporary Third World ideologies of self-reliance and self-centered development. What makes Rousseau's position worthy of attention, however, is that he was aware not only that his advice was utterly impracticable in the modern world, but that such encouragement of radical parochialism was unsatisfactory at the highest theoretical level. Indeed, Rousseau is the only political philosopher besides Kant who squarely faces the problem of international relations or, more precisely, of the necessary plurality of political communities and the difficulty it poses for the construction of a good society, whether at the global level or the local one. Previous thinkers had ignored this implication of the multiplicity of independent societies or had at best provided a secondary treatment of it. The great thinkers seem to deal with this question in footnotes, postcripts, or outlines of unwritten works. To be sure, the same might be said of Rousseau himself, who never wrote the section of the *Social Contract* devoted to international relations that he announced both there and in *Emile*.[3] Even so, he stands out for proclaiming that the unavoidable plurality of civilized societies both undermines the benefits of their common civilization and jeopardizes the possibility of each one's achieving a good political order within its own boundaries.

There are three logical approaches to the problem of the plurality of human societies. Of these, two try to circumvent it, the first by isolating the good community and the second by expanding it into a universal empire. The third approach is to accept the multiplicity of states as inevitable but contrive to make it more tolerable than the state of nature among individuals. Plato and Aristotle, even if they do not believe in the possibility—perhaps even the desirability—of complete isolation, accord a clear priority to the domestic order of the city over its foreign relations, a priority corresponding to those of peace over war and of leisure over work. Dante, Kant, and Hegel believe in their different ways in some kind of universal order. Both Hobbes and Locke recognize the paradox that whereas individuals enter civil society to safeguard their life and property, states remain in the state of nature and hence of war, thereby continuing to pose a threat to these very goods. They believe, however, that violence is less inevitable among states than among individuals, since the former can contrive institutions, agreements, and rules for maintaining a partial and precarious peace. They hope that an emergent world society, resting on a way of life that is commercial rather than warlike, will mitigate the continuing plurality and rivalry of states.

Rousseau does not simply dismiss any of these positions, but ultimately he finds all of them wanting. While categorically rejecting universal monarchy or any other version of a worldwide political order, he accepts the partial validity of a "general society of the human race." He argues, however, that such a society exists in pure form only as an abstraction of philosophers. In political life, it cedes to the inevitable priority of the multiplicity of real communities. Any bond of sentiment attaching us to the human race as a whole is only an extrapolation, and a weak one, from the solidarity that flourishes within certain particular societies, primarily small republics. It is true that "our needs bring us together in proportion as our passions divide us, and the more we become enemies of our fellow men, the less we can do without them."[4] Rousseau draws from this contradiction, however, a conclusion opposite that of Locke and Montesquieu, which prevailed in his time. Mutual dependence breeds conflict, not cooperation, and needs do not supersede the passions but exacerbate them. This is one reason the state of nature, contrary to Hobbes and Locke, is more violent among states than among individuals. Another is that amour propre runs rampant among states: there is no natural equality among nations as there was among individuals in the state of nature. Since the greatness of nations is entirely relative, they cannot but compare themselves with one another, and their quest for self-aggrandizement is inevitably endless and limitless. Nor are states restrained by compassion or humanity. Feelings belong to individuals, not to collective beings, and war is a relation not between men but between states.[5]

Rousseau seems, then, to be drawn to the classical position—that is, to the search for the best regime within a particular community and to the preference for the small, isolated republic. Such indeed is what he recommends to the Poles and the Corsicans. On the other hand, Rousseau knows first that the conditions of modern life have made isolation and virtue almost impossible; at most the Poles and Corsicans are rare exceptions to this rule. Second, the horror in which he holds both war and amour propre leaves him ambivalent toward the warlike virtues privileged by the classical position. Third and perhaps most important, the philosopher himself cannot be content with the freedom and peace of the virtuous community, not only because of their fragility in a corrupt and warlike environment, but because his own compassion and indignation cannot accept confinement within the borders of his city. He cannot entirely accept that the freedom and happiness of the fraction of mankind to which he belongs should depend on abandoning the rest of it to tyranny and war.

Rousseau states the last of these points most forcefully in a passage of the *State of War.*

> Permeated with [the] persuasive talk [of the philosophers], I lament the miseries of nature, admire the peace and justice established by the civil order, bless the wisdom of public institutions and console myself for being a man by looking upon myself as a citizen. Well versed in my duties and happiness, I shut my book, leave the classroom, and look around me. I see unfortunate nations groaning under yokes of iron, the human race crushed by a handful of oppressors, a starving crowd overwhelmed with pain and hunger, whose blood and tears the rich drink in peace, and everywhere the strong armed against the weak with the formidable power of the law.
>
> All this happens peacefully and without resistance. It is the tranquillity of Ulysses's comrades, shut in the cave of the Cyclops, waiting to be eaten. One must groan and keep silent. Let us draw a veil over these horrifying subjects. I raise my eyes and look into the distance. I see fires and flames, the countryside deserted, towns pillaged. Savages, where are you dragging these unfortunate people? I hear a terrible noise; what an uproar! I draw near; I see a scene of murder, ten thousand butchered men, the dead piled in heaps, the dying trampled under horses' hooves, everywhere the face of death and agony. So this is the fruit of these peaceful institutions! Pity and indignation rise from the bottom of my heart. Barbarous philosopher! Come and read us your book on the field of battle![6]

This text seems to imply that all efforts toward the good and legitimate society, including Rousseau's own in the *Social Contract,* are vain and obscene as long as war and oppression are not eradicated everywhere. At any rate, what happens within one community cannot ignore the fundamental obstacle posed by the plurality of states.

> The first thing I notice, in considering the condition of the human species, is an open contradiction in its constitution, which causes it to vacillate incessantly. As individual men, we live in a civil state

subject to law, as peoples we each enjoy a natural liberty; this makes our position fundamentally worse than if these distinctions were unknown.

Living simultaneously in the social order and in the state of nature, we are subjected to the inconveniences of both, without finding security in either: in the mixed condition in which we find ourselves, whichever system we prefer, making too much or too little of it, we have achieved nothing and are in the worst state of all. That, it seems to me, is the true origin of public disasters.[7]

In *Emile*, where almost the same statement occurs, Rousseau insists that "the continual action and reaction" of states is "responsible for more misery and loss of life than if men had all kept their initial freedom," and he denounces again "this partial and imperfect association which produces tyranny and war."[8]

The question is where Rousseau goes from here. He has identified the "mixed state" of "partial and imperfect association" resulting from the plurality of states as the main cause of the worst plagues of humanity, tyranny and war. Of course the central thrust of this positive doctrine is precisely to avoid at all costs ambiguity, ambivalence, and division within the city and within the soul, by educating men into being either completely citizens or completely men, and escaping the conflicting pressures of self-love, of patriotism, and of cosmopolitanism. Yet it is my contention that in his practical answers concerning international relations Rousseau does not succeed in avoiding the very contradictions and ambiguities he wants to suppress. Although it was precisely this ambivalence that enabled him to inspire both nationalism and humanitarianism, to accuse both commerce and war, to foster nostalgia for civic heroism and natural peaceful isolation alike, the diversity of his influence was at the price of much hesitation and an ultimate failure to cut the Gordian knot of the "mixed state." These vacillations pervade his stance on a variety of issues, whether plans for perpetual peace, the limitation of damage within the "state of war," the fostering of the unity and identity of political communities, or the respective virtues of the citizen and the thinker.

Perpetual Peace or Power Politics?

For several years, during the time he was preparing the *Social Contract* and *Emile*, Rousseau worked at the request of his protector Madame Dupin on a digest of twenty-three posthumous volumes left by the abbé de Saint-Pierre, and in particular on the latter's project for perpetual peace. The upshot of these labors was two pieces, of which one purported to be a presentation of Saint-Pierre's project, although in Rousseau's words and, as he warns us, containing some of his own arguments. The second work, which was published only after Rousseau's own death, contains his *Judgment* on the abbé's project. As already suggested, however, the separation between the two texts is less than clear-cut. The first already contains quite a few critical remarks, and the second is less categorically critical than one would think. The purpose and the meaning of the whole enterprise remain ambiguous. Many illustrious readers over the years, including Voltaire, Madison, Kant, and Kenneth Waltz, have identified Rousseau with Saint-Pierre and have seen in him a utopian pacifist. Others, correctly noting that Rousseau's pessimism concerning international relations and the wisdom of rulers is at the opposite pole from the naive optimism of Saint-Pierre, dismiss the whole business as a chore performed to please Madame Dupin. Although it seems reasonable to think that left to his own devices Rousseau would not have chosen the good abbé and his twenty-three volumes as the most appropriate vehicle for his own message, it also seems likely that the abbé's subject at least was close to his heart. The involved, ambiguous, and even contradictory character of his comments on the good abbé appears to be related to his own hesitations and to that other Rous-seauian mystery, his failure to complete his *Institutions politiques* with that treatment of international affairs without which, as we have seen, he declared his whole political system worthless.

The proof that Rousseau's examination of Saint-Pierre's project bears the imprint of his own meditations on the central problem of international relations is that it begins with the now familiar denunciation of the mixed state and its contradictions. It continues by foreshadowing Kant in proposing the solution of peace through law. "If there is any way of reconciling these dangerous contradictions, it is to be found only in such a form of federal government as shall unite nations by bonds similar to those which already unite their individual members, and place the one no less than the other under the authority of the law." Rousseau, however, immediately betrays his lack of confidence in the likelihood of such a universal federation. "Even apart from this, such a form of government seems to carry the day over all others; because it combines the advantages of small and large states, because it is powerful enough to hold its neighbors in awe, because it upholds the supremacy of the law, because it is the only force capable of holding the subject, the ruler, the foreigner equally in check."9 Although escaping the state of nature between nations through a universal federation may be utopian, the second-best alternative, a variety of federations as a means to creating islands of peace within the state of war, does seem feasible in Rousseau's eyes.

After having signaled this ambiguity in his presentation of federation, Rousseau proceeds in truly dialectical fashion by describing first, in glowing terms, the special bonds of religion, customs, and commercial interests that unite the powers of Europe; then, in equally eloquent but scathing terms, he details the rivalries, cruelties, hatreds, and dangers of war that these very bonds of mutual dependency encourage. Finally he concludes that those very bonds that are dangerous and harmful at present could easily become factors of peace and happiness if organized under the rule of law in accordance with Saint-Pierre's system of the guarantee of existing borders and of arbitration by a high council.

Rousseau proceeds, however, to reverse himself yet again, by deriding the simplicity of Saint-Pierre in relying on the merits of his project to persuade the rulers of Europe that it would be in their unanimous interest to adopt it. Rousseau stresses the prevalence of passions over reason, of apparent interests over real interests. Princes will always prefer their immediate advantage to their long-term interest and their separate interests, which satisfy their thirst for power and superiority, over their common interests, which being common are felt only faintly. Once functional, Saint-Pierre's system would be difficult to overthrow, but it was most unlikely ever to be adopted. Even so, Rousseau hastens once again to defend it against those who deride it as impractical. He notes that Henry IV of France and his minister Sully had proposed a very similar system. The difference was that they relied not on its abstract persuasiveness but on a patient political strategy, conducted from a position of strength, and appealed to each of the other powers of Europe in terms of its particular interests. Given a propitious constellation of power, a new Henry IV might succeed with such a project, but probably not without the use of force.

> Beyond doubt, a lasting peace is, under present circumstances, a pretty ridiculous project. Give us back Henry IV and Sully, however, and it will once more become a reasonable proposal. Or rather, while we admire so fair a project, let us console ourselves for its failure by the thought that it could be carried out only through violent means, which would be dangerous for humanity. One does not see how federal leagues can be established other than through revolutions, and, under these circumstances, which

one of us could say if this European league is to be desired or to be feared? It would perhaps do more harm in a moment than it would prevent for centuries.[10]

Is this conclusion, at the same time skeptical, resigned, and ironic in tone, Rousseau's last word on peace, revolution, and the use of force? Or is it written with tongue in cheek? It is difficult to say. What remains clear is Rousseau's pessimism about the "mixed state" and his willingness to seek partial measures intended to reduce its violence.

One such measure is the reform of international law and particularly the law of war. While pouring scorn on Grotius and the whole existing corpus of international law, Rousseau proposes principles of his own on such topics as noncombatant immunity and the duty to spare prisoners. These principles follow from his definition of war as a relation between states rather than individuals.[11]

We have already mentioned another even more important measure: the encouragement of federations, which Rousseau never tires of recommending as the only way toward a solution. Federations raise as many problems as they solve, but by making war less likely and more distant, though they do not eliminate it, they do help reduce its impact on daily life.[12] Together the member states are supposed to wield enough defensive force to preserve them from foreign attack, yet too little offensive force to undertake conquests. All obviously depends, however, on the nature of both the component units and the bonds that unite them. If federations appeal to Montesquieu and Rousseau inasmuch as they combine the advantages of large states and small ones, that is because both thinkers regard small states as the only good ones from the point of view of domestic politics. They alone can be virtuous republics, where citizens know and identify with each other and their city while keeping for-eigners at a distance. But don't these very features of small republics pose problems for other aspects of Rousseau's thought?

Polis or Nation?

To begin with, the very notion that war is a relation between states, not individuals, loses its power when individuals identify themselves with the state via the general will and patriotism.[13] Is it possible, then, to maintain the principle of noncombatant immunity? This seems all the more problematic in that even in the case of Poland Rousseau recommends abolishing professional armies in favor of popular "defensive defense," using guerilla tactics (*petite guerre*) and avoiding technological warfare.[14] It seems that apart from a general plea against cruelty and inhumanity, Rousseau offers two sets of proposals. The first is for corrupt states ruled by selfish princes: here he tries above all to limit the scope and destructiveness of war by casting doubt on its legitimacy. The second, more important set of proposals is for small republics that are still capable of good laws and of education to virtue. The wars of these states will likely be defensive in nature, since most conquests originate in rulers' desire to consolidate their tyranny at home. When republican citizens fight in defense of their homeland, the heroic virtues of patriotism to which they have been educated will make life miserable for the invader.[15] Still, if they are to deter potential aggressors more powerful than themselves they have no choice but to federate.

Isn't there a tension, though, between the very idea of a federation and the total identification of the citizen with his fatherland and fellow citizens? Doesn't federation imply multiple loyalties and Rousseau's citizenship an exclusive one? Rousseau complains of Frenchmen and Englishmen becoming too much alike and advises Poles to be as distinct from foreigners as possible. He recommends that the Corsicans admit no more than one foreigner a year to permanent residence and praises the Spartans for having practiced iniquity abroad and equity only at home. He describes patriots in general as "harsh to foreigners," since these "are only men . . . nothing in [their] eyes." One wonders how solid a federation of republics of this stamp could be.

As for Poland, which is too large a nation to become a virtuous republic, Rousseau advises it to give up part of its territory and to adopt a federal form of government, dividing itself into a number of states and subdividing these into an equal number of smaller units. At the same time he warns the Poles to "define their limits carefully and be sure that nothing can break the bond of common legislation which unites them, or disturb their common subordination to the body of the republic."[16] It is clear that patriotism and citizenship are to be vested in Poland, not in its constituent parts. In short, the classic dilemma of federations, that they risk being either too much or too little, seems particularly acute in Rousseau's case. Poland, though decentralized, would still be a large nation-state. As for the federal links among small, virtuous republics, these would ultimately rest on common interest and institutions, which Rousseau teaches us are more than fragile in the absence of a common civic education.

The instance of Poland raises another important issue, the relation between nation and people or republic. It is in the *Government of Poland* that Rousseau most often speaks of the national. He writes of "national institutions which shape the genius, the character, the tastes and the manners of a people; which give it an individuality of its own; which inspire it with that ardent love of country, based on ineradicable habits, which make its members, while living among other people, die of boredom though surrounded by delights denied them in their own land." "Incline the passions of the Poles in a different direction [from the growing tendency toward homogeneity in Europe], and you will give their souls a *national* physiognomy which will distinguish them from other peoples, which will prevent them from mixing, from feeling at ease with these peoples, from allying themselves with them."[17]

These are the passages that, more than any other, have earned Rousseau the title father of modern nationalism. Could it be that he stresses this theme for Poland because it is a modern state that is prevented by its size, by its hierarchical order, and by its environment from attaining the civic virtue of the small republic? In the absence of the unity and identity produced by the general will, might nationalism be the only means of keeping a people united and distinct from its neighbors?

Anne M. Cohler, in her highly interesting *Rousseau and Nationalism*, attributes to the concept of the nation a more fundamental role in Rousseau's thought. She stresses the prepolitical character of the nation. In this she relies above all on Rousseau's assertion in the *Second Discourse* that long before the establishment of government "men, who until this time wandered in the woods, having adopted a more fixed settlement, slowly come together, unite in different bands, and finally form in each country a particular *nation*, unified by custom and character, not by regulations and laws but by the same kind of life and foods and by the common influence of climate." Cohler further notes Rousseau's claim in his *Essay on the Origins of Languages* that "language distinguishes nations from each other," and that "speech, being the first social institution, owes its form to natural causes alone."[18]

One is tempted, then, to assign to the Rousseauian concept of nation both a prepolitical, or quasi-natural, and a postpolitical, or juridical, status. Only the people of a nation in the latter sense is essentially political and molded by legislation and education. It is, however, this latter sense of nation that proves primary for Rousseau. He defines patriotism not in terms of ethnic ties but as based on the relation between the particular will and the general will. "It is neither walls nor men that constitute the fatherland. It is laws, mores, customs, government, constitution, the manner of being which results out of all this. The fatherland lies in the relations of the state to its members; when these relations change or are destroyed, the fatherland vanishes."[19]

Cohler herself notes that "nationalism is an appeal to a pre-existing group which will be radically changed by the government which is to be established upon it."[20] Thus in the passages I have quoted from the *Government of Poland*, the "national genius" and the "national physiognomy" are the result of the institutions (and even the manipulations) of the legislator. In this they do not differ so very much from Plato's "noble lie." The principal difference with the ancients lies elsewhere: in the complex interplay between nationalism and cosmopolitanism and, in the last analysis, among reason, spiritedness (Platonic *thumos*) and feeling.

Spiritedness, Reason, or Feeling?

From Plato and Aristotle to Hegel and Nietzsche, the relation between patriotism and cosmopolitism is problematic for every political philosopher, but for none more than for Rousseau. There could be no starker contrast than that between Rousseau's two treatments of this question in *Emile*.

> To prevent pity from degenerating into weakness it must be generalized and extended to the whole of mankind. For the sake of reason, for the sake of love of ourselves, we must have pity for our species still more than for our neighbor. . . . The less the object of our care is immediately involved with us the less the illusion of particular interest is to be feared. The more one generalizes this interest, the more it becomes equitable, and the love of mankind is nothing other than the love of justice.[21]

Thus book 4 of *Emile*. In book 1, by contrast, one finds the same praise of patriotism and critique of cosmopolitanism encountered in the *Discourse on Political Economy* or the *Government of Poland*.

> Every particular society, when it is narrow and unified, is estranged from the all-encompassing society. Every patriot is harsh to foreigners. They are only men. They are nothing in his eyes. This is a drawback, inevitable but not compelling. The essential thing is to be good to the people with whom one lives. Abroad, the Spartan was ambitious, avaricious, iniquitous. But disinterested-

ness, equity and concord reigned within his walls. Distrust those cosmopolitans who go to great length in their books to discover duties they do not deign to fulfill around them. A philosopher loves the Tartars so as to be spared having to love his neighbors.[22]

Of course this is not so much a contradiction as an expression of Rousseau's famous dictum that "forced to combat either nature or the social institutions, one must choose between making a man or a citizen, for one cannot make both at the same time." Even so, it would be too simple to leave it at saying that the passage in book 4 concerns the education of a man while that in book 1 concerns that of a citizen. The question is whether even in his conception of the citizen Rousseau can entirely avoid the contradictions of the mixed state, which he exposes so forcefully in his famous critique of the bourgeois.[23] It is whether the Rousseauian citizen is entirely "denatured" or whether he in some decisive respects bears the marks of natural man, of Rousseauian man, and perhaps of Christian or modern man.

There is in the first place the paradox—already present in Plato and Aristotle—of conceiving the desirable society as one of warriors without wars, one that manages to be both militaristic and peaceful. The best city should be small, isolated, dedicated to its domestic harmony and shunning expansion and conquest; at the same time, it not only should be ready to defend itself, but should revolve around those virtues of patriotism, courage, and sacrifice that flourish in wartime. If the city remains at peace, are these virtues likely to flourish? Conversely, if they flourish, is the city likely to remain at peace? If they wither away, will it remain strong and free?

Here the implicit answers of the classics and of Rousseau appear to diverge. For the classics too, the necessities of war may bring the city to grief by forcing it to choose between the maintenance of its freedom and its fostering of virtue. In a striking and mysterious sentence, Leo Strauss identifies the exigencies of defense as the Achilles' heel of the polis and technological innovation as the Trojan horse of its corruption.[24] For the classics, however, the warlike character of civic virtue reflects not only the necessities of external defense but the character of the desired domestic order. The thirst for dominion and mastery shades over into that for nobility: both are grounded in the spirited part of the soul. Rousseau, however, although he never tires of extolling antique virtue at the expense of modern corruption, so detests cruelty and war as to be open to the prospect of the eventual withering away of virtue. In the *Abstract of the Project of the Abbé de Saint-Pierre*, he considers the objection that in the event of perpetual peace, armies will lose their courage and discipline. "[In that case] it is true that there will be no more hardening for war. But neither will there be any more need for it. Of what use would it be to train for war, when you have no intention of ever making it? And which is the better course—to cultivate a pernicious art, or to destroy the need of it forever?"[25]

That the art of war is pernicious seems indeed to be one of Rousseau's most settled convictions.

> [From the division of mankind into political societies] arose all those horrible prejudices which rank the honor of shedding human blood among the virtues. The most decent men learned to consider it one of their duties to murder their fellow-men; at length men were seen to massacre each other by the thousands without knowing why; more murders were committed in a single day of fighting and more horrors in the capture of a single city than were committed in the state of nature during whole centuries over the entire face of the earth.[26]

In the education of Emile, accordingly, the teaching of history, occupied as it is primarily with wars and revolutions, plays a brief and subordinate role. "Even Thucydides [otherwise the greatest of historians] always speaks of war, and one sees in his narratives almost nothing but the least instructive thing in the world, that is battles." Rousseau denies for his part not only the moral value of war but much of its historical significance. "One often finds in a battle won or lost the reason for a revolution which, even before this battle, had already become inevitable. War hardly does anything other than make manifest outcomes already determined by moral causes which historians rarely know how to see." Emile's study of great conquerors will focus primarily on their private lives. Conquest itself will be studied once Emile's education has prepared him to despise it. "He will be indignant in seeing the whole of humankind its own dupe, debasing itself in these children's games. He will be afflicted at seeing his brothers tear one another apart for the sake of dreams and turn into ferocious animals because they do not know how to be satisfied with being men." Pyrrhus and Augustus will be studied in order to show the vanity of ambition.[27]

This criticism of ambition is not forgotten even when Rousseau returns to his praise of heroic virtues. In the *Government of Poland*, he speaks of creating "courageous and unselfish souls" among whom one must preserve and revive simple customs and wholesome tastes and "a warlike spirit devoid of ambition" (*un esprit martial sans ambition*).[28] Such a combination is by no means impossible, as is confirmed to some extent even by modern examples such as the Swiss of Rousseau's day and the Israelis of our own. These very examples, however, attest at the same time to the fragility of this combination. This fragility follows not only from the corrosive effects of luxury and commerce but from the tension between love of humanity and love of fatherland. "The love of humanity inspires many virtues such as tenderness, equity, moderation, charity, indulgence, but it does not inspire courage, firmness, etc.; and it does not give them this energy which they get from the love of fatherland which elevates them toward heroism."[29]

Yet as I have already suggested, Rousseau does not opt for the political virtues over the demands of equity and charity. While he shares the classics' rejection of unrestrained commerce and acquisitiveness, his reservations about spiritedness align him rather with the moderns. While he rejects Montesquieu's substitution of commerce and humanity for austerity and war, his own hope is to combine the refusal of wealth with that of inhumanity. This intention reminds of that of Christianity. He may then be vulnerable to his own critique of the latter as subversive of genuine citizenship.

Rousseau's differences with the classics obtrude even or above all on the level of the transpolitical, where the balance shifts in both cases from patriotism to cosmopolitanism. The "great cosmopolitan souls" who overcome "the imaginary barriers that separate peoples" do so, for Plato and Aristotle, through their exercise of universal reason. For Rousseau they do so through having preserved their natural compassion; it is thus that "they include the whole human race in their benevolence." True, as Orwin points out in his chapter in this volume, compassion becomes love of humanity only through the good offices of imagination, whose development presupposes reason. But the fact remains that compassion, which occupies a subordinate place in the classical view, becomes central in Rousseau only through the demotion of both philosophy and politics in favor of the primacy of humane sentiment.[30]

Conversely, it is the conscription of reason and moral indignation under the banner of sentiment, and above all of compassion, that forms Rousseau's major legacy in international politics. More than his ambiguous statements on nationalism and internationalism, what has changed the world is the revolutionary potential of the conclusion of the *Discourse on the Origins of Inequality*, with its explosive indictment of the global inequality of masters and subjects, rich and poor, "since it is manifestly against the law of nature, in whatever manner it is defined, that a child command an old man, an imbecile lead a wise man, and a handful of men be glutted with superfluities while the starving multitude lacks necessities."[31]

Rousseau in Perspective: The Philosophy of History and the Historical Experience

On the question of war and peace proper, beyond the structural and permanent problem of the plurality of states, Rousseau's central message concerns the character of modern society. For Locke and Montesquieu, the advent of commercial society affords at least a partial solution to the problem of strife by substituting interests for passions and humanity for fanaticism. Rousseau reverses this judgment by asserting that mutual dependence and competition will make war more likely and true peace impossible. Kant, Hegel, and Marx accept this reversal but reverse it in turn: competition and commerce, inequality and wealth do lead to division and war, but this process in turn leads through the "cunning of nature" or "of reason" to the unification of the planet, to the education of man, and to inherently peaceful political regimes.

In some respects history justifies both Rousseau and his philosophic or revolutionary successors. Optimism about the peaceful character of commercial and industrial society (about the primacy of the economic over the military), though widespread in the nineteenth century, was reduced to black humor by the two world wars and two totalitarian regimes of the twentieth. Today, with the collapse of the second of these regimes, the notion of the obsolescence of war in Western society is enjoying a resurrection. Michael Doyle argues that Kant was right, that liberal democracies do not make war on each other, and that this has much to do with factors alleged by Kant such as economic interdependence and the rising costs of war.[32] Francis Fukuyama argues that Hegel (in the guise of Kojève) was right and that our time has reached the end of history—that is, of war and revolution.[33] Of course, even if true, this may amount only to the West's becoming a kind of "island of the last man": none can deny that violence continues unabated in the rest of the world. The question, then, would be that of the relations between center and periphery, between a liberal or posthistorical West and an anarchic tyrannical or threatening East and South. Here Rousseau becomes relevant once again. At one level, one of Kant's formulations that seems most prophetic concerns cosmopolitan right. Today "a violation of right at one point of the planet is felt everywhere."[34] CNN lends concrete content to Kant's insight. So does economic interdependence, which confirms the eighth proposition of the *Idea for a Universal History with a Cosmopolitan Intent:* "The influence that the shattering of a state exerts upon all others (given the strong ties of each with the others on our continent through their industries), compels the others to offer themselves as arbiters."[35]

What does all this mean, however, in terms of real solidarity and a real ability to bring a free and peaceful order to the planet? What is the moral and political impact of the progress in communication and commerce? Both Kant and Hegel were aware that a world based on the search for economic satisfaction alone could not provide the basis of a genuine peace. Kant, the philosopher of peace, counted on disinterested morality, Hegel, the philosopher of war, counted on patriotic sacrifice to restore a dimension of nonmercenary citizenship to a world dominated by possessive individualism. Obviously they both failed to prevent the rise of the last man. Rousseau, on the other hand, warned that the homogeneity of Enlightenment would yield men who were only Europeans or, even worse, only men—that is, nothing. Nor would he have been surprised by the reassertion of difference, whether rhetorical or violent and whether in the guise of nationalism, ethnic revival, communitarianism, or simply tribal or gang warfare.

Rousseau and the International Relations of Today

But what would have been Rousseau's response to the current situation? Which side would he have taken in our current debates? The answer seems easy in two respects (military intervention and economic interdependence) and difficult in two others (national identity and humanitarian solidarity).

In spite of being favorably disposed toward the notion of international organization as proposed by the abbé de Saint-Pierre, today Rousseau would most probably have been a neoisolationist. Much as he hated war and loathed conquest, he would likely have balked at any suggestion of a war to end all wars, at any intervention to punish aggression, or even at any alliance intended to deter it and to protect potential victims. His distrust of the motives of rulers and the consequences of wars would have aligned him with the critics of an active great power policy, especially one involving force.

Rousseau's stance would have been even less ambiguous on issues of economic interdependence. He would have condemned, deplored, or derided the ideological victory of free trade and welcomed resistance to it. He would have sided with American unions against NAFTA, with French farmers and artists against the GATT, with Third World radicals and the *dependencia* school for "self-centered development" and against "unequal exchange" and "the imperialism of free trade."

The ambiguities as to a contemporary Rousseauian position begin with a third dimension of our current situation—which is both the most modern and the most Rousseauian—social interpenetration. Political societies correspond less and less to the Rousseauian ideal of internal unity and external isolation; they are more and more afflicted by both the internal divisions and the external influences Rousseau denounced so forcefully. But by the same token, they experience conflicting aspirations—the need for distinctiveness and self-closure, on the one hand, and the broadening of compassion to the whole human race, on the other—both of which are of Rousseauian inspiration.

Since the end of the Cold War, the double process of fragmentation and interpenetration has only accelerated. States lose their grip on their societies because they have to compete for the loyalties of their citizens with the claims both of smaller, subnational communities and of external transnational influences, ranging from mass media to mass migrations and from religious movements to criminal mafias. The breakdown of the communist pseudofederations such as the Soviet Union and Yugoslavia has provided the most spectacular examples of the emergence of such issues as minorities and refugees, borders and migrations. The problems, however, are still more general than these. They concern both the nature of national identity and the duties and power of the international community. In one sense these preoccupations pull in opposite directions: fragmentation and the politics of ethnicity, globalization and the politics of humanitarian intervention. In another sense, we can reconcile the two in the principle of solidarity for oppressed groups, especially where these are national minorities. But the very factor that lends force to this principle also accounts for its fragility: it rests on humanitarian sentiment more than on calculations of economic viability or military feasibility.

As regards the first of these issues—ethnicity and nationalism—Rousseau's thought is at the center of the discussion, at least in France. This is shown nicely in Liah Greenfield's *Nationalism*.[36] She employs two oppositions: ethnic versus civic nationalisms and individualistic versus collectivist. In terms of this schema, British and American nationalism is civic and individualistic, while the German and Russian versions are ethnic and collectivist. Only the French notion of nationalism is both civic and collectivist, because it bases sovereignty not on individual rights nor again on ethnic identity, but on the abstract notion of the general will. So the French notion of the nation is informed by Rousseau. In a more general and less sophisticated way, discussion of the differences between France and Germany often features the opposition between Rousseau and Herder, who, like Renan and Fichte, are supposed to represent two versions of national identity, the civic or democratic and the ethnic or romantic.

In fact, however, Rousseau cannot be reduced to either of these alternatives. Without going as far as Cohler, we have seen the importance both of the prepolitical roots of the nation and of the deliberate exploitation and encouragement of national differences through the civil religion and civic education. Similarly, though Rousseau cannot be charged with favoring conquest or any form of expansionist nationalism, the encouragement of xenophobia for domestic and defensive purposes cannot but risk provoking the very international conflict it aims at avoiding.

The relevance of Rousseau's thought to understanding the complementary trend of humanitarian solidarity is even more striking—as is the ambiguity or ambivalence of his teaching. We have seen how, in Rousseau's view, the compassion of modern man is both more extensive and weaker than that of the true citizen, thus contributing to the dilemmas of nationalism and cosmopolitanism. Could it be that the mass media, and in particular television, have blazed a trail out of this dilemma? Certainly international compassion today plays a role undreamed of in Rousseau's time. Certainly, too, this is due in great part to what is often called "the CNN factor"—that in the "global village" the horrors of war and famine come home to the average citizen. Losing the abstractness of far-off sufferings commented on by both Rousseau and Voltaire, these now become catalysts for global change. They evoke an impulse "to do something," thus fostering transnational movements like Amnesty International or humanitarian organizations like Doctors without Borders.

Rousseau would surely have sympathized with these impulses, so akin to his evocation in the *State of War* of the philosopher on the battlefield. At the same time, he would have foreseen their fragility and fickleness, as one horror show replaces another before the eyes of the public. He would not have been surprised to see that, very often, the *répugnance à voir souffrir* that is the source of compassion may lead us to change channels rather than the policies of our governments, especially if the latter choice involves risk and sacrifice for ourselves. He stressed that compassion was at its most powerful when it did not conflict with our interests, as he emphasized that states were far more prone to pursue the latter. The nonintervention of the West in Yugoslavia attests only too clearly to this truth. The hesitation, unease, and, more often than not, hypocrisy that governments and public opinion have demonstrated in the face of this last crisis confirm that when it comes to humanitarian issues we remain today deeply divided—among nations, within nations, and within ourselves. It appears that the curse of the "mixed state" is with us as much as ever.

NOTES

1. Jean-Jacques Rousseau, *Considerations on the Government of Poland*, in *Rousseau on International Relations*, ed. Stanley Hoffmann and David Fidler (Oxford: Clarendon Press, 1991), 92; for the original, see Rousseau, *Oeuvres complètes*, 5 vols., ed. Bernard Gagnebin and Marcel Raymond (Paris: Bibliothèque de la Pléiade, 1959–95), 3:1037–38.

2. Jean-Jacques Rousseau, *Constitutional Project for Corsica*, in Hoffmann and Fidler, *Rousseau*, 141–43 (*Oeuvres complètes* 3:903–4).

3. Jean-Jacques Rousseau, *On the Social Contract, with Geneva Manuscript and Political Economy*, ed. Roger D. Masters, trans. Judith R. Masters (New York: St. Martin's Press, 1978), 132 (bk. 4, chap. 9; *Oeuvres complètes* 3:470); *Emile*, trans. Allan Bloom (New York: Basic Books, 1979), 466–67 (*Oeuvres complètes*, 4:848–49).

4. First version of the *Social Contract*, chap. 2, "On the General Society of the Human Race," in Hoffmann and Fidler, *Rousseau*, 102 (*Oeuvres complètes*, 3:281–82).

5. *The State of War*, in Hoffmann and Fidler, *Rousseau*, 40–41 (*Oeuvres complètes*, 3:604–8).

6. Ibid., 42–43 (3:609).

7. Ibid., 44 (3:610).

8. *Emile*, 466 (*Oeuvres complètes*, 4:848).

9. *Saint-Pierre's Project for Peace*, in Hoffmann and Fidler, *Rousseau*, 54–55 (*Oeuvres complètes*, 3:564).

10. Ibid., 100 (modified translation) (3:599–600).

11. *Fragments on War*, in Hoffmann and Fidler, *Rousseau*, 48–52 (*Oeuvres complètes*, 3:613–16); *The Social Contract*, 1.4, in *Social Contract*, ed. Masters, 50–51 (*Oeuvres complètes*, 3:356–58).

12. *Saint-Pierre's Project for Peace*, in Hoffmann and Fidler, *Rousseau*, 81–84 (*Oeuvres complètes*, 3:584–86).

13. Cf. the definition of virtue as the conformity of the particular will with the general will and the statement that "the greatest miracles of virtue have been produced

by patriotism." *Discourse on Political Economy*, in Rousseau, *On the Social Contract*, ed. Masters, 217–19 (*Oeuvres complètes*, 3:252–55).

14. *Government of Poland*, chap. 13, "The Military System," in Hoffmann and Fidler, *Rousseau*, 182–91 (*Oeuvres complètes*, 3:1012–20).

15. Ibid., 182–89 (3:1013–18).

16. Ibid., 173–75 (3:970–71).

17. Ibid., 168–69 (3:960–61).

18. Jean-Jacques Rousseau, *Discourse on the Origins of Inequality*, in *The First and Second Discourses*, ed. Roger D. Masters, trans. Roger D. Masters and Judith R. Masters (New York: St. Martin's Press, 1964), 148 (*Oeuvres complètes*, 3:169); Anne M. Cohler, *Rousseau and Nationalism* (New York: Basic Books, 1970), 119.

19. Letter to Colonel Pichet of 1 March 1764 (*Oeuvres complètes*, 3:1535).

20. Cohler, *Rousseau and Nationalism*, 34.

21. *Emile*, 253 (*Oeuvres complètes*, 4:548).

22. Ibid., 39 (4:248–49).

23. Ibid., 40–41 (4:249–51).

24. Leo Strauss, *Thoughts on Machiavelli* (Glencoe, Ill.: Free Press, 1958), 298.

25. Jean-Jacques Rousseau, *Saint-Pierre's Project for Peace*, in Hoffmann and Fidler, *Rousseau*, 83–84 (*Oeuvres complètes*, 3:586).

26. *Discourse on the Origins of Inequality*, in *Discourses*, ed. Masters, 161 (*Oeuvres complètes*, 3:179).

27. *Emile*, 239–42 (*Oeuvres complètes*, 4:532–34).

28. *Government of Poland*, in Hoffmann and Fidler, 176 (*Oeuvres complètes*, 3:1003–4).

29. *Fragments politiques*, in *Oeuvres complètes*, 3:536.

30. *Discourse on the Origins of Inequality*, in *Discourses*, ed. Masters, 160–61 (*Oeuvres complètes*, 3:178); Clifford Orwin, "Rousseau and the Discovery of Political Compassion," chapter 14 below.

31. *Discourse on the Origins of Inequality*, in *Discourses*, ed. Masters, 181 (*Oeuvres complètes*, 3:194).

32. Michael Doyle, "Kant, Liberal Legacies and Foreign Affairs," *Philosophy and Public Affairs* 12, nos. 3 and 4 (1983): 203–35, 324–53.

33. Francis Fukuyama, *The End of History and the Last Man* (New York: Simon and Schuster, 1992).

34. Immanuel Kant, *Perpetual Peace*, third final article, in *The Philosophy of Kant*, trans. Carl J. Friedrich, Modern Library Edition (New York, 1946), 446.

35. Immanuel Kant, *Idea for a Universal History with a Cosmopolitan Intent*, in *Philosophy of Kant*, 127.

36. Liah Greenfield, *Nationalism: Five Roads to Modernity* (Cambridge: Harvard University Press, 1992).

❧ 11 ❧
Rousseau, Ethnicity, and Difference

H. D. FORBES

The practical problems of nationalism and world government are now entangled with the deep divisions within many nation-states owing to ethnic differences and the "politics of difference."[1] The problem illustrated with startling clarity by Canada's ongoing constitutional difficulties is found elsewhere in more muted but still threatening forms. Dedication to ethnic accommodation is no guarantee that it can be achieved in practice.

Discussion of these matters is hobbled by the ambiguity of some key terms and by the need always to be coping with the very disagreements we are trying to understand. What is a nation, and how does it differ from an ethnic group? Do nations even exist, or are they just imaginary creations? Where should one look for the sources of nationalism? Does it have more to do with politics, language, religion, or ethnicity? How should one understand the opposition that is now frequently observed between traditional nationalism or patriotism and intense loyalties to more "partial"—but possibly more extensive—groups like languages, religions, races, and genders?

The previous chapters by Marc Plattner and Pierre Hassner have explained why Rousseau is often called a founder, even *the* founder, of nationalism, but also why he can be regarded as a source of modern internationalism. They have set the discussion of nationalism and internationalism within a framework of broader considerations having to do with the fundamental tensions in Rousseau's thought. I shall go over the same ground with a view to further clarifying Rousseau's relation to our contemporary politics of difference. I shall work my way into this subject by following the lead of Charles Taylor, a moderate advocate of "difference," particularly "multiculturalism," who stresses both the influence of Rousseau on current thinking and the limitations of his thought as a basis for dealing with our current practical problems.[2] Taylor's observations and suggestions are rooted in a remarkable knowledge of modern political theory. Some of his formulations are misleading, I shall try to show, but all are revealing. The politics of difference comes to light, in his presentation, as an alternative to the liberal theory and practice of individual rights. It borrows some of Rousseau's objections to individual rights but rejects his fundamental principles. Its relation to Rousseau may be clearest if we focus, as Taylor does, on ethnicity.

Practical Differences

Allan Bloom liked to inveigh against abstractions, particularly the abstractions of modern social science.[3] Serious confusion can result from employing weighty words like "culture" and "values" outside any definite context of practical controversy. "Difference" too is a rather vague and potentially misleading term. One of the real merits of Taylor's main discussion of Rousseau and difference, his essay "The Politics of Recognition," is its surprisingly clear discussion of two important practical problems. In the last two sections of the essay Taylor discusses, first, Quebec's demand for a new constitutional status within Canada and, second, the question of the "canon" of accredited authors in the humanities departments of American universities. Let me quickly outline the main differences between them and Taylor's practical recommendations.

For many years Canada has been in the grip of a dangerous conflict between Quebec, the federal government, and the other provinces centering on Quebec's demand for more autonomy. A generation ago a new "separatist" nationalism displaced the older French-Canadian nationalism that was compatible with Canadian federalism. Taylor presents the resulting conflicts as essentially a clash between "communitarian" and "procedural" liberalism rather than between Quebec and Canada, or French and English, or the federal government and the provinces. The clash that most concerns Taylor came to a head in the late 1980s over a package of constitutional amendments, the Meech Lake Accord, which would have officially recognized Quebec as a "distinct society" within Canada and would thus have loosened slightly the "equal protection" provisions of the Canadian Charter of Rights and Freedoms.[4] Had the amendments been adopted, they would have implicitly legitimized Quebec's existing restrictions on the rights of its "anglophone" and "allophone" citizens and would have opened up the possibility of different rights in different parts of the country. Adopting the amendments would have provided at least a temporary respite in Canada's constitutional battles. In fact, had the Meech Lake Accord been accepted quickly and with good grace by English Canada, Taylor and many others believe, it would have "settled" the problem of Quebec nationalism or separatism for at least a generation and possibly much longer. Canadians would not be facing, as they are now, a resurgent separatist movement that is threatening to destroy their country.

Opponents of the Meech Lake Accord, most notably a former prime minister, Pierre Elliott Trudeau, objected to any special recognition of Quebec or the Québécois, arguing that it would be incompatible with the equal recognition owed all ethnic or national groups.[5] They also found the prospect of different rights in different parts of the country fundamentally unacceptable. According to the "procedural" conception of liberalism they seemed to espouse, no "collective goals" can be permitted to override "individual rights." In their view, according to Taylor, a truly liberal society must not adopt any public definition of the ends of life. "A liberal society must remain neutral on the good life, and restrict itself to ensuring that however they see things, citizens deal fairly with each other and the state deals equally with all."[6] From this perspective, a state like Quebec that espouses collective goals on behalf of its "national" majority is inherently discriminatory. It implicitly denies equal respect to those of its citizens who do not belong to the favored ethnic or national group. Moreover, it sets a bad example: if Quebec were permitted to discriminate on behalf of its cultural majority, the "proceduralists" implied, then why should the larger society—Canada as a whole—not have an equal right to discriminate on behalf of *its* majority? Why should sauce for the goose not be sauce for the gander? What if Canada were to pass a law making English the only official language from coast to coast? If the government of Quebec can use legislation to give Quebec a "French" look, why should the federal government not be able to give Canada as a whole an "English" look by banning French or any other language from outdoor signs? And if English-speaking Canadians were trying to achieve the same results quietly by doing nothing—by protecting free individual choice of language in the context of a majority English society—how can the Québécois who espouse "collective goals" really complain?

Defenders of Quebec like Charles Taylor tended to see things differently. In their view the Québécois are a *minority* and should be encouraged to affirm their cultural distinctiveness within Canada by adopting laws in Quebec, where they are a *majority*, that reinforce their cultural distinctiveness. The refusal of liberals like Trudeau to recognize that "standard schedules of rights might apply differently in one cultural context than they do in another," and "that their application might have to take account of different collective goals," just lent credence to the view that liberalism is unable to acknowledge distinct cultural identities, and it pushed the Québécois toward separation.

Taylor supports Quebec but also defends liberalism against some of its more extreme detractors. He denies that liberalism need be set against difference. He rejects the "proceduralist" criterion of liberalism and offers instead a more "communitarian" test, according to which a society can be called liberal even when it is "organized around a definition of the good life" and so has "strong collective goals," provided it also shows respect for diversity. To do so, Taylor says, it must protect the *basic* rights of all its citizens, including of course those who do not share its collective goals. "But now the rights in question are conceived to be the fundamental and crucial ones that have been recognized as such from the very beginning of the liberal tradition: rights to life, liberty, due process, free speech, free practice of religion, and so on." The right to send one's child to an English-language school and the right to post a sign in English in front of one's store are not among these *fundamental* rights, Taylor implies. "One has to distinguish the fundamental liberties, those that should never be infringed and therefore ought to be unassailably entrenched, on the one hand, from privileges and immunities that are important, but that can be revoked or restricted for reasons of public policy"—for example, in order to promote the survival or protect the integrity of a minority / majority culture like that of the Québécois.[7]

Taylor discusses the Canadian case at some length to illustrate the current division within liberalism regarding "difference." Procedural liberalism, he concludes, is indeed inhospitable to difference because it insists on the same rights for all, without exception, and because it makes no provision for the collective goal of cultural survival. "I think this form of liberalism is guilty as charged by the proponents of a politics of difference." Communitarian liberals, by contrast, are more accommodating. They distinguish basic rights from "the broad range of immunities and presumptions of uniform treatment that have sprung up in modern cultures of judicial review." They defend basic rights, but not the "immunities and presumptions" that work against cultural survival. "They are willing to weigh the importance of certain forms of uniform treatment against the importance of cultural survival, and opt sometimes in favour of the latter." Taylor aligns himself with this second kind of liberalism, because "more and more societies today are turning out to be multicultural," and "the rigidities of procedural liberalism may rapidly become impractical in tomorrow's world."[8]

Turning to the United States, Taylor urges Americans to accept changes in the curriculum of schools and colleges to recognize more fully the cultural contributions of their minority ethnic and other groups. Practically speaking, he explains, the problem of multiculturalism in the United States is the problem of "the canon."[9] The traditional "Eurocentric" curriculum is said to convey the message, between the lines, that all creativity and worth inhere in dead white males of European provenance. This is unacceptable to women and to people of color. The curriculum must therefore be changed, not to provide everyone with a broader culture, but to give due recognition to the hitherto excluded. "Just as all must have equal civil rights and equal voting rights, regardless of race or culture, so all should enjoy the presumption that their traditional culture has value."[10]

Taylor ignores the practical objection to this multiculturalism, that all cultures cannot be crammed into one curriculum (let alone one *course*), to focus on the theoretically more interesting problem of justifying the necessary judgments of value. If there are indeed grounds for such judgments, then they cannot be demanded as a right. "A favorable judgment on demand is nonsense. . . . The giving of such a judgment on demand is an act of breathtaking condescension."[11] Aware of this difficulty (and perhaps others), most partisans of difference, Taylor observes, now tend to embrace the "subjectivist, half-baked neo-Nietzschean theories" associated with Foucault and Derrida, which simply deny that there is any "objectivity" to judgments of value. The whole problem of justification then seems to fall away, since properly speaking one is no longer making judgments that can be right or wrong but is merely accepting or rejecting "cultures" without reference to their merits or shortcomings. Unfortunately, the easier recognition is to acquire, the less it is worth. "The act of declaring another culture's creations to be of worth and the act of declaring oneself on their side, even if their creations aren't all that impressive, become indistinguishable."[12] So the old problem returns in a slightly different guise. Those who demand recognition want *respect*, not a condescending acceptance.

What then should contemporary academics do, facing demands for a more inclusive curriculum? Whatever they may think, Taylor says, they must not say what Saul Bellow is reputed to have said: "When the Zulus produce a Tolstoy we will read him."[13] This may well have been an honest expression of Bellow's convictions, but it is also a quintessential expression of Eurocentric arrogance. It would clash with any authentically Zulu estimation of Zulu culture, and by making Tolstoy the standard of cultural excellence, it denies the very principle of human equality. Influential writers and teachers have a responsibility to show more sensitivity and tolerance, it seems. But not too much more. Well-meaning professors falling over each other to embrace exotic cultures they know nothing about (and may secretly despise) can be insufferably patronizing. Their prematurely favorable judgments can be ethnocentric in a more subtle way. Rushing to curry favor, they cannot help but praise the other for being like themselves.

So there must be a middle way, Taylor concludes, between openly ethnocentric rejection of the other and inauthentic, condescending recognition. He finds his middle way by speaking of a *presumption* of equal worth of different cultures—all those "that have provided the horizon of meaning for large numbers of human beings, of diverse characters and temperaments, over a long period of time."[14] Since this presumption can be put to the test of "further study" only in the future, it avoids awkward practical problems in the present. And in the future we may discover a providential harmony of all these great cultures, as Herder seems to have believed, or perhaps just a deeper sense of how far away we remain from "that ultimate horizon from which the relative worth of different cultures might be evident."[15] But in any case, by putting off the difficult judgments of relative worth, without simply denying their possibility, we slip nicely between the rock of relativism and the hard place of absolutism and solve our immediate problem.

Different practical problems evidently call for different practical prescriptions. In both his discussion of Quebec's place in Canada and his discussion of the curriculum in American universities, Taylor shows himself sympathetic to "difference" without being simply its partisan. But in the Canadian case he sides with "dualism" against multiculturalism, whereas in the American case, he favors multiculturalism over Eurocentrism. In the Canadian case he affirms the right of a local majority to insist on assimilation among minorities resident on its territory. In the American case, for easily understandable historical reasons, he puts less emphasis on releasing local majorities from the supervision of the Supreme Court or encouraging them to affirm their distinctive cultures.

Taylor is on solid ground insofar as he is simply defending the Meech Lake Accord and lamenting the failure of English-speaking Canadians to embrace it. But insofar as he is offering general principles for the resolution of ethnic conflicts, he seems to be on shaky ground, since his more relaxed "communitarian" liberalism seems to provide support, in principle, for the demands of practically every ethnic group, majority and minority alike. Why should it not be welcomed even more warmly by the English, dreaming of a unilingual Canada, or by Canada's smaller ethnic minorities, dreaming of a *truly* multilingual and multicultural Canada, than by the French in Quebec, trying to defend their language and culture? In the United States, why should it not be welcomed as warmly by the white "European" majority as by the various relevant minorities?

One may be tempted to conclude that terms like "difference" and "multiculturalism" hide crucial distinctions between these cases. Taylor emphasizes their similarities, however. The practical demands in question spring from a common source, it seems, and that source—Rousseau—can also be held responsible for some of our difficulties in dealing with them in a reasonable and flexible way.

Authenticity and Recognition

Taylor presents the politics of difference as the latest expression of a broader "politics of recognition." The first form of this politics, "the politics of universalism" or "equal dignity," emerged centuries ago out of Christian and humanist sources.[16] Since the eighteenth century it has developed along two different lines, one stemming from Rousseau, the other from Kant. More recently the Kantian line has produced two further variants, one more strictly "liberal," the other (which Taylor favors) more "communitarian." Out of the inner tensions of all these developments has emerged our contemporary "politics of difference."

The older principles of "equal dignity" and current theories about "difference" are alike insofar as both involve demands for equality. Both require that human beings conventionally defined as "inferior" be treated as the natural equals of their "superiors." "Dignity" differs from "difference" because different groups are typically making the relevant demands and because the demands themselves are different. "The politics of equal dignity" refers to the long struggle against class and religious privilege that came to a head two or three generations ago. It began as a demand for purely legal or political rights (legal equality, religious toleration, universal suffrage, etc.) and gradually, by a familiar process, became a struggle for material redistribution (the *social* justice of the trade union and socialist movements). "The politics of difference," by contrast, refers to the current struggle against *gender* and *national, racial,* or *ethnic* privilege. It aims to achieve what might be called *cultural* justice. Its main beneficiaries are to be women, gays, lesbians, blacks, Chicanos, and other marginalized and oppressed minorities. They seek recognition not just of their legal equality as citizens, but of their social equality as representatives of different cultures or ways of life. Its key contention is that "our identity is partly shaped by recognition or its absence, often by the *mis*recognition of others, and so a person or group of people can suffer real damage, real distortion, if the people or society around them mirror back to them a confining or demeaning or contemptible picture of themselves. Nonrecognition or misrecognition can inflict harm, can be a form of oppression, imprisoning someone in a false, distorted, and reduced mode of being."[17]

Our ancestors not so long ago would have stared at us uncomprehendingly, Taylor notes, had we complained to them that a lack of recognition was imprisoning us in a "false, distorted, and reduced mode of being." But today this "discourse of recognition and identity" is familiar and in a sense easily understood. Where does it come from? What thoughts does it express?

According to Taylor, the most important source of the politics of recognition in all its contemporary forms is "the massive subjective turn of modern culture, a new form of inwardness, in which we come to think of ourselves as beings with inner depths." In an earlier age, apparently, "being in touch with some [external] source—for example, God, or the Idea of the Good—was considered essential to full being." Now, however, our moral salvation is seen to involve connection with a source deep within ourselves, and for this we are indebted to Rousseau. "The most important philosophical writer who helped to bring about this change was Jean-Jacques Rousseau." (In "The Profession of Faith of the Savoyard Vicar," for example, Rousseau presents morality as a matter of following an "immortal and celestial voice" that proclaims inborn principles of justice and virtue.) "This voice is often drowned out by the passions that are induced by our dependence on others, the main one being our pride. Our moral salvation comes from recovering authentic moral contact with ourselves."[18] This self-contact, or capacity to listen to our inner voice, takes on independent and crucial moral significance, Taylor says, when it is believed that "each of our voices has something unique to say." Then the "accent" shifts from listening for a "voice of nature," which is in principle the same for all, to "realizing a potentiality which is properly my own." "There is a certain way of being human that is *my* way. I am called upon to live my life in this way, and not in imitation of anyone else's life. . . . If I am not [true to myself], I miss the point of my life; I miss what being human is for *me*."[19] This is the idea of individuality or originality, and it requires that we all resist the pressures toward outward conformity. We must all strive to be *authentic*.[20]

What is the connection between this "powerful moral ideal of authenticity" (involving an "inward turn" like that of the Savoyard vicar) and the outward demands for recognition noted earlier (so unlike the vicar's resignation to being a vicar rather than a parish priest)? Taylor finds it in a "crucial feature of human life," namely, "its fundamentally *dialogical* character." We discover our inner depths through interaction with "significant others," and we can enjoy a secure feeling of authenticity, or a positive identity, only if those others freely recognize what we see in ourselves. A successful search within is thus indistinguishable from a successful negotiation with "significant others." In striving for authenticity we are really "aspiring to a certain kind of dialogicality."[21] Those who are denied this "dialogicality" suffer real harm.

The fundamental demand, then, of the newest form of the politics of recognition—namely, the politics of difference—is for the external validation of internally generated identities at odds with those of the majority or the dominant group in a society. This demand has deep roots; it grows naturally out of the transformations in our society and in our moral thinking in the past centuries. Rousseau helped to uncover (or create) this demand, but, as we shall see, his political theory provides no way of meeting it.

Rousseau's Political Theory

A standard objection—perhaps *the* standard objection—leveled at Rousseau's political theory is that it fails to recognize inviolable natural rights. By putting no limits except procedural ones on what "the state" can do to "society" or "the individual," it subordinates individual rights and the state-society distinction to the right the community has over all. According to Rousseau, political institutions are to be understood not as means that men develop for better protecting their prior natural rights, but rather as changes in their way of living (indeed, in their very nature) that *create* rights, and only such rights as the sovereign people decide. "It is contrary to the nature of the body politic for the sovereign to impose on itself a law which it cannot break," Rousseau says, and worse still, individuals can be "forced to be free."[22] These famous teachings of Rousseau, his liberal critics say, are really monstrous errors with terrible practical consequences.

In recent years this familiar objection has been recast, and Rousseau is now attacked from a new direction. The emphasis has shifted from individual to group rights, and he is blamed not for failing to protect "individuality," but for implicitly denying "difference." The source of difficulties may still be his radical egalitarianism, which threatens individual eccentricity and dissent as well as class privilege, but his contemporary critics, unlike their predecessors, seem drawn to the idea that privacy hides oppression ("the personal is political") and eager to use the state to overcome inequalities they attribute to society. What they dispute is Rousseau's assumption that the state can be understood as a contract among undifferentiated individuals. It should not proscribe "partial societies" as a threat to its general will, as Rousseau argued, but rather should treat their accommodation as its main task.

Taylor illustrates this new critical tack. He presents Rousseau's theory as one designed to overcome the "bad other dependence" of a society of "masters and slaves." In such a society, individuals compete for a good, which is "positional" or "differential" honor or esteem, that none can truly have. All are caught in a pointless struggle because, whatever the outcome, no one can be truly satisfied: if there are to be winners there must be losers, and the winners can at best enjoy the worthless esteem of "losers." "Master and slave corrupt each other," he quotes Rousseau as saying. The only solution, which Rousseau's theory apparently provides, is a society of equal mutual recognition and esteem. No longer will there be masters and slaves, with the masters as dependent on the good opinion of their slaves as the slaves are on the good opinion of their masters. Instead there will be a society of equal citizens free of any *personal* dependence. All will be equally subordinate to, or dependent on, "the general will." In short, there will be a society in which no one governs anyone else but in which all govern all.[23]

In such a society, Taylor seems to think, every individual purpose would yield to the generally agreed "common project." Valuing their equality of dependence and esteem, individual citizens would forgo their individual desires (power, wealth, etc.) that put them in competition with each other. They would be wholeheartedly devoted to attaining the collective goal.

How exactly would such devotion ensure equality, and to what extent? Taylor's brief remarks about equality are open to conflicting interpretations. Sometimes he says that every citizen in Rousseau's "healthy republic" would enjoy exactly the same esteem as every other citizen. "In republican society . . . all can share equally in the light of public attention." He contrasts such a society of equal sharing with "a system of hierarchical honor" in which "one person's glory must be another's shame, or at least obscurity." Rousseau's great contribution, he says, was to recognize "the importance of equal respect, and, indeed, [to deem] it indispensable for freedom." But Taylor also says that Rousseau requires equal respect only for the *virtuous* citizens of his healthy republic. "The society is one in which all the virtuous will be esteemed equally." "Under the aegis of the general will, all virtuous citizens are to be equally honored."[24] In other words, favorable public attention will go to the virtuous, not the vicious. Praise will be distributed as unequally as virtue and vice. Nothing is said about the crucial difference between these contrasting formulations.

Taylor is also confusing when he says that the tight unity of purpose Rousseau demands is incompatible with any differentiation of roles. In a healthy republic, it seems, all citizens must play the same role. But which role? Will they all be tinkers, tailors, soldiers, or sailors? How can a collectivity pursue a common goal of any kind, except perhaps strict equality, without some division of tasks? Again Taylor's meaning is obscure.

> The key to a free polity for Rousseau seems to be a rigorous exclusion of any differentiation of roles. Rousseau's principle seems to be that for any two-place relation R involving power, the condition of a free society is that the two terms joined by the relation be identical. $x R y$ is compatible with a free society only when $x = y$. This is true when the relation involves the x's presenting themselves in public space to the y's, and it is of course famously true when the relation is "exercising sovereignty over." In the social contract state, the people must be both sovereign and subject.[25]

There seems to be an equivocation here like that between equal esteem and unequal esteem, but harder to pin down. Does Rousseau demand $x = y$ generally or only in "public space"? What is public space? What does the relation between the people as sovereign and the people as subject have to do with the relations, public or private, between individual members of the "public person"?

At any rate, Rousseau apparently goes astray as a political theorist after he contrasts the present depraved, unequal condition of mankind with a healthy condition of "freedom-in-equality." At present all individuals—superiors and inferiors alike—are slaves to the good opinion of others, since they are all "pulled outside themselves" by their craving for honors that only some can have. In a healthy republican society, by contrast, "all can share equally in the light of public attention" because "a perfectly balanced reciprocity takes the sting out of our dependence on opinion, and makes it compatible with liberty." A condition for this healthy "reciprocity" and "equality of esteem" is, unfortunately, a common purpose or project shared by all citizens. Only by letting it take precedence over all their individual projects or purposes can they escape competition with each other. Only in such a society of equal subordination to "the general will," it seems, can citizens be protected from wanting to win the favor of others with goals different from their own, and so from the misfortune of being "pulled out of themselves" and "alienated."[26]

Taylor acknowledges that this "Rousseauean model of citizen dignity" has its attractive side: it is said to inaugurate the modern politics of equal dignity. But he finds it "crucially flawed" because it promises equality of esteem only on condition that all accept "a very tight common purpose." The model links freedom to "a rigorous exclusion of any differentiation of roles." It demands that people be identical, at least in public space, and so can provide no positive sense of difference. Only one type of human being—the type fitted to play the society's one legitimate role—could be recognized in such a "healthy republic." Racism, sexism, homophobia (or heterophobia), ageism, and ableism would presumably run rampant within it. For Taylor, this is unacceptable. He finds Rousseau "guilty of imposing a false homogeneity." Indeed, Rousseau's formula for overcoming dependence on others ("we must all be dependent on the general will") is condemned as having been "the formula for the most terrible forms of homogenizing tyranny, starting with the Jacobins and extending to the totalitarian regimes of our century."[27]

Theory and Practice

A practical test may be the wrong one to apply to Rousseau's reflections on ethnicity and difference. Readers of Rousseau often seem to find themselves wondering whether what he says may be true even if it offers no simple solutions for our pressing practical problems. Taylor seems to me too quick to condemn Rousseau without paying sufficient attention to some of his most interesting observations—for example, about the effects of mixing peoples in great modern cities like Montreal. In fact, such cities seem to be the breeding grounds of the conflicts associated with nationalism, separatism, and difference.

Rousseau was certainly aware of the ethnic diversity of modern cities, and much like some of Quebec's separatists, he connected it with the corruption of nations.[28] He saw that the increasing contact between different peoples was gradually obliterating their differences and thought that it was everywhere requiring the same maxims of hierarchy and accommodation. "There is now a hundred times more contact between Europe and Asia than there formerly was between Gaul and Spain. Europe alone used to be more diverse than the whole world is today. . . . The Europeans are no longer Gauls, Germans, Iberians, and Allobroges. They are nothing but Scythians who have degenerated in various ways in their looks and still more in their morals."[29] In "The Politics of Recognition," Taylor neglects comments like these, and the whole vexed question of Rousseau's "sexism," to focus on his criticism of hierarchical honor and his advocacy of an egalitarian social contract. He praises Rousseau as a psychologist who discovered a human need, *recognition,* but faults him for proposing political institutions that would deny the need he discovered its proper satisfaction. His ideal state, though democratic, would have difficulty recognizing difference.

How might Rousseau react to Taylor's praise and blame? Might he smile at the praise, frown slightly at the blame, but pass on in silence? More likely he would protest vigorously about once again having been misunderstood. As he grew older, Rousseau became more contentious and more suspicious. He resented his contemporaries' failure to appreciate him at what he thought was his true worth. Would he be any more indulgent with twentieth-century philosophes?

He might begin by disputing Taylor's comments about "equality of esteem" and "rigorous exclusion of any differentiation of roles." Rousseau would presumably not disown radical egalitarianism. His political works and other writings provided a profound criticism of the aristocratic society of eighteenth-century France. In his personal life, he maintained an attitude of prickly independence toward his social superiors, even refusing a pension from Louis XV. But in his writings he says nothing to suggest that a healthy republic would be without winners and losers. Indeed, arguing that elective aristocracy is the best form of government ("it is the best and most natural order for the wisest to govern the multitude"), Rousseau says that the elected magistrates would be a small number of "venerable senators" chosen by their fellow citizens because of their "probity, enlightenment, experience, and all the other reasons for public preference and esteem."[30] Taylor himself quotes the passage from the *Government of Poland* in which Rousseau refers approvingly to those

Greek games where successful contestants were "crowned amidst applause from all their fellow-citizens" and that rekindled their "spirit of emulation and love of glory."[31] To illustrate what he means by sharing equally in the light of public attention, Taylor cites Rousseau's encouragement of simple public festivals: "Plant a stake crowned with flowers in the middle of a square; gather the people together there, and you will have a festival." But nothing in this passage suggests a law requiring the more attractive and graceful citizens, dancing around the maypole, to get exactly the same number of admiring glances as the less attractive, clumsier ones.[32]

What about "rigorous exclusion of any differentiation of roles"? Rousseau might press Taylor to explain the complaints among our contemporaries about his "patriarchalism" and "sexism." Can there be so much smoke and no fire? *Emile*, where Rousseau discusses "Sophie, or the Woman," is admittedly not a treatise on the healthy republic, but the points he makes there about the differences between the sexes seem to have a wider bearing. And Rousseau could again point to the chapters on government in the *Social Contract:* if the distinction between magistrates and other citizens is not a differentiation of roles "in public space," what is? A strict interpretation of the "no differentiation" rule would obviously condemn humanity to a primitive simplicity even greater than that enjoyed by noble savages. In the *Social Contract*, was Rousseau recommending such a regression?

Taylor might brush these objections aside as mere quibbles. The main issue, he might insist, is *difference*, which means essentially the accommodation of racial and ethnic minorities. Rousseau may have been right to see vanity everywhere; right to reject the traditional moral authorities; right to elevate the general will above individual claims to various abstract "rights"; and right to see democratic participation as a way to build consensus; but he was wrong to see freedom in society as simply the collective exercise of sovereignty, with all this implies about the homogeneity of a healthy republic. In fact, as Rousseau should have seen more clearly, pluralism, or a complex society that sustains many ways of life, is a condition for meaningful human freedom. Rousseau's insistence on uniformity is unhelpful: it provokes demands for equal recognition while blocking any satisfaction of those demands. It just aggravates our present problems.

This imaginary rebuttal applies a practical test to Rousseau's theory, which he might well dispute. He was in the habit of contrasting the demands of society with the needs of those few cosmopolitan souls like himself who were devoted to truth and who tried to penetrate to the heart of things. He might point out that practical remedies of the sort Taylor recommends often suffer from detached contemplation, working better the less closely they are examined. Practice creates problems for theory, and theory for practice. In neither his political nor his educational writings was Rousseau especially practical. Perhaps he was right to suggest, as he sometimes does, that a reasonable individual, adequately informed, would choose to detach himself as much as possible from the main currents of modern life.[33] The increasing scale of contemporary political life may be even more of a problem than Taylor suspects. The very complaints about alienation, inauthenticity, and lack of identity that define the politics of difference may flow directly from it.

Man and Citizen

"One can say that there are two roads from the state of nature and that they do not meet, the one leading to civil society, the other to the condition of men like Rousseau," whose great theme, one could say, is man's natural goodness and his corruption in society.[34] Very briefly, Rousseau thought that false sociability was the bane of society, and especially of modern "bourgeois" society, where all is politeness and deceit. Men are educated to be neither simply men nor truly citizens, but somehow both at once, which is impossible. Their amour propre causes them to become strangers to themselves, each fashioning a character designed to please or impress others. Always striving for preeminence, they lack integrity; they deceive themselves even as they try to deceive others. They learn to live outside themselves, depending on others for their sense of themselves. The highest possibilities of social life—friendship, virtue, honor, and wisdom—are corrupted and perverted by their envy and distrust. Admittedly, no one need suffer terribly under this regime, but no one can be truly happy, and all have a vague sense of emptiness, futility, weakness, and inner conflict. All are servile; none are truly free.

Rousseau finds the root of the problem in a faulty education, one fit only for making "double men," devoted in appearance to serving others, but always relating everything to themselves alone. They are selfish, but they crave the approval of others, so they are indecisive, confused, and wavering, unable to speak and act in a lofty, noble way. "He who in the civil order wants to preserve the primacy of the sentiments of nature does not know what he wants. Always in contradiction with himself, always floating between his inclinations and his duties, he will never be either man or citizen. He will be good neither for himself nor for others. He will be one of these men of our days: a Frenchman, an Englishman, a bourgeois. He will be nothing."[35] Rousseau's remedies for this divided condition consist essentially in forcing a choice between the demands of nature and those of citizenship. Education must make either men or citizens.

"The social contract" represents one possible remedy for the ills of personal dependence and the pathological amour propre associated with it. These ills can be overcome—to the extent that they can be overcome at all within society—only by reducing and rationalizing the inequalities among citizens. In the healthy republic Rousseau outlines, all citizens would have equal standing as members of the sovereign people, and this people would be bound together not just by the laws they freely adopt and thus feel obliged to respect, but by some prior union of "origin, interest, or convention."[36] The false sociability and degenerate morality of bourgeois society can be overcome, it seems, only in a state based on some kind of "national feeling" or "ethnicity."

Rousseau's theory has some affinity to *nationalism*, meaning by that term the theory that the boundaries of the state should correspond to those of a "prepolitical" or "sociological" entity, the nation, defined by a common language or way of life. But the earlier chapters by Marc Plattner and Pierre Hassner have shown how difficult it is to reduce Rousseau's thought on these matters to any simple formula. In particular, both emphasize the differences between the small republics Rousseau admired and the large modern states associated with nationalism. Here it must suffice to point out that Rousseau, when he spells out the conditions for legislation, implies that not every aggregate of individuals can be formed into a well-governed state. He recognizes that laws influence manners and morals, but he also insists that laws be adapted to them, so that the people are naturally inclined to love their country and to feel bound to their fellow citizens by ties of sentiment and affection. The same laws will not suit different peoples with different *moeurs*, he notes, and different laws in different parts of a country just create confusion. Citizens ought to know one another and their leaders, and they must be able to move about freely and to intermarry without losing track of what is truly theirs. They must see themselves as naturally belonging together and sharing a common fate. They must be set apart from the rest of the world by more than just a line on a map, and they must be able to see their fellow citizens as beings like themselves, not just as strangers. A condition for patriotism (*amour de la patrie*) is that the homeland be something more for its citizens than it is for foreigners, that it accord them some things that it refuses others.[37]

Rousseau, despite his travels and his reading, was clearly no cosmopolitan in the ordinary meaning of that term. He was inclined to point out, as he does in the *Discourse on Political Economy*, that "the sentiment of humanity evaporates and weakens as it is extended over the whole world, and that we can't be moved by calamities in Tartary or Japan as we are by those of a European people."[38] Interest in others must be somehow confined and compressed before it will be active. It can gain real force, he seems to think, only when it is concentrated on fellow citizens we identify with because of common interests and habits of association. He looks with a certain equanimity on the narrowness or blindness, and even the enmities and injustices, that are commonly associated with intense patriotism. He seems to rank Cato above Socrates, for example.[39] In the *Social Contract* he even dares to object to Christianity that its ideal of universal brotherhood, and the detachment from worldly things it cultivates, are entirely contrary to *l'esprit social*.[40] Defending himself later, he points out that it is the vices of mankind that make political institutions necessary and their passions that make them work, and he echoes the passage at the beginning of *Emile* where he says that "every patriot is harsh to foreigners" and that "the essential thing is to be good to the people with whom one lives."[41]

The homogeneity Rousseau recommended, not just of class but of ethnic background, would mitigate the bad effects of the personal interdependencies that would remain in his healthy republic. Citizens would need to cooperate with each other, but in the situation he envisions, they would know each other and would share more or less the same "second nature." They would all be inclined to see each other as members of a single team, more concerned with their common successes and failures against external rivals than with their internal relations of superiority and inferiority toward each other, and so they would be less sensitive to affronts. The laws would be strong and men generally law-abiding, so their behavior would be predictable. This is the crucial condition: only when men's behavior is predictable can one depend on *it* without depending on *them*. Only then is one freed from the need to flatter others in order to secure their services, for they simply do what the laws (in the context of the *moeurs*) require.

In a large state, made up of diverse peoples, with a government dedicated to the celebration and cultivation of difference, by contrast, this kind of reliability suffers. The need for cooperation is broadened to include strangers whose customs and values are unknown and whose reactions to one's own opinions and behavior are even less predictable than the reactions of one's ethnic compatriots. The laws are relaxed. Habits and tastes previously repressed emerge from hiding. Sensitivities increase as people are encouraged to demand respect for their distinct cultures, identities, and lifestyles. If such recognition is deliberately or even unintentionally withheld, they have a legitimate grievance. They may refuse their cooperation or even retaliate against the offender. The "general will" becomes ever more elusive. It threatens to become a broad new injunction that is impossible to fulfill: "Be true to yourself and give all others what they think they deserve." The result, Rousseau might have predicted, will be an ever more inflamed amour propre, endless edgy negotiation of "identities," and a growing sense of universal falseness and alienation from public life.

A deepening of this alienation is in a sense Rousseau's second, individualistic remedy for mankind's divided condition. In his autobiographical writings as well as in his Savoyard vicar's profession of faith, Rousseau tries to show a way back to natural goodness from civilized corruption. The individual adopting this remedy—it makes no sense to think of a whole society doing so (except perhaps at church)—must withdraw from society, turning away from the endless quest for recognition from others. He must cultivate solitude and introspection, finding the sense of his own existence within himself. He must detach himself from the goods that make him dependent on the opinion of others and must learn to live apart, a solitary dreamer, unconcerned with the reactions of others to his awkward unsociability.

Rousseau might be tempted to illustrate his ideas by pointing to Taylor himself, who puts his finger on a real problem when he says, in effect, that academics and others are now being forced to give the outward signs of a respect many of them do not feel, and the result is restiveness, resentfulness, and rebellion. The restiveness of those claiming oppression needs no elaboration: they want to be respected for who they are. But what about their alleged oppressors? Can they too demand respect for who they really are? Some of them think, for example, that academics have a right ("academic freedom") to ignore the demands emanating from "state" and "society" that they show respect for cultures and ways of life they are naturally disposed (by their education and experience) to patronize or to greet with indifference, annoyance, or contempt. No, Taylor says: university professors are obliged to teach and act on the assumption that all relevant cultures are equal.

Rousseau could point out here that the procrastination and make-believe Taylor recommends are not integrity. Can one say in a lofty style, with a firm sense of inner conviction and courage in standing up for what one truly believes, "Let's pretend for a while that all cultures are equal and leave for another day the discussion of whether it's true"? If the marginal have a right to express their needs and feelings without inhibition, why should famous writers and scholars have to adopt such transparent evasions?

Taylor seems to have a tin ear for what Rousseau was saying about honor and authenticity. For Rousseau, society and authenticity are necessarily at odds, since society engages our vanity (amour propre) to get us to deny our primary concern with our own well-being (our self-interest or *amour de soi*). Authenticity means recovering a proper sense of ourselves out of the false sociability of our socialization. In Taylor's discussion of "the ethics of authenticity," by contrast, there is no hint that the desire for recognition might be at the root of *inauthenticity*. Taylor wishes to refute the idea, which he associates with Allan Bloom, that the striving for authenticity is ethically (or morally) questionable. He does so (so to speak) with a definition. What is authenticity for Taylor? It is choosing a "meaningful" life or identity from the many offered by one's tradition or horizon of meanings, that is to say, one's compatriots.[42]

Taylor's authentic individual with a secure positive identity is really one of Rousseau's "double men." He listens to the voice of nature within himself but wants the approval of others. Not for him an old-fashioned life of self-denial and self-deception, rooted in the need to conform to others or the wish to shine in their eyes. He knows, as Taylor puts it, that "our moral salvation comes from recovering authentic moral contact with ourselves."[43] But he also knows, thanks to George Herbert Mead and Frantz Fanon, that he should not underestimate "the place of the dialogical in human life." A positive identity cannot be defined apart from others, since "in the nature of the case, there is no such thing as inward generation, monologically understood."[44] Try as we may to detach ourselves from others and their judgments of us, we cannot escape the dialogical character of human life. Our identities are always socially derived and sustained. "We define our identity always in dialogue with, sometimes in struggle against, the things our significant others want to see in us." So the authentic individual has to negotiate with others, and paradoxically, according to Taylor, Rousseau's development of an ideal of inwardly generated identity gives a new importance to outward recognition. As Taylor sums it up, "my own identity crucially depends on my dialogical relations with others."[45] They hear me, therefore I am.

Conclusion

Taylor's strongest argument for "difference" and against Rousseau is one he never states clearly. We are committed to conducting politics on a "national" and "international" scale because that is how we think we can best achieve world peace and domestic tranquillity.[46] Accommodation between different cultures is necessary, it is said, because the alternative is war. In the "global village," we must move toward some form of international organization—a world government of some sort—in which a common citizenship and universal human rights independent of race, creed, or national origin will be recognized everywhere. And the struggle for this new world order must begin at home. Only by overcoming boundaries, sovereignty, and nationalism or ethnocentrism in our own lives can we merit immunity from the horrors of technological war and terrorism. To this end, all must perhaps profess certain merely conventional judgments of equality, and all may have to learn to live in an atmosphere of cynicism, inauthenticity, and alienation; but if so, it's a small price to pay for peace and prosperity.

Rousseau differs most clearly from liberals like Taylor, as well as from more "postmodern" partisans of difference, by rejecting internal ethnic diversity. Like them, Rousseau treats ethnicity as something valuable, not something to be ignored or suppressed when establishing political institutions. (In his imaginary world of small republics, each would be homogeneous, but the world as a whole would be diverse: close by there would always be other small republics, with different laws and institutions.) For Rousseau, however, any attempt to go from smaller to larger political units—to get beyond "tribalism" or "ethnicity" to "nationality" or "humanity"—is fraught with difficulties. Legitimate government, whether democratic, aristocratic, or monarchic in form, must rest on a "social contract" or "general will," and there is no such thing when peoples are bitterly and intolerantly opposed to each other because of differences in the laws (or "histories" or "revelations") under which they live. Indeed, they may have little patience for any would-be legislator who tries to convince them that their antipathies create serious practical problems and that all would be better off if they could just agree to disagree, treating Moses and Mohammed, say, as enriching sources of identity for a multicultural society. Heaven should perhaps favor such peoples with a new revelation that would get them out of their difficulties, but in the meantime they must live with their old ones, which leave them in a state of nature vis-à-vis each other. Superstition precedes tolerance in Rousseau's ordering of things, and the obligation to be tolerant is a consequence, not a condition, of a social compact.

The fundamental question, then, from the standpoint Rousseau provides, is whether the differences we now think of as "ethnic" should be within or between states. Rousseau's answer cannot be reduced to any simple rule like the "principle of nationalities." But he denied, in effect, that there can be large, well-governed states established to protect and promote every sort of ethnic diversity in the name of individual and group rights. He accepted a certain "ethnocentrism" as the unavoidable basis of good politics. He treated ethnic differences as a means by which wise legislators and good governments elevate amour propre into *amour de la patrie*. Vast modern states with their huge "multicultural" populations clamouring for recognition he would surely regard with a skeptical eye. Their festivals of diversity he would probably see as failures of the legislator's art. Contemporary aspirations to "universality" he might connect with earlier ones, which he deplored. He evidently saw no prospect of eliminating or enclosing all ethnic differences without destroying patriotism, and no way of encouraging ethnic differences without dividing a state against itself and its citizens more deeply against themselves.

Rousseau's political psychology is currently unwelcome, and perhaps it was always irrelevant, practically speaking. When Rousseau set his face against the Enlightenment, he was putting himself in opposition to the whole course of modern European history, and indeed that of the world. However well grounded his political principles might be "in theory," they could have little relation to practice and are almost sure to be misunderstood when they are thought to have such a relation. But to complain that by clarifying some of our problems Rousseau aggravates them is like blaming the little boy for the uproar that followed his famous comment about the emperor's fine new clothes. As Rousseau himself said, we should not flatter ourselves that we can avoid the natural consequences of the greatness we seek, and "the abuses of large States must not be raised as an objection to someone who wants only small ones."[47]

NOTES

1. Many now say that conventional ideas of equality, even liberal or progressive ideas, ignore or deny "difference." The partisans of difference struggle to work out the theory and practice of a new, "postmodern" politics that will sever concepts like justice, freedom, fairness, and authority from any controversial notions of the good. They speak for a broad coalition of racial and ethnic groups, feminists, gays, lesbians, and others who complain of their oppression under conventional definitions of beauty, health, intelligence, and morality. Mere skepticism or moral relativism offers them no lasting relief. Nor can they be content with a simple substitution of, say, gay definitions for straight ones: some might benefit, but the coalition would suffer. The partisans of difference wish to uphold a demanding political morality without devaluing or excluding any particular culture or way of life. For a useful survey of themes and proposals, see Iris Marion Young, *Justice and the Politics of Difference* (Princeton: Princeton University Press, 1990).

2. Taylor's most important discussion is his essay "The Politics of Recognition," in Charles Taylor et al., *Multiculturalism and "The Politics of Recognition,"* ed. Amy Gutmann (Princeton: Princeton University Press, 1992), 25–73, which is reprinted in Taylor's *Philosophical Arguments* (Cambridge: Harvard University Press, 1995), 225–56. The essay draws on Taylor's analysis of the problem of relativism and authenticity in *The Malaise of Modernity* (Toronto: Anansi, 1991), published in the United States as *The Ethic of Authenticity* (Cambridge: Harvard University Press, 1991), which draws in turn upon Taylor's *Sources of the Self: The Making of the Modern Identity* (Cambridge: Harvard University Press, 1989). This large "essay in retrieval" is designed to show that the moral imperatives of modern culture have deep, strong sources. All these publications argue that accepting "authenticity" as a moral ideal need not mean encouraging "individualism" or the neglect of civic duties. Taylor accuses Allan Bloom, in particular, of disparaging "the moral ideal of authenticity" by confounding it with "a non-moral desire to do what one wants without interference." Taylor, *Malaise of Modernity*, 15, 21.

3. For example, Allan Bloom, *The Closing of the American Mind* (New York: Simon and Schuster, 1987), 238: "That gray net of abstractions, used to cover the world in order to simplify and explain it in a way that is pleasing to us, has become the world in our eyes. The only way to see the phenomena, rather than sterile distillations of them, to experience them in their ambiguity again, would be to have available alternate visions, a diversity of profound opinions." See also Allan Bloom, *Giants and Dwarfs* (New York: Simon and Schuster, 1990), 238.

4. The Accord failed because two provinces, Manitoba and Newfoundland, refused to adopt the required amendments. Their refusal was supported by a large body of opinion in English-speaking Canada. The main practical question in the background had to do with the language laws Quebec had adopted in the 1970s. "One regulates who can send their children to English-language schools (not francophones or immigrants); another requires that businesses with more than fifty employees be run in

French; a third outlaws commercial signage in any language other than French." Taylor, *Multiculturalism*, 52–53. For more details, see Peter H. Russell, *Constitutional Odyssey: Can Canadians Become a Sovereign People?* 2d ed. (Toronto: University of Toronto Press, 1993).

5. For example, *With a Bang, Not a Whimper: Pierre Trudeau Speaks Out*, ed. Donald Johnston (Toronto: Stoddart, 1988), 34: "The crucial importance of the Charter meant that we all share a set of common values and that all Canadians are thence on an equal footing; whether they be Quebecers, Albertans, French, English, Jewish, Hindu, they all have the same rights. No one is special. All Canadians are equal, and that equality flows from the Charter."

6. Taylor, *Multiculturalism*, 57.

7. Ibid., 59. The "and so on" presumably refers to property.

8. Ibid., 61.

9. Other practical controversies associated with multiculturalism in the United States, as in Canada, have to do with affirmative action, censorship, and free speech. See Dinesh D'Souza, *Illiberal Education: The Politics of Race and Sex on Campus* (New York: Free Press, 1991), and Richard Bernstein, *Dictatorship of Virtue: Multiculturalism and the Battle for America's Future* (New York: Knopf, 1994).

10. Taylor, *Multiculturalism*, 26, 65–66, 68. How much value? In *Malaise of Modernity*, 47–52, Taylor explains why it must be *equal* value.

11. "If the judgment of value is to register something independent of our own wills and desires, it cannot be dictated by a principle of ethics. On examination, either we will find something of great value in culture C, or we will not. But it makes no more sense to demand that we do so than it does to demand that we find the earth round or flat, the temperature of the air hot or cold" (Taylor, *Multiculturalism*, 69–70). A similar problem arises with respect to individual I: it makes no more sense, strictly speaking, to demand that we find something of great moral or intellectual value in a particular individual than it does to demand that we find him or her tall or short. A theory like the one Taylor proposes elsewhere, which distinguishes persons from other living things based on differences in their capacity to reflect on the principles underlying their actions, implies a scale of "personality" according to which some human beings are "tall" and others "short." See Charles Taylor, "The Concept of a Person," *Philosophical Papers* 1 (1985): 97–114.

12. Taylor, *Multiculturalism*, 69.

13. Ibid., 42.

14. Taylor, *Multiculturalism*, 72. This codicil takes care of aberrant phases of the history of great nations, like the Soviet communist phase of Russian history. It raises the question, however, of the relation between time and numbers in qualifying for a presumption of equality. Taylor is silent, for example, about how the shorter but more numerous following for Soviet communist culture compares with the longer but less extensive influence of, say, Haitian voodoo culture.

15. Ibid., 73.

16. Cf. ibid., 26–28, and Taylor, *Sources of the Self*, 111–98. Taylor downplays the

detailed examination of individual thinkers such as Rousseau in favor of a broader examination of the complex, constantly changing network of ideas, intuitions, "accents," and assumptions characteristic of an age.

17. Taylor, *Multiculturalism*, 25.

18. Ibid., 28–29.

19. Ibid., 30.

20. Taylor associates this "powerful moral ideal" of authenticity with the writings of Herder, who applied it not just to individuals but to peoples, with their unique cultures. "Just like individuals, a *Volk* should be true to itself, that is, its own culture. Germans shouldn't try to be derivative and (inevitably) second-rate Frenchmen, as Frederick the Great's patronage seemed to be encouraging them to do. The Slavic peoples had to find their own path. And European colonialism ought to be rolled back to give the peoples of what we now call the Third World their chance to be themselves unimpeded. We can recognize here the seminal idea of modern nationalism, in both benign and malignant forms." Ibid., 30–31.

21. Ibid., 32, 34.

22. Jean-Jacques Rousseau, *On the Social Contract*, bk. 1, chap. 7, in *On the Social Contract, with Geneva Manuscript and Political Economy*, ed. Roger D. Masters, trans. Judith R. Masters (New York: St. Martin's Press, 1978), 54–55.

23. Taylor, *Multiculturalism*, 45–46, 48–51. The quotation is from Jean-Jacques Rousseau, *Emile, or On Education*, trans. Allan Bloom (New York: Basic Books, 1979), 85: "Dependence on things, since it has no morality, is in no way detrimental to freedom and engenders no vices. Dependence on men, since it is without order, engenders all the vices, and by it master and slave are mutually corrupted. If there is any means of remedying this ill in society, it is to substitute law for man and to arm the general wills with a real strength superior to the action of every particular will."

24. Taylor, *Multiculturalism*, 35, 45, 48, 49.

25. Ibid., 50–51.

26. Ibid., 35, 48–49.

27. Ibid., 44, 51; Young, *Justice and the Politics of Difference*, 42–45, 47, 108–11, 229–30, provides a more "postmodern" statement of this objection. Rousseau is said to lack a proper understanding of social groups defined by a shared sense of identity in opposition to other groups. "Groups" are neither "aggregates" (mere collections of people sharing common attributes) nor "associations" (constituted by individuals for particular purposes). Rousseau is in the grip of "Cartesian" assumptions about the priority of selfhood to language and social relations; so his social contract theory is "methodologically individualist" or "atomist," and consequently it provides no basis for needed "institutions that promote reproduction of and respect for group differences without oppression." In fact, it expresses an "urge to unity" that "denies, devalues, or represses the ontological difference of subjects, and seeks to dissolve social inexhaustibility into the comfort of a self-enclosed whole."

28. *Emile*, 468–69.

29. Ibid., 453, 468.

30. *Social Contract*, bk. 3, chap. 5, ed. Masters, 86.

31. Jean-Jacques Rousseau, *Considérations sur le gouvernement de Pologne*, in *Oeuvres complètes*, 5 vols., ed. Bernard Gagnebin and Marcel Raymond (Paris: Bibliothèque de la Pléiade, 1959–95), 3:958. Cf. Taylor, *Multiculturalism*, 46.

32. See Jean-Jacques Rousseau, *Letter to M. d'Alembert on the Theatre*, in *Politics and the Arts*, trans. Allan Bloom (Ithaca, N.Y.: Cornell University Press, 1960), 126, which continues: "I need not have recourse to the games of the ancient Greeks; there are modern ones which are still in existence, and I find them precisely in [Geneva]. Every year we have reviews, public prizes, kings of the harquebus, the cannon, and sailing. Institutions so useful and so agreeable cannot be too much multiplied; of such kings there cannot be too many."

33. This seems to be the result of Emile's two years roaming the great states of Europe and learning the science of political right. It seems to cure him of political hopes and to teach him to look for happiness in the abode where he has lived.

34. Allan Bloom, "Jean-Jacques Rousseau," in *History of Political Philosophy*, 3d ed., ed. Leo Strauss and Joseph Cropsey (Chicago: University of Chicago Press, 1987), 578, and Arthur M. Melzer, *The Natural Goodness of Man: On the System of Rousseau's Thought* (Chicago: University of Chicago Press, 1990).

35. *Emile*, 40.

36. *Social Contract*, bk. 2, chaps. 9, 10, ed. Masters, 74. Similarities of this sort are not a sufficient condition for good legislation, however, and an excess of them may create as many problems as a deficiency. The people must not be refractory, Rousseau says. Neither customs nor superstitions must have struck such deep roots as to make them recoil from the legislator's care, which is above all concerned with the gradual rectification of manners, morals, customs, and opinions (*Social Contract*, bk. 2, chaps. 8, 12).

37. Jean-Jacques Rousseau, *Discourse on Political Economy*, in *On the Social Contract, with Geneva Manuscript and Political Economy*, ed. Roger D. Masters, trans. Judith R. Masters (New York: St. Martin's Press, 1978), 222.

38. Ibid., 219. He was perhaps even more inclined to censure those who made cosmopolitanism an excuse for avoiding the obligations of patriotism. "Distrust those cosmopolitans who go to great length in their books to discover duties they do not deign to fulfill around them. A philosopher loves the Tartars so as to be spared having to love his neighbors" (*Emile*, 39).

39. *Political Economy*, 219; also *Letter to d'Alembert*, 29.

40. *Social Contract*, bk. 4, chap. 8, ed. Masters, 128.

41. *Emile*, 39. Cf. Jean-Jacques Rousseau, *Correspondance complète de J. J. Rousseau*, ed. R. A. Leigh (Geneva: Institut et Musée Voltaire, 1964–), 17:63 and 16:127: "The spirit of patriotism is an exclusive spirit that makes us look upon all except our fellow citizens as strangers and almost as enemies."

42. "The agent seeking significance in life, trying to define him- or herself meaningfully, has to exist in a horizon of important questions. That is what is self-defeating in modes of contemporary culture that concentrate on self-fulfillment *in opposition* to the demands of society, or nature, which *shut out* history and the bonds of solidarity. . . . To

shut out demands emanating from beyond the self is precisely to suppress the conditions of significance, and hence to court trivialization. . . . Authenticity is not the enemy of demands that emanate from beyond the self; it supposes such demands." In short, the self can serve others in many meaningful ways—as a doctor, a lawyer, etc.—but not, it seems, as a solitary dreamer. "I couldn't just *decide* that the most significant action is wiggling my toes in warm mud" (Taylor, *Malaise of Modernity*, 36, 40–41). All this may be true, but it clashes with the idea that our moral salvation involves resisting the demands of external conformity, and it points in the direction Allan Bloom indicated, of trying to judge the demands of others by a standard beyond them.

43. Taylor, *Multiculturalism*, 29.

44. Ibid., 32.

45. Ibid., 34.

46. "There are other cultures, and we have to live together more and more, both on a world scale and commingled in each individual society," since "all societies are becoming increasingly multicultural, while at the same time becoming more porous. . . . Their porousness means that they are more open to multinational migration." Ibid., 63 and 72. Apart from these few vague comments about how the world is changing, Taylor never explains the good beyond accommodation that accommodation serves and that naturally determines its limits.

47. *Social Contract*, bk. 3, chap. 13, ed. Masters, 100.

❦ IV ❧
Our Virtues: Community, Sincerity, Compassion

❧ 12 ❧
Privacy and Community

Steven Kautz

Here is a notable peculiarity of our moral experience: we love our privacy, yet we long for community. What is more, our two loves—our love of privacy (or the idea of privacy) and our love of community (or the idea of community)—are strangely marked by a sort of fanaticism, born of (illiberal) despair in face of the "inconsolable coldness of modernity."[1] We have been driven by some mysterious force to embrace ever more unbounded modes of *idiosyncratic privacy*, on one hand, and *constitutive community*, on the other hand; we have thereby abandoned a more sober (liberal) view of the reasonable bounds of privacy and community, and so of the possible harmony between them.

I propose to consider here this aspect of contemporary moral life, primarily by means of a discussion of a recent book by a formidable contemporary Rousseauian, Richard Rorty. Rorty's *Contingency, Irony, and Solidarity* (1989) is valuable for this reason above all: it provides an uncommonly precise and comprehensive account of prevailing moral opinions (or at least prevailing elite moral opinions) in "postmodern bourgeois" society. Rorty thus shows how apparently contradictory aspects of our moral experience can be traced to a fundamental common root: the postmodern flight from reason and embrace of "contingency." What seems messy is really tidy once one grasps this common root. In particular, the apparently disparate impulses toward idiosyncratic privacy and constitutive community can both be traced to the moral experience of contingency: to the anxious recognition that "socialization, and thus historical circumstance, goes all the way down" and that there is no way to "refer back to something beyond the reach of time and chance" as a ground, beyond contingency, of our own "most central beliefs and desires."[2]

But first I will say a few words about Rousseau, for this peculiarly postmodern sort of spiritual dissonance is a distant (and perhaps somewhat corrupt) legacy of Rousseau.

249

I

As Allan Bloom has demonstrated, the foundation of Rousseau's moral and political thinking is his devastating assault on the soul of the bourgeois, "that debased form of the species."

> This phenomenon, the *bourgeois*, is the true beginning point of Rousseau's survey of the human condition in modernity and his diagnosis of what ails us. The *bourgeois* stands somewhere between two respectable extremes, the good natural man and the moral citizen. The former lives alone, concerned with himself, his preservation, and his contentment, unconcerned with others, hence wishing them no harm. The latter lives wholly for his country, concerned solely with the common good, existing only as a part of it, loving his country and hating its enemies. Each of these two types, in his own way, is whole—free of the wasting conflict between inclination and duty that reduces the *bourgeois* and renders him weak and unreliable. He is the individualist in society, who needs society and its protective laws but only as means to his private ends. . . . The *bourgeois* is a hypocrite, hiding his true purposes under a guise of public-spiritedness. . . . The *bourgeois*'s morality is mercenary, requiring a payoff for every social deed. He is incapable of either natural sincerity or political nobility.

Or, as Bloom was fond of saying, "to describe the inner workings of his soul, he is the man who, when dealing with others, thinks only of himself, and on the other hand, in his understanding of himself, thinks only of others."[3] In Rousseau's famous formulation: "He who in the civil order wants to preserve the primacy of the sentiments of nature does not know what he wants. Always in contradiction with himself, always floating between his inclinations and his duties, he will never be either man or citizen. He will be good neither for himself nor for others. He will be one of these men of our days: a Frenchman, an Englishman, a bourgeois. He will be nothing."[4] Here, then, is Rousseau's diagnosis of our civilized ills: the souls of human beings in the modern liberal world are divided, between a *privacy* that is no longer quite natural and a *community* that is not yet quite moral; the civilized human being is too dependent to be wholehearted in (natural, selfish) pursuit of private goods, yet too egoistic to be wholehearted in (moral, selfless) devotion to the community. As Arthur Melzer says, "his soul is divided by a *selfish selflessness*."[5]

And so it is that there are (at least) two Rousseaus: the sentimental, aesthetic, romantic individualist of the *Reveries* and (sometimes) *Emile* and other "private" works; and the virtuous, patriotic, democratic collectivist of the *Social Contract* and other "political" works (the "Citizen of Geneva"). As Melzer stresses, Rousseau undertakes to "cure" humanity by teaching modern would-be solitaries and citizens how "to embrace totally either side of the contradiction: complete selfishness or complete sociability." This dual aspect of Rousseau's thought helps to explain certain apparent "antitheses" in his writings: "the praise of solitude and also the praise of community; of idleness and laziness and also of activity and vigor; of sincerity, naturalness, and spontaneity and also of self-conquest and social control; of sensitivity, gentleness, sentimentality, and compassion and also of manliness, courage, hardness, and patriotism"; and so on. If the problem of the bourgeois (liberal) soul is its lack of unity, then the solution is to radicalize our love of privacy or our love of community, and thereby to recover, as far as is possible in the civilized world, the wholeheartedness (if nothing else) of the natural man. And so Rousseau offers a gallery of portraits of human beings who achieve a kind of sentimental wholeheartedness that is akin to natural goodness, and one or two portraits of the less natural or more moral wholeheartedness of the patriotic citizen. Thus "Rousseau's constructive thought necessarily bifurcates into two conflicting ideals: extreme individualism and extreme collectivism."[6] Here is one of the roots of our tendency to embrace (at least in speech) remarkably unbounded modes of privacy and community; this is among the most fundamental of the legacies of Rousseau.

In his *Reveries*, Rousseau speaks of his "intense desire for solitude," his late rediscovery "that the source of true happiness is within us." He describes certain "moments of rapture" during "solitary walks" and "reveries": "These hours of solitude and meditation are the only ones in the day during which I am fully myself and for myself, without diversion, without obstacle, and during which I can truly claim to be what nature willed." So, for example:

> I would slip away and go throw myself alone into a boat that I rowed to the middle of the lake when the water was calm; and there, stretching myself out full-length in the boat, my eyes turned to heaven, I let myself slowly drift back and forth with the water, sometimes for several hours, plunged in a thousand confused, but delightful, reveries which, even without having any well-determined or constant object, were in my opinion a hundred times preferable

to the sweetest things I had found in what are called the pleasures of life.

If true happiness is possible for a human being, it consists in recovering "the sentiment of existence" ("in itself a precious sentiment of contentment and of peace") during such utterly private moments of self-absorbed and idiosyncratic rapture: "During these wanderings, my soul rambles and glides through the universe on the wings of imagination, in ecstasies which surpass every other enjoyment," including the enjoyments of thought or reflection, "a painful and charmless occupation for me."[7] Indeed, Melzer argues that Rousseau's account of the sentiment of existence is founded on a new theory of self-love: "Rousseau's theory of self-love leads to a radical new kind of individualism, not merely political but, as it were, ontological"; the human being "has no essential connection to anything outside him, whether social or metaphysical"; "our being *is* our presence to ourselves, our sentiment of existence."[8] In his contribution to this volume, Melzer further portrays the "new Rousseauian self": emphatically private; sentimental rather than rational; spontaneous rather than moral ("I must 'be myself' regardless of *what* I may be"); "particular, unique, and idiosyncratic" rather than "my share of universal human nature."[9] Here is the Rousseau who is the teacher of poets and lovers and solitary walkers: the apostle of a new and more authentic privacy or individuality, a new way of being alone that does not admit the vices of the bourgeois soul.[10]

And yet there is that other Rousseau, the "Citizen of Geneva" whose praise of patriotic virtue is unbounded and uncompromising. In the passage from *Emile* that immediately precedes the denunciation of the bourgeois soul quoted above, Rousseau offers this splendid, awful praise of republican citizenship:

> The Lacedaemonian Pedaretus runs for the council of three hundred. He is defeated. He goes home delighted that there were three hundred men worthier than he to be found in Sparta. . . . This is the citizen.
>
> A Spartan woman had five sons in the army and was awaiting news of the battle. A Helot arrives; trembling, she asks him for news. "Your five sons were killed." "Base slave, did I ask you that?" "We won the victory." The mother runs to the temple and gives thanks to the gods. This is the female citizen.

So virtue is patriotism: the citizen's wholehearted love of his community, of the republic, "exclusive of himself."[11] If this is unnatural, as surely it is, then "one who dares to undertake the founding of a people should feel that he is capable of changing human nature, so to speak; of transforming each individual, who by himself is a perfect and solitary whole, into a part of a larger whole from which this individual receives, in a sense, his life and his being." Such virtue is utterly incompatible with privacy or individuality: in the best case, "each citizen is nothing, and can do nothing, except with all the others"; the human being must somehow be transformed from a natural integer into a civil fraction.[12] As Montesquieu too shows, the patriotic virtue of a citizen, whose devotion to the community is unmixed with the private motives and dependencies that corrupt the bourgeois soul, requires "a continuous preference of the public interest over one's own"; indeed, such love of the (republican) community "is a renunciation of oneself, which is always a very painful thing."[13] Here is the Rousseau who is teacher of the republican zealots of the French Revolution, and perhaps also of their tamer descendants among today's communitarians: a "democratic absolutist," as Melzer says, who embraces an illiberal politics that aims in various ways (making use of what Montesquieu calls "the full power of education") to build "a spontaneous, all-encompassing communal feeling" that is surely more than rational and contrary to nature.[14]

And so Rousseau despises liberal society and its bourgeois politics of "self-interest rightly understood." Liberal societies rest on a politics of fearful accommodation among naturally lawless enemies who have somehow learned that it is reasonable to seek peace together in order to pursue happiness alone: the liberal social contract is a sort of peace treaty; and the liberal citizen is a prudent solitary. In certain promising liberal communities, the pursuit of happiness has taken a commercial form: the pursuit of happiness is mostly the pursuit of private property. And commerce, which makes possible a certain comfortable security, is itself among the firmest guarantors of civil peace. Finally, in advanced liberal communities ("great") politics has withered away, so to speak, as it has been supplanted by institutions of "indirect government" (including representation, among others) that moderate or tame the warlike passions of partisans and sectarians.[15] As is well known, Rousseau repudiates all of this. For Rousseau it is not reasonable fear but pity that is the true origin of the virtues: "For all their morality, men would never have been anything but monsters if Nature had not given them pity in support of reason." The attempt to turn private vices into public virtues must fail: what is real about the liberal project is the private vices, no more. Commerce softens the morals and tastes of human beings, and so perhaps it renders them peaceful, but this is a peace suitable only for intemperate slaves: "With money one has everything except morals and Citizens." And liberal political institutions, which turn citizens into private persons who are more or less indifferent to public life, purchase moderation at the price of freedom: "As soon as public service ceases to be the main business of citizens, and they prefer to serve with their pocketbooks rather than with their persons, the State is already close to its ruin."[16] There is no place for "political nobility" in the liberal polity.

So too, Rousseau despises the liberal at home or in society. As Bloom remarks, "Rousseau's *bourgeois* is identical to Locke's rational and industrious man, the new kind of man whose concern with property was to provide a soberer and solider foundation to society." But Rousseau is not impressed by this liberal imagination of a "rugged individualist" who seeks neither to enslave others nor merely to gratify them and who is prepared to live and let live in a peaceful community where rights and privacy are respected. He sees, rather, hypocritical slaves who have "reduced the Art of pleasing to principles," cowardly conformists ("constantly one follows custom, never one's own genius") whose petty vices are tamed only by their fear of incurring the disapprobation of "the herd that is called society." The bourgeois is not free, says Rousseau, because he is not able to stand alone. In many ways, but above all in his pursuit of comfortable security through the acquisition of property, the bourgeois is utterly dependent on others, obliged therefore to please and to deceive them in order to achieve a private prosperity. More generally, the vaunted individualism of liberal society is a fraud: our souls are the souls of small businessmen, however much we may affect an authentic freedom from the prevailing habits and vices of bourgeois society. And finally, the bourgeois not only fails to achieve a life of "rugged individualism" but also abandons the ordinary decency of those "simple souls" whose "morals were rustic but natural." In short, there is no place for "natural sincerity" in liberal society.[17]

Rousseau stands at the beginning of an enduring tradition of thought whose aim is to restore the "respectable extremes"—natural privacy and moral community—that have been destroyed by the rise of the bourgeois. Such thinkers (and artists, and sometimes even politicians) seek to radicalize our love of privacy or our love of community, in Rousseau's spirit if not always in his manner. To be sure, our sometimes radical thoughts about privacy and community coexist uneasily with conventional bourgeois practices of privacy and community: that is, we despise ourselves. Thus a postmodern sort of spiritual dissonance (born of our awareness of the inauthenticity of bourgeois life) now further fragments the souls of those already suffering from the spiritual dissonance of modern bourgeois life that was diagnosed by Rousseau.

II

When I say "we," I refer above all to those Richard Rorty calls "postmodern bourgeois liberals" or "liberal ironists." Most of us, I suppose, are somehow postmodern bourgeois liberals: who among us, to take a simple but revealing case, still holds these truths to be self-evident, that all men are created equal and all the rest? Postmodern liberal intellectuals have by now (as Rorty argues) achieved a sort of "cultural hegemony." For the postmodernist, "questions of ends as opposed to means—questions about how to give a sense to one's own life or that of one's community—are questions for art or politics, or both, rather than for religion, philosophy, or science." The postmodern intellectual recognizes that nature "teaches no moral lesson, offers no spiritual comfort," but he is able to live with this hard fact, more or less, since it is after all possible and perhaps even better to create one's own moral lessons, or to find spiritual comfort in the embrace of one's community. And yet, to complete Rorty's portrait, these postmodern bourgeois intellectuals are (for no good reason, but no good reason is needed) liberals too. That is, they believe that "cruelty is the worst thing we do"; they admit that for us as citizens "*nothing* is less dubious than the worth of [the] freedoms" of liberal democratic political communities; and they are committed to a humane egalitarianism that enables us "to *create* a more expansive sense of solidarity than we presently have" and teaches us how to expand our sense of who counts as "we" and thereby to diminish our sense of who counts as "they." And so the liberal political community is not especially in need of the sustenance provided by classical liberal philosophy, which seeks "foundations" for liberal principles and institutions that are unnecessary and anyway unavailable. Rather, the liberal polity stands in need of better liberal poetry, says Rorty, which can enable us to imagine what we can never really know (since "humanity" is not the name of a "natural kind")—that is, to imagine our "solidarity" with those who seem at first glance to be "they" and not "we."[18]

Here is our problem, or part of it: we are divided against ourselves, torn between our love of privacy and our love of community. We are now driven toward ever more solitary and idiosyncratic modes of privacy, and toward ever more authoritative and constitutive modes of community—not so much in practice as in thought, but the practice will surely follow the thought soon enough. The tidy old-fashioned harmony of civil society and liberal polity has somehow been destroyed, and so our privacy is now too lonely, our community too stifling. Let us begin with privacy.

For the postmodern soul, described so well by Rorty, "privacy" is not merely the sphere within which we have a right to undertake the "pursuit of happiness," unfettered and indeed almost unnoticed by the liberal state, guided rather by our religious faith, by our parents, by who knows what, to choose a straight and true path toward happiness. "Privacy" today describes nothing so cozy and homey as "civil society" or "friendship" or "family" or "church." Rather, postmodern "privacy" is a sphere of willful, anxious self-expression and even "self-creation" where human beings reside in utter solitude, inspired by a lonely "terror" to choose their own "private poems," idiosyncratic paths away from contingent pasts toward equally arbitrary (but heretofore unimagined) futures. The "triumph" of a human life, says Rorty, is not self-knowledge but "self-overcoming"; not the discovery of a tried and true path toward human happiness (not even the discovery of an untried but true path), but rather the embrace of one or another private and "ludicrous obsession" capable of liberating a human being as far as possible from the ugly fate, indeed the "'horror,'" of "'finding oneself to be only a copy or replica'" of something, some way of life, that already was. (Not in the end, it should be noted, far enough from this fate to enable any human being to altogether overcome the "terror" that "one might end one's days in . . . a world one never made, an inherited world"—since every private poet's self-creation is at best "marginal" and "parasitic on her precursors.") Not happiness but perfect and therefore idiosyncratic freedom is the aim of our postmodern privacy; such perfect freedom is always willful or perverse, for otherwise it would be constrained by the authority of some past; what is more, it is inevitably incomplete, and thus desperate. Human life is in the best case (the case of Rorty's "strong poet") a progress from one perversion of prevailing practices to the next that ceases only in death.[19]

This is postmodern "privacy." The moral revolution that is implicit in this way of understanding privacy is clear in Rorty's account. Consider the following discussion of Freud's novel way of talking about the idiosyncratic and often fantastic memories or incidents that "dramatize and crystallize a human being's sense of self-identity," which I quote at length because it is so revealing:

To appreciate Freud's point would be to overcome what William James called "a certain blindness in human beings." James's example of this blindness was his own reaction, during a trip through the Appalachian Mountains, to a clearing in which the forest had been hacked down and replaced with a muddy garden, a log cabin, and some pigpens. As James says, "The forest had been destroyed; and what had 'improved' it out of existence was hideous, a sort of ulcer, without a single element of artificial grace to make up for the loss of Nature's beauty." But, James continues, when a farmer comes out of the cabin and tells him that "we ain't happy here unless we're getting one of those coves under cultivation," he realizes that "I had been losing the whole inward significance of the situation. Because to me the clearings spoke of naught but denudation, I thought that to those whose sturdy arms and obedient axes had made them they could tell no other story. But when *they* looked on the hideous stumps, what they thought of was personal victory. . . . In short, the clearing which to me was a mere ugly picture on the retina, was to them a symbol redolent with moral memories and sang a very paean of duty, struggle and success. I had been as blind to the peculiar ideality of their conditions as they certainly would also have been to the ideality of mine, had they had a peep at my strange indoor academic ways of life at Cambridge." I take Freud to have spelled out James's point in more detail, helping us overcome particularly intractable cases of blindness by letting us see the "peculiar ideality" of events which exemplify, for example, sexual perversion, extreme cruelty, ludicrous obsession, and manic delusion. He let us see each of these as the private poem of the pervert, the sadist, or the lunatic: each as richly textured and "redolent of moral memories" as our own life. He lets us see what moral philosophy describes as extreme, inhuman, and unnatural, as continuous with our own activity.

Freud, says Rorty, "breaks down all the traditional distinctions between the higher and the lower, the essential and the accidental, the central and the peripheral. He leaves us with a self which is a tissue of contingencies rather than an at least potentially well-ordered system of faculties." (This "helps explain how someone can be both a tender mother and a merciless concentration-camp guard.")[20]

Rorty argues that the human self has no "core," that there is no true self that a human being should strive to awaken or discover; that is, the postmodernist liberal sees "the self as centerless, as a historical contingency all the way through." The human self is merely a "network of beliefs, desires, and emotions with nothing behind it—no substrate behind the attributes." This network is, in the first place, the creation of the community; Rorty argues that "there is nothing much to 'man' except one more animal, until culture, the meshes of power, begin to shape him into something else." And yet "who gets to do the socializing is often a matter of who manages to kill whom first," and so this account of the self might seem to justify the spiritual enslavement of all human beings to their community, and even to those in the community who most effectively use force or fraud to impose their idiosyncratic ways of thinking and acting on the rest of us (perhaps the "strong poets").[21]

We may escape this slavish condition, says Rorty, only if we somehow create ourselves anew, through the continual "reweaving" of this network of beliefs and desires. But there is no essential humanity or true self that can be the object of our aspirations, or guide our quest for freedom: "There is only the shaping of an animal into a human being by a process of socialization, followed (with luck) by the self-individualization and self-creation of that human being through his or her own later revolt against that very process." Self-creation is a kind of freedom from the community, then, but it is a freedom that is not directed by any law of nature or by reason. Moral freedom is above all the recognition of contingency, says Rorty; thus the greater slavery consists in "obedience to permanent nonhuman constraints," like God or nature, not in obedience to the "conversational constraints" imposed by our various communities. The philosophical or religious attempt to escape the contingency of community, according to Rorty, only turns human beings into "properly-programmed machine[s]." And so Rorty's creative individuals accept no guidance from God or nature in their revolt against their socialization but instead undertake to write their own "private poems." Idiosyncratic experimentation with one's self is for him the way of life of the truly free human being, the strong poet, who escapes the terrible fate of those who live in an inherited world, but without falling into the slavish habits of those who obey imaginary masters.[22]

Something akin to Rorty's understanding of privacy is often reflected in our ordinary language of privacy. Let me here offer a trivial example, or anyway a more mundane consequence, of the postmodernist reinterpretation of the idea of privacy. I mean the argument that follows to illustrate a more general point; nothing much rides on the particular example, since the general phenomenon is recognizable. That general phenomenon is the emptiness, and the whining tone, that marks so much of our talk about privacy today.

Consider, for example, the recent Supreme Court decision concerning the so-called right of privacy, *Planned Parenthood v. Casey* (the 1992 abortion case). I have no desire to discuss the question of the provenance of this constitutional right here. But the pivotal opinion in this case, like a number of other opinions of the Court in this area, also addressed a more fundamental question, the moral meaning of the idea of privacy: what is this privacy that is somehow central to our notions about "liberty"? The failure of the Court's various attempts to provide a moral foundation for the idea of privacy is palpable and well known. Let me quote the most recent example—but there are many others—of such a failed attempt. Here is a passage from the Joint Opinion (Justices O'Connor, Kennedy, Souter) in *Planned Parenthood v. Casey*, on the extent of the substantive sphere of liberty protected by the Fourteenth Amendment, including a certain "private realm" into which the state may not enter:

> These matters ["personal decisions relating to marriage, procreation, contraception, family relationships, child rearing, and education"], involving the most intimate and personal choices a person may make in a lifetime, choices central to personal dignity and autonomy, are central to the liberty protected by the Fourteenth Amendment. *At the heart of liberty is the right to define one's own concept of existence, of meaning, of the universe, and of the mystery of human life.* Beliefs about these matters could not define the attributes of personhood were they formed under compulsion of the State. (Emphasis added)

Empty pieties of this sort regarding liberty and privacy abound in recent Supreme Court decisions. Indeed, it is striking how far the language of the law, including the language of the Supreme Court, has been influenced by a view of privacy and freedom that is akin to Rorty's view. It would not be difficult to cite many other passages describing liberty in these terms, more or less: as a private and idiosyncratic ("define one's own concept") quest for "meaning," where this meaning is somehow a "mystery," and where meaning is "defined," not discovered. But let me generalize, so as not to rest the whole argument here on my distaste for this particular passage.[23]

Here is my suggestion: When we speak about privacy today, our talk is commonly empty, formal, self-indulgent, even desperate. Private life is for many of us a "journey" of self-disclosure or self-creation rather than self-discovery or self-knowledge. We love our privacy, but we are not especially confident that we know very well what to do with it. Compare Rorty's self-creator, or the empty pieties of the Joint Opinion, with the more robust self-confidence of old-fashioned "rugged individualists," the sorts of liberals who invented (more or less) the distinction between private and public that is now so central to our moral vocabulary. Who is the rugged individualist? He is, roughly and briefly, a reasonable and free moral agent who is the author of his own way of life and who possesses grounds of self-esteem that are independent of his "community" or "home." Such a liberal is able to stand alone, if need be, or in the company of a few friends, against the intolerance or even the contempt of his community. But he knows well where he stands. When such a liberal says "privacy," or when he speaks of "the right to be let alone—the most comprehensive of rights and the right most valued by civilized men," he is thinking about some private way of life that is worth a fight. When he says privacy, he means "freedom of religion" and he is fighting for his God; or he means "freedom of speech" and thought and he is fighting for the chance to persuade his fellow citizens of what he thinks is right; or he means "family" and he is fighting for the right to educate his children in his own way in pursuit of a particular way of life; or whatever.[24] But this is not the character of much contemporary talk about privacy. Our postmodern talk about self-creation and self-expression is empty and formal: what counts is the liberating experience, the rebellion, not the chosen way of life. What is more, our privacy is commonly restless, anxious, "experimental": always in search of something new and exotic, never altogether at home in a private way of life. And this new experience of privacy is founded on new thoughts about privacy.

Enough on privacy. What about community? Here too Rorty and others radicalize the liberal idea. Again and again Rorty urges us to "identify" with our own community, at least in our thoughts, and especially when we speculate or worry about what gives moral meaning and dignity to our lives. In this respect, if in no other, he is a communitarian theorist. In an essay titled "Pragmatism, Relativism, and Irrationalism," for example, Rorty contrasts the postmodernist's acceptance of the necessarily contingent starting points of all thought with the Platonic (as well as Christian and Kantian) effort to "evade this contingency" by discovering a starting point that is beyond contingency, in nature (or God, or reason). For Rorty, all thinking properly begins with the recognition that "our inheritance from, and our conversation with, our fellow-humans [is] our only source of guidance": we must begin where we are, as participants in a continuing dialogue among members of a particular historical community. Rorty denounces the "hope" that possesses the Platonic philosopher and others, who seek to step outside this conversation and gain access to "the ahistorical and nonhuman nature of reality itself." The philosopher is not animated by an irresistible urge to know, or constrained above all by the necessity to follow the argument; on the contrary, he is in fact propelled by a need for a certain "metaphysical comfort," to believe that the world has a certain intelligible order, or to "find something ahistorical and necessary to cling to." But for Rorty, recognition of the authority of one's community is not only a philosophical necessity that thoughtful human beings must accept; identification with one's community is also a moral good that decent citizens come to cherish. We should "cling" to community, then, for both theoretical and moral reasons. And so Rorty also praises the postmodernist's acceptance of contingency on the grounds that it makes possible a "renewed sense of community," even an "identification with our community"; this identification can finally emerge "when we see this community as *ours* rather than *nature's, shaped* rather than *found*," and it is much stronger than the more modest identification with one's community that is possible for the philosopher and others (like classical liberals) who elevate "objectivity" over "solidarity." Thus Rorty seeks to replace the philosophic quest for an uncertain metaphysical comfort (that the world should be intelligible) with a communal quest for a certain moral comfort (that we should have a home here): "In the end, . . . what matters is our loyalty to other human beings clinging together against the dark, not our hope of getting things right." On Rorty's account, the issue between postmodernism and Platonism is simply a question of what we ought to "cling" to: nature, or our community.[25]

Indeed, Rorty argues that "morality" is no more than "the interest of a historically conditioned community," and that "human dignity" is similarly "derivative from the dignity of some specific community": "loyalty to [our society] is morality enough." Indeed, Rorty is arguably one of our most radical partisans of community. Other communitarians are content to say, with Michael Sandel, that *certain* "loyalties and convictions" acquire *some* "moral force" *partly* because these moral commitments are essentially bound up with our various self-understandings as members of particular communities. We know ourselves not simply as lonely individuals, but also as loyal members of various communities. These various belongings have a moral force that obligates us in important ways; for Sandel, such obligations go beyond, but apparently do not altogether supplant, more universal duties—including not only those that we incur through our free and rational choices as individuals, but also (what is more important) those that bind us as human beings simply. But Rorty characteristically goes much further; in his response to Sandel, he affirms that identification with one's community is the *only* warrant for moral judgments and moral duties:

> I would argue that the moral force of such loyalties and convictions consists *wholly* in this fact, and that nothing else has *any* moral force. There is no "ground" for such loyalties and convictions save the fact that the beliefs and desires and emotions which buttress them overlap those of lots of other members of the group with which we identify for purposes of moral or political deliberations.

In matters of morality, according to Rorty, we may *never* appeal to the idea of natural duties or to the virtue of humanity (except perhaps rhetorically, among fools or children), since these notions are based on the old-fashioned and now discredited philosophical aspiration to see the natural human being as he really is, stripped of all cultural or conventional accretions; on the contrary, since "there is nothing to people except what has been socialized into them," we are only able to justify our moral choices in the language, and according to the standards, of the community with which we happen to identify (for whatever historical or idiosyncratic reasons). For Rorty, a human being "really is" nothing more than what his community has made him.[26]

Here is Clifford Geertz's splendid description of this sort of posture toward one's community. Such a view of community or culture, says Geertz,

> certainly strikes a contemporary chord. The attractions of "deafness to the appeal of other values" and of a relax-and-enjoy-it approach to one's imprisonment in one's own cultural tradition are increasingly celebrated in recent social thought. Unable to embrace either relativism or absolutism, . . . our philosophers, historians, and social scientists turn toward the sort of we-are-we and they-are-they *imperméabilité* Lévi-Strauss recommends. Whether one regards this as arrogance made easy, prejudice justified, or as the splendid, here-stand-I honesty of Flannery O'Connor's "when

in Rome do as you done in Milledgeville," it clearly puts the question of . . . cultural diversity . . . in rather a new light.[27]

Rorty does offer a kind of solution to one aspect of the problem I am discussing here. It is indeed the main business of *Contingency, Irony, and Solidarity* to show that these two quests (for private self-creation and for solidarity with one's community) can *both* be accommodated within a liberal "utopia." "The closest we will come to joining these two quests is to see the aim of a just and free society as letting its citizens be as privatistic, 'irrationalist,' and aestheticist as they please so long as they do it on their own time—causing no harm to others and using no resources needed by those less advantaged." Here is the formula, then: Nietzsche plus J. S. Mill plus Rawls equals a liberal utopia. Those (as Rorty elsewhere says) "who have a taste for sublimity will have to pursue it in their own time, and within the limits set by *On Liberty*." Or finally and most bluntly, each liberal human being must learn to "divide herself up into a private self-creator and a public liberal"; it is an error to suppose "that the same person cannot be, in alternate moments, Nietzsche and J. S. Mill."[28] Here is the liberal as Clark Kent: Superman and mild-mannered citizen.

To be sure, Rorty's utopia is a *liberal* utopia. That is, Rorty remains committed to more or less conventional liberal aspirations and principles, both procedural and substantive: "cruelty is the worst thing we do"; "*nothing* is less dubious" than "the value of the democratic freedoms and relative social equality which some rich and lucky societies have, quite recently, come to enjoy"; "our human rights culture" is "morally superior to other cultures"; "in respect to words as opposed to deeds, persuasion as opposed to force, anything goes"; the liberal practice of privacy must "[cause] no harm to others and [use] no resources needed by those less advantaged"; and we must "try to extend our sense of 'we' to people whom we have previously thought of as 'they.'"[29] In this respect at least, Rorty's postmodern liberal politics have little in common with the politics of many other postmodernists today. But these liberal principles of justice are not, on Rorty's account, universal principles that can be defended on neutral grounds: "When the value of such institutions is challenged . . . no direct answer can be given, because there is no neutral ground," says Rorty; or again, "There is no *neutral*, noncircular way to defend the liberal's claim that cruelty is the worst thing we do, any more than there is a neutral way to back up Nietzsche's assertion that this claim expresses a resentful, slavish attitude." And so we must "[give] up the idea that liberalism could be justified, and Nazi or Marxist enemies of liberalism refuted, by driving the latter up against an argumentative wall—forcing them to admit that liberal freedom has a 'moral privilege' which their own values lacked."[30]

Here is the problem: if it *"just happened* that Europe began to prize benevolent sentiments and the idea of a common humanity," and if it *"may just happen* that the world will wind up being ruled by people who lack any such sentiments and any such moralities," then how can we be confident that liberal polities will long be able to sustain themselves, especially in an era of liberal self-doubt and even self-loathing, once they have abandoned, or been compelled to abandon, the old-fashioned Enlightenment aspiration to build just societies on the ground of our essential humanity—not to speak of self-evident truths?[31] To begin: Is it "psychologically" possible "to be someone for whom 'cruelty is the worst thing we do,' and to have no metaphysical beliefs about what all human beings have in common"? Next: Will the "general adoption of antimetaphysical, antiessentialist views about the nature of morality and rationality and human beings . . . weaken and dissolve liberal societies," or "strengthen" them? Rorty's postmodern liberalism is simply "a hazardous experiment": to test the proposition that the postmodern soul will, often enough, be a liberal soul. And so when Rorty says that "our human rights culture" is "morally superior to other cultures," he is making a prediction, not advancing a claim about "universal human nature." Rorty argues that the new postmodern conceptions of privacy and community comport well with liberal democracy; that postmodern liberals will be "nice, tolerant, well-off, secure, other-respecting" rather than willful or self-satisfied or dogmatic or desperate, and that they will choose to defend liberal principles when brought face to face with the charms of one or another form of illiberal politics. Besides, "nobody who has experienced both [liberal and illiberal societies] would prefer the latter." In a postmodern world, Rorty seems to say, the liberals will sooner or later win.[32] Now it is not my purpose here to criticize this admittedly "hazardous" experiment, although it seems to me that it is (for both psychological and political reasons) hard to imagine its success.[33] But it is worth remarking that many of Rorty's critics, from all parts of the political spectrum, have argued that Rorty here seems remarkably complacent about the security—not to mention the justice—of liberal principles and habits. In John Gray's words, Rorty seems to be subject to "one of the illusions of the age," the view that "the future of liberal institutions is underwritten by the imperatives of modernity." And Jean Bethke Elshtain argues that Rorty "links his commitment to contingency to a rough-and-ready progressivist teleology (even though he cannot permit himself teleological arguments, he relies tacitly on Whiggish history)": "the contingencies seem to be on 'our side'"; "the good guys appear to be winning, more or less." But there are good reasons, as Elshtain shows, to suspect that Rorty's confidence is misplaced.[34]

Rorty's imaginary liberal utopia is not merely a philosopher's dream. For it is surely a problem for us today to imagine a way to bring about political unity from a diversity that is more profound than that imagined by, say, the authors of the *Federalist Papers*. And this new sense of diversity has its roots (at least in part) in the new conception of self and community that is offered by postmodern theorists like Rorty. When, for example, New York is described as a "gorgeous mosaic," the image is one that Rorty would approve. Such images are fast supplanting that other more traditional image for transforming many into one: the melting pot. Consider another long passage from an essay by Rorty, "On Ethnocentrism," a response to the Geertz essay just quoted:

> I shall conclude these comments by turning to Geertz's claim that "we have come to such a point in the moral history of the world that we are obliged to think about [cultural] diversity rather differently than we have been used to thinking about it." He develops this point by saying that "we are living more and more in the midst of an enormous collage," that "the world is coming at each of its local points to look more like a Kuwaiti bazaar than like an English gentlemen's club." These latter descriptions seem right to me. . . .
>
> Like Geertz, I have never been in a Kuwaiti bazaar (nor in an English gentlemen's club). So I can give free rein to my fantasies. I picture many of the people in such a bazaar as preferring to die rather than share the beliefs of many of those with whom they are haggling, yet as haggling profitably away nevertheless. Such a bazaar is, obviously, not a community, in the strong approbative sense of "community" used by critics of liberalism like Alasdair MacIntyre and Robert Bellah. You cannot have an old-timey *Gemeinschaft* unless everybody pretty well agrees on who counts as a decent human being and who does not. But you *can* have a civil society of the bourgeois democratic sort. All you need is the ability to control your feelings when people who strike you as irredeemably different show up at City Hall, or the greengrocers, or the bazaar. When this happens, you smile a lot, make the best deals

you can, and, after a hard day's haggling, retreat to your club. There you will be comforted by the companionship of your moral equals.

Wet liberals will be repelled by this suggestion that the exclusivity of the private club might be a *crucial* feature of the ideal world order. It will seem a betrayal of the Enlightenment to imagine us winding up with a world of moral narcissists, congratulating themselves on neither knowing nor caring what the people in the club over on the other side of the bazaar are like. But if we forget about the Enlightenment ideal of the self-realization of humanity as such, we can disassociate liberty and equality from fraternity. If we attend rather to the reports of our agents of love, our connoisseurs of diversity, we may agree with Lévi-Strauss that such exclusivity is a necessary and proper condition of selfhood. By attending to the reports of our agents of justice, we can see how such strong, ethnocentric, exclusivist selves might cooperate in keeping the bazaar open, in keeping the institutions of procedural justice functioning.[35]

Again, I do not mean to consider whether such a utopia is imaginable.[36] The question I raise here, rather, is whether the new doctrines of self and community are compatible with classical liberal ways of conceiving of individual and community, public and private. Are we capable any longer of describing a privacy and a community that can sustain classical liberal politics?

III

The prevailing extremism in our speech about idiosyncratic privacy and constitutive community drives us away from a more sober liberal consensus about the meaning of the ideas of privacy and community.[37] This extremism has its roots in Rousseau's assault on the bourgeois soul, an assault that culminates in an effort, as Bloom argues, to restore the "respectable extremes, the good natural man and the moral citizen": the origin of the project of radicalizing our love of privacy and our love of community is contempt for the bourgeois or liberal soul. It is worth remarking, however, that the tendencies I have been describing have now become prevalent in liberal political thought as well. Consider, for example, the increasingly widespread view that it is the business of the liberal community, perhaps even its main business, to provide communal support for self-esteem by teaching and even enforcing a right to "equal concern and respect," as Dworkin puts it. That is a novel way of bringing together idiosyncratic privacy and constitutive community while striving to maintain a liberal commitment to tolerance and diversity: on one hand, the new liberal orthodoxy affirms a right to equal respect for every private way of life, however idiosyncratic and whatever its quality, since judgments regarding the quality of private choices are now thought by such liberals to be illicit in principle; on the other hand, the new liberals admit that there is no reasonable ground of self-esteem beyond the (constitutive) community, so that a failure to "recognize" or esteem alien private choices "can inflict harm, can be a form of oppression."[38] The combination of these two dispositions produces a remarkable transformation of liberal moral psychology: from a doctrine of proud individualists who insist on the right to be left alone to a doctrine more suitable for the desperately lonely, "clinging together against the dark." "Mind your own business!" has become "I'm OK! You're OK!"

The moral experience I have been describing can perhaps be traced to Rousseau in one other respect—only at a greater distance. Both aspects of the prevailing moral extremism have another common root: the conviction that human beings are by nature homeless, that nature and God offer us no guidance as we move through a world that speaks no moral language (indeed, speaks no language at all, on Rorty's account), so that we must make up a language (or several) for ourselves, as self-creative individuals or as loyal members of a constitutive community. The effect of this doctrine is to push us toward a solitude that will enable us to fashion novel ways of life for ourselves, and toward a community that will somehow help us to feel at home. No wonder, then, that the doctrine is accompanied by an experience of terror, as Rorty and others acknowledge. Barber, for example, speaks of the "inconsolable coldness of modernity" that is born of a liberation won "at the price of deracination (the absence of roots and meaning)."[39]

How far is this despair a legacy of Rousseau? Rousseau was among the first to teach that human beings are by nature homeless; that nature teaches very few moral lessons; that the human being is almost infinitely malleable and so the range of possible human lives, including happy ones, is indeterminate; that the history of the human species (or the progress of civilization) so distances us from our original natures that it is hard to see any longer what guidance our speculations about nature or human nature can provide for our various pursuits of happiness. In short, there is no very useful blueprint written someplace in nature or in a book, whose discovery might provide a model of our essential humanity to guide those human beings who are able to find it and to follow it. As Melzer says: "Having gone irrevocably beyond his natural life as an animal, man is now on his own, homeless and free, without nature or instinct to guide him, an accidental being who must try to invent an altogether new life and happiness for himself."[40] All of this is the beginning of the inquiry, not the end. Liberalism stands or falls on its capacity to make the case for the dignity of private life. In establishing a liberal community, we admit that the only truly common goods are peace and the means to peace. Peace or security is most nearly achieved where partisan and sectarian doctrines about putative common goods are not heard in political debate; in a liberal world, such high-minded moral and political aspirations have their proper places outside the sphere of common deliberation and common action. Liberals must therefore admit that the political way of life is not an end in itself; the ways of life of citizens and statesmen are soon deprived of their former dignity—statesmen are supplanted by bureaucrats, citizens by entrepreneurs. Liberal politics, in short, is boring: we refrain from more exciting or inspiriting political and moral partisanship because we worry that such quarrels are often merely more or less quiet modes of civil war. And so we liberal citizens are deprived of some of the greatest joys of political association, including above all the sometimes agreeable but often dangerous business of common deliberation about what is a good and just and happy human life, and about how the political community can educate human beings who will discover such lives. Since we may not pursue happiness (or establish justice, or serve God) through partisan or sectarian political activity in common with kindred spirits, liberals are obliged to undertake such pursuits only in private, or in the liberal "society." For this reason, and especially in the face of new and illiberal doctrines regarding the nature of the self and its relation to community, partisans of liberalism must think again about the moral meaning of the idea of privacy. This at any rate is a legacy of Rousseau: that it is no longer so easy to describe a mode of privacy that is compatible with moderate liberal community.

The challenge of postmodern liberalism, then, points partisans of a more classical liberalism toward a reconsideration of the thought of Rousseau, in order to see whether liberalism has within itself the resources to resist the contemporary impulse to abandon sober liberal rationalism and moderation in favor of a more exhilarating (self-creative, self-expressive) way of life. Can the way of life of the bourgeois, praised by Locke and even Tocqueville, be defended against the assault of Rousseau? Rousseau's criticism of the bourgeois remains persuasive today, and it is somehow even now at the root of our confusions about "privacy." And yet the tradition of thought about privacy inspired by Rousseau has itself perhaps reached a dead end. Besides, it is striking how far the virtues of the bourgeois still bind even his critics, including Rorty—virtues like tolerance, civility, humanity. So perhaps it is time to take up the quarrel between Locke and Rousseau once again.

NOTES

I thank the Earhart Foundation for its generous support of this work. I am also grateful to Wilson Carey McWilliams and to the editors for helpful comments on an earlier version of this chapter.

1. Benjamin R. Barber, *The Conquest of Politics* (Princeton: Princeton University Press, 1988), 179.

2. Richard Rorty, *Contingency, Irony, and Solidarity* (Cambridge: Cambridge University Press, 1989), xiii, xv.

3. Allan Bloom, *Giants and Dwarfs* (New York: Simon and Schuster, 1990), 179, 180, and chapter 7 above, 146–47.

4. Jean-Jacques Rousseau, *Emile, or On Education*, trans. Allan Bloom (New York: Basic Books, 1979), 40.

5. Arthur M. Melzer, *The Natural Goodness of Man* (Chicago: University of Chicago Press, 1990), 76. "Yes, you men in society do not feel your enslavement, Rousseau's argument continues, but only because you have internalized it. . . . You know that your life is not in your own hands. Consequently, while you remain fundamentally selfish, your life and death dependence on other human beings has molded your habits so that you instinctively act as society requires. Unlike the patriotic citizen, you do not genuinely love and live for society, which remains for you a mere means. But it is a means so necessary and general as to be more important to you than any momentary and particular selfish end. Thus your very selfishness has trained you to serve society eagerly and habitually if ultimately insincerely" (ibid., 75; see generally, ibid., 29–85, for a splendid account of the origin and nature of this civilized disunity of soul).

6. Ibid., 89–91.

7. Jean-Jacques Rousseau, *The Reveries of the Solitary Walker*, trans. Charles E. Butterworth (New York: Harper and Row, 1979), 31, 12–13, 66, 69, 91; see also 16, 66–69, 95, 110, 119.

8. Melzer, *Natural Goodness*, 41–42; see generally 31–46.

9. Arthur M. Melzer, "Rousseau and the Modern Cult of Sincerity," chapter 13 below, 288–90. Or again: "Men's lives grow from within, and the core of their existence is not reason, which is inherently common and public, but feeling, which is private and idiosyncratic. Thus Rousseau has a keen sense of how trapped we all are in our own unique perspectives" (Melzer, *Natural Goodness*, 46; see also 42).

10. See Allan Bloom, *Love and Friendship* (New York: Simon and Schuster, 1993),

39–265; see also Christopher Kelly, *Rousseau's Exemplary Life* (Ithaca: Cornell University Press, 1987).

11. Rousseau, *Emile*, 40; see also Jean-Jacques Rousseau, *First Discourse*, in *The First and Second Discourses Together with the Replies to Critics and Essay on the Origin of Languages*, ed. and trans. Victor Gourevitch (New York: Harper and Row, 1986), pt. 1; cf. Montesquieu, *The Spirit of the Laws*, trans. Anne M. Cohler, Basia Carolyn Miller, and Harold Samuel Stone (Cambridge: Cambridge University Press, 1989), 3.3, 4.5, 5.2–3; and see Leo Strauss, "On the Intention of Rousseau," *Social Research* 14 (December 1947): 457–61.

12. Jean-Jacques Rousseau, *On the Social Contract*, in *On the Social Contract, with Geneva Manuscript and Political Economy*, ed. Roger D. Masters, trans. Judith R. Masters (New York: St. Martin's Press, 1978), bk. 2, chap. 7. See too bk. 2, chap. 4, bk. 4, chaps. 7–8.

13. Montesquieu, *Spirit of the Laws*, 4.5; see also 3.5, 5.5–7, 7.2, 7.8–12. See Plato, *Republic*, trans. Allan Bloom (New York: Basic Books, 1968), 457c–465e, 416c–417b.

14. Melzer, *Natural Goodness*, 95, 98; Montesquieu, *Spirit of the Laws*, 4.5; see also 4.6–7, 5.2–7. And see generally Melzer, *Natural Goodness*, 94–113, for the various ways, including public moral education, a small and homogeneous community, sumptuary laws and other laws designed to curb commerce and limit inequality, public festivals, public religion, and other modes of censorship, and others—all imposed by means of "the awesome force of the democratic absolutist state . . . exercised through general laws" (99). Cf. Michael Walzer, *Obligations* (Cambridge: Harvard University Press, 1970), 77–98.

15. Walter Berns, *In Defense of Liberal Democracy* (Chicago: Regnery Gateway, 1984), 29–62; Berns, "Taking Rights Frivolously," in *Liberalism Reconsidered*, ed. Douglas MacLean and Claudia Mills (Totowa, N.J.: Rowman and Allanheld, 1983), 51–66; Harvey C. Mansfield Jr., "Hobbes and the Science of Indirect Government," *American Political Science Review* 65 (March 1971): 97–110; idem, "Modern and Medieval Representation," in *Nomos X: Representation*, ed. J. Roland Pennock and John W. Chapman (New York: Atherton Press, 1968), 55–82.

16. Jean-Jacques Rousseau, *Second Discourse*, in *The First and Second Discourses Together with the Replies to Critics and Essay on the Origin of Languages*, ed. and trans. Victor Gourevitch (New York: Harper and Row, 1986), 161–62; Rousseau, *First Discourse*, in ibid., 16–20; Rousseau, *Social Contract*, bk. 3, chaps. 13–15, esp. bk. 3, chap. 15 on representation: "The English people thinks it is free. It greatly deceives itself; it is free only during the election of the members of Parliament." See also *Second Discourse*, 187: "I know that the former do nothing but incessantly boast of the peace and quiet they enjoy in their chains, and that *they call the most miserable servitude peace:* but when I see . . . multitudes of completely naked Savages scorn European voluptuousness and brave hunger, fire, the sword, and death in order to preserve nothing but their independence, I feel that it is not for Slaves to reason about freedom."

17. Bloom, chapter 7 above, 146–47; for "political nobility" and "natural sincerity," see 147. For Rousseau's attack, see *First Discourse*, 4–7, 27; see also *Second Discourse*, 167–68, 175–84, and the passage from the preface to *Narcissus* quoted in

Melzer, *Natural Goodness,* 79–80. See Melzer, *Natural Goodness,* 69–85, for an analysis of Rousseau's account of personal dependence. For a portrait of a more dignified liberal soul, see Nathan Tarcov, *Locke's Education for Liberty* (Chicago: University of Chicago Press, 1984).

18. Rorty, *Contingency,* xv, 3, 196–97, 20; Richard Rorty, *Objectivity, Relativism, and Truth* (Cambridge: Cambridge University Press, 1991), 197–98. See generally Rorty, *Contingency,* xiii–xvi, 44–69, 82–95, 173–77, 189–198; Rorty, *Objectivity,* 197–202, 203–10. The paragraph in the text refers to Rorty, but the ideas are in the air. Rorty's recent work is an uncommonly revealing mirror of contemporary moral opinion, for he brings together apparently contradictory interpretations of our moral world, scattered here and there in the work of less comprehensive contemporary theorists, into one more or less coherent whole.

19. Rorty, *Contingency,* 24, 29, 38, 41; the "'horror . . . replica'" language quoted by Rorty is from Harold Bloom, *The Anxiety of Influence* (Oxford: Oxford University Press, 1973), 80 (on "'the strong poet's anxiety of influence'"). Perhaps I exaggerate the aspect of anguish in this portrait of the postmodern idea of privacy; after all, Rorty often prides himself on his playfulness in the face of questions that everyone else takes altogether too seriously, or so he says. But I do not think so: see the chapter "The Contingency of Selfhood," *Contingency,* 23–43, which is explicitly presented as a reinterpretation of our fear of death or fear of extinction, in the form of an idiosyncratic reading of a poem by Philip Larkin.

20. Rorty, *Contingency,* 37–38, 32. See too Richard Rorty, "Robustness: A Reply to Jean Bethke Elshtain," in *The Politics of Irony,* ed. Daniel W. Conway and John E. Seery (New York: St. Martin's Press, 1992), 220–23.

21. Rorty, *Objectivity,* 188, 199; Richard Rorty, *Consequences of Pragmatism* (Minneapolis: University of Minnesota Press, 1982), 208 (cf. xlii); Rorty, *Contingency,* 185 (cf. 45, 177).

22. Rorty, *Objectivity,* 199; Richard Rorty, "Education without Dogma," *Dissent* 36 (spring 1989): 200; Rorty, *Consequences,* 165–66. See also Rorty, *Objectivity,* 31–32, 184–92, 199–202; Richard Rorty, *Essays on Heidegger and Others* (Cambridge: Cambridge University Press, 1991), 143–63, 193–98; Rorty, *Contingency,* 23–43, 45–46, 96–137, 189–91.

23. *Planned Parenthood v. Casey,* 112 S.Ct. 2791 (1992), at 2807. For a few other instances: see Justice Douglas's concurring opinion in *Doe v. Bolton,* 410 U.S. 179 (1973), and *Roe v. Wade,* 410 U.S. 113 (1973) at 211–15; Justice Stevens's concurring opinion in *Thornburgh v. American College of Obstetricians,* 476 U.S. 747 (1986), at 777; and Justice Blackmun's dissent in *Bowers v. Hardwick,* 478 U.S. 186 (1986), at 204–6. On the same point, see also Laurence H. Tribe's effort to fill this gap (which he recognizes as a gap in the opinions of the Court) in the argument in the chapter "Rights of Privacy and Personhood" in his *American Constitutional Law,* 2d ed. (Mineola, N.Y.: Foundation Press, 1988), 1302–1435, which seems to me to fail on the same grounds. Or consider a related issue in the law: the idea that "freedom of expression" is an adequate gloss of "freedom of speech" is another instance of illiberal irrationalism in the law.

24. Justice Brandeis is the author of the passage quoted in the text, in dissent in *Olmstead v. United States*, 277 U.S. 438 (1928), at 478. Consider too Justice Harlan's dissent in *Poe v. Ullman*, 367 U.S. 497 (1961), the forerunner of *Griswold v. Connecticut*, 381 U.S. 479 (1965), and still the most impressive argument for a right of privacy in a Supreme Court opinion, where the right is explicitly and emphatically associated with an account of the place of the family in a liberal regime (at 545–55). In this connection, recall that at the beginning of the recent history of the right of privacy, that right was often traced to the argument for parental rights in *Meyer v. Nebraska*, 262 U.S. 390 (1923), and *Pierce v. Society of Sisters*, 268 U.S. 510 (1925); cf. *Prince v. Massachusetts*, 321 U.S. 158 (1944), at 166, on a "private realm of family life which the state cannot enter," cited often in later cases. Cf. Tribe, *American Constitutional Law*, 1300, on "some form of 'family' as a focal point for human feeling and solidarity"; and Justice Powell's plurality opinion in *Moore v. City of East Cleveland*, 431 U.S. 494 (1977). This history makes intelligible (as Justice White's opinion itself does not) the emphasis on "family, marriage, or procreation" in *Bowers v. Hardwick*, 478 U.S. 186 (1986), at 191. The growing abstraction of our moral ideas about privacy makes it increasingly difficult to mark the boundary of the legal right in a principled way.

25. Rorty, *Consequences*, 165–66; on "Solidarity or Objectivity?" see Rorty, *Objectivity*, 21–34.

26. Rorty, *Objectivity*, 197–202, quoting Michael J. Sandel, *Liberalism and the Limits of Justice* (New York: Cambridge University Press, 1982), 179; Rorty, *Contingency*, 177 (see also xiii–xvi, 44–69, 185, 189–98).

27. Clifford Geertz, "The Uses of Diversity," *Michigan Quarterly Review* 25 (winter 1986): 108. Lévi-Strauss is Geertz's immediate object here, but he argues in the essay that Lévi-Strauss and Rorty share a "to-each-his-own morality" that rests on "a common view of cultural diversity" (111).

28. Rorty, *Contingency*, xiv–xv, 85; Richard Rorty, "Posties," *London Review of Books*, 3 September 1987, 11–12.

29. Rorty, *Contingency*, xiv–xv, 52, 146, 192, 197; Richard Rorty, "Human Rights, Rationality, and Sentimentality," in *On Human Rights: The Oxford Amnesty Lectures 1993*, ed. Stephen Shute and Susan Hurley (New York: Basic Books, 1993), 116.

30. Rorty, *Contingency*, 197, 53. And see Rorty, *Objectivity*, 208: "The ideals of procedural justice and human equality are parochial, recent, eccentric cultural developments," not universal principles justified by "appeal to neutral criteria"; see also *Objectivity*, 175–96. Rorty denies that his affirmation that "our human rights culture" is "morally superior to other cultures" requires any claim about "a universal human nature" (Rorty, "Human Rights," 116).

31. Rorty, *Contingency*, 185.

32. Rorty, *Contingency*, 85; cf. 192, on "moral progress"; Rorty, *Objectivity*, 29, 178; Rorty, "Robustness," 222–23; Rorty, "Human Rights," 116, 127, 129, 133–34.

33. For a discussion of the psychological consequences of this postmodern liberalism, see Steven Kautz, "The Postmodern Self and the Politics of Liberal Education," *Social Philosophy and Policy* 13 (winter 1996): 164–89.

34. John Gray, "Why Irony Can't Be Superior," *Times Literary Supplement*, 3 November 1995, 5; Jean Bethke Elshtain, "Don't Be Cruel: Reflections on Rortyian Liberalism," in Conway and Seery, *Politics of Irony*, 201. See further Elshtain's challenges to Rorty on the cruelties of the French Revolution, 204–6, and on the cruelties of our century, 211–14; and compare Elshtain, 206–7, with Rorty, "Robustness," 219–20; and see Rorty, "Human Rights," 134, on "moral progress."

35. Rorty, *Objectivity*, 208–10.

36. For a further discussion of Rorty's liberal politics, see Steven Kautz, *Liberalism and Community* (Ithaca: Cornell University Press, 1995), 77–106.

37. See Kautz, *Liberalism and Community*, 51–76, for an account of the liberal mode of reconciling privacy and community, focusing on the case of toleration. I have not described that liberal view here.

38. Bloom, chapter 7 above, 146; Ronald Dworkin, *A Matter of Principle* (Cambridge: Harvard University Press, 1985), 181–213, 335–72; Charles Taylor, *Multiculturalism and "the Politics of Recognition"* (Princeton: Princeton University Press, 1992), 25; cf. Kautz, *Liberalism and Community*, 64–75. Consider Taylor's account of the "Politics of Recognition": on one hand, "our moral salvation comes from recovering authentic moral contact with ourselves" (29, citing Rousseau on the "sentiment of existence"); on the other hand, "due recognition is not just a courtesy we owe people. It is a vital human need" (26). See generally Taylor, *Multiculturalism*, 25–44.

39. Barber, *Conquest of Politics*, 177–84.

40. Melzer, *Natural Goodness*, 89.

Rousseau and the Modern Cult of Sincerity

ARTHUR M. MELZER

We are all engaged in the effort to know ourselves—and know what is good—and to move the former a little closer to the latter. We are engaged in this effort not because we are professors or students, but because we are human beings. But self-knowledge is notoriously difficult; as Nietzsche says, each is always furthest from himself.[1] The same point is made by an old joke: "We don't know who discovered water, but we're pretty sure it wasn't a fish."

The point is that we cannot see the things we are immersed in. And this crucial fact gives rise to a specific strategy for attaining self-knowledge: we can see and know ourselves best by getting outside ourselves through the study of other places and times, for example, through travel and especially through the study of history—time travel, as it were.

But this historical strategy for self-knowledge, which is necessary for human beings as such, everywhere and always, is doubly necessary for us modern or (if you like) postmodern human beings. Doubly necessary because we live in a uniquely artificial or technological world, a world brought into being by the political inventions and intellectual revolutions of the past several centuries. We are uniquely historical beings, and therefore we, more than others, need to study our history in order to know ourselves.

This fact is what makes the present volume, *The Legacy of Rousseau*, so vital. The thought of Jean-Jacques Rousseau played so great a role in shaping our current selves, in creating the world of beliefs and sentiments that make us who we are, that one is almost entitled to say we cannot know ourselves without understanding Rousseau.

At any rate, Rousseau is especially helpful for answering the particular question about ourselves that I want to raise here: Why are we so obsessed with sincerity? For the canonizing of sincerity or authenticity, its elevation to the highest or most fundamental human virtue, seems to be one of the defining characteristics of our age. This has been the observation of a long line of critics.

One might immediately object, of course, that the goal we are truly obsessed with is wealth or material success. But one of the strangest things about our society is that while everyone chases money, few wholeheartedly believe in it. Virtually every American will tell you that Americans are too materialistic and sell out too easily. Somehow we have all internalized the old critique of bourgeois culture; we are all critics of our own lives. And on this second, critical level, when we ask ourselves what it means *not* to sell out, a little voice within us always gives the same reply: "Be true to your inner self." This is our obsession with sincerity.

Thus, by the ideal of sincerity I mean something very general—more general, perhaps, than is sanctioned by common usage. In the largest sense, I mean the phenomenon Allan Bloom describes in saying that in our thinking about human happiness and human excellence, we have replaced the traditional vocabulary of virtue and vice with such new pairs of opposites as inner-directed/other-directed, real self/alienated self, sincere/hypocritical.[2]

For example, if one asks what character trait has been the single greatest subject of condemnation and loathing by the intellectuals and artists of the past two centuries, one would have to answer: hypocrisy. Even today, as Judith Shklar remarks: "Hypocrisy remains the only unforgivable sin, perhaps especially among those who can overlook and explain away almost every other vice, even cruelty. However much suffering it may cause, and however many social and religious rules it may violate, evil can be understood after due analysis. But not hypocrisy, which alone now is inexcusable."[3] Conversely, if one seeks to name the positive characteristic that our culture uses to define the happy and healthy soul, one would have to say "being oneself." If the modern age had a theme song, it would be "I Gotta Be Me."

But also included in the ideal of sincerity is the assumption that the self I gotta be is the private self, even the secret self. Thus the turn to sincerity also entails the "fall of public man," to use the title of a well-known work of sociology, that is, the demotion of the public, political realm of life and the concomitant elevation of the world of the personal, the private, and the intimate.[4]

Thus, for example, Lionel Trilling suggested that the new ideal of sincerity was responsible for the sudden florescence—during the seventeenth century—of such sincere art forms as autobiography, memoir writing, and portrait painting.[5] And certainly this tendency continues today in our self-obsessed society, with its hunger for every form of personal disclosure and disburdening self-display from psychoanalysis to tell-all memoirs to EST to Oprah Winfrey. And so when Christopher Lasch speaks of our "culture of narcissism" this too seems yet one more feature of our new world of sincerity.[6]

But sincerity is not to be confused with frankness or plain speaking, an opposite virtue and very much on the wane in our age of euphemism and sensitive speech. A person is supposed to show himself to others, not others to themselves. The frankness of one would only inhibit the sincerity of another. Nor is today's sincerity the same as old-fashioned honesty. Was George Washington *sincere*? Honesty involves a self-disciplined adherence to the truth or to one's word; sincerity, an adherence to the self.

So in sum, if it is true that we are obsessed with sincerity—that above everything else, we loathe hypocrisy, cherish self-disclosure, and long to be ourselves—the question is why. How did this ideal emerge?

Sincerity as an Outgrowth of Democratic Egalitarianism

Let me make a first stab at an explanation—a first stab that will prove inadequate and thus prepare the way for a somewhat different approach. In seeking to understand any major feature of American life, usually the best place to begin is with Tocqueville's *Democracy in America*. One consults him first to see if he explicitly discusses the issue in question, and if he does not—as is more or less the case with sincerity—then one can at least attempt to apply his general method of explanation. This method, which as I understand it is a variation on a long tradition dating back to Plato and Aristotle, endeavors to understand every characteristic of a given society as an outgrowth of the fundamental political principles structuring that society—in the case of America, the principles of equality and freedom. In Tocqueville's view, for example, even our penchant for materialism ultimately derives from these more basic principles.[7]

So can we understand the ideal of sincerity as a direct outgrowth or expression of the democratic principles of equality and freedom? Ultimately, I think the answer is no. But it is likely that our love of sincerity springs from more than one source, and certainly one of these sources is our hunger for equality. So let us very briefly consider this Tocquevillian explanation before moving beyond it.

To begin with the points Tocqueville himself makes, the equality, freedom, and mobility of democratic society destroy the rigid hierarchy and ceremonious formality of aristocratic life, liberating men for greater spontaneity, sincerity, and naturalness. "Democracy loosens social ties, but it tightens natural ones."[8] In the realm of social etiquette, to take the most obvious example, "democratic manners are neither so well thought out nor so regular [as aristocratic ones], but they often are more sincere [*sincère*]. They form, as it were, a thin, transparent veil through which the real feelings and personal thoughts of each man can be easily seen."[9] Similarly, the democratic family, being more egalitarian, dispenses with cold, aristocratic formality, and appeals instead to natural affection, openness and intimacy.[10] Above all, aristocratic societies "liked to entertain a sublime conception of the duties of man"; and these lofty morals, straining human nature, inevitably were honored more in speech than in deed. Strenuous ideals generate hypocrisy. Democratic equality, by contrast, encourages a more realistic and open acknowledgment of human selfishness and thus engenders a moral doctrine—"self-interest properly understood"—that is "wonderfully agreeable to human weaknesses." As such, it is followed more easily and so also more sincerely.[11]

All these points show how a decrease in aristocratic hypocrisy and a corresponding increase in sincerity are unintended by-products, as it were, of democracy and equality. They do not, however, address just the phenomenon we are examining, which presumably was not yet present in Tocqueville's America: the rise of sincerity as a conscious goal, indeed as the highest ideal and virtue.[12]

Thus, still in the spirit of Tocqueville but beyond the letter, we might add the following points relating equality to the *virtue* of sincerity. Sincerity calls on us to admit and reveal our true inner feelings, and this means especially the feelings we would otherwise want to hide, that is, the base and shameful ones. There is no virtue, after all, in revealing our most noble impulses. Thus the ideal of sincerity serves equality, because it encourages self-unmasking, self-debunking, and the public renunciation of the pretense to superiority. Sincerity would have all of us declare, "Beneath my public mask, I too am weak."

Taken to an extreme, sincerity is even more leveling. On television talk shows, for example, we see a daily parade of reformed drug addicts, child molesters, and other moral unfortunates who, speaking loquaciously of their crimes, end up receiving the admiration of the audience for their courageous openness and sincerity. The more horrible their secrets, the nobler *they* are for revealing them. Thus, on a certain level, the worse they are, the better they are: heroes of sincerity are to be found only among the most unfortunate or depraved. In short, the ideal of sincerity, when taken to an extreme, has that

transvaluing power—made famous by Nietzsche—by which established hier-
archies and inequalities are not only subverted but reversed.

Sincerity as a Countercultural Ideal

Notwithstanding all this service that sincerity renders to equality, however,
it still seems one cannot rest with a Tocquevillian explanation. One cannot
adequately explain the rise of sincerity as an *ideal* as a direct outgrowth of the
principle of equality that stands at the core of our regime. A new kind of
analysis is needed.

My primary reason for saying this is that the ideal of sincerity did not first
arise from *within* our liberal, democratic regime, but rather was a reaction
against it. As is well known, sincerity was first embraced by intellectuals and
artists who, standing outside and against the dominant bourgeois culture,
denounced it for its rampant hypocrisy and conformism. In other words, what
is crucial for understanding the virtue of sincerity and our obsession with it is to
see that it is a new kind of virtue—a "countercultural virtue" if you like. It is
distinguished from other virtues in at least three ways.

First, as we have just seen, it is not a *direct* virtue embodying the ideals of the
society, but a reactive or countercultural one, embraced out of revulsion for
our direct traits and primary impulses. Sincerity was canonized not because it
expressed the regime and its principles, but because it seemed so clearly
missing from the regime.

Second, sincerity is, at least in its origins, not a collective virtue, stemming
from the principles or conscience of the nation as whole, but rather a specialized virtue, being the discovery and unique property of the intellectual class
that stands in an adversarial relation to the culture at large.

And third, because sincerity is defined against the prevailing culture, it is
not a "natural" virtue like courage that grows out of permanent features of the
human condition, but rather a historical virtue, arising in reaction to specific,
historically contingent conditions. Courage, for example, is recognized pretty
much everywhere as a virtue and as at least a contender for the highest virtue,
whereas sincerity is much less often singled out for praise and, before our time,
has perhaps never been viewed as the highest virtue.

Now if it is true that sincerity is not a natural but a historical virtue, then to
understand it fully we ought to study it historically. And if we search back to
find the first emergence of the ideal of sincerity in the full modern sense, we

come eventually to Rousseau. The proof of this assertion will require the rest of my essay, but for initial evidence let me offer three observations.

One, Rousseau was the first philosopher to adopt the posture of the modern alienated intellectual—the first who stood outside society not to escape or transcend it, but to look back in criticism and blame.

Second, if we look at the content of this criticism and blame, we find that the fundamental vice for which Rousseau condemns the men of his time is insincerity and hypocrisy.[13] Indeed, he is the inventor of the critical concept of "bourgeois hypocrisy."

Third, if we turn to the positive goal Rousseau promotes, we find at its core a new ideal of sincerity, understood for the first time as an end in itself. This ideal, moreover, is illustrated and exemplified in the life of Rousseau himself, who was the only philosopher whose longest writing is his autobiography. And this writing focuses not primarily on the events of his life or on his ideas but on his inner feelings and sentiments. It is a document committed to intimate self-disclosure, recounting in excruciating detail, for example, his youthful desire to expose himself and his protracted love affair with a woman he liked to call Mama.

So if we are seeking the historical origins of our peculiar ideal of sincerity, I believe Rousseau is our man. Let us then ask him our question: Why are you so obsessed with sincerity?

I think he would give a two-part answer—the first part concerning the unique prevalence of hypocrisy or insincerity in modern or bourgeois society, the second concerning the unique goodness of sincerity as such. Let us consider each in turn.

But an initial word of caution. We will be examining one particular strand of Rousseau's thought—an especially important one, but still not the whole garment. Rousseau's attack on hypocrisy is something he never mutes or qualifies. His positive ideal of sincerity, on the other hand, is meant to apply, undiluted, only to those enabled or compelled to live isolated, withdrawn, private lives. It does not apply to that alternative ideal of Rousseau's works: the denatured, public-spirited citizen living in the legitimate state. There is no talk of sincerity in the *Social Contract.* To be sure, the citizen is no hypocrite, like the people Rousseau sees about him in Paris. He is sincere in the important sense that he is self-consistent and acts as he speaks. But since he places loyalty to the fatherland and the general will above loyalty to his unique inner self, indeed since he is a self-combater, continually at war with his most natural impulses, he is not sincere in the deepest sense. Similarly, Rousseau believes that even in private life it is never good for a young woman to be altogether sincere. He considers female sexual modesty to be necessary precisely because it is untrue.[14] Again, Rousseau makes it quite clear that strict honesty or sincerity is not wholly compatible with the role of the great legislator who founds a nation, or with that of the tutor who raises Emile, or even with that of the philosophic writer of books.[15] Thus the ideal of sincerity, though in a sense the deepest stratum of Rousseau's thought, nevertheless had an elaborately hedged and qualified status in his writings that it has mostly lost in our own time and that at any rate must be abstracted from in the analysis to follow.

The New Prevalence of Hypocrisy

Rousseau would say that if he seems obsessed with insincerity, constantly railing and fulminating against hypocrisy, that is only because hypocrisy is the most fundamental and characteristic feature of the men of his time. Many others, in fact, had pronounced the same judgment, including Montesquieu, who wrote a brief essay titled *A Praise of Sincerity*. In this work, which is roughly contemporaneous with Rousseau's writings and thus a useful term of comparison, Montesquieu calls flattery and false politeness "the virtue of the century; it is the whole study of today."[16] He attributes this regrettable situation partly to the natural preference men always have for pleasant flattery over troublesome frankness and partly to the influence of the French monarchy of his time, which produced and propagated the courtier spirit.[17]

Rousseau's description of the same situation, as well as his explanation for it, is far more radical. He describes how

> everything being reduced to appearances, everything becomes factitious and deceptive: honor, friendship, virtue, and often even vices themselves about which men finally discover the secret of boasting; how, in a word, always asking others what we are and never daring to question ourselves on this subject, in the midst of so much philosophy, humanity, politeness, and sublime maxims, we have only a deceitful and frivolous exterior.[18]

This condition of hypocrisy is certainly not natural or historically universal, according to Rousseau, who maintains, on the contrary, that men are naturally good. Therefore this vice must result from certain corrupting social conditions. It is not a natural vice but a historical one. Furthermore, according to Rousseau, the historical cause of our hypocrisy is not anything isolated or specific to a particular form of government. The French courtliness Montesquieu criticized is only one manifestation, if an egregious one, of a much broader phenomenon. The true source of our hypocrisy is to be found in the fundamental structure of modern society as such.

To understand this, let us begin somewhat further back. Rousseau adopts but radicalizes the theoretical individualism of the thinkers he is attacking, the early modern thinkers like Hobbes and Locke whom Rousseau blames for the new prevalence of hypocrisy. Human beings, in his view, are not by nature social, but rather are solitary and selfish. They can, however, be artificially transformed and made into social beings by properly devised political institutions—those that can engender sympathetic fellow feeling and a patriotic love of the common good. To the extent that a society succeeds in thus denaturing human beings and transforming them into patriotic citizens, these human beings will live happy, healthy, and free of hypocrisy.

But according to Rousseau, the defining characteristic of modern societies is their conscious renunciation of this difficult effort to transform men into citizens. Encouraged by the theoretical individualism of such thinkers as Hobbes and Locke, modern or bourgeois societies attempt the experiment of leaving men as they are, as naturally selfish individuals, and uniting them by showing them that cooperation with others is in their own selfish interest.[19]

The crucial modern claim, then, is that selfishness of the proper kind actually fosters sociability. The more selfish people are, after all, the more they feel the need of things; the more they need things, the more they depend on other men to supply them; and the more they depend on others, the more they must be willing to serve others so that these others will serve them in return. In this way sociability can be generated from selfishness.

But in Rousseau's view this grand modern experiment is an unmitigated disaster. He agrees that materialism, individualism, and selfishness can indeed be used to hold people together in society through bonds of self-interest, but such a society will have the unavoidable effect of forcing each of its members to become a phony, an actor, and a hypocrite.

The reason is beguilingly simple. The whole idea of generating sociability from selfishness relies—obviously—on a *contradiction* within human selfishness: The more selfish I am, the less I love others, but the more I need them. Thus the more I care only about myself, the more I am driven to seek the services of others. And this elemental contradiction is what creates the modern character: the *other-directed egoist,* who is prevented by his need to use others from ever being himself. "He is the man," in Allan Bloom's description, "who, when dealing with others, thinks only of himself, and on the other hand, in his understanding of himself, thinks only of others."[20]

Think it through. The egoistic individual is forced by his very selfishness to appear just and benevolent toward others—so that they will help him—but because he is selfish, he never sincerely desires to be this way for its own sake. The same thing that makes him need to appear moral—his selfishness— makes him dislike being moral. In short, among selfish but mutually depen- dent human beings, it is necessarily bad to *be* what it is necessarily good to *seem.* In such a society there is an unavoidable gulf between seeming and being; and this is why it becomes psychologically necessary that all men become phonies, actors, role players, and hypocrites.

> From now on we must take care never to let ourselves be seen such as we are: because for every two men whose interests coincide, perhaps a hundred thousand oppose them, and the only way to succeed is either to deceive or to ruin all those people. That is the fatal source of the violence, the betrayals, the deceits and all the horrors necessarily required by a state of affairs in which everyone pretends to be working for the others' profit or reputation, while only seeking to raise his own above them and at their expense.[21]

In sum, the modern commercial republic, generating sociability from selfish- ness, necessarily creates a society of smiling enemies, where each individual pretends to care about others precisely because he cares only about himself.[22]

So this is the first half of Rousseau's answer to our question: Why is he, and why are we in his footsteps, so obsessed with sincerity? His answer is that, for the reasons just given, hypocrisy is everywhere; it is the universal and essential characteristic of the man of our time, the modern bourgeois. And indeed, since Rousseau, the concept of "bourgeois hypocrisy" and the irritable tendency to find it everywhere has been a staple of Western literature and philosophy.[23]

The Character of Bourgeois Hypocrisy

Before going on to the second half of Rousseau's response to our question, we need to evaluate at least briefly this first argument, which, despite its considerable influence, seems too extreme. Why must we all be secret enemies, one wants to ask, given the relative harmony that exists among our selfish interests? Rousseau anticipates the objection: "If I am answered that society is so constituted that each man gains by serving the others, I shall reply that this would be very well, if he did not gain still more by harming them. There is no profit, however legitimate, that is not surpassed by one that can be made illegitimately, and wrong done to one's neighbor is always more lucrative than services."[24] But does this statement remain true if one looks not only at immediate profit, but at one's long-term self-interest? Perhaps one should rather conclude with Adam Smith that for people in the middle classes, who have no significant power other than their reputation, success "almost always depends upon the favor and good opinion of their neighbors and equals; and without a tolerable regular conduct, these can very seldom be obtained. The good old proverb, therefore, that honesty is the best policy, holds, in such situations, almost always perfectly true."[25]

Indeed, honesty seems to be the characteristic bourgeois virtue. If Rousseau failed to see this, it is because (his terminology notwithstanding) the world he observed was late aristocratic, not bourgeois. And honesty does not flourish in corrupt aristocracies, as Montesquieu pointed out and Smith goes on to argue: "In the superior stations of life the case is unhappily not always the same. In the courts of princes, in the drawing-rooms of the great, where success and preferment depend, not upon the esteem of intelligent and well-informed equals, but upon the fanciful and foolish favour of ignorant, presumptuous, and proud superiors, flattery and falsehood too often prevail over merit and abilities."[26] More generally, in traditional and aristocratic societies, where people are bound to one another with a hundred duties not of their own choosing, doubtless one of them is honesty; but should a person find it necessary on occasion to lie—like the "wily Odysseus"—his standing as a man of honor and virtue need not be fundamentally compromised. But in a bourgeois society, where this web of duties has been swept away and where people face each other as free, atomized, but needy individuals, almost all serious human relationships are voluntarily contracted based on free promise or consent. Here agreement and trust are everything. Precisely here, then, a man is only as good as his word. Thus, as W. E. H. Lecky remarks in his *History of European Morals*:

> Veracity is usually the special virtue of an industrial nation, for
> although industrial enterprise affords great temptations to decep-

tion, mutual confidence, and therefore strict truthfulness, are in these occupations so transcendently important that they acquire in the minds of men a value they had never before possessed. Veracity becomes the first virtue in the moral type, and no character is regarded with any kind of approbation in which it is wanting. . . . This constitutes probably the chief moral superiority of nations pervaded by a strong industrial spirit.[27]

Even if all of this is granted, however, Rousseau would not be without reply. Under the right social and economic conditions, he might argue, people's long-term self-interest may indeed incline them to behave honestly, especially if this calculation is buttressed by additional moral or religious impulses (as in fact Locke, Smith, Tocqueville, and Weber, among others, all assume). But the question is, What is the character of this bourgeois honesty and respectability? No matter how deeply ingrained, Rousseau suspects, at bottom it is false. It still grows out of the fundamental contradiction of selfish sociability or egoistic other-directedness. It is not a virtue embraced for its own sake as something intrinsically good, but is adopted only for the useful impression it makes on others. It is only a necessary evil. Each man earnestly praises it in public—to encourage others to be honest and to convince them that he is so—but in private he knows that it contradicts his heart's desire. Thus the bourgeois may indeed be honest, but he is not sincere; his whole moral posture is a mask worn for others—an act, a role, a lie.[28]

This is the account of bourgeois hypocrisy in its toned-down form, the form that flourished during most of the nineteenth century. In the past fifty years, however, the old, straitlaced honest bourgeois seems gradually to have given way to a new type, closer in many respects to Rousseau's original model. Such writers as C. Wright Mills, Eric Fromm, and above all David Riesman have argued that the increasing bureaucratization of the corporation and the state have revived something like the old courtier spirit. The "inner-directed" man of early capitalism—whose hypocrisy always remained a somewhat controversial hypothesis—is being replaced by the "other-directed" man—whose eager posturing, conformity, and hollowness are far more widely acknowledged.[29]

At any rate, without trying to settle here the precise degree of prevalence of bourgeois hypocrisy, it should be possible, in light of the preceding discussion, at least to characterize more exactly this new kind of hypocrisy identified by Rousseau and note how it differs from earlier forms. Wherever there is a lofty and strenuous moral ideal, as in aristocratic societies or piously Christian ones, there will inevitably be moral hypocrites. But in most cases such persons might more accurately be called "boasters" because their claims ultimately stem from a genuine (if wavering) admiration for the prevailing moral ideal, and they err only in exaggerating their attainment of it.

The new, bourgeois hypocrisy is fundamentally different. The skeptical unmasking of Christian and aristocratic moral hypocrisy is the very precondition for the emergence of the new hypocrisy of interest. Liberated from the pretense to aristocratic self-sufficiency and to divine protection, the bourgeois faces, unprotected, his mortal exposure, his selfish neediness, and therefore his utter dependence on others. Thus, when he raises his exaggerated claims to honesty, he does so not from a genuine faith in or admiration of honesty (as a Christian or aristocratic hypocrite might), but from a calculated desire for the material benefits of being thought honest. Unlike the moral hypocrite, that is, he has no genuine desire to *be* what he endeavors to *seem;* on the contrary, a contradiction exists between his claims and his motive for asserting them. His other-directedness is egoistic. He pretends to care for others because he really cares only for himself.

That is why the bourgeois hypocrite seems so loathsome. The claims he makes for himself are surely less grandiose and probably even less false (as judged by behavior) than those of the aristocratic or Christian hypocrite, but they are more profoundly insincere. He is no longer merely boasting; he is dissimulating, acting, role playing. His public claims constitute a direct denial of his true self. For this reason his hypocrisy is actually worse the more it is successful, for it involves a falsification of the inner life, a fundamental self-betrayal. That is why, in confronting this new hypocrisy, Rousseau and those who follow him invent a new vocabulary of criticism, unknown to earlier moralists, involving such terms as inner nothingness, emptiness, hollowness, phoniness, inauthenticity, and so forth.

Related to this are two other distinctive features of the modern preoccupation with hypocrisy, which also point to its Rousseauian provenence. The condemnation of hypocrisy is obviously not new. The most prominent earlier example is perhaps the Sermon on the Mount. But in all earlier condemnations this vice is regarded as a moral problem of the individual, a natural human foible like cowardice or immoderation. By contrast, in Rousseau and in the view prevailing after him, hypocrisy is regarded as a social and historical problem: it is seen as a widespread deformity of character systematically produced by the evils of modern society. It is "bourgeois" hypocrisy. Conse-quently, hypocrisy in the modern understanding is necessarily a counter-cultural concept—indicting the existing social order—and the attack on it has more the character of social criticism than of moral exhortation.

Moreover, because this vice is blamed on society, the specifically modern concept of hypocrisy tends to go along with the view that only the bohemian intellectual, who is defined by his stance outside and against society, can free himself from this deformity and so recognize it. And this in turn leads to the view that the intellectual has the unique ability and therefore the unique duty to act as the conscience of society and to denounce its hypocrisy wherever and whenever he sees it.[30]

In sum, Rousseau and those who followed him were obsessed with hypoc-risy because of the new prevalence of this vice, resulting from the rise of the bourgeois state, and because of their perceived duty as intellectuals to de-nounce it. And since Rousseau's time this duty has been well fulfilled, produc-ing a torrent of antibourgeois attacks on hypocrisy.

Sincerity as the Highest Good

There is a second part, however, to Rousseau's explanation for his obses-sion with sincerity. If the first points to the prevalence of hypocrisy in his time, the second gives new arguments for the positive good of sincerity. This second part is indeed a necessary addition to the first because the mere fact that hypocrisy is bad and prevalent by no means proves that sincerity is the highest good. The Sermon on the Mount, for example, contains a famous attack on hypocrisy, but this leads not to a praise of sincerity as such but rather to the praise of piety—sincere piety. There is no suggestion here that the nonbeliever could justify himself before God by emphasizing his sincerity.

Similarly, in Shakespeare and Molière we find much emphasis on the falseness of men's claims to virtue and nobility, but the opposite of hypocritical nobility is still taken to be genuine nobility—not sincerity as such. Thus Rousseau (and we after him) is doing something fundamentally new when he makes the seemingly obvious move from blaming hypocrisy to praising sincerity—that is, praising not sincere piety, or sincere righteousness, but sincerity itself and by itself. In other words, Rousseau is the first to define the good as being oneself regardless of what one may be. And that is a radically new position—a position that is at the core of his and our unique obsession with sincerity.

To uphold this new view is the point of the second part of Rousseau's answer, which consists of a defense of the goodness of sincerity as such. But this argument actually brings us into the most fundamental level of Rousseau's thought, for his defense of sincerity is really a consequence of his whole new understanding of human nature, his comprehensive redefinition of the human self.

According to Rousseau, the fundamental principle of human nature is self-love: the innate inclination to delight in, preserve, and actualize ourselves.[31] But this claim is certainly not new; many earlier thinkers had taken such a view. The crucial issue is, What is the human self that we incline to delight in, preserve, and actualize? Here is where Rousseau will give a new answer.

Aristotle, for example, makes the famous statement that man is a political animal. And by this he means that the true human self is a public or communal self, that a human being cannot be himself by himself, that he can truly realize himself and come into his own only by performing his function within the larger political whole. Plato maintains that our truest self is our reason or mind, and that we actualize ourselves most fully through the act of philosophic contemplation. Saint Augustine holds that our highest good and truest self is God; and that self-love, fully conscious of itself, is the same as the love of God.

Rousseau rejects all these earlier accounts. The starting point for his new reflections on the self is the same as that, seen above, for his analysis of the modern state and the origins of hypocrisy: the theoretical individualism of early modern thought—only deepened and radicalized.

Rousseau maintains that the true foundation of the human self is not God or reason or the community but the elemental self-consciousness of the individual. Although he does not present a systematic derivation of his views, Rousseau's argument seems to run as follows. In every act of awareness or perception, I am always simultaneously aware that I perceive. And furthermore, in thus perceiving that *I* perceive, I necessarily perceive myself. Therefore there is a self-awareness that necessarily accompanies every act of awareness as such. This is the famous "sentiment of existence": the sheer awareness that I am, that I exist. And it is in this elemental self-consciousness that Rousseau locates the true human self and the foundation of our being. Somehow a human being exists not through his relation to God or to the essence of man, but through a relation to himself. Our being is our presence to ourself, our sentiment of existence.[32]

The exact meaning and ground of these claims are, to be sure, not altogether clear. But what can be seen fairly clearly are their consequences, which emerge if we plug them back into the theory of self-love we began with. The fundamental human inclination, we have seen, is self-love, which impels us to preserve and actualize ourselves. We want, as fully as possible, to become what we are, to realize ourselves, to become as alive and actualized as possible, to really live. But how, concretely, we ought to go about this depends on the true nature of the human self.

In this context Rousseau's new definition of the self has the following meaning: The true way to actualize oneself is not through the love of God, or philosophic contemplation of the cosmos, or participation in the political order, but through withdrawal from everything else and communion with one's inner self.

Here, in short, is Rousseau's argument for the positive good of sincerity. As we can see now, it is not merely an ethical argument praising the morally virtuous character of sincerity. Nor is it a political argument about the social usefulness of sincerity. Rather, it is an argument issuing from the deepest claims regarding the nature of human existence. Rousseau argues that sincerity is the highest good in life because it is the essential path to genuine selfhood and self-realization. What piety is for Saint Augustine, what contemplation is for Plato, sincerity is for Rousseau. It is the unique means through which we draw closer to Being and make ourselves most real.[33]

Let me try to elaborate this point, and render it more specific, by distinguishing six fundamental characteristics of the new Rousseauian self and by showing how each of these, in its own way, leads to the canonization of sincerity as the royal road to self-realization. In doing this I may be forced, in places, to extend Rousseau's ideas beyond his own formulations of them—yet not beyond the general tendency of his thought, or so I believe.

First, because the sentiment of existence is completely internal, the true self is emphatically private. The real me is not my social self or communal self: it is not what I am in other people's eyes, nor is it my role in the community, my public activity and political participation. The real me is the one that is there when I am alone.

Rousseau is aware that the public world of honor, power, and status seems to us more real and important. But he endeavors with all his force to convince us that this is a deadly illusion: that the public world is an alienation from the true self, that the private world of feelings and intimacies is actually the more real one. Rousseau consciously strives to subvert the public world and to make people more withdrawn, inward, intimate, self-absorbed, and introspective.

Of course Rousseau also knows, indeed emphasizes, that for civilized, socialized, and especially urbanized human beings it is no easy matter to get free of the social self, which does not simply disappear behind closed doors. But he believes that those who live in relative isolation, or are willing to retreat there, if they will commune with themselves in the company of nature and a few close friends or family members, can succeed over time in recovering contact with a good part of their natural sentiments and selves. In other words, Rousseau has a faith, if a very qualified one, in the power of introspection—a crucial presupposition of the ideal of sincerity. Self-knowledge does not require a rigorous dialectical examination of our opinions and beliefs or an externally applied psychoanalytic examination of the subconscious mind. The Rousseauian self is more immediately accessible. Ultimately, we can find and know and be ourselves through introspection and sincerity.[34]

Second, for Rousseau the true self is not the rational self. We are not our intellect, our mind, but our feelings. The ground of our being is the sentiment of existence, which is a sentiment, a feeling: "to exist, for us, is to feel [*sentir*]."[35]

As for reason, in Rousseau's view it is recently acquired and rather unnatural. It may indeed be the most impressive or powerful of our faculties, but it is not a very deep part of us: that is, it does not control our behavior and, more important, it is not the ground of our being or existence. Therefore we actualize ourselves not by reasoning or contemplating reality, but by communing with our sentiments and feelings. From the standpoint of Rousseauian selfhood, it is less important to be true to reality than to be true to oneself. So the ideal of wisdom must be replaced with that of sincerity.

Third, the true self is not the moral self. Rousseau knows that human beings, though by nature solitary and free, have the capacity to invent laws, contract obligations, create ethical and religious duties, and then force themselves to comply with these. Civilized human beings are self-overcoming animals who will conquer and repress their spontaneous inclinations and natural selves in the name of certain ethical ideals.

Rousseau sees this as socially salutary, indeed necessary, and spends much time admiring it; but ultimately he sees it as unnatural. The true self is the spontaneous self, not this invented and forcibly imposed moral character. The real me is the one that remains when I let go and stop trying, when I just let it be. I truly find myself when, rejecting all the strenuous talk about my higher self, and liberated from shame and guilt, I just freely observe and sincerely acknowledge all that goes on within my soul. I must "be myself" regardless of *what* I may be. So again, the true me is accessed through sincerity.[36]

Fourth, my true self is not primarily what I have in common with others— my share of universal human nature—but rather what is particular and unique to me. For in nature only the individual or particular is real; everything universal is a human creation, indeed a falsification, a distorting imposition on reality. Thus everything in myself that I have in common with others probably derives from the alien influence of society. Everything in me that is particular, unique, and idiosyncratic is likely to derive from my true inner self.[37]

One consequence of this is as follows. If my truest being were something universal—like participation in the universal nature or essence of man—then I could come to recognize and understand myself best through a kind of rational knowledge. Then the Delphic imperative to "know thyself" would mean "know human nature." But if the deepest thing in me is unique, then I can only know myself personally, and the whole enterprise of rational self-knowledge must be replaced by each individual's introspection and sincerity.

Fifth, just as the Rousseauian self is not universal but rather particular, so also it does not have the character of a form or a formal cause. The elemental self-consciousness that is the ground of our being does not have any form or idea or essence: it is a pure sentiment of *existence*. It is a pure awareness *that* we are—without any specification of *what* we are. Thus the human self has the character not of a form but, as it were, of a source or a wellspring. And so self-realization does not mean arranging one's soul in the proper order, or being in conformity with the formal essence or objective nature of man. Rather, it means being in touch with our source, "connecting" with our wellspring, being "on-line." For Rousseau, being oneself does not mean corresponding to oneself but rather *coming from* oneself—and thus it means sincerity. For the sincere person is he who always makes his true self his source and origin.

The sixth and last characteristic involves a twist. The true self is "expansive." After one has finally retreated from all the social sources of falsehood and hypocrisy and turned back to the plenitude of the natural self, one finds that an important part of that self is a quasi-erotic inclination to "expand" the self outward in pursuit of a still greater aliveness.[38] The presence of other human beings alienates me from myself so long as I hold up my social self to greet and confront theirs. But when, withdrawing within, I discover my true, private self, it also becomes possible to discover and "identify with" theirs, to connect inside to inside, to be witness to the intense, trembling reality that another's life has for him, and in this way to excite and heighten the experience of my own life, to make my existence more real to me. To the extent, then, that the Rousseauian self seeks to connect to some larger reality, it is to the inner flow of human life and suffering. Rousseau, one might say, replaces classical contemplation with a caring voyeurism. And once again, sincerity, both one's own and others', is the essential condition of this experience.[39]

Conclusion

In sum, Rousseau radically reinterprets the character of human existence, arguing that the true human self, rooted in the sentiment of existence, is private rather than public, sentimental rather than rational, spontaneous rather than moral, unique rather than universal, originary rather than formal, and compassionately expansive rather than closed. And each one of these changes, in a different way, makes sincerity the key to self-actualization. This fact, together with the new prevalence of hypocrisy in the emerging bourgeois order, explains why Rousseau was so obsessed with sincerity. And I believe that an experience of hypocrisy and a conception of the self similar to Rousseau's lies behind much of our own preoccupation with sincerity.

By way of conclusion, I shall briefly speculate on how the character of Rousseau's argument may also help us understand one further feature of our love of sincerity. As we have seen, the hatred of hypocrisy and longing for sincerity first emerged not as an expression of the dominant culture, but as a reaction against it, as a countercultural ideal employed by bohemian intellectuals in their critique of bourgeois society. But in recent decades the ideal of sincerity has clearly become general, permeating the whole of society. Today everyone denounces conformity and longs for sincerity. In other words, as suggested above, one of the strangest characteristics of our society is that in some measure everyone has internalized the intellectual critique of bourgeois life. Everyone contains some mix of culture and counterculture. And everything that once seemed so resolutely antibourgeois has now come to light as only late bourgeois.

If this observation is correct, it might be useful to look once again to Rousseau for an explanation. We have seen that the theoretical principles underlying both parts of Rousseau's analysis are largely borrowed from the very thinkers he is attacking. Specifically, Rousseau's central premise, his extreme individualism, is only an extension and radicalization of the bourgeois individualism of Hobbes and Locke. But this means that Rousseau's critique of modern culture is essentially a dialectical critique: he shows that the very principles of that culture, when thought through in all their inner tensions, lead one to a countercultural stance. Rousseau's main argument is indeed that modern society builds on a massive contradiction: it is based on individualism, and for this very reason it destroys all sincere individuality. Both sides of this contradiction combine, in Rousseau, to produce an intense and redoubled longing for individuality—an obsession with sincerity.

Nothing prevents others from eventually reenacting this same dialectical process. Indeed, if one can generalize from the argument and the example of Rousseau, it seems that bourgeois culture contains the seeds of its own critique, and that the antibourgeois intellectual is the inevitable outgrowth of the thing he criticizes. But if he is that, then he is also an outgrowth that will tend to spread. To generalize still further, it looks as if a society based upon Lockean individualism will tend sooner or later to generate a kind of Rousseauian anti-Lockeanism which will slowly become general while remaining in permanent and unresolved tension with the original, Lockean substratum. Some such process, at any rate, appears to be at work in our ever-spreading and ever-frustrated longing for sincerity.

NOTES

1. Friedrich Nietzsche, *On the Genealogy of Morals*, trans. Walter Kaufman and R. J. Hollingdale (New York: Random House, 1967), 15.

2. Allan Bloom, introduction to Jean-Jacques Rousseau, *Emile, or On Education*, trans. Allan Bloom (New York: Basic Books, 1979), 4.

3. Judith N. Shklar, *Ordinary Vices* (Cambridge: Harvard University Press, 1984), 45.

4. Richard Sennett, *The Fall of Public Man: On the Social Psychology of Capitalism* (New York: Vintage Books, 1974).

5. Lionel Trilling, *Sincerity and Authenticity* (Cambridge: Harvard University Press, 1971), 23–25.

6. Christopher Lasch, *The Culture of Narcissism: American Life in an Age of Diminishing Expectations* (New York: W. W. Norton, 1979). Lasch also points out that practicing psychiatrists have reported "a shift in the pattern of the symptoms displayed by their patients. The classic neuroses treated by Freud, they said, were giving way to narcissistic personality disorders" (238).

7. Alexis de Tocqueville, *Democracy in America*, ed. J. P. Mayer, trans. George Lawrence (Garden City, N.Y.: Doubleday, 1969), 530–34.

8. Ibid., 589.

9. Ibid., 607.

10. Ibid., 587–89.

11. Ibid., 525–27.

12. It should also be said that, whereas Tocqueville sees democratic citizens as free of aristocratic formality and hypocrisy, he emphasizes that they tend to their own unique form of hypocrisy and conformism—stemming, in his view, from the tyranny of the majority.

13. This fact, observed by many interpreters, is the great theme of Jean Starobinski's study, *Jean-Jacques Rousseau: La transparence et l'obstacle* (Paris: Gallimard, 1971).

14. See *Emile*, 358–60, 370–71, 385, 387.

15. See Jean-Jacques Rousseau, *On the Social Contract, with Geneva Manuscript and Political Economy*, ed. Roger D. Masters, trans. Judith R. Masters (New York: St. Martin's Press, 1978), 69; *Emile*, 120; *Preface of a Second Letter to Bordes*, in *The First and Second Discourses*, ed. and trans. Victor Gourevitch (New York: Harper and Row, 1986), 114–15. See also Starobinski, *La transparence et l'obstacle*, 125–26; and Judith N. Shklar, "Rousseau's Images of Authority," in *Hobbes and Rousseau: A Collection of Critical Essays*, ed. Maurice Cranston and Richard S. Peters (Garden City, N.Y.: Doubleday, 1972), 333–65.

16. Montesquieu, *Eloge de la sincérité*, in *Oeuvres complètes*, ed. Roger Caillois (Paris: Gallimard, 1949), 1:101. This essay seems to have been written sometime between 1716 and 1728. See also the passage from Duclos's *Considerations sur les moeurs de ce siècle*, quoted by Rousseau in *Emile*, 338.

17. Ibid., 102, 104–5.

18. Jean-Jacques Rousseau, *Second Discourse*, in *The First and Second Discourses*, trans. Roger D. Masters and Judith R. Masters (New York: St. Martin's Press, 1964), 180. See also 156, 194; *First Discourse*, 36–39; *Emile*, 230.

19. See *First Discourse*, 51; preface to *Narcissus*, in *First and Second Discourses*, trans. Gourevitch, 105.

20. Introduction to *Emile*, 5.

21. Preface to *Narcissus*, 105. See also *Second Discourse*, 156, 172–75, 193–95; *Discourse on Political Economy*, in *On the Social Contract, with Geneva Manuscript and Political Economy*, ed. Roger D. Masters, trans. Judith R. Masters (New York: St. Martin's Press, 1978), 216–17; *Letter to Beaumont*, in *Oeuvres complètes*, ed. Bernard Gagnebin and Marcel Raymond (Paris: Bibliothèque de la Pléiade, 1959–69), 936.

22. These points are argued at greater length in Arthur M. Melzer, *The Natural Goodness of Man: On the System of Rousseau's Thought* (Chicago: University of Chicago Press, 1990), 59–82.

23. It will seem strange to call the man of Rousseau's aristocratic age a "bourgeois," but that is Rousseau's own usage (see *Emile*, 40), adopted in full knowledge of its provocative character (perhaps on the model of Molière's comic title *Le bourgeois gentilhomme*—only reversed). Rousseau does not accept the traditional distinction of classes. The true class division of the human species, after all, should follow the division

of the truest social good—which for Rousseau is neither wealth nor privilege but freedom. Thus there are three classes of men. The first is the "citizen," who enjoys "civil freedom" because, while needing other human beings, he also loves and lives for them. A second class is the asocial "savage" (and to some extent the free peasant), who, neither needing others nor loving them, enjoys "natural freedom." Virtually all the rest of humanity forms a third, slavish class midway between the other two: the social individual—archetypally the "town dweller," the urban noncitizen—who, while needing others, loves and lives for himself alone. This is the "bourgeois." It includes the French aristocracy, for "one who believes himself the master of others is nonetheless a greater slave than they" (but see *Emile*, 346, 451, for the conventional use of "bourgeois").

24. *Second Discourse*, 194–95.

25. Adam Smith, *The Theory of Moral Sentiments* (Indianapolis: Liberty Classics, 1969), 128.

26. Ibid., 129.

27. W. E. H. Lecky, *History of European Morals from Augustus to Charlemagne*, 2 vols. (New York: D. Appleton, 1879), 138; cf. 155. See also Schopenhauer's "The Wisdom of Life," in *The Essays of Arthur Schopenhauer*, trans. T. Bailey Saunders (New York: Willey Books, 1935), 70–73.

28. Bourgeois honesty will be less hypocritical, of course, in the degree to which the "additional moral or religious impulses" mentioned above are dominant. The bourgeois virtues become genuinely and intrinsically attractive through the nobility of "self-reliance," the pleasures of sympathy and approbation, the proto-Kantian dignity of foresighted self-denial and rational self-mastery, and the religious faith that God helps those who honestly help themselves. But Rousseau, who doubted man's natural sociality, had little faith in the power of any morality outside the total moralizing environment of the militantly patriotic city-state. In general, the more skeptical one is, the more hypocrites one sees.

29. See Mills's account of the "new entrepreneur" in C. Wright Mills, "The Competitive Personality," *Partisan Review* 13 (September 1946): 433–41, and Eric Fromm's description of the "marketing orientation" in *Man for Himself: An Enquiry into the Psychology of Ethics* (New York: Fawcett Books, 1947), 75–89. See David Riesman with Nathan Glazer and Reuel Denny, *The Lonely Crowd: A Study of the Changing American Character* (New Haven: Yale University Press, 1950), esp. 17–24, 45–48.

Although there is wide consensus concerning the conformist character of contemporary American life, there remains some disagreement as to its cause. The primary non-Rousseauian line of explanation derives from Tocqueville and John Stuart Mill (augmented by Nietzsche and Ortega y Gasset), who blame equality and the tyranny of the majority more than competitive individualism.

30. See, for example, *Dialogues*, in *Oeuvres complètes*, 1:936; *Letter to Beaumont*, 965; *Emile*, 474; letter to Perdriau, 28 September 1754, in *Correspondance complète*, ed. R. A. Leigh (Geneva: Institute et Musée Voltaire, 1969).

31. *Emile*, 212–13; *Second Discourse*, 95, 221–22.

32. Consider *Second Discourse*, 142; *Emile*, 42, 61; *Oeuvres complètes* 2:1124–25; *Dialogues*, 805–6.

33. On the argument of the last several paragraphs, see also Melzer, *Natural Goodness of Man*, 35–46, and Pierre Burgelin, *La philosophie de l'existence de Jean-Jacques Rousseau* (Paris: Presses Universitaires de France, 1952), 115–48.

34. Here again we see a stark contrast with Montesquieu's *Praise of Sincerity*, the first premise of which is that self-knowledge through introspection is impossible. That is precisely why "sincerity" is so crucial: others must frankly tell us the truth about ourselves, for we have no other means of discovering it (see 99–102). In this essay Montesquieu is really praising "frankness" about others, and precisely on the premise that true Rousseauian sincerity—that is, accurate self-disclosure—is impossible.

For Rousseau's own later misgivings about the adequacy of introspection, see his *The Reveries of the Solitary Walker*, trans. Charles E. Butterworth (New York: New York University Press, 1979), 43, 75. See also Starobinski, *La transparence et l'obstacle*, 216–17.

35. *Emile*, 290 (I have altered the translation). See *Dialogues*, 806; *Lettres morales*, in *Oeuvres complètes*, 4:1109.

36. Consider *Dialogues*, 668–71, 822–25; *Reveries*, 77. From here one sees most clearly the fundamental difference between Rousseau's new concern with hypocrisy and sincerity—his increased "inwardness"—and the apparently similar concern found in the Gospels (and in the late Stoics, such as Marcus Aurelius). The latter clearly grows from a heightened longing for moral purity. It calls for inwardness, self-scrutiny, and confession in order to increase our moral striving and to intensify our repentance. Rousseauian sincerity, by contrast, intends and produces the opposite effect: it encourages self-acceptance and the release from shame. It would have us acknowledge our inner weaknesses, saying: "This is the way I am. I cannot change how I feel. I will not lie about it." It makes the acknowledgment of vice into a virtue. The only true sin is insincerity itself.

37. See *Emile*, 91, 94, 97; *La nouvelle Héloïse*, in *Oeuvres complètes*, 2:563, 568.

38. See *Dialogues*, 805–6, 1324–25; *Emile*, 67, 159, 168; *Reveries*, 92, 95. See also Ronald Grimsley, "Rousseau and the Problem of Happiness," in Cranston and Peters, *Hobbes and Rousseau*, 437–61.

39. See *Reveries*, 81; *Emile*, 220–31. One sees from this point the essential inner connection between sincerity and compassion, that other great idol of Rousseau's thought and of our world. This connection, in turn, further grounds or justifies the ideal of sincerity, by reassuring us that "being oneself" will in fact make one, if not actively moral or "virtuous," then at least "good," that is, compassionate and disinclined to harm others.

❦ 14 ❧
Rousseau and the Discovery
of Political Compassion

CLIFFORD ORWIN

No one can doubt that the rhetoric of compassion has helped shape democratic politics. The American presidential election of 1992 featured not only
"the economy, stupid," but a perceived contrast between a more compassionate candidate and a less compassionate one. This perception may have been
unfair to President Bush, who had sought to evoke a "kinder, gentler America"; if he failed to convince the voters that he felt for them, it was not for want
of trying. Even politicians with hard noses have endorsed the necessity of a
warm heart: Lyndon Johnson once remarked that John Connally didn't "have
even the tiniest trace of compassion; . . . that'll keep him from the top."[1] Nor
did the Republican landslide of 1994 in any way refute Johnson's premise.
"Compassion for victims, not criminals": the voters of America punished the
Democrats for their *lack* of sympathetic concern—for being "out of touch"
with decent, hardworking, sorely beleaguered people like themselves. To say
nothing of the fact that with the end of the Cold War the issue of "humanitarianism" now dominates Western debate about foreign policy.[2]

Although many factors have promoted the rise of compassion in the modern era, that thinker whose contribution was greatest was Rousseau. He pre-
sided over the dawn of political compassion: we might almost say he staged it.
Christian charity long antedates him, but charity is not compassion, however
we may tend to confuse them. Charity is divine in origin and otherworldly in
intention: to love one's fellow as Christ loves him is to strive for the salvation of
his soul. Compassion by contrast is purely human (humanity is almost a
synonym for it) and is altogether this-worldly. Whereas charity requires that
the Christian rise above his sinful human nature (invoking the assistance of
divine grace), compassion is a merely natural sentiment, which attests to the
goodness or innocence of our nature. As such it is from the Christian perspective self-indulgent: a form of pride or even idolatry.[3]

If compassion was not a theological virtue, neither had the older philosophers promoted it. On this consider the judgment of Victor Hugo. "Plus saint

que Socrate, plus grand que Platon": thus in his poem "Le crapaud" does he eulogize a donkey who steps out of his way to avoid crushing a toad.[4] Bathetic Hugo may have been, but he was not misinformed. Socrates and Plato had not championed compassion; God knows how many trodden toads littered the road to Academe. As for Plato's pupil Aristotle, he treats pity not in the *Ethics*, his account of the virtues, but in the *Rhetoric*, his account of the passions, those dark irrational movements of our soul that virtue enables us to master.[5]

With Rousseau, by contrast, compassion seizes center stage as *the* morally fruitful sentiment. To grasp the implications of this, it is necessary to consider both why morality becomes in Rousseau a matter of sentiment rather than of grace or of reason and why compassion is the sentiment so favored.

It was the *Discourse on Inequality* that made Rousseau's reputation as the apostle of compassion. The *Discourse* charts man's progression from the innocent contentment of the state of nature to the frightful disorder, oppression, and misery of civil society. It fosters either or both of two apparently opposite attitudes, each wholly novel to political philosophy. On the one hand, radical despair or nostalgia for a lost wholeness and innocence that cannot be regained; on the other, radical hopefulness concerning the possibility of recreating that wholeness in some future civil society. Each is a possible interpretation of the central theoretical achievement of the work, Rousseau's historicization of the question of human nature. Each found many takers.

Compassion, like other major themes of the *Discourse*, must be related to this theoretical core, and it partakes of this crucial ambiguity. In one of the most fervent passages of a fervent work, Rousseau offers compassion as the only pure, the only natural morality, a precious remnant of man's pristine goodness.[6] He presents it as the still small voice of primordial sentiment among the delirious passions of us so-called rational beings. His official argument is that, as reason and amour propre wax, compassion must inevitably wane. The solidarity that prevailed among men by nature depended on their lack of reason and therefore of individuality; now that reason has come between them natural pity may be regretted, but it cannot be regained. Pity thus furnishes one eloquent plank of Rousseau's eulogy of the state of nature and his corresponding blame of civil society.

On the other hand, and for the same reason, compassion looms within the *Discourse* as *the* moral standard for civil man. Rousseau's very presentation of today's compassion as a faded relic of its resplendent natural self aims to goad us and to fortify it. There remains for us a natural alternative; we are not completely forlorn. Compassion is the last refuge of nature in our state of greatest estrangement from it. It constitutes the sole remaining possibility of communion or intimacy with our fellow human beings. As the alternative to reason and amour propre, it figures in the rhetoric of the *Discourse* as the genuine, sincere, or authentic—in a word, natural—response to the present unnatural human condition.

I have mentioned Socratic justice and Christian charity as predecessors of (and alternatives to) Rousseauian compassion, to which we might add the enlightened self-interest of Hobbes and the other thinkers of the Enlightenment. However little these three moral strategies might otherwise have in common, all, according to Rousseau, are deficient for the same reason. They all presume human beings to be more rational than they are. None founds morality in the only place it can be founded, in sentiment rather than in reason. Rousseau embraces compassion for the very reason Aristotle had rejected it: because it is subrational, because indeed it and rationality are at odds. "Although it may behoove Socrates and Minds of his stamp to acquire virtue through reason, the human Race would have perished long ago if its preservation had depended only on the reasoning of its members."[7]

Although critics of compassion may condemn it as soft, Rousseau's reasons for promoting it are harsh, indeed Machiavellian. He offers it not as the most perfect basis for morality but as the most effective. His praise of compassion is one aspect of his moral realism. Consider the following note to book 4 of *Emile*, which goes even further than the passage just cited from the *Discourse*, for it traces even what was there described as "the sublime precept of reasoned morality" to the collaboration of reason and sentiment:

> Even the precept of doing unto others as we would have them do
> unto us has no true foundation other than conscience and senti-
> ment; for where is the precise reason for me, being myself, to act as
> if I were another, especially when I am morally certain of never
> finding myself in the same situation? And who will guarantee me
> that in very faithfully following this maxim I will get others to
> follow it similarly with me? The wicked man gets advantage from
> the just man's probity and his own injustice. He is delighted that
> everyone, with the exception of himself, be just. This agreement,
> whatever may be said about it, is not very advantageous for good
> men. But when the strength of an expansive soul makes me iden-
> tify myself with my fellow, and I feel that I am, so to speak, in him,

it is in order not to suffer that I do not want him to suffer. I am interested in him for love of myself, and the reason for the precept is in nature itself, which inspires in me the desire of my well-being in whatever place I feel my existence. From this I conclude that it is not true that the precepts of natural law are founded on reason alone. They have a base more solid and sure. Love of men derived from love of self is the principle of all human justice. The summation of all morality is given by the Gospel in its summation of the law.[8]

Reason divides men; only sentiment reliably unites them. Each of these points requires emphasis. Against Hobbes and Locke and their followers, Rousseau insists that no amount of reasoning based on self-interest ever leads to true concern for one's fellow as opposed to a fraudulent show of it. It is not merely that Enlightenment thought overestimates the possibilities of reason, however, but that it underestimates those of sentiment. His invocation of the gospel is misleading, for what the Evangelist derives from God's wholly selfless love for us (and from our consequent obligation to return it), Rousseau derives from the love of each of us for himself.

From this derivation of compassion from the sentiment of self-love, it follows that the more complete our identification of ourselves with the other, the more perfect and powerful our compassion for him.

Even should it be true that commiseration is only a sentiment that puts us in the place of him who suffers—a sentiment that is obscure and strong in savage man, developed but weak in civilized man—what would this idea matter to the truth of what I say, except to give it more force? In fact, commiseration will be all the more energetic as the observing animal identifies himself more intimately with the suffering animal. Now it is evident that this identification must have been infinitely closer in the state of nature than in the state of reasoning. Reasoning engenders vanity (*amour-propre*) and reflection fortifies it; reason turns man back upon himself. . . . His fellow man can be murdered with impunity right under his window; [the philosopher] has only to put his hands over his ears and argue with himself a bit to prevent nature, which revolts within him, from identifying him with the man who is being assassinated.[9]

Rousseau offers this reductionist analysis of the psychology of pity not spontaneously, but as a concession to a hypothetical objection. Still, it is the only analysis of its psychology that he offers, and other evidence in the passage supports the suspicion that it is his own. Compassion thus understood as depending on "identification" is in a sense unreasonable; "reason turns man back upon himself" by reminding him that the sufferer is someone else, that he himself is quite all right. Compassion must have been stronger in the state of nature than it is in society, because there it would have faced no challenge from reason. The state of human bestiality must have been the lost golden age of the power of compassion.

If we could rest content with this argument for the inverse relation of reason and pity (and therefore of society and pity), Rousseau's presentation of compassion would seem relatively straightforward (and straightforwardly elegiac). In fact, however, this argument, though not entirely misleading, does prove to be overdrawn. Bestiality is not simply friendly to compassion, or society simply harmful to it.

In the first place we must note a crucial qualification of the very passage just cited. Compassion is *obscure* and strong—or lively (*vif*)—in savage man, *developed* but weak in civilized man. Rousseau does not deny that there is a respect in which pity as we know it, however enfeebled, is actually superior to that of our presumed feral forebears. And though he does not state the implications of this concession, he quietly provides evidence that he has reflected on them.

There is no question but that compassion is weak in comparison with the other passions of social man, and that reason and amour propre do collude to establish that distance from the sufferings of our fellow that Rousseau presents as so repulsive. Yet it follows both from Rousseau's formulations and from the weight of his examples that in instances where no selfish passion obtrudes, compassion is actually more powerful in society than in the state of nature. It is, for example, not to natural commiseration but to "pity modified by reason" (reason, the rhetorical villain in the piece) that Rousseau credits what he calls the "social virtues" of humanity, benevolence, clemency, friendship, and generosity. If pity is more lively in natural man, that is indeed because he lacks the reasoning required to disengage himself from his identification with his suffering fellow. For this very reason, however, his pity is "obscure": it will never rise above mere mute, self-absorbed horror.[10] Natural man is nothing if not literal-minded. "His imagination paints nothing for him." "Imagination does not speak to his heart." Imagination, as Rousseau stresses in every other context, develops only with reason.

Reason cuts both ways; if its progress weakens commiseration in some respects, it expands its possibilities in others. The tyrant Sulla, who, arriving at the theater stained with the blood of his fellow citizens, cannot refrain from weeping at the sorrows of Hecuba,[11] is far more sensitive to human suffering than natural man could have been. He is also, however, more capable of steeling himself against it. The weakness of compassion in society is not absolute but relative. Stronger absolutely through the development of reason and imagination, it is weaker relatively because this same development has fed the passions with which compassion must compete.

Without some grasp of reason's positive contribution to compassion, we cannot comprehend the peak of Rousseau's presentation of pity in the *Discourse:* his evocation of the "great cosmopolitan souls." These few sages "breach the imaginary barriers that separate peoples and, following the example of the sovereign Being that created them, include the whole human race in their benevolence."[12] The great cosmopolitan soul is not the least but the most reasonable of men, who rises furthest above the conventions that hamper the rest of us like blinders. Compassion figures here as the basis of a new morality that, while surely not founded solely on reason, is open only to those few human beings whose vision is clearest.

In the end the very realism that compels Rousseau to prefer a sentimental basis of morality to a rational one also compels him to co-opt reason for his project. Whatever may have been the basis of compassion in the state of nature, in society it depends on the proper education of our sentiments by means of both reason and imagination. Rousseau's rhetorical strategy is intended to further such an education, and the *Discourse* itself offers a fine example of this strategy. From it we are to come to see as never before the preponderance of suffering in social life, and so to learn to be ashamed of our past lack of response to it. In this respect the *Discourse* aims to provide an experience not unlike that of Lear on the heath.

This emphasis on education to compassion will explain why it is not the *Discourse* but rather *Emile,* Rousseau's treatise on education, that contains his definitive treatment of compassion. Compassion furnishes one of the great themes of *Emile,* but like all the others it can be interpreted only within the context of the work as a whole. It is therefore necessary to begin this aspect of our discussion by taking a few steps backward.

Within the context of *Emile*, the greatest importance of compassion is not to society but to Emile himself. It sees him through the most difficult stage of education, that beginning with puberty. The perils of puberty include precocious sexual experience, which both coarsens and depletes human character, and a ruinous explosion of amour propre. From the first of these evils, the second would be sure to follow: precocious sexuality would plunge Emile into a maelstrom of comparisons and render him dependent on the wills of others. "From the bosom of so many diverse passions I see opinion raise an unshakable throne, and stupid mortals, subjected to its empire, basing their own existence on the judgments of others."[13]

The alternative to ruinous precocity proves to be sublimation. Of this last Rousseau is the great discoverer and apostle, for he is the first to interpret the whole of the "higher" life of man in terms of the sublimation of the lower.[14] Because nature has no clear intentions for human sexuality beyond mere feral copulation, imagination must (and will) supply the want of a higher natural end (i.e., of the *eros* of the Greek philosophers). He who guides the imagination of the adolescent thus disposes of an enormous reservoir of vitality, effervescent but without a determinate object, susceptible then to being diverted into a variety of channels.

Only with adolescence, then, is compassion possible for Emile, and only then is it necessary for him. It is sensuality that awakens in him the capacity for compassion, and it is compassion that furnishes the salutary alternative to precocious sexual experience. If properly sublimated, his new ardor will nourish the moral element in human life, which raises us above the beasts and "humanizes" our relations with others.

The first of the sublimations on which morality depends is the one that issues in compassion. "It is man's weakness which makes him sociable; it is our common miseries which turn our hearts to humanity."[15] Where Hobbes had sought to reform human life through appealing to rational self-interest, Rousseau seeks to do so through evoking fellow feeling. Yet this very departure from Hobbes discloses Rousseau's indebtedness to him. If, as already noted, Rousseau rejects Hobbes's rationalism, he ratifies Hobbes's fateful decision to refound human life on a negative orientation rather than a positive one. He agrees with Hobbes that what unites human beings is not (as earlier thinkers had claimed) a natural common good, but merely a common natural frailty. Hobbes, however, had sought to build on our fear of incurring suffering ourselves, and on an alleged rational self-interest grounded in this fear: thus would we refrain from harming others simply out of concern for ourselves. Rousseau, by contrast—convinced of the infeasibility of this scheme—solicits a response to the sufferings of others founded on our experience of our own. He appeals not to selfish interest but to genuine mutual concern.

Again I must stress that Rousseau is not a more "idealistic" thinker than Hobbes—on the contrary, he rejects Hobbes's argument precisely for its excessive "idealism."[16] His turn from self-interest to compassion reflects his determination that the former, no matter how cleverly manipulated, is unequal to the task of reforming social life. The faith in its sufficiency thus stands revealed as utopian. Compassion emerges by contrast as a social resource worth exploiting. This is not to say that his understanding of it is mushy. His exposition of pity in *Emile* features three maxims that summarize this understanding (although they cannot be said to exhaust it).[17] In keeping with Rousseau's moral realism, these maxims have in common that they stress not only the power but the limits of compassion.

First maxim: "It is not in the human heart to put ourselves in the place of people who are happier than we are, but only in that of those who are more pitiable." The superior good fortune of others does not touch us; or rather, it touches us with envy, driving a wedge between us and them. Apparent exceptions to this harsh rule are merely apparent. Where the contentment of the other is fully within our own reach (is such that we can condescend to it, as with the amusements of children and rustics), then indeed we can share it. Otherwise the happiness of others adds nothing to our own and in no way draws us closer to them.

With this maxim Rousseau reveals the distance that separates him from his sometime reader Adam Smith, for whom "sympathy" figures as the basis of a morality of the "impartial spectator."[18] According to Rousseau it is impossible to achieve impartiality through sympathy, for our capacity even for the latter is strictly limited by the primacy of our self-concern.

"It follows, therefore, that in order to incline a young man to humanity, far from making him admire the brilliant lot of others, one must show him the sad sides of that lot; one must make him fear it." What this implies is in the first instance that the tutor must begin the education of Emile's sentiments by exposing him not to cases of seeming good fortune—for this would only embitter him—but to those of the most obvious misery: wretched illness and poverty and the like.

Second maxim: "One pities in others only those ills from which one does not feel oneself exempt." Here Rousseau cites Virgil's Dido: "Non ignora mali, miseris succurrere disco" ("No stranger to affliction, I learn to succor the wretched").[19] "I know nothing so beautiful, so profound, so touching, so true as this verse." This maxim helps Rousseau explain why the upper classes are so harsh toward the poor; even should they acknowledge the latter's misery, that misery is nothing to them. Emile by contrast is to be raised to feel keenly his exposure to the winds of fortune and to natural human frailty. He must come "to feel that not all human prudence will be able to answer whether in an hour he will be alive or dead, whether the sufferings of the nephretic will not before nightfall be causing him to grind his teeth, whether in a month he will be rich or poor, whether in a year, perhaps, he will not be rowing under the lash in the galleys of Algiers." If Emile is to excel at sympathizing with the misfortunes of others, he must excel at imagining his own.

Third maxim: "The pity one has for another's misfortune is measured not by the quantity of that misfortune but by the sentiment that one attributes to those who suffer from it." Here is yet another aspect of compassion's dependency on imagination: we are only as sensitive to the sufferings of others as we are capable of imagining them to be sensitive to them. Thus, Rousseau explains, "the rich console themselves for the harm that they do the poor in supposing them so stupid that they don't feel any of it." Universal compassion requires education in the common sensibility of mankind: the tutor must liberate Emile from what today would be called classism.[20]

We have already noted the realism of these three maxims. This realism follows from their emphasis on the *relativity* of compassion. Why is it that (as expounded in the first maxim) to comtemplate the pleasures of another is bitter but to contemplate his pains is somehow sweet? Based on both the doctrine and the examples of the *Discourse on Inequality*, we might have expected that compassion, as a sympathetic identification with the sorrows of our fellow, would itself be painful.[21] Sometimes it is. In fact, however, as the maxims remind us, the compassion we extend to others is not typically painful for us; we are even likely to cherish the experience.[22]

We can account, according to Rousseau, for the sweetness of compassion only by the relativity it shares with all the sentiments of civil man. As Rousseau presents us, once in society we are social to the core: aware of the intersubjectivity of human life, we can no longer see ourselves except in relation to others—or others except in relation to ourselves. We strive not for the good or to be good, but to be first: that is, to be better than others in whatever respect.

Our very happiness is thus relative rather than absolute, a function of our perception of our relation to the other.[23]

The tenor of our response even to the sufferings of our fellow will therefore depend primarily on the *comparison* between his lot and ours. For the very reason that it is painful to return from another's superior good fortune to confront our lack of it, it is pleasant to return from his bad fortune to our comparatively good one. Our sentiment is predominantly pleasant or painful not in agreement with the sentiment of the other—not, then, in agreement with a simple principle of sympathy—but in keeping with the primacy for us of sentiments of "relativity."[24]

This is not to deny the element of discomfort in compassion. One of the factors that moves us to help the other is the agitation induced in us by our perception of his suffering. As suggested by my quotation of Rousseau on page 299 above, this element of "identification" remains the basis of the whole experience of compassion. Still, that experience is highly complex, and even the element of "identification" will prove to be not simply painful. Compassion is distinct from suffering, commiseration from misery. The distinction inheres in just that element of distance that is the contribution of "relativity."

Compassion is not (as the *Discourse* seemed to suggest) simply opposed to amour propre. If amour propre in its broadest sense means to live compara-tively, then compassion is closely linked with it. Pity takes us "outside ourselves"—one of Rousseau's most common descriptions of amour propre— and is therefore inevitably followed by a return to ourselves. Our vicarious experience of the misery of others is mitigated by our simultaneous awareness of our freedom from it. Pity is "the first relative sentiment" for Emile[25]—in place of the envy or emulation that otherwise would have been. A relative sentiment, however, is a sentiment of amour propre. Indeed, immediately after his most ringing declaration in *Emile* that compassion is a pure emanation of *amour de soi-même*, Rousseau retracts this view with astonishing abruptness.

> Since my Emile has until now looked only at himself, the first glance he casts on his fellows leads him to compare himself with them. And the first sentiment aroused in him by this comparison is the desire to be in the first position. This is the point where love of self [*amour de soi-même*] turns into *amour-propre* and where begin to arise all the passions that depend on this one. But to decide whether among these passions the dominant ones in his character will be humane and gentle or cruel and malignant, whether they

305

will be passions of beneficence and commiseration or of envy and covetousness, we must know what position he will feel he has among men, and what kinds of obstacles he may believe he has to overcome to reach the position he wants to occupy.[26]

Rousseau here states as clearly as one could wish that commiseration is a passion that depends on amour propre. Pity is sweet in good part because the delights of feeling that I don't suffer outweigh the discomforts of feeling that you do. First of all, it is pleasant simply to feel that we are free of the pain that afflicts another. This we might describe as the "Lucretian" element in compassion; like Lucretius, we must emphasize that it does not consist in pleasure in the misfortune of others, but only in relief at one's freedom from these.[27] Second, we take pleasure in the victim's need of us. (Rousseau here clearly anticipates Nietzsche's critique of the hidden imperialism of the do-gooder.)[28] For us to assist the victim both relieves the discomfort we take in his suffering and enhances the delight we take in our superiority. Indeed, Rousseau had even argued (in a draft of his exposition of his first maxim) that one basis of the interest we naturally take in the sufferings of our fellow is the hope that if we assist him he will reward us.[29]

Although Rousseau's rhetoric of pity is sentimental, his psychology of it is harsh. The delights of compassion, however, are not only those of amour propre. For even our primary act of identification with our suffering fellow is, according to Rousseau, commonly more invigorating than painful.[30] This conclusion follows from Rousseau's novel doctrine of the expansiveness of being. He follows both Hobbes and the Stoics in asserting that what is primary for human beings is self-love. But whereas the Stoics had interpreted self-love as revealing a strong positive attachment to life as good and an inclination to the fulfillment of the lofty ends prescribed for us by nature, Hobbes had broken with them on both these points, insisting that our fundamental experience is not the goodness of life but rather the badness of death, and denying that nature sets any ends for man. Rousseau, for his part, understands self-love positively but not teleologically. He asserts that it involves not mere self-preservation but a natural delight in increasing or extending the fullness of our being through an impulse toward expanding it. Expansion, then, is as natural to us as being itself.[31] Our expansiveness is formless or protean, and therefore malleable; because nature prescribes no clear goal or object for it, we take delight in expansion as such. Identification even with the sorrows of another is therefore sweet even in itself because it entails a fuller and deeper experience of our being. The compassionate man is like the athlete for whom the very strain of exertion is pleasant in contributing to a heightened sense of his vitality.[32]

Rousseau's understanding of compassion thus takes its place within the framework defined by his doctrines of our expansiveness as natural beings and our relativity as social ones. Before turning to the question of the legacy of this understanding, it remains to discuss the role of compassion in the later stages of Emile's education. In keeping with the first of the maxims of compassion, the tutor's strategy is to expose Emile not to the delights but to the sorrows of others. Here too he will make the comparison of their lot with his own, but so long as his glance falls only on others more wretched than himself, he will never recoil from it with anger, shame, and bitterness.[33]

Once Emile has learned to pity, it is crucial that he learn whom to pity. Having already exposed Emile to physical sufferings (the only ones readily intelligible to him), the tutor now expands his repertoire to include moral ones. Carefully guided by the tutor, Emile must learn to pity those who suffer from the vices of society—all, that is, who inhabit the delusional world of amour propre. Learning to pity these, Emile will learn to shun those vices, which will first come to light for him as painful maladies of the soul. In short, no sooner has Emile acquired that compassion that can flower only in the absence of the ravaging passions of amour propre, than Rousseau puts it to work to preempt the birth of those passions.[34]

Finally, Emile is to learn the ways of the world by continuing to exercise his compassion: rather than acting on his own behalf (and falling prey to the distortions of self-interest), he is to act on behalf of the less fortunate. We can call this the epoch of knight-errantry in Emile's education—or more pro-saically, that of social work. The main point to grasp, however, is that here as at every stage of the education, Emile's compassion proves to be even better for him than it is for his neighbors.[35]

Although compassion is to be important to the mature Emile's relations with his fellows, Rousseau does not present it as sufficient for them. Rousseau himself never elaborates a morality of pure compassion. In fact he explicitly denies that one is possible. The possibilities of compassion are great, but so are its limitations. Stated most briefly, compassion must be supplemented by a proto-Kantian morality of generality. This last is necessary to redress the *inequities* of compassion, arising from its necessary focus on such particular sufferings as may grip the imagination. Fired with the sufferings of a visible victim, Emile may lose sight of the common good; succumbing to pity for a criminal, he may neglect the interests of society.[36]

Thus we have come full circle: as we needed a compassionate morality to supplement the coldness of reason, we need a rational one to restrain the impulsive warmth of compassion. The affective basis of that morality remains, to say the least, up in the air. Rousseau apparently implies in *Emile* that the sentiment of compassion will continue to sustain the morality that requires its generalization. Kant, however, in a pivotal work written in response to *Emile*, suggests that the more general morality becomes, the less compassion supports it. In the end we must doubt whether a truly general compassion is possible for us.[37] In so arguing, Kant merely develops certain suggestions of Rousseau himself. The maxims of compassion, after all, stress the dependence of compassion on imagination and therefore its inevitable particularity or partiality. Even earlier Rousseau had declared that "it seems that the sentiment of humanity evaporates and weakens as it is extended over the whole world," and that "commiseration must in some way be confined and compressed to be activated."[38] He thus variously indicates the necessity of grounding morality on sentiment, the necessity of generality to true morality, and the difficulty of grounding a properly general morality in compassion (or perhaps in any other sentiment).[39] Given these difficulties it is not surprising that Kant, having begun by questioning compassion, should go on to dismiss it in his mature writings as of no moral value.[40]

Last, Emile's education in compassion and even his proto-Kantian morality must be supplemented both by natural religion and by his marriage with Sophie. The natural religion is clearly necessary to support the proto-Kantian morality. As for marriage with Sophie, Emile is not so immune to the shocks and blandishments of the greater society as not to require an alternative society. Again we recall that his education in compassion is indeed to sensitize him to the sufferings of others, but that its main purpose is to inoculate him against them. He is no Don Quixote, no "knight of the sorrowful countenance"; he is not being groomed to live for others. Emile, like the solitary walker, is in but not of bourgeois society. Compassion ensures at the same time Emile's concern with society and his detachment from it; practically speaking, however, detachment is to predominate.

By now the reader may wonder whether Rousseau, having articulated so precisely the limits of compassion, does not stand refuted out of his own mouth. For I began by touting his moral realism, and his interest in compassion as an instance of it. But how realistic, on his own showing, is a morality of compassion? In particular, how realistic is it for bourgeois or commercial or post-Christian society? Whatever may be the case with Emile (who is, after all, imaginary) the typical bourgeois will rarely be open to compassion. Drifting, divided, and burdened with a thousand futile cares, he will have little sensibility to spare for the troubles of others. His preferred experience of sympathy will be the sterile one of the theater: there he will suffer delightful tremors that, while demanding absolutely no action on his part, will permit him to congratulate himself on his sensitivity.[41] In the real world compassion may stir him very occasionally, but even then, in the absence of generalization, its justice will remain highly suspect.

Still, a moralist (especially a "realistic" one) must work with what circumstance permits him, and according to Rousseau this remains compassion. In many respects, moreover, a morality of compassion is well suited to bourgeois society. Compassion does not presuppose a healthy public life (that informed by the general will) but offers a kind of alternative to one. As a redresser of specific grievances and a consoler for specific sorrows, it will never lack for trade in bourgeois society. Its justice is indeed imperfect, but then (according to Rousseau) injustice is so rampant in such a society—and justice so little to be hoped for in it—that we may as well settle for compassion. In short, in a society whose typical inhabitant Rousseau describes as "nothing," compassion, with its appeal to a new and distinctly modern or post-Christian sensibility, furnishes a moral strategy that is somewhat better than nothing.[42]

It was in the course of thus promoting the cause of decency in bourgeois society that Rousseau imparted to compassion its distinctive modern political coloring. He was the first to promote compassion as an affair of social class, as something owed by the rich just because they were rich to the poor just because they were poor. It was he who first dared tell the rich that they were unjust simply by virtue of being rich, and that the poor, conversely, were oppressed simply by virtue of being poor.

Rousseau's presentation of the people is less sentimental than his reputation might lead us to suppose: "The people show themselves such as they are, and they are not lovable."[43] Yet he more than makes up for this by the hatefulness of his presentation of the rich: "But society people have to be disguised: if they were to show themselves such as they are, they would be disgusting."[44] This last verdict proves true in two particularly damning respects. The first has to do with the heartlessness of the rich, which I take to be the one of their qualities most in need of concealment. (They disguise it by means of the various rationalizations that Rousseau ascribes to them.) That hypocrisy is even more hateful than in any previous secular understanding follows from another central plank of Rousseau's new (post-Christian, post-Enlightenment) moralism—the glorification of sincerity.[45] Indeed, it seems fair to say that the only vice in the Rousseauian canon that is as odious as hypocrisy is lack of compassion, and it is just these two vices that he presents as typical of the rich.

It is true, of course, that on Rousseau's own showing the rich are desperately unhappy, but he cautions against our commiserating with the ills of the rich as with those of the poor. "Were [the rich man] unhappier than the poor man himself, he would not be pitiable, because his ills are all his own doing, and whether he is happy depends only on himself."[46] The misery of the rich is "imaginary"; they are not starving, no-one beats them.

Yet (again on Rousseau's own showing) is this not to abstract from the responsibility of "society" for the ills of social man, whether he is rich or poor? Are these "imaginary" ills of the rich really within their power to vanquish? Only if we regard the problem of amour propre or of social dependency as a superficial and contingent one. In fact it is for Rousseau identical with the problem of society itself. Something like this ambiguity recurs in Marx, for whom the bourgeois is simultaneously predator and victim, oppressor and mere cog of an oppressive system that prolongs his unhappiness as surely as that of the proletarian.

I do not believe that Rousseau himself hated the rich: even in the context of one of his most blistering criticisms of them, he makes it clear that Emile must learn "to love all men, even those who despise men."[47] He was, however, the first philosopher to teach the rich to hate themselves. This he did in the hopes of nudging them toward behaving less hatefully toward the poor. His readers were primarily the well-to-do, and his rhetoric was intended primarily for them. We might say that Rousseau invented liberal guilt; before him the proponents of enlightened modernity had been conspicuously free of guilt.

Rousseau thus politicized compassion in the hope of moderating the arrogance of the rich in a society that still belonged to them. In teaching them to hate themselves, however, he could not but encourage the rest of us to hate them. Rousseau blames the ills of the poor on the rich (who compound their responsibility for these by their indifference to them), and he blames the ills of the rich on the rich (to which we should therefore respond with indifference).

In berating them as wholly insensitive in order to stimulate their sensitivity, he left the impression that, unwilling to extend compassion, they could lay no claim to receive it. He thus contributed to the discourse of the French Revolution and of all the revolutions to follow.

However much historians may disagree as to Rousseau's influence on the Revolution, it certainly offered the first example of the power of his rhetoric of political compassion. Robespierre and Saint-Just presented the Terror itself as the vanguard of the compassionariate. They promoted compassion as the basis of a new politics of reconciliation between rich and poor, powerful and weak: it was the means by which the rich would achieve solidarity with the poor. For this very reason, however, anyone rich or powerful who lacked it consigned himself to extirpation. To be a true revolutionary (among so many false ones) was to take upon oneself the burden of the suffering masses and to feel it even more keenly then they themselves did. It was thus to evoke an anger in oneself as boundless, as oceanic as that suffering. It is in this last highly dubious sense that, according to Hannah Arendt, the best men of every modern revolution have been men of compassion.[48] They have resembled Stevie, the innocent half-wit of Joseph Conrad's *The Secret Agent*, who is induced to try to plant a bomb in Greenwich Observatory by an appeal to his inchoate rage at that suffering due to cruelty that he himself has known only too often. They have lacked only the half-wittedness that justifies describing Stevie as innocent.

Yet clearly the prestige of compassion in the nineteenth century exceeded even that of revolution. Rousseau the apostle of humanity transcended Rousseau the political agitator. Already in 1787, Goethe replied to a letter from the humanitarian Frau von Stein: "Also, I must say myself, I think it true that humanity will triumph eventually, only I fear that at the same time the world will become a large hospital and each will become the other's humane nurse."[49] Goethe clearly saw the problem that was, a century later, to preoccupy Nietzsche: the dynamic by which all were to become both sick and caretakers for the sick, sufferers and alleviators of suffering. Clearly Goethe relished neither outcome; he thus fired the first tentative salvo against the moral authority of compassion. If Rousseau's influence was pervasive in the nineteenth century, so too was the struggle against that influence.

The great systematizer of the morality of pity was Schopenhauer. Schopenhauer was anything but an agitator, and the pity he preached was profoundly unpolitical. No special class of human beings but the human condition as such was pitiable. Schopenhauer thus sought to popularize and even to radicalize

Rousseau's education of Emile; at the same time he denied that pity (and therefore morality) was a subject in which human beings were educable. Eschewing all psychologizing, he attempted what Rousseau had not, a metaphysics of compassion—in his case inspired by Eastern religions.[50] He thereby glorified pity even more than Rousseau had done—while yoking it to the denial of life and to a rejection of Western civilization.

No wonder then that Nietzsche was to complain in the preface to his *Genealogy of Morals* of the "ever-spreading morality of pity that had seized even on philosophers and made them ill."[51] Precisely because he accepted Schopenhauer's link between pity and the denial of life (and argued that this denial informed all displays of "humanitarianism"), he was moved to renounce pity almost as thoroughly as Schopenhauer had affirmed it. For him the apparently nonpolitical character of his predecessor's doctrine concealed an objective that was ambiguously political and antipolitical: the revenge of sick, dwindling, pain-wracked forms of life against flourishing ones. Nietzsche hoped to inspire a politics of the repudiation of pity.[52] That politics fell into the wrong hands. Yet to return to the case of Jacobinism is to be reminded that the politics of compassion is itself highly ambiguous. The extremes meet, and they do so by making demands, whether of compassion or of cruelty appropriate only to superhuman beings.

It is a mark of Rousseau's greatness (as well as of the doubtfulness of his legacy) that the thinker in him anticipated and criticized almost all the excesses of the rhetorician and thus of his erstwhile disciples. He was both the proximate source and the most prescient critic of the leading trends of thought of the nineteenth century; this was true in the case of compassion as in so many others. For as I have tried to argue, his attempt to tap the power of compassion was informed by a clear awareness of its limits.

It is always risky to reanimate a figure of the past as a critic of the present. I will conclude, however, by noting one development of our day that it is reasonable to suppose Rousseau would have presented with bitter irony. This is the routinization of compassion in massive public bureaucracies of caring. In the March 1992 issue of the *Atlantic* one could read about Dr. Ralph G. H. Siu, author of *Less Suffering for Everybody*.[53] Dr. Siu is the founder of the new science of panetics, which aims to help reduce suffering by designing scientific criteria for quantifying it. (He has named his proposed unit of suffering the dukkha, from the Pali language spoken by the Buddha.) Having determined the quotient in dukkhas of every known kind of suffering, we could construct dukkha flow diagrams, which would display the net suffering costs (or benefits) of policy alternatives by charting the degree to which the sum of dukkhas inflicted by a given policy would exceed (or fall short of) that of the dukkhas relieved by it. "Someday," Dr. Siu has suggested, "you could diagram the whole United States. Can you imagine all the thousands, all the millions, of streams of dukkhas going in and out?"[54] Employing such data, we could design public policies that would be suffering efficient.

Dr. Siu is an honorable man, but his scheme seems worthy of Swift's Projectors. And like the schemes Swift ascribed to them, this caricature of the modern project captures a real difficulty with it. The institutionalization or rationalization of the struggle against suffering does indeed imply its quantification or depersonalization. Yet suffering, at least insofar as it is distinctly human, is always personal suffering, which as such defies quantification. What would Dr. Siu say to (or of) Anna Karenina? Would her dukkha count soar off his chart? Or (in a world where so many suffer physical privation and oppression) would it fail to rate inclusion on it? In Solzhenitsyn's novel *Cancer Ward*, the deportee Elizaveta Anatolyevna suggests that Anna's sufferings were such as no one in this century could take seriously. "These literary tragedies are just laughable compared to the ones that we've lived through."[55] This claim is worth pondering. Whatever our final verdict on it, it confirms the difficulties of designing a dukkha meter. Obviously some sufferings are greater than others; but just as obviously some people (like Anna) suffer more deeply than others.

Such perplexities recall a seeming incongruity of Rousseau's advocacy of compassion: his opposition to the structures of modernity. From its outset modernity aimed at the alleviation of suffering: think of Bacon's slogan "the relief of man's estate." And Rousseau himself seems to approve of this goal, in particular of the modern resolve to improve the lot of the poor. In his elaboration of his third maxim of compassion, for instance, he denounces what has come to be called "blaming the victim"—that is, blaming the poor for their poverty, which is in fact the result of circumstances beyond their control. Rousseau endorses the view that "man is the same in all stations" (a position friendly to compassion toward the poor), but not that of "our sages" who claim that "there is . . . the same proportion of happiness and misery in every station—a maxim as deadly as it is untenable." "If all are equally happy, what need have I to put myself out for anyone?" Listing the ills to which the poor are condemned by their poverty, Rousseau denounces the passivity of the rich in the face of these. As for the stolidity of the poor, it evinces their good sense:

they see that they have no choice but to adapt to their misery.[56] Rousseau thus appears to leapfrog the reformers of the nineteenth century who sought to better the lot of the poor by improving their morals, to alight at the head of those reformers of the twentieth, for whom the poor are the victims not of their bad habits but of a "system" to which these habits present a sensible (even a defiant) response.

Is Rousseau then a patron of the welfare state? Yes and no. Obviously he gave a tremendous impetus to reformism of all kinds, and not just in France. On the other hand, it cannot have been his purpose to encourage the systematic promotion of the poor to the ranks of the middle class within the framework of commercial society. It is true that Rousseau anticipates a fundamental error of Marx by arguing that the necessary tendency of commerce (or "luxury") is toward the concentration of wealth in the hands of the few and the ever greater impoverishment of the many. Still, this is not his only or even his principal objection to commercial society. He assails the prosperity at which commerce aims as much for its effects on those who enjoy it as for its effects on those who are deprived of it. If all denizens of bourgeois society were thoroughly middling, they would still be thoroughly miserable. Rousseau is the forerunner of all those social critics who seek not so much to integrate the poor into liberal society as to cast their existence as a standing and permanent reproach to it.

Insofar as modern philanthropy expresses itself above all through its promotion of modernity (political, economic, ideological, and technological), Rousseau insists that it is misguided at best. He was the first to claim that despite its pretenses modernity actually increases human suffering, that its progress is inseparable from that of a distinctly modern misery. Modernity or Enlightenment begins by fanning all manner of hopeful and acquisitive passions, thereby aggravating discontent even as it pretends to assuage it. Further, it favors vast impersonal political structures, as "alienating" as they are oppressive; new concentrations of wealth, and hence massive new inequalities; the uprooting of stable and healthy modes of existence; the mass dissemination of modes of thought corrosive of decency and contentment; frenetic activity on every front that is productive only of unhappiness; and the poisoning of human relationships at the source, relegating us to loneliness, distrust, and insincerity. Worst of all, modernity does not loosen but tightens the bonds of personal dependency.

By now this diagnosis has become not merely familiar but ingrained, and by proclaiming it Rousseau anticipates the subsequent modern obsession with addressing these symptoms. He also foreshadows, however, our discontent with the institutionalization even of efforts to alleviate them. To begin with, he clearly declares compassion incompatible with any way of life professionally devoted to the relief of suffering. "It is thus by dint of seeing death and suffering that priests and doctors become pitiless."[57] Compassion withers in the face of routinization. As it withers, those who make a career of caring will come to be actuated by less benevolent sentiments. Relations of caring and helping too are relations of dependency. As with all social relationships, this dependency is mutual. The clients depend on the patrons, but so do the patrons on the clients. And dependency, always presented by Rousseau as the fundamental human evil, will breed, as it always does, contempt and resentment, superiority and hatred, never compassionate concern. "Organized compassion" emerges from Rousseau as a contradiction in terms, for every organization (including a therapeutic one) is a structure of dependency that as such fosters the very misery that therapy professes to address.[58]

The problem does not lie, however, merely with the distortions of society. It lies also (as implied by the remark about priests and doctors) with the weakness of natural beneficence. Only in the *Reveries of the Solitary Walker*, his last and most personal work, does Rousseau explore the social possibilities of compassion unfortified by any interested passion. There he recalls how he had fallen into giving alms to a certain beggar boy he encountered each day in the course of his walk. At first he looked forward to their meetings. He soon discovered, however, that he had begun to take a detour to avoid the spot where the boy awaited him. An act of spontaneous humanity had dwindled into a habit and an obligation, a burden instead of a pleasure. The Rousseau of the *Reveries* presents himself as the most beneficent of men—and his concern with others as fitful, self-indulgent, and unproductive of obligations of any kind. Man is not by nature social, and compassion, being natural, affords no basis for lasting society. He whose relations with his fellows rest exclusively on natural beneficence proves to be he who least enters into relations with them.[59]

NOTES

Versions of this paper were delivered at the John M. Olin Center of the University of Chicago on 26 January and 22 May 1993, at the Centre Raymond Aron de Recherches Politiques of the Ecole des Hautes Etudes en Sciences Sociales, Paris, on 14 June 1993, and at Kenyon College on 10 February 1994. I am grateful for these invitations and for the spirited discussions that ensued. I had addressed these issues earlier in my Harvard doctoral dissertation of 1976 and in my essay "Compassion," *American Scholar* 49, no. 3 (summer 1980): 309–33, republished in French translation as "Le triomphe de la compassion," *Commentaire* (Paris), no. 43 (autumn 1988): 613–23; no. 44 (winter 1988–89): 955–62. I am grateful to Harvey C. Mansfield Jr. and the late Judith N. Shklar for supervising the dissertation, to Joseph Epstein for his encouragement of the essay, and to Pierre Manent of *Commentaire* for supervising its translation. I am also grateful to Ernest L. Fortin for first urging me in 1985 to work up a lecture on Rousseau and compassion that has since passed through several incarnations.

1. Johnson delivered himself of this verdict in conversation with George Ball early in the Johnson administration. It formed the climax to a declamatory set piece that he had begun by posing the question of what it was that was sure to keep Connally from the top. Johnson then proceeded to detail the many strengths that would otherwise have promised Connally the presidency, thus setting the stage for this final dramatic flourish. Recounted in James Reston Jr., *Lone Star: The Life of John Connally* (New York: Harper and Row, 1989), 418.

2. On contemporary issues of humanitarianism see Luc Boltanski's remarkable work *La souffrance à distance: Morale humanitaire, médias et politique* (Paris: Métailié, 1993); also the reflections of Pierre Hassner in the essay he has contributed to this volume (chapter 10), as well as those in his *La violence et la paix: De la bombe atomique au nettoyage ethnique* (Paris: Editions Esprit, 1995). Cf. also Clifford Orwin, "Distant Compassion," *National Interest* 43 (spring 1996): 42–49, and *Books in Canada* 25, 3 (1996): 21–24.

3. For a summary of the most powerful post-Rousseauian critique of compassion from a Christian perspective, see Nicholas Berdyayev, *Dostoyevsky* [1923], trans. Donald Attwater (1934), (New York: Meridian Books, 1957), 116–27. See also Max Scheler, *The Nature of Sympathy* (*Wesens und Formen der Sympathie* [1922]), trans. Peter Heath (1954) (New York: Archon Books, 1970), with its critique of "naturalistic" theories of pity, its argument for the dependence of pity upon love, and its praise for the understanding of love articulated by Saint Francis of Assisi.

4. Victor Hugo, *La légende des siècles*, 13 ("Maintenant"): "Le crapaud," 1.152, in Hugo, *Poésie*, Collection "L'Intégrale" (Paris: Editions du Seuil, 1972), 2:115. Cf. Hugo's later, longer, and even more lugubrious "La pitié suprême" (ibid., 592–607).

5. Aristotle, *Rhetoric*, 2.8.

6. Jean-Jacques Rousseau, *The First and Second Discourses*, ed. Roger D. Masters, trans. Roger D. Masters and Judith R. Masters (New York: St. Martin's Press, 1964), 130–33; reprinted in Rousseau, *Discourse on the Origins of Inequality*, ed. Roger D. Masters and Christopher Kelly, vol. 3 of *The Collected Writings of Rousseau* (Hanover, N.H.: University Press of New England, 1992), 36–38. Hereafter I will cite both editions in the following manner: *Discourse on the Origins of Inequality*, 130–33 (36–38). I will also cite the French text of this and other writings of Rousseau by the standard Pléiade edition: Jean-Jacques Rousseau, *Oeuvres complètes*, ed. Bernard Gagnebin and Marcel Raymond, 5 vols. (Paris: Editions Gallimard, 1959–95). I will cite this edition as follows: *Oeuvres complètes*, 3:154–57 (for the present passage). Be advised, however, of the recent publica-

tion of the first true critical edition of the *Discourse on the Origins of Inequality:* Rousseau, *Diskurs über die Ungleichheit / Discours sur l'inégalité,* ed. Heinrich Meier, 2d ed. (Paderborn: UTB / Ferdinand Schöningh, 1990).

7. Rousseau, *Discourse on the Origins of Inequality,* 133 (38; *Oeuvres complètes,* 3:156–57).

8. Rousseau, *Emile, or On Education,* trans. Allan Bloom (New York: Basic Books, 1979), 235n (*Oeuvres complètes,* 4:523n).

9. Rousseau, *Discourse on the Origins of Inequality,* 132 (37; *Oeuvres complètes,* 3:155–56).

10. Consider in this connection Rousseau's examples of alleged feral "pity," as well as that drawn from Mandeville's *Fable of the Bees.* The examples drawn from beasts are even more important than may at first appear. Not only do they provide the only directly observable evidence for the existence of pity among human beings in the natural state, but they should also (by the logic of Rousseau's argument) display the characteristics of such pity. There being in this state no difference between the affects of men and those of beasts, natural man should be capable only of such pity as other beasts are capable of. See Rousseau, *Discourse on the Origins of Inequality,* 130 (36; *Oeuvres complètes,* 3:154). For discussions of the objections to ascribing effective pity to natural man, see Roger D. Masters, *The Political Philosophy of Rousseau* (Princeton: Princeton University Press, 1968), 136–57; Victor Goldschmidt, *Anthropologie et politique: Les principes du système de Rousseau* (Paris: Vrin, 1973), 331–56; John Charvet, *The Social Problem in Rousseau* (Cambridge: Cambridge University Press, 1974), 17–19; Clifford Orwin, "Humanity and Justice: The Problem of Compassion in the Thought of Rousseau" (Ph.D. diss., Harvard University, 1975), 67–90; Marc F. Plattner, *Rousseau's State of Nature: An Interpretation of the Discourse on Inequality* (DeKalb: Northern Illinois University Press, 1979), 82–87.

11. Rousseau, *Discourse on Inequality,* 131 (36; *Oeuvres complètes,* 3:155).

12. Ibid., 160–61 (54; *Oeuvres complètes,* 3:178).

13. *Emile,* 215 (*Oeuvres complètes,* 4:494). For the broader discussion of puberty, see *Emile,* 211–35 (*Oeuvres complètes,* 4:489–523).

14. The finest discussions of this side of Rousseau's thought are those of Allan Bloom, in his introduction to his translation of *Emile* (*Emile,* 15–27) and in his *Love and Friendship* (New York: Simon and Schuster, 1993), 39–140.

15. *Emile,* 221 (*Oeuvres complètes,* 4:503).

16. Arthur M. Melzer, *The Natural Goodness of Man: On the System of Rousseau's Thought* (Chicago: University of Chicago Press, 1990), 110–11.

17. *Emile,* 223–26 (*Oeuvres complètes,* 4:506–10).

18. Adam Smith, *The Theory of Moral Sentiments* [6th ed., 1790] (Indianapolis: Liberty Classics, 1982), 9–26.

19. Virgil, *Aeneid,* 1.630.

20. Indeed, Rousseau's exposition of this maxim further raises the specter of that other current stigma, "speciesism." In commenting on man's inhumanity to man he also elucidates his inhumanity to beasts—which he ascribes to the very same cause. Cf. the remarkable manifesto by Claude Lévi-Strauss, "Rousseau fondateur des sciences de

l'homme," in *Jean-Jacques Rousseau*, ed. Samuel Baud-Bovy, Robert Derathé, et al. (Neuchatel: Editions de la Baconnière, 1962), 239–48.

21. Rousseau, *Discourse on Inequality*, 130 (36; *Oeuvres complètes*, 3:154).

22. *Emile*, 221–22, 223, 229 (*Oeuvres complètes*, 4:503–4, 506, 514–15).

23. Ibid., 212–15, 221–22, 223, 227–29, 235–37, 241–43 (4:491–94, 503–4, 506, 512–15, 522–25, 533–35). Cf. Rousseau, *Discourse on Inequality*, 115 n. i, 130 n. o, 133–34, 149–50, 155–56, 174–75 (26 n. 7, 36 n. 12, 38, 47–48, 51–52, 63; *Oeuvres complètes*, 3:142 n. IX, 3:154 n. XV, 157, 169–70, 174–75, 188–89). One could adduce many other passages in many others of Rousseau's works.

24. *Emile*, 221–22, 223, 227–29, 235 (*Oeuvres complètes*, 4:503–4, 506, 512–15, 523–24).

25. Ibid., 222 (4:505).

26. Ibid., 235 (4:523–24). The immediately preceding ringing declaration to the opposite effect is the one I have cited at pp. 298–99 above.

27. Lucretius, *De rerum natura* (*On the Nature of Things*), 2:1–62.

28. Friedrich Nietzsche, *Daybreak*, secs. 133, 136; *The Gay Science*, secs. 13, 14, 118, 377. Cf. *Genealogy of Morals*, Third Essay, secs. 11–22; *Ecce Homo* (the chapter on *Daybreak*, sec. 2). For a revelation of the surprising parallelism between Nietzsche's interpretation of the psychology of pity and Rousseau's, see *Daybreak*, sec. 133.

29. *Emile*, 223 n. 4 (*Oeuvres complètes*, 4:506 n. [a]).

30. Ibid., 229 (4:514–15).

31. For an excellent articulation of this issue, to which my account is indebted, see Melzer, *Natural Goodness of Man*, 36–48.

32. I should further note that by contending that it is nascent sensuality that awakens the capacity for compassion, Rousseau casts the expansiveness of adolescence as a flow of sexual energy. The intimacy of pity is sweet for Emile because he craves intimacy, and it is electric because it fails of consummation. Rousseau does not dwell on this implication of his teaching, which moreover does not belong in the hands of a pedant. The reader is therefore referred to a work of delicacy and wit, Laurence Sterne's *Sentimental Journey through France and Italy*.

33. *Emile*, 221–22, 226–29 (*Oeuvres complètes*, 4:503–4, 512–15).

34. Ibid., 236–44 (4:525–36).

35. Ibid., 249–53 (4:543–48).

36. Ibid., 253 (4:548).

37. Ibid., 252–53 (4:547–48); Immanuel Kant, *[Remarks to the] Observations on the Feeling of the Beautiful and Sublime* (*Bemerkungen zu den Beobachtungen über das Gefühl des Schönen und Erhabenen* [1764–65]), trans. J. T. Goldthwait (Berkeley: University of California Press, 1960), 57–62. For an incisive analysis of the *Remarks* see Richard L. Velkley, *Freedom and the End of Reason: On the Moral Foundation of Kant's Critical Philosophy* (Chicago: University of Chicago Press, 1989), 61–88 (on our problem, 82–84).

38. *Discourse on Political Economy*, in Rousseau, *On the Social Contract, with Geneva Manuscript and Political Economy*, ed. Roger D. Masters, trans. Judith R. Masters (New York: St. Martin's Press, 1978), 219 (*Oeuvres complètes*, 3:254–55).

39. For a discussion of grounding morality in the generalization not of compassion but of amour propre, see *Emile*, 252–53 (*Oeuvres complètes,* 4:547–48). This passage immediately precedes the admonition to correct the deficiencies of pity through generalizing it; it seems that the generalization of whichever sentiment yields justice in Rousseau's understanding. For an example of what Rousseau may have meant by the generalization of amour propre, see *Social Contract,* bk. 1, chap. 8.

40. Cf. Immanuel Kant, *Groundwork of the Metaphysics of Morals,* trans. H. J. Paton (1948) (New York: Harper and Row, 1964), 65–66; *Critique of Practical Reason,* pt. 2 ("Methodology of Pure Practical Reason"), trans. T. K. Abbott (London: Longmans, Green, 1923), 252–57; *The Doctrine of Virtue* (pt. 2 of the *Metaphysics of Morals*), "The Ethical Doctrine of Elements, 2: On Duties of Virtue to Others"), trans. Mary J. Gregor (New York: Harper and Row, 1964), 125–26. Cf. also the transitional *Lectures on Ethics,* pt. 2 ("On Duties to Others"), trans. Louis Infield (New York: Methuen, 1930), 191–95.

41. See the discussion of theatrical compassion in Christopher Kelly's contribution to this volume (chapter 2). For an insightful treatment of the related themes of pity, amour propre, and theater in Rousseau, see also David Marshall, *The Surprising Effects of Sympathy: Marivaux, Diderot, Rousseau, and Mary Shelley* (Chicago: University of Chicago Press, 1988), 135–77.

42. On the bourgeois as "nothing," see *Emile*, 40 (*Oeuvres completes,* 4:249–50).

43. Cf. the fragment that Rousseau's editors have titled "Un ménage de la rue St-Denis" (*Oeuvres complètes,* 2:1256).

44. *Emile*, 225 (*Oeuvres complètes,* 4:509); punctuation slightly altered.

45. On which see Arthur Melzer's contribution to this volume (chapter 13).

46. *Emile*, 225 (*Oeuvres complètes,* 4:509).

47. Ibid., 226 (4:510).

48. For a controversial but suggestive treatment of the role of compassion in the French Revolution, see Hannah Arendt, *On Revolution,* rev. ed. (New York: Viking Press/Compass Books, 1966), 53–110. Cf. Jan Marejko, *Rousseau et la dérive totalitaire* (Lausanne: L'Age de l'Homme, 1984), 83–85. Ran Halévi has suggested to me that Rousseau was more than just one generation ahead of his time: that the Jacobins (even the most radical ones) characteristically thought in terms of the nobles and the people (branding all alleged opponents as "aristocrats"), and that the clear perception of the political problem in terms of the social classes of rich and poor had to await the nineteenth century. On Rousseau's influence on the French Revolution see François Furet's contribution to this volume (chapter 8).

49. "Auch muss ich selbst sagen halt ich es für wahr dass die Humanität endlich siegen wird, nur fürcht ich dass zu gleicher Zeit die Welt ein grosses Hospital und einer des andern humaner Krankenwärter werden wird." Letter from Rome of 8 June 1787, in *Goethes Briefe* (Hamburg: Christian Wegner, 1964), 2:60. In the text I have employed the translation of Walter Kaufmann in his edition of Nietzsche's *On the Genealogy of Morals* (New York: Vintage Books, 1967), 124 n. 3.

50. Arthur Schopenhauer, *On the Basis of Morality* (*Über die Grundlage der Moral*

[1841]), trans. E. F. J. Payne (Indianapolis: Bobbs-Merrill/Library of Liberal Arts, 1965), esp. 138–214.

51. Friedrich Nietzsche, *On the Genealogy of Morals* (1887), trans. W. Kaufmann and R. J. Hollingdale, published with *Ecce Homo* (New York: Vintage Books, 1967), 19 (preface, sec. 5).

52. Nietzsche, *Daybreak*, secs. 132–39, 146, 467; *Gay Science*, secs. 289, 338, 345; *Thus Spoke Zarathustra*, 1.9, 2.3, 4.2; *Beyond Good and Evil*, secs. 62, 82, 199, 202, 206, 222, 225, 260, 293; *Genealogy of Morals*, Third Essay, sec. 14; *Twilight of the Idols*, "Expeditions of an Untimely Man," 37. For a recent treatment of Nietzsche's thought on compassion and the profundity and ambiguity of its influence on subsequent reflection on the subject, see Boltanski, *La souffrance à distance*, 189–214.

53. Cullen Murphy, "The First Brick," *Atlantic*, March 1992, 20–22.

54. Ibid., 22.

55. Alexander Solzhenitsyn, *Cancer Ward*, trans. Nicholas Bethell and David Burg (New York: Bantam Books, 1969), 479.

56. *Emile*, 225–26 (*Oeuvres complètes*, 4:508–10).

57. Ibid., 231 (4:517).

58. For a contemporary critique of the consequences of the institutionalization of compassion in the welfare state, see Marvin Olasky, *The Tragedy of American Compassion* (Indianapolis: Henry Regnery, 1992). Olasky's critique comes from "the Right"; on the intellectual Left there are striking parallels between Rousseau's argument and Michel Foucault's celebrated contention that the methods of modern therapy are above all methods of control. This contention has generated a vast body of literature whose theme is the critique of the welfare state. Cf. Boltanski, *La souffrance à distance*, 247 n. 3. On related issues of international politics see note 2 above.

59. Jean-Jacques Rousseau, *Reveries of the Solitary Walker*, trans. Charles E. Butterworth (New York: New York University Press, 1979), Fifth Reverie, 66–67 (Rousseau as the benefactor not of human beings but of rabbits); Sixth Reverie, 74–78 (the incident of the beggar boy and the reflections it gave rise to); Ninth Promenade, 127–31 (Rousseau's easy beneficence). For the French originals of these passages see *Oeuvres complètes*, 1:1044, 1050–54, 1090–94. Cf. *Emile*, 344–355 (*Oeuvres complètes*, 4:678–91), on the sort of beneficence Rousseau would practice if he were free to choose his way of life.

❧Contributors❧

ALLAN BLOOM (until his death in 1992) was John U. Nef Professor in the Committee on Social Thought at the University of Chicago. He was the translator of Plato's *Republic* and Rousseau's *Emile*, and author of *The Closing of the American Mind* and *Love and Friendship*.

WERNER J. DANNHAUSER is professor emeritus of government at Cornell University and visiting professor in the Department of Political Science at Michigan State University. He is the author of *Nietzsche's View of Socrates*.

H. D. FORBES is professor of political science at the University of Toronto. He is the author of *Nationalism, Ethnocentrism, and Personality: Social Science and Critical Theory*.

FRANÇOIS FURET is director of studies at the Ecole des Hautes Etudes en Sciences Sociales, director of the Institut Raymond Aron, and Raymond W. and Martha Hilpert Gruner Professor in the Committee on Social Thought at the University of Chicago. He is the author of *Interpreting the French Revolution* and *Le passé d'une illusion*.

PIERRE HASSNER is a director of studies at the Centre d'Etude de Recherches Internationales and professor at the Institut d'Etude Politiques, Paris. He is the author of *La violence et la paix*.

STEVEN KAUTZ is associate professor of political science at Emory University. He is the author of *Liberalism and Community*.

CHRISTOPHER KELLY is associate professor of political science at the University of Maryland, Baltimore County. He is the author of *Rousseau's Exemplary Life: "The Confessions" as Political Philosophy*. He is the editor, with Roger Masters, of *The Collected Writings of Rousseau*.

ROGER D. MASTERS is professor of government at Dartmouth College. He is the author of *The Political Philosophy of Rousseau* and *The Nature of Politics*. He is the editor, with Christopher Kelly, of *The Collected Writings of Rousseau*.

ARTHUR MELZER is associate professor of political science at Michigan State University. He is the author of *The Natural Goodness of Man: On the System of Rousseau's Thought*.

CLIFFORD ORWIN is professor of political science at the University of Toronto. He is the author of *The Humanity of Thucydides*.

MARC F. PLATTNER is the director of the International Forum for Democratic Studies and the editor of the *Journal of Democracy*. He is the author of *Rousseau's State of Nature: An Interpretation of the Discourse on Inequality*.

JOEL SCHWARTZ is the author of *The Sexual Politics of Jean-Jacques Rousseau* and of several studies of Freud.

SUSAN SHELL is professor of political science at Boston College. She is the author of *The Rights of Reason: A Study of Kant's Philosophy and Politics* and *The Embodiment of Reason: Kant on Spirit, Generation, and Community*.

NATHAN TARCOV is professor of political science and in the Committee on Social Thought and the College at the University of Chicago. He is the author of *Locke's Education for Liberty* and the translator, with Harvey C. Mansfield, of Machiavelli's *Discourses on Livy*.

RICHARD VELKLEY is associate professor of philosophy at Stonehill College. He is the author of *Freedom and the End of Reason: On the Moral Foundation of Kant's Critical Philosophy*.

❧Index❧

Schopenhauer, Arthur, 13, 311–12
self, selfhood, xi, 67–68, 74, 76, 157, 258, 275–76, 285, 287–91; and community, 258, 265–66, 268. *See also* honesty; hypocrisy; sentiment of existence; sincerity
self-awareness. *See* sentiment of existence
self-interest, 28, 114, 147, 149, 157, 160, 164–65, 281, 283, 299, 302–3
selfishness, 281–82, 285
self-knowledge, 274, 289, 295n. 34. *See also* sincerity
self-love. *See amour de soi*
self-preservation, 7, 66, 76
self-sacrifice, 78–79
self-sufficiency. *See* individual, autonomy
sentiment of existence, 68, 252, 287–91
Sermon on the Mount, 285–86
sex, sexuality, 58–59, 87, 94, 96–105, 280, 302, 318n. 33; child, 88, 92–94, 96, 101–3, 134. *See also* Freud
Shakespeare, William, 286
Shelly, Percy Bysshe, 32
Shklar, Judith, ix, 275
Sieyès, abbé Emmanuel, 169, 173–74
sincerity, xi–xii, 147, 254, 274–79, 282, 284, 286–92, 295n. 34, 295n. 36, 295n. 39, 310. *See also* authenticity; honesty; hypocrisy
Siu, Dr. Ralph G. H., 312–13; *Less Suffering for Everybody*, 312
Smith, Adam, 116, 283, 303; *Wealth of Nations*, 152
Snow, C. P., 110
social behavior, 126, 128, 133
social competition, 114
social contract, 131–32, 135, 140n. 49, 143, 147, 151, 157, 164, 180, 186, 230, 232, 235, 239, 243n. 27, 253
socialism, 146
sociality, xii, 294n. 28
socialization, 146, 249, 258
social man, 58, 178, 180
society: and art, 21, 32; bourgeois (*see* bourgeois society); civil (*see* civil society); civilized (*see* civilized society); evolution of, 132; versus government, xii; and human nature, 111, 132–33, 146; industrialized, 131–32, 214; liberal (*see* liberal society); modern (*see* modern society); versus nature (*see under* nature); savage (*see* savage society); stateless, 128–29
Socrates, 30, 297–98

solitude, 237, 251–53, 256, 281. *See also* individual; privacy
Solzhenitsyn, Aleksandr, *Cancer Ward*, 313
Sophie, 102, 253, 308. *See also* Emile
soul, 56, 65, 69, 74, 158, 254, 290, 297, 307; bourgeois (*see under* bourgeois); divided, 89, 250; healthy, 275; liberal, 264; modern, 6; postmodern, 256, 264
sovereignty, 171, 174–76, 179, 233; of people, 169, 171, 174, 176, 194–95, 230, 235
Soviet Union, 216
Sparta, 6, 115, 148–49, 159, 185–86, 194, 208, 210, 252
speech, xi, 30, 121, 124, 135
Spengler, Oswald, 65
Spinoza, Baruch, 110
Starobinski, Jean, 112
state: and civil society, 9; formation of, 131; size of, 159, 185, 189, 193–94, 207–9, 235–36, 239–40 (*see also* city, best; government, best form of)
stateless society, 128–29
state of nature, 34, 49, 58, 69, 135, 155, 180, 212, 240, 299–301; versus civil state (*see under* civil society); equality in (*see under* equality); freedom in (*see under* freedom); Hobbesian (*see under* Hobbes); pure, genuine, 111, 113–15, 120, 122, 126–29; Rousseauian, 77; as social, 133; among states, 187, 201, 205; and transparency, 122; wholeness in, xi, 70
Stoics, 306
Strauss, Leo, 5, 110, 211; *Natural Right and History*, 5
sublimation, xi
suffering, 26–27, 59, 114, 301–3, 304–7, 311–15. *See also* compassion; pity
Sulla, Lucius Cornelius, 301
Sully, Maximilien de Béthune, duc de, 206
Switzerland, 192
sympathy, 303–4

Talmon, Jacob, 172
Taylor, Charles, 220–34, 237–39; "Politics of Recognition," 221, 232
theater, 22–24, 30–31, 39n. 12. *See also* arts
Thoreau, Henry David, 145, 165
Tocqueville, Alexis de, 5, 12, 17, 145, 165–66, 175, 268, 276–78, 293n. 12; *Ancien Régime*, 175; *Democracy in America*, 6, 276
Trilling, Lionel, 275